THE QUEEN'S EMBROIDERER

# THE QUEEN'S EMBROIDERER

*A True Story of Paris, Lovers,
Swindlers, and the First Stock
Market Crisis*

## JOAN DEJEAN

BLOOMSBURY PUBLISHING
NEW YORK · LONDON · OXFORD · NEW DELHI · SYDNEY

BLOOMSBURY PUBLISHING
Bloomsbury Publishing Inc.
1385 Broadway, New York, NY 10018, USA

BLOOMSBURY, BLOOMSBURY PUBLISHING, and the Diana logo are trademarks of
Bloomsbury Publishing Plc

First published in the United States 2018

ISBN: HB: 978-1-63286-474-1; ePub: 978-1-63286-476—5

LIBRARY OF CONGRESS CATALOGING-IN-PUBLICATION DATA IS AVAILABLE

2  4  6  8  10  9  7  5  3  1

Typeset by Westchester Publishing Services
Printed and bound in the U.S.A. by Berryville Graphics Inc., Berryville, Virginia

To find out more about our authors and books visit www.bloomsbury.com and sign up
for our newsletters.

Bloomsbury books may be purchased for business or promotional use. For information
on bulk purchases please contact Macmillan Corporate and Premium Sales Department at
specialmarkets@macmillan.com.

CONTENTS

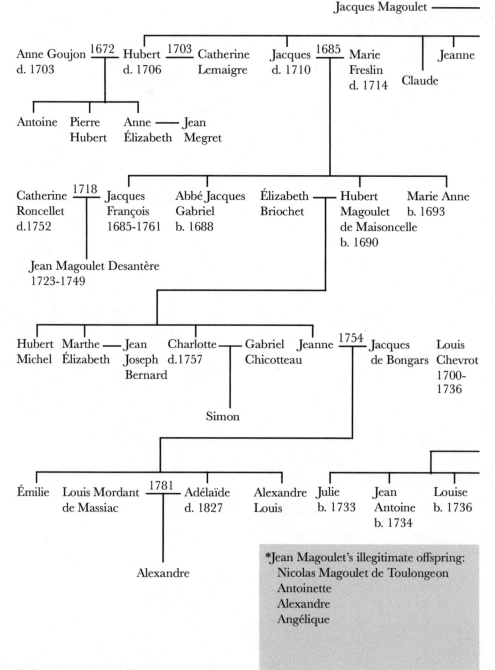

Jacques Magoulet ———

Anne Goujon —1672— Hubert —1703— Catherine    Jacques —1685— Marie    Jeanne
d. 1703    d. 1706    Lemaigre    d. 1710    Freslin
   d. 1714    Claude

Antoine    Pierre    Anne ——— Jean
   Hubert    Élizabeth    Megret

Catherine —1718— Jacques    Abbé Jacques    Élizabeth —— Hubert    Marie Anne
Roncellet    François    Gabriel    Briochet    Magoulet    b. 1693
d.1752    1685-1761    b. 1688    de Maisoncelle
   b. 1690

Jean Magoulet Desantère
1723-1749

Hubert    Marthe —— Jean    Charlotte —— Gabriel    Jeanne —1754— Jacques    Louis
Michel    Élizabeth    Joseph    d.1757    Chicotteau    de Bongars    Chevrot
   Bernard    1700-
   1736

Simon

Émilie    Louis Mordant —1781— Adélaïde    Alexandre    Julie    Jean    Louise
   de Massiac    d. 1827    Louis    b. 1733    Antoine    b. 1736
   b. 1734

Alexandre

*Jean Magoulet's illegitimate offspring:
   Nicolas Magoulet de Toulongeon
   Antoinette
   Alexandre
   Angélique

# MAGOULET FAMILY TREE

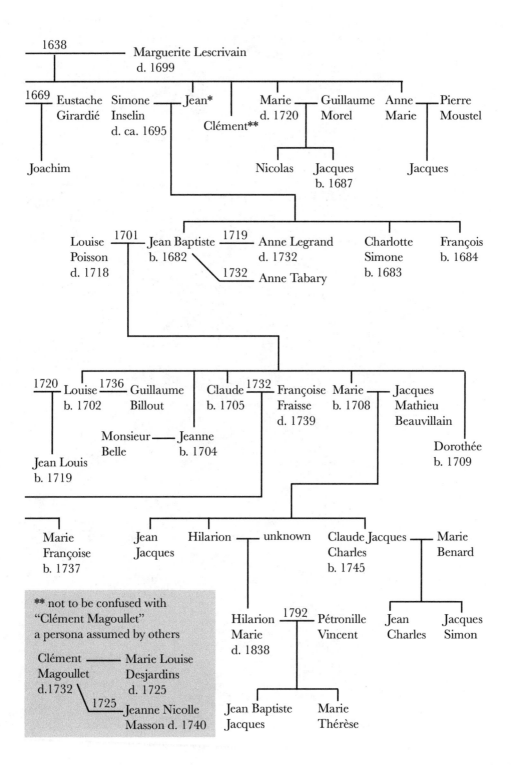

1638 ── Marguerite Lescrivain
d. 1699

1669 ── Eustache    Simone ── Jean* ──    Marie ── Guillaume    Anne ── Pierre
Girardié     Inselin           Clément**    d. 1720   Morel          Marie   Moustel
d. ca. 1695

Joachim                                        Nicolas    Jacques                Jacques
                                                          b. 1687

Louise ── 1701 ── Jean Baptiste ── 1719 ── Anne Legrand    Charlotte    François
Poisson           b. 1682                   d. 1732         Simone       b. 1684
d. 1718                  1732 ── Anne Tabary               b. 1683

1720 ── Louise ── 1736 ── Guillaume    Claude ── 1732 ── Françoise  Marie ── Jacques
        b. 1702           Billout      b. 1705           Fraisse    b. 1708   Mathieu
                                                         d. 1739            Beauvillain

                  Monsieur ── Jeanne                                        Dorothée
                  Belle       b. 1704                                        b. 1709

Jean Louis
b. 1719

Marie           Jean        Hilarion ── unknown    Claude Jacques ── Marie
Françoise       Jacques                            Charles            Benard
b. 1737                                            b. 1745

** not to be confused with
"Clément Magoullet"
a persona assumed by others          Hilarion ── 1792 ── Pétronille    Jean     Jacques
                                     Marie              Vincent        Charles  Simon
Clément ── Marie Louise              d. 1838
Magoullet  Desjardins
d.1732     d. 1725
    \ 1725 ── Jeanne Nicolle          Jean Baptiste    Marie
              Masson d. 1740          Jacques          Thérèse

*Paris in the early eighteenth century.*

NOUVEAU
PLAN DE PARIS
et de ses
FAUBOURGS

| | |
|---|---|
| 1594 | Henri IV, the first Bourbon monarch, wins control of Paris |
| 1610 | Henri IV assassinated |
| 1610–1643 | Reign of Louis XIII |
| 1618–1648 | Thirty Years' War |
| 1643–1715 | Reign of Louis XIV |
| 1660 | Louis XIV marries Marie-Thérèse of Spain |
| 1682 | French court moves to Versailles |
| 1683 | Death of Queen Marie-Thérèse |
| 1685 | Huguenots banished from France |
| 1686 | The League of Augsburg formed |
| 1688–1697 | Nine Years' War/War of the League of Augsburg/War of the Grand Alliance |
| 1693–1694 | Famine in Europe |
| 1701–1714 | War of the Spanish Succession |
| 1708–1709 | The Great Winter |
| September 1, 1715 | Death of Louis XIV |
| 1715–1723 | Regency of Philippe d'Orléans |
| May 1716 | Founding of the General Bank |
| August 1717 | Founding of the Western Company |
| May 1718 | Founding of New Orleans |
| December 1718 | Founding of the Royal Bank |
| May 1719 | The Western Company and the Indies Company merge |
| June 1719 | First slaves arrive in Louisiana |
| December 1719 | Shares in the Indies Company reach 10,025; the ship *Mutinous* sails for Louisiana with 150 Frenchwomen on board |
| Summer 1720 | Runs on the Royal Bank; riots in Paris |
| September 1720 | South Sea Bubble bursts in London |
| December 1720 | Shares in the Indies Company at 1,000; John Law flees France |
| 1721 | Publication of Montesquieu's *Persian Letters* denouncing the effects of Law's system |
| 1723–1774 | Independent reign of Louis XV |
| 1733 | Publication of Voltaire's *Letters Concerning the English Nation*, harbinger of the movement now known as the Enlightenment |
| 1774–1792 | Reign of Louis XVI |
| 1789 | French Revolution begins |

One August afternoon in France's National Archives, I found two documents listed under the name of Jean Magoulet, official embroiderer to Louis XIV's queen. The first, Magoulet's letter of appointment as the Queen's Embroiderer, was no surprise, but the second, a royal decree, stopped me in my tracks: "August 5, 1719. Lock Marie Louise Magoulet up in prison and ship her off to Louisiana."

In 1719, such an official pronouncement was unequivocal: Marie Louise Magoulet had been accused of prostitution and was being deported to the newly founded city of New Orleans as an undesirable.

Minutes later, I was racing through the streets of Paris' Marais, bound for the Arsenal Library, where the records of the Bastille prison are housed. Before the afternoon was out, I had learned that Louise Magoulet was indeed, as I had suspected, the daughter of the Queen's Embroiderer. I had also learned that the charge of prostitution had been trumped up by her very own father. I had even glimpsed the outline of a great love affair, between Louise Magoulet and Louis Chevrot.

Well before I realized that various Magoulets and Chevrots would crisscross the globe and that this family saga would play out over two full centuries, I already knew that it would be no easy task to retrace the Magoulet family's path from Versailles' magnificence to prison squalor. I walked away from this project several times but always came back: I couldn't get Louise Magoulet's star-crossed love story out of my mind.

She and Louis Chevrot deserved so much more than life gave them.

# THE QUEEN'S EMBROIDERER

CHAPTER ONE

# The Queen's Embroiderers

T HIS IS AMONG the earliest surviving depictions of the interior of an
  authentic shop, the emporium of a known merchant, in this case, Jean
Magoulet. Magoulet is identified in the caption printed below the handsomely
etched image as "brodeur ordinaire," or official embroiderer in the service of
the queen—that is, Queen Marie-Thérèse, the Spanish infanta who from the
time of her marriage in 1660 to her death in 1683 ruled France as Louis XIV's
wife. The caption adds that the queen is "deceased," so we know that the
scene depicted took place after 1683.

Jean Magoulet, the Queen's Embroiderer, wears the accoutrements of everyday
aristocratic dress—a perfectly curled periwig, fine muslin cuffs and cravat—
and his younger assistant is similarly attired. But one element is missing, and
that absence distinguishes the merchants' dress as infinitely less costly than the
garments worn by the great aristocrat who is Magoulet's potential client. The
merchants' attire, while elegant, is unadorned, whereas the cuffs and the front
panels of the nobleman's handsome *justaucorps* (the ancestor of today's suit jacket)
are richly ornamented with the kind of embroidery for which Magoulet was
famous.

Across the back wall hang official garments of various kinds: the cross of the
Saint-Esprit, or Holy Spirit, the highest chivalric distinction that could be
conferred on French noblemen; a chasuble, the principal vestment worn by a
priest when celebrating mass; and a *housse*, the decorative cloth placed under
the saddles of horses on ceremonial occasions. This *housse*, featuring a fleur-
de-lis pattern, seems destined for the mount of a royal guard.

*Advertisement for the Parisian shop of the Queen's Embroiderer, Jean Magoulet.*

The noblewoman examines an embroidery pattern, more of which are scattered over the tablecloth. These were presentation designs, created by renowned embroiderers as samples of their work to be used just as Magoulet is doing, to generate custom. The shop assistant displays for the nobleman's perusal a panel destined to become part of either a waistcoat or a jacket similar to the one the client is wearing but embroidered in a style evidently so eye-catchingly different from everything already in his wardrobe that, leaning forward in his chair and hand on hip, the aristocrat is giving it his full and rapt attention.

The shopping scene conveys the message that Jean Magoulet's emporium featured a stock of embroidery fit for a queen—or a bishop, or a cavalry officer, or the highest nobles in the land. The image was designed as a promotional tool to entice anyone with the means to afford luxurious adornments to Magoulet's elegant boutique.

In the 1680s, when this etching first circulated, such a clientele would naturally have been drawn to Magoulet's work, for it had been rewarded with the ultimate seal of approval: that of the court at Versailles. At the center of the caption, the coat of arms of France's deceased queen is prominently featured, so no one could forget that Magoulet was an official purveyor to the French crown.

Today, Versailles has attained the status of a mythical court, probably the most famous court of all time. In the 1680s, that myth was just taking shape. Louis XIV's château was not yet complete when king and queen and courtiers moved to Versailles from the Louvre in May 1682. The palace's iconic space, the Galerie des Glaces, or Hall of Mirrors, was opened to the public the following December. From then on a great whirl of parties, receptions, and court festivities of all kinds began; those celebrations would transform the name Versailles into a European legend. And no space witnessed more of those brilliant displays of French style and magnificence than the Hall of Mirrors.

Modern tourists who marvel at this legendary space are dazzled above all by its vast expanse of mirrored glass. They also look up to admire the monumental vaulted ceiling covered with paintings depicting the high points of the Sun King's reign, produced by the workshop of royal artist Charles Le Brun.

The grand gallery is more than forty-one feet high, so it is hard to appreciate Le Brun's masterpieces, only dimly visible on the ceiling far above. This would have been all the more true in the seventeenth century, when evening festivities were only softly lit by candlelight. And in any event those magnificent paintings and the gallery's best-known feature, its mirrors, were not compatible in any way. Indeed, for what was in 1682 an inconceivably vast and wildly costly display of mirrored glass to pay off, the gallery had to be filled with bright and shiny things whose reflection would bounce off the mirrors to create an overall effect of brilliant shimmering. Rather than the mirrors in which they were reflected, those glittering surfaces were what the seventeenth-century precursors of today's tourists remembered from their visits to Versailles' grand gallery.

There was the legendary silver throne installed on a dais at one end of the gallery, used on ceremonial occasions to convince notable foreign visitors of France's supremacy. The steps leading up to the throne were literally dripping with embroidery; on the uppermost step the most precious needlework was displayed, embroidery so delicate it was described as "lacework"—all of it executed with outrageously expensive metallic thread. Surrounding that storied throne were eight monumental panels, neither oil paintings nor tapestries, but paintings in needlework, masterpieces of French royal embroidery fifteen feet high. Each magnificent panel featured a pavilion embroidered in gold surrounded by figures worked in silver. With its blatant display of precious metal, embroidery rather than painting was the art form emblematic of the Sun King's Versailles.

The panels showed off a technique known as embroidery in the round. The principal design elements were cut out in a paper padding, which was shaped and stitched onto cloth; metallic threads were then laid down in parallel lines over the padding underneath. The motifs thus rendered acquired precise contours, a sensuous depth, a variety of finish. The prolific use of metal thread gave embroidery the light-reflecting capacity essential in spaces lit by candlelight. In a technique known as *or nué*, or shaded gold, multiple shades of gold were juxtaposed and the tones were modulated through a gradation of hues; because of the contrasting reflective surfaces, the panels glimmered with a sheen more complex than the throne's more ordinary glow. In candlelight, the brightest areas functioned as highlights and attracted illumination. So much precious metal coated the vast quantity of thread required to execute intricate designs that the panels were incredibly weighty, unlike the throne, which was in fact made of wood and merely covered with a thin layer of silver.

In this context, the Sun King always chose outfits embroidered *en plein*, a phrase that literally means "fully." As indeed they were: the monarch's jackets and waistcoats were often so densely embroidered that not a speck of the fabric underneath could be glimpsed: he thus seemed garbed solely in gold and silver, reflecting light with every turn. Even in such a wildly glittering setting as the Galerie des Glaces, the monarch stood out as the most sparkling object of all.

The many pounds of precious metal required to paint in needlework explain why we can no longer admire such masterpieces. Like the king's silver furniture, the greatest royal embroidery was destroyed in 1689 when the monarchy was desperately short of coin. The ostentatiously visible wealth of gold and silver embroidery was melted down to finance the monarch's ever more ruinously expensive wars.

Jean Magoulet was named to his position as the Queen's Embroiderer in 1677, just as work on Louis XIV's château was moving into high gear. When the court formally settled in Versailles in May 1682, he was still serving the queen. He was thus in the right place at absolutely the right time: the only moment in Versailles' long history when no expense was spared to make the palace's ruler and everything in it glisten and gleam.

And Magoulet's career did not end with the queen's death: he was soon best known for his accomplishments in another area, what we call haute couture, perhaps the most expensive couture ever created.

In the early 1680s, Paris was only just acquiring the reputation it still enjoys, as the European capital of style. A fashion industry worthy of the name was able to develop when the taste for fabulous garments spread beyond the court to an ever larger public of wealthy men and women. When high fashion became a middle-class pursuit, embroidery found a new calling.

*Habit d'Hyuer*

*Tour de plumes a deux pointes*
*Castor gris blanc*
*Perruque noüeé*
*Colet rond Brodé*
*Manteau de drap de Hollande couleur de feu doublé de velours noir ou pluche de couleur*
*Manchon de pluche de couleur*
*Iuste-au corps gris brodé de soye de couleur doublé de satin et la veste de mesme*
*Broderie plate d'or et d'argent*
*Canons a la Royale brodez coupez en botte tenant au bas*
*Souliers noirs lustrez et tirerez d'or*

*In 1678, a Parisian newspaper ran the first ad ever for a man's high-fashion outfit—richly embroidered with gold and silver thread.*

In January 1678, a Parisian newspaper, *Le Mercure galant* (*The Gallant Mercury*), included news never before seen in the periodical press: it discussed in detail the latest fashions for winter and included illustrations of the season's iconic garments. The paper ushered in modern fashion journalism with men's fashions, such as this "winter outfit"; women's garments followed. And the description of every outfit was focused on embroidery's central role.

The original male fashion plate was decked out in all the latest trends. His many stylish adornments—from his collar and his cloak to his jacket—owe their status as fashions of the moment to the fact that they were covered with embroidery in the kind of intricate patterns for which the Queen's Embroiderer was renowned, designs worked in gold and silver thread.

The *Mercury*'s illustration is in a sense a royal affair—one design is even named "à la royale"—but the man of mode it features is not depicted wearing a sword as French nobles did. With this choice, the paper suggested that the new fashions for winter 1678 were trends not designed exclusively for members of the court but instead styles to be copied by anyone who could afford them.

At the moment when the French fashion industry was taking shape, Magoulet was producing for his clients embroidery so heavily encrusted with metallic thread that no creation produced by Chanel Haute Couture today can even begin to compare. A truly extravagant outfit of the time might require ten or more pounds of precious metal.

Famous embroiderers were gifted draftsmen, with exceptional skill at imagining and planning memorable patterns. Their work would thus make or break an important new garment. This explains why the nobleman in Magoulet's shop image is examining the sample so intently. This was where his sense of style would be on display: the cut of a man's jacket changed far less often and less radically than did embroidery motifs, and the kind of trendsetting whimsy evident in an embroidery pattern had no equivalent in tailoring. In the power dressing of Louis XIV's Versailles and the Paris fashion scene, the embroiderer was responsible for the glitz and glamour that made an outfit memorable.

And if you wanted embroidery fit for the king of France, you sought out Jean Magoulet. Magoulet had ready access to the secrets of the Garderobe du Roi, the King's Wardrobe, the name given to the extended machinery that made possible the lavish outfits and frequent costume changes that were the day-to-day stuff of life at the Sun King's court.

On August 3, 1679, the scion of the House of Lorraine, the Prince d'Harcourt, contacted the Queen's Embroiderer with an urgent request. The prince was so enamored of "the jacket with gold embroidery" that he had just seen the king wearing at Versailles that he was after a copy that would be "indistinguishable," perfect "down to the last stitch." Magoulet went straight to Étienne Cagnyé, Sieur de La Greffe, who served every July as the first valet of the King's Wardrobe; Cagnyé had thus handed that memorable jacket to the king on the day when it had caught the prince's eye. Cagnyé came through for his colleague and quickly turned over the embroidery pattern that had served for the royal garment, "sealed with his coat of arms" as proof of its accuracy. Magoulet assured the prince that "everything would be absolutely identical."

Naturally, that combination of insider information and remarkable skill came at a price, and a very high one indeed.

In 1690, Jean-Baptiste Colbert, Marquis de Seignelay, son of the elder Jean-Baptiste Colbert, the Sun King's most trusted adviser, decided it was time to renew his collection of *justaucorps*. The monarch's valued collaborator in his own right, Seignelay served the crown as *Secrétaire d'État à la Marine*, Navy Secretary. A man in Seignelay's position had his pick of luxury goods purveyors; only the finest received a contract to work for him.

The marquis ordered a first jacket from master tailor Jean de La Lande, in black velvet extensively trimmed with gold braid. Even with the added expense of the braid, Seignelay paid only 20 livres. (In 1690, a livre could buy ten pounds of good bread or four pounds of high-quality meat.) Seignelay also desired a second jacket. The marquis picked out a striped cotton textile in the newly fashionable shade of brown known as musk. On March 1, 1690, when Seignelay bought the cloth from fabric merchant Barbe Indienne, she charged 3 livres. He then turned the textile over to the Queen's Embroiderer. For Magoulet's creation, "an outfit fully embroidered in gold," France's navy secretary received a bill on April 20 for 580 livres—29 times more than the total outlay for the Marquis' velvet jacket, and 193 times the price paid for the cloth.

Purchases made that same year for the wardrobe of Seignelay's wife confirm this vast cost differential between the price of embroidery and all other expenditures in the acquisition of a high fashion garment. She acquired two *aunes* (a unit of measure equivalent to about 1.25 yards) of fine silk brocade for 33 livres. To transform the cloth with "embroidery in gold with flowers in a raised design in gold and silver," Magoulet charged 631 livres, more than nineteen times the cost of the sumptuous textile.

Royal artisans lived an elegant public life: they interacted on a regular basis with the court at Versailles; they had business dealings with members of France's first families; they created fabulous objects, veritable works of art, which they sold for major sums; they maintained luxurious shops in Paris' best neighborhoods; and they might even live nearby, as Magoulet did. In all these capacities, they had to dress and act the part, to own the right clothes and wigs and to wear them with just the right attitude.

Because of their proximity to king and court and as a recognition of their exceptional talent, royal artists also gained social status and erased many of the negative connotations of earning a living through sales and the work of their hands, and even to some extent their lack of a birthright. Look at Magoulet's self-depiction in his shop image: there's no stain of manual labor on this man, who appears more a trusted confidant than a simple merchant. Magoulet's art was a social anchor for him. His title "the Queen's Embroiderer" elevated him within the carefully nuanced ranks of the French middle classes.

In the Parisian luxury goods industry, success was defined as the ability to improve one's lot professionally, socially, and financially: Magoulet's story must have seemed a perfect example of the French dream.

But behind the glamorous façade that the depiction of Magoulet's shop was designed to promote was a dense web of lies. This was equally true of his eldest son, who also became a noted embroiderer and who also used the title the Queen's Embroiderer. Both these great artists were at the same time individuals with an elegant public image and men who devoted enormous energy to hiding their secret lives from those closest to them.

Both royal embroiderers appeared constitutionally incapable of living within their means, even when those means should have proved amply sufficient to maintain their households. They became poster children for a society increasingly addicted to credit. Whenever their wild overspending led them into a level of debt that they could not sustain, they tried to make a quick windfall. Then, as each risky venture fell through, they turned on their family.

Both royal embroiderers abused their familial duties: they spent money that belonged to their wives; they tapped into funds legally set aside as an inheritance for their children. And if a spouse or a child threatened to expose their mismanagement, they struck back—and they took no prisoners. Time and again, they lashed out with cold-blooded ruthlessness: abusive behavior seems to have come as naturally to them both as the ability to imagine gorgeously intricate designs. The story of the two Queen's Embroiderers is thus equal parts nightmare and fairy tale, as much a saga of intimate violence as of needlework so exquisite and technically demanding that its cost would be prohibitive today.

In the course of their attempts both to get rich quickly and to save their skin when they got into bad straits, the Queen's Embroiderers became imposters, tricksters, con artists nonpareil. They lied about everything and to everyone: to the police, to notaries, to their in-laws. They lied about their ages and those of their children, about their professional accomplishments and their net worth. They caroused; they philandered; they made a mockery of the laws of church and state. The only truly authentic thing about them was their extraordinary talent and their ability to weave gold and silver thread into the kind of garments that seemed the stuff of dreams. In their lives and on an almost daily basis, haute couture crossed paths with high crime.

Savage beauty indeed.

# CHAPTER TWO

# Star-Crossed

I N PARIS IN early 1719, you could have filled your lungs with the heady air of fast money. High rollers roamed the city's streets looking for ways to spend the gargantuan profits they had accumulated virtually overnight: prior to this, no one had ever been able to make so much money so quickly. Everything about them screamed *nouveau riche*, a term recently coined to characterize individuals distinguished solely by their vast and instant wealth. Pickpockets loved them because they carried on their persons prodigious quantities of an entity the French had only lately discovered: paper money. Paper was so much lighter than coin that the newly rich had in their pockets far more cash than urban dwellers had been able to walk around with before: because of the nouveaux riches of 1719, the use of wallets became common. Those early wallets were stuffed with freshly minted banknotes, the first that the French had touched. Those crisp bills were their earnings from the first stock market bubble the world had known.

The parvenus and the pickpockets of Paris had one man to thank for their good fortune: the Scottish economic theorist John Law, who introduced the French to the wonders of paper money and high-risk speculation. The attraction of instant, easy wealth proved irresistible to many, including two upwardly mobile Parisians: a fabled embroiderer, the younger Jean Magoulet, and a well-connected financial administrator, Antoine Chevrot.

Philippe, Duc d'Orléans, the regent governing France for the future Louis XV, was the first to fall under Law's spell. In August 1717, the regent put him in charge of the Compagnie d'Occident, the Western Company, which controlled trade between France and its North American colonies, including the gigantic tract of land depicted in this 1718 map by Nicolas de Fer.

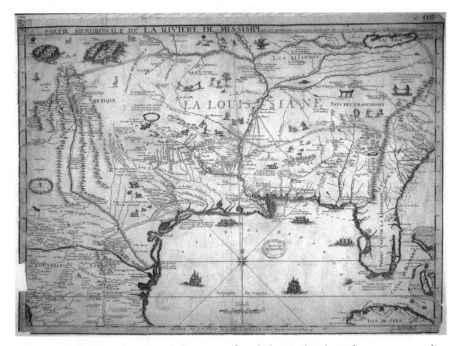

*In 1718, the year that New Orleans was founded, Nicolas de Fer's map presented the territory known as "the Mississippi" or "the Louisiana."*

The French colony established in 1699 and known at first as "the Mississippi" or "the Louisiana" covered most of the Mississippi River valley, stretching from the Gulf of Mexico north to the Great Lakes, from the *presqu'île* or "peninsula of Louisiana" (Florida) west to the edge of New Spain. French authorities were convinced that Louisiana had the potential for rapid and spectacular growth. All that was needed was the workers necessary, in the words of one royal decree, "to extract the fruit of this commerce." In its September 12–14, 1717 issue, the London periodical the *Post Man* reported that the French crown had made "a free gift" to Law's enterprise of the ships, merchandise, and construction already "in the Louisiana" on one condition: "the company shall within 25 years transport into the Louisiana 6000 Whites and 3000 Negroes."

In 1718, New Orleans was founded: from then on, Louisiana had a focal point. By 1719, not even three hundred French had settled in the city, whereas there were well over five thousand French colonists on the island of Martinique. When Law was given control over Louisiana, slavery had not yet been developed: perhaps a dozen Africans were present in its vast expanse. In contrast, the first slaves had reached Jamestown in 1619; a century later, the institution was expanding rapidly in the English colony. And already in 1700 there were more than eleven thousand slaves in Martinique.

On June 6, 1719, two French ships, the *Duc du Maine* and the *Aurore* (Aurora), reached Louisiana. Because of Law's pledge to "transport . . . 3000 Negroes," a new age had dawned for the colony: slavery had officially arrived. The ships had sailed from Saint-Malo for lands the French then referred to as Juda (today's Togo and the Republic of Benin) and the Guinea Coast (now the Republic of Guinea), where their captains had purchased hundreds of slaves. But it was some time before the next ships from Africa reached New Orleans. Law turned his attention instead to those six thousand white laborers, a promise that proved far trickier to fulfill, in part because of the problem of their sex.

French colonial administrators had long been concerned that the virtually total absence of white women would encourage unions between French male settlers and Indian women. The first mass arrival of black slaves fostered anxiety about a type of miscegenation the French had never previously had reason to fear. In 1719, pressure was on to find white women to populate New Orleans—to hunt them down straightaway and to use any means necessary to get them onto ships as quickly as possible.

The mission's control center was La Salpêtrière, the division of Paris' vast internment facility, the Hôpital Général (General Hospital) that served as a workhouse and prison, largely for women. Every Frenchwoman forced onto a ship bound for the fledgling colony had transited through the Salpêtrière and had been personally selected by that institution's notoriously harsh warden, Marguerite Pancatalin.

Pancatalin was the first to realize that female colonists had become a priority for the new powerhouse in the world of French finance, John Law. On June 27, 1719, Warden Pancatalin drew up a list of 208 women already interned in the Salpêtrière whom she considered *bonnes pour les îles*, "fit for the islands." She did so despite the fact that the official royal declarations from January 8 and March 12, 1719 that outlined the practice of identifying settlers for expulsion to Louisiana spoke only of men: the idea of deporting female prisoners was not mandated by royal decree but was the private initiative of Law and Pancatalin.

The window during which Law and Pancatalin were able to act with impunity was small: it opened in June 1719, the month when the first slave ships docked in the French new world, and it closed before the end of that year. By early 1720, rumors were flying in the streets of Paris about the sudden disappearance of young people who had been arrested by officers of the crown. Soon, angry mobs were protesting the practice of forced deportation.

*The 1719 list of women deemed "fit for the islands" and destined for forced deportation to New Orleans.*

Awareness of what was going on became widespread only in 1720 because in the second half of 1719, Parisians were obsessively focused on what we know as the stock market. The moment during which young Frenchmen and women were permanently spirited away corresponded exactly to the period of the most unbridled financial risk Europe had ever seen and the most frenzied speculation France has ever known. During those months, it became possible for any Parisian with ready cash to acquire shares of stock and believe he or she would get a quick and spectacular return on his or her investment.

In his journal, the Marquis de Dangeau, a diplomat and military man, tracked every change in price, beginning with May 12, 1719, when the bank of Law's company opened its doors for business and began a public offering of its stock at 500 livres per share. By May 24, he reported, shares "had already gained 30%"—"and M. Law guarantees that stock will be far higher before the end of the year." And M. Law's prediction proved correct.

Already on September 11, shares passed the symbolic 5,000 mark. On October 8, Dangeau noted that "the ardor to possess stock in the company is greater than ever." On December 12, he recorded the first sign of the bubble's end when stock suddenly began to plunge. The free fall continued during the early months of 1720, just as opposition to the exile of prisoners to Louisiana was finally building. By May 12, 1720, when a royal decree put an end to the deportations Law had counted on to supply workers for the new colony, Dangeau reported that because of speculation, "most people consider themselves ruined."

France's brief experiment with the expulsion of undesirables yielded but a few hundred colonists for New Orleans. The young men forced onto boats were either homeless beggars, vagabonds, or smugglers who had slipped into the capital from the provinces and were caught without identity papers. The profile of the women shipped off was more complex.

Pancatalin prepared a blunt dossier on each of the candidates she proposed. More than half of the women she had selected had either been born in the French provinces or were foreigners (Irish, German); some were described as Gypsies. No one in Paris would have been alarmed at their sudden disappearance. The overwhelming majority were charged with either petty theft or "prostitution," a term that covered activities ranging from streetwalking to having an affair with a married man. The one trait the women had in common was their modest birth: they were the daughters of parents without influence, low-income workers of various kinds.

Law's plan was thus able to move ahead as smoothly and swiftly as his company's stock. By the time Parisians' speculation frenzy was at its most feverish, the cargo had been assembled for still another of the economist's innovative ideas: a ship that would transport only female undesirables. In the entire slick operation, there was only one anomaly, one young woman who did not fit Pancatalin's profile: Louise Magoulet.

Louise was the daughter and the granddaughter of the two brilliant Queen's Embroiderers, Jean Magoulet father and son. When Louise's mother died during the night of November 10, 1718, her father, the second Queen's Embroiderer, found himself with five minors between the ages of nine and seventeen in his care. Magoulet's propensity for risky investments had saddled him with considerable debt. He quickly found a personal lifeline: Anne Legrand, an exceedingly wealthy older woman, also newly widowed but with no desire to take on five children along with the younger man who had so successfully charmed her. Five years later, when Magoulet's children were old enough to tell their story, they explained to the head of the Parisian police that, rather than devote their mother's dowry to their care as French law mandated, their father had simply turned them loose on the streets soon after her death.

Louise Magoulet and Louis Chevrot had already met and fallen in love by the time her mother died. They could have been introduced by the mutual friends who later helped them escape their fathers' wrath. Since family members shared the same parish church, Louise and Louis could have spotted each other in adjacent pews at Sunday mass.

When her father forced her out of her home after her mother's death, seventeen-year-old Louise turned to Louis for help. She became pregnant almost immediately, by late November or early December 1718. And even though Louis later said that the minute he had set his eyes on her, "he had known that Louise Magoulet would be his wife," by the time they could have been sure of her pregnancy, the couple would have realized that they had no way of winning their fathers' consent to their union.

In order to marry, a young woman of any social status required not only her family's approval but a dowry, and a handsome one at that if she hoped to prove attractive to someone like Louis' father, Antoine Chevrot. All his life, Antoine had aspired to one thing alone: fine titles and the social prominence they brought. Antoine would have turned a blind eye to a less than robust dowry only in the case of a potential daughter-in-law with an aristocratic title.

Jean Magoulet and Anne Legrand married on Saturday, June 3, 1719. By then, his daughter Louise was about five months pregnant. Shares in Law's company were just starting to climb, and the hunt for young Frenchwomen mandated by Law was beginning to heat up.

Louis and Louise's fathers, Antoine Chevrot and Jean Magoulet, became mortal enemies, even though they were united in their opposition to the match. They were both cash-strapped when the dream of instant riches for anyone able to invest in Law's stock began to gain traction. Their eldest children could have raised the kind of capital both fathers badly wanted by marrying into money; no other kind of union would have won their blessing.

In Louise's case, neither Pancatalin nor the police had to track her down: she was denounced to them as a "depraved prostitute" by her own father; he even made arrangements for her arrest. Everything that happened to Louise Magoulet can be explained by the financial "ardor" that gripped France in 1719. Her family's story is a textbook example of behavior that becomes conceivable when people suddenly find themselves able to make so much money that there is no longer a bottom line, when they lose their moral compass in the face of windfall profits.

Only four days after Louise's arrest, the list of prisoners submitted by Pancatalin was finally approved with this annotation: "public and scandalous prostitutes." This gave Louise's thoroughly corrupt arresting officer, Jean Bourlon, the chance to make sure that Jean Magoulet's wishes for his daughter were carried out to the letter. Magoulet had written Louis Charles de Machault, lieutenant general of the Parisian police, to describe his seventeen-year-old daughter as "ruined by venereal disease" because "she had given herself to many men." He asked that Louise first be locked up in the Salpêtrière and then *faire passer es îles*—"sent off to the islands."

On October 6, 155 lowborn women selected by Law from among the 208 on Pancatalin's list were taken from the Salpêtrière, bound for the port of Le Havre and a ship destined for New Orleans. The women traveled in straw-filled carts, chained at the waist in groups of sixteen. Only days before their departure, Bourlon, the officer assigned to carry out Machault's decree, had added Louise Magoulet to their number. Two days after the women left Paris, Dangeau reported that stock market fever was hotter than ever before. All eyes were on those magic numbers.

The ship designed to carry some 150 Frenchwomen to "the Louisiana" was the unique vessel of its kind. In the face of mounting protests from the people of Paris, Law's company never again tried to fill one of its ships with a cargo of women. From then on, deportation was never again practiced on a large scale. Instead, the number of African slaves sent to Louisiana was dramatically increased.

Louis and Louise, the young lovers whose hopes for marriage were thwarted when Louise was banished from Paris in the company of alleged thieves and prostitutes, were not their fathers' sole victims. In the end, Jean Magoulet and Antoine Chevrot tore their families apart, leaving in their wake a trail of ruined lives and squandered talent as well as mountains of unmanageable debt. "Old sins cast long shadows," as the proverb goes.

Their families also left behind a paper trail of epic proportions. Two centuries of legal documents, police files, church records, and prison registers make it possible to retrace both the unfolding of a great love story and the scandalous history of the two houses determined to destroy it.

The chronicle you are about to read is true. No names have been changed, for I do not believe that there are any innocents left to protect. The two families whose trajectories intersected so disastrously in 1719 have died out. An online check of French telephone directories in 2016 revealed that, three centuries later, in the entire country not a single Magoulet remains. Individuals named Chevrot did turn up, but none of them can be a direct descendant of the Antoine Chevrot who opposed his son's marriage with Louise Magoulet.

My protagonists' lives prove once more just how right Mark Twain was: real life can be so much more amazing than invented plots because "Fiction is obliged to stick to possibilities; Truth isn't." Readers will find at the end a full record of the evidence on which this book is based, a list of all the documents

I consulted, mainly in the French National Archives and the archives of the Bastille prison.

It's never possible to verify absolutely everything about lives lived so long ago: time takes its toll on the historical record. The most significant loss to French archives took place because of the fire that in 1871 gutted Paris' Hôtel de Ville, or City Hall. Among the records then destroyed were the archives from Parisian churches that had been moved there in the aftermath of the Revolution of 1789. As a result, the exact dates of the births and deaths of early Parisians are seldom known.

Prior to the 1871 fire, a specialist in Parisian luxury goods merchants, Alexandre Laborde, combed the records of many churches in the city and compiled a catalog of baptisms and marriages involving these craftsmen, particularly those who had worked for the French court. The title "the Queen's Embroiderer" naturally caught his eye. Laborde's registry has survived; because of it, I am certain of many key facts of the Magoulet family's history, key birth dates in particular.

In France's National Archives in Paris, the past is found packaged in boxes measuring roughly 15 by 11 inches and 4 to 7 inches high, made of sturdy dark green cardboard and tied with dingy beige ribbons. Into those utilitarian cartons are crammed the stuff of the everyday life, across the centuries, of Parisians male and female, ordinary and elite.

Countless thousands of those cardboard boxes contain the documents Parisians signed in the presence of the hundreds of notaries active in the city at any given moment. For most Parisians these documents are few in number: at most, the contract drawn up to establish the terms for their marriage and the occasional lease signed when they changed address. The individuals key to this story were of a different breed. They signed contracts establishing the terms on which they borrowed or lent money, contracts specifying the kinds of work they would produce and at what cost. The list goes on and on—obligations, agreements, negotiations and renegotiations.

Still other green boxes contain the juiciest documents of all: those that record the day-to-day activities of the Parisian police. Beginning in the late seventeenth century, Paris was divided into administrative areas, somewhat like precincts, with officers known as *commissaires* assigned to each of them. It's impossible to establish exact correlations between different national police forces today, much less between modern forces and those of centuries past. *Commissaires* shared some of the administrative and supervisory duties of modern police commissioners; they also directed criminal investigations as today's chief inspectors do. I will refer to them as either *commissaires* or inspectors.

*Commissaires* were responsible for keeping the peace in Paris and for guaranteeing that the citizens of the city obeyed royal laws and ordinances. In this capacity, they were the recipients of all criminal complaints made to the police and were charged with the inquiry into whatever offense was alleged. Vast numbers of these reports have survived. They range from allegations of domestic violence to attempts to settle disagreements that pitted one business partner against another, husband against wife, or father against son. All these were areas of dispute in which the Magoulets and the Chevrots excelled.

The police archives include the agreements drawn up to appoint legal guardians for children upon the death of a parent. They also contain the records of another duty that fell within the *commissaires'* mandate: the fixing of the seals. Immediately after a death, a listing of the individual's possessions was established. To protect valuables until a formal inventory was drawn up, bailiffs then ran ribbons across doors and the drawers of storage furniture all over the residence; these were held in place at each end with wax imprinted with a judicial seal. Those fastenings had to be broken before access could be obtained so that the final inventory could take place. *Scellés*, or "seals," can speak volumes about the secrets and lies that had governed the lives of the apartment's inhabitants: the body found in an unexpected bedroom or children frantic to locate a parent's will.

No official ever tried to get to the bottom of the crimes I will describe; no officer of the law took the side of those falsely accused and tried to establish their innocence. The police officials assigned to the investigations at the time invariably seemed to have been immediately dazzled when they heard titles such as "the Queen's Embroiderer."

Finally, some background on what was upon this occasion truly the root of all evil: money. In France under the Bourbon monarchy, everyday commercial transactions were usually made using actual gold, silver, and copper coins, but vast numbers of purchases were also made on credit. Individuals ran up accounts with merchants; they freely exchanged promissory notes, financial instruments that contained a promise by one party to pay another a fixed sum either on demand or at a specified date. These practices were so widespread that it's clear that, as the eighteenth century progressed, more and more individuals were living almost exclusively on credit and thus were carrying an ever heavier debt load. In fact, the only people who seemed unable to obtain credit were those known to be indigent.

At certain moments of crisis in the late seventeenth and the early eighteenth century, France experienced critical shortages of precious metals: at those times, both the country's economy and the finances of all Frenchmen were absolutely dependent on credit. Individuals who had lived well beyond their means in better times easily became caught in a downward spiral. The most horrendous deeds committed by the fathers at the center of this story were carried out during such a credit crisis.

During those times of monetary emergency, some individuals also used a type of currency with which the country had had no prior experience: paper money. The downfall of the Magoulets and the Chevrots was directly related to the most ambitious early experiment with paper in any European country: France's introduction in 1719 to the concept of "fiat money," paper currency not convertible into coin of equivalent worth.

Those lucky enough to have real money in their pockets carried valuable coins known as *écus* and *louis* as well as smaller ones. When they took on debt or engaged in financial transactions, they always calculated in a money of account for which there was no equivalent coin: the *livre tournois*, usually called simply the *livre*. A livre contained twenty *sous*; a sous contained twelve *deniers*. *Livre* means "pound," but to avoid confusion with the pound sterling, I will not translate *livre*, which I will write simply "livre."*

The fate of two families was determined in December 1718, when the Queen's Embroiderer could not get his hands on 3,000 livres.

---

*To give some sense of the livre's fluctuating purchasing power, I have included a price index as an appendix.

# CHAPTER THREE

# Upward Mobility 1: Salt and Taxes
# The Chevrots: 1604–1698

FOR GENERATIONS, THE Magoulets and the Chevrots, like most families anywhere and at any time, were aspirational. Each set of parents wanted their children to be wealthier and more socially prominent. Both of these families began their ascension early in the seventeenth century with a young man from the provinces traveling to Paris to make a name for himself.

In seventeenth-century Paris, there were two clear paths to upward mobility. If you had the talent, you could work in the rapidly developing luxury goods industry, as did the two Queen's Embroiderers. You could also become part of an ever-expanding administration that managed the finances of the monarchy and governing bodies, such as the Parisian Parlement. This was the path chosen by the Chevrots. Before the century's end, the finance industry and the luxury goods industry dominated an economy that was the envy of the rest of Europe. The most sought-after artisans in the Western world produced the luxury goods that were a mainstay of the French economy: by 1700, all over the Continent, well-heeled Europeans would buy only fans and scarves, shoes and gowns and jackets made in France. The finance industry raised and managed the funds that made it possible to build the palace of Versailles and to wage the wars that gave France much of the territory it still occupies.

Early in the seventeenth century, these two Parisian families began what for decades seemed an unstoppable rise. The Chevrots were a family of gifted lawyers who were employed either as advisers to the Parisian Parlement or in financial administrations. Each successive patriarch managed the Chevrot family's own financial affairs in time-honored ways.

Each Chevrot married off his eldest son with great care to a woman from a well-connected and wealthier family, thereby ensuring the next generation's increased prosperity.

This part of their strategy can be traced to February 22, 1604. On that day, in the office of a Parisian notary, a wedding contract was signed. Such agreements were milestones in a family's legal life. A marriage settlement set out each family's financial contributions to the union and determined their distribution among future generations.

In February 1604, the first Antoine Chevrot in seventeenth-century Paris was ready to take a wife. His marriage contract reveals a young man on the move, eager to make his mark.

The first witness to sign on Antoine's behalf was not the most important family member, as was traditionally the case, but Rolain de Saint-Étienne, identified as a "noble homme," whom Antoine described as "a friend." The description "noble homme" was not a sign of noble birth but meant simply that Antoine's friend was the most prominent person in the room that day. Saint-Étienne's distinction was professional: he held a position in the financial administration in Normandy. A second "friend" also stood up for Antoine: an attorney who worked for the Parisian police. To vouch for him that day, Antoine had thus chosen not family members but "friends" who were also useful business associates.

The two friends represented the circles in which all the successive Antoine Chevrots would live their professional lives: finance and its administration, justice and the law. And indeed the groom had already established this pattern: he identified himself as a *huissier des tailles* in the Parisian Tribunal, an officer who carried out judges' orders relating to the collection of the *taille*, the principal direct royal tax.

In 1604, the royal taxation administration offered an ambitious young man the ideal opportunity to get ahead. King Henri IV's reign was still new; he had only recently brought peace to his kingdom after decades of war between Protestants and Catholics. When after many attempts he had finally won Paris in 1594, Henri IV had found a battered capital, its finances in ruins just like its streets. The monarch had great plans for Paris: within a decade, construction had been completed on the city's first modern bridge, the Pont Neuf, and work had begun on Paris' first modern square, the Place Royale, today's Place des Vosges. The king desperately needed revenue to subsidize such costly urban renewal projects (as well as the high cost of waging war), and the *taille* was an evident source. Henri IV also needed men on whom he could rely to make sure that payments were up to date and that all who should be paying tax were doing so. Those in his employ moved up quickly, and in the process they made essential contacts. Those loyal to Henri IV remained loyal to one another as well.

The groom further stated that he was *majeur*, "of age," over twenty-five. It was then common in Paris for men to marry at about thirty; all the future Antoine Chevrots did just this. The bride's connections were excellent, exactly what an ambitious young man required. Her father, Antoine Gillot, as well as other family members, were *marchands de bois*, merchants who dealt in firewood and timber. They exercised a virtually recession-proof trade: Parisians always needed wood, and never more than in the early seventeenth century, when a building boom was on and wood was the principal material used for Parisian housing. In 1612, a French periodical informed its readers that "as soon as Henri IV had become master of Paris, you could see new construction all over the city." Antoine Chevrot made a most opportune match.

Marie Gillot, born in 1577, was also "of age." She brought to the table a substantial dowry: 4,500 livres in cash, an annuity worth 1,500 more, and an additional 800 in personal effects. The bride's family provided her husband with the contacts he needed to get ahead in his newly adopted city. Her three younger brothers were destined to become major players in various financial administrations. In 1622, Marie's brother Germain, then already the chief controller for the Parisian salt tax, married the daughter of one of the country's most powerful financiers, Jean Duhamel, chief controller of the national salt tax administration.

Marie Gillot even had her own handsomely furnished apartment in a good neighborhood, on the rue de la Poterie near Paris' Hôtel de Ville. She listed her abundant possessions, which included a bed and bedding, a good supply of sheets and towels, dishes, tables and chairs, a pair of fine walnut wardrobes, even paintings on the walls—in short, everything a young couple needed in order to start a life together.

The cash was handed over immediately. All Antoine Chevrot had to do was sign the contract, collect the money, and move in. Sign he did, and with a very firm and well-formed signature, whereas Marie Gillot stated that she could neither read nor write. Although this was perhaps surprising for someone from her socioeconomic milieu, early in the seventeenth century this was not unusual in France and even in Paris, where literacy was traditionally the highest in the kingdom. Even at the century's end and in the largest cities, barely half of all Frenchwomen could sign their names. In the country as a whole, only 14 percent of women could do so.

It was less common for someone who was neither a member of the clergy nor a professional scholar to write as fluently as Antoine Chevrot did. His marriage contract provides the first illustration of a cardinal rule of this family saga: the ability to write well conferred authority and status.

That 1604 settlement plainly testifies to what mattered to Antoine Chevrot. The contract is equally eloquent in its silence.

No family member was present on that February day to stand up for the groom. In fact, Antoine made no mention of any family ties whatsoever: he did not even state the names of his parents, a ritual gesture almost always observed in such documents, even for a man already of age and thus with no need for parental consent. This indicated that his family was not Parisian—he had moved to the French capital in order to work for the most important tax office in the kingdom—and also that there was nothing to brag about in his family's social status. In this official context, Antoine Chevrot did not want to call attention to his roots. It was not his family's past that mattered: his future alone counted. Indeed, he even made a most unusual promise to the family that was accepting him into its ranks: that he would soon "find a better situation for himself." To do so, he required a substantial capital investment.

In seventeenth-century France, no appointment was possible without cold hard cash. Every single position occupied by every Chevrot and Magoulet— every post in every one of the various administrations they served, even that of Queen's Embroiderer—was purchased, and always for sums larger than Marie Gillot's dowry. Jean I Magoulet, for instance, paid 6,000 livres for the privilege of embroidering for Queen Marie-Thérèse.

Antoine Chevrot was thus a self-made man, the first of his family to live in Paris, the first Chevrot with the ambition to take advantage of the social mobility that, in the course of the seventeenth century, became increasingly possible in the French capital for those clever enough to negotiate the machinery of power. He was determined to make the name that he signed so forcefully mean something.

The young man from nowhere would surely have been well satisfied with his family's future achievements. For more than a century, until Louis Chevrot met and fell in love with Louise Magoulet, the Chevrot dynasty's familial strategy was so crystal-clear that it produced a family tree that is astonishing in its simplicity.

For an entire century and through four generations, the line went forward, from one Antoine Chevrot to the next, with each subsequent marriage moving the family up a notch in the two worlds that counted in its members' eyes: Paris and the French court. Each successive Antoine Chevrot was a form of capital:

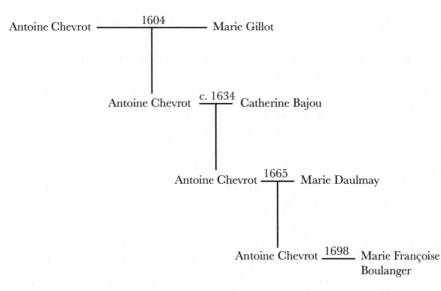

Antoine Chevrot ——— 1604 ——— Marie Gillot

Antoine Chevrot — c. 1634 — Catherine Bajou

Antoine Chevrot — 1665 — Marie Daulmay

Antoine Chevrot — 1698 — Marie Françoise Boulanger

he brought to the table a combination of ambition, drive, and self-confidence that, along with a superior education, promised professional success—or so it seemed to the families into which each Antoine married.

The wisdom of a cornerstone of the Chevrot strategy is obvious: only one child, to concentrate resources; a son, to continue the line. In an age when infant and child mortality were brutally high, their policy would have been more than risky. In seventeenth-century France, roughly 25 percent of children did not live to see their first birthday; at least 50 percent did not reach the age of ten. But wills and inventories and other Chevrot family documents are clear—and this was a family of jurists and counselors, so there were always abundant legal documents: in each generation, there was a sole heir, always a son, always named Antoine.

Shortly after that 1604 marriage, the Chevrots shared in a dream of many Parisians: owning a piece of their city's choice real estate. The property selected in 1612 was located in a highly desirable spot, the area that would later be known as the Marais.

Paris' Marais neighborhood has regained of late the reputation it acquired in the second half of the seventeenth century: that of being, in the words of a 1715 guidebook to the city, "the fun part of town." Tourists from all over the globe flock there today. In their strolls through the Marais, it's unlikely that many venture just beyond the Picasso museum to explore one of the neighborhood's smallest streets, the rue du Perche. That street, named for a French province that was eliminated in 1789, now seems perfectly unobtrusive.

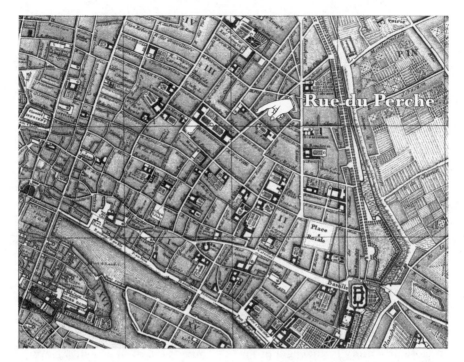

Rue du Perche

Extending a mere two blocks (and short ones at that), it's barely 25 feet wide. But in the early seventeenth century, the rue du Perche was a model of urban modernism.

It was then a brand-new street in an equally new neighborhood, one that Henri IV had designed in an effort to anchor into Paris' urban fabric an innovative city square, to be named the Place de France. When Henri IV was assassinated in 1610, the project was aborted. After the monarch's death, the land set aside for the Place de France was acquired by Michel Pigou, a straw man acting on behalf of powerful figures in Paris' financial administration. New streets were laid out, including the rue du Perche, and plots of land were sold.

On January 25, 1612, Nicolas Bajou became the original owner of one of the smallest houses on the street: he acquired the property directly from Gérard Gippon, the mason who had bought the land and done the construction. The sales document describes it as "very near the rue Vieille-du-Temple." Bajou's house still stands, at number 3 rue du Perche, just off the intersection with the rue Vieille-du-Temple.

Number 3 is today a modest house. Only two windows wide, it has lived on, slight and unassuming, behind its unadorned, whitewashed façade. Almost all the neighboring homes are considerably wider and of less primitive design: number 3 has clearly remained a stonemason's work.

On the ground floor when you enter, to the left is a single, nearly square room, originally the shop, the commercial establishment that stood at street level in all but the grandest Parisian residences. A staircase leads up to a series of small apartments. In the seventeenth century, these would have been the family's living quarters, one room to a floor. The house is one story taller today than it was then, but all in all, number 3 rue du Perche is still essentially the house Bajou acquired in 1612.

Bajou was then a young man, an officer of the judicial administration of the city of Paris, the Châtelet. During all his married life, he lived in the house with his wife, Geneviève Bajou; her younger sister Catherine was married to the second Antoine Chevrot, also in the Châtelet's employ, as a lawyer in charge of defense appeals.

The Bajou marriage was childless. On January 26, 1665, only weeks before she died, Geneviève Bajou, still living in the rue du Perche house, made a will. She was clearly quite elderly: her signature at the end is shaky. It's the kind of tidy document one might expect from someone who had spent her life in close proximity to the legal profession. She disposed of absolutely everything: the amber necklace "around my neck" was left to her goddaughter, the bonnet on her head to her servant, Marie du Croissy.

The entire estate of this quietly prosperous family—her home, a sizable farm near Paris, cash, and financial assets—she bequeathed to her sister Catherine. Upon her sister's death, the estate would go to Catherine's *fils unique*, her sole son and heir, the fortunate third Antoine Chevrot. His aunt asked only that Antoine pay her "modest" debts, which were tiny indeed.

And thus it was that the house on the rue du Perche came to be part of the Chevrot family estate. No Chevrot ever made the house a family home; by 1665, it was far from grand enough for their taste. Instead it became rental property; for well over a century, a succession of Chevrots leased the house to a succession of Parisian *vinaigriers*, merchants who made and sold vinegar and mustard. In typical Parisian merchant style, these *vinaigriers* used the downstairs shop as a commercial space and lived in the rooms upstairs.

Two sisters and only one heir: the third Antoine Chevrot was their golden boy and hope for the future. And it's easy to see why. By 1665, Antoine was already a member of the most elite circle in the Parisian judicial world. He served as an *avocat au Parlement*, a jurist in the employ of the Parisian Parlement. These lawyers were a class apart from the average Parisian barrister:

they were considered the best legal minds of the day, those most knowledgeable in the increasingly intricate procedures that governed the increasingly large number of cases brought to judgment before the Parlement. The Parlement's lawyers enjoyed enhanced social status and useful political connections as well.

The third Antoine Chevrot, a lifetime *avocat au Parlement*, was clearly a prudent man. In 1665, he had not yet married: he had waited to cash in on his professional calling card until the moment when he could make the best match possible. The death of Geneviève Bajou, with the promise of the substantial estate that would be his upon his mother's death, set the stage for a brilliant union.

Six decades of the patient construction of a dynasty paid off handsomely only four months after Geneviève Bajou made her will, when the young lawyer was wed. His aunt was not present; she had evidently died during the interval. Antoine's bride was an heiress to a fortune founded on a commodity that for centuries had the power to build and to destroy empires: salt.

On May 21, 1665, their marriage contract was drawn up. This time the parties did not meet at the notary's office, as was common practice. They gathered instead in a grand Parisian residence, and the notary came to them.

Today, documents recorded by Parisian notaries are piled together in boxes in the French National Archives, located around the corner from the rue du Perche. In this context, most documents appear identical, and the differences between rich and poor are erased: the will of a powerful man might turn up right after a lease signed by a merchant of modest means. Even so, occasionally documents stand out because they feature an evident status indicator.

By 1665, some notaries had recently adopted a practice designed to flatter their wealthiest clients: major acts relating to their families were bound not with the simple stitches usually used, but with color-coded ribbons: black for probate inventories, red or pink for marriages. Antoine's contract features a jaunty silk bow: it has faded over the centuries to a very pale pink. The notary who chose it was the family notary of the bride's family, the Daulmay dynasty of merchants.

The bride, Marie Daulmay, was the daughter of Jean Daulmay, who identified himself as a *commis aux aides*, someone employed by the Fermiers Généraux, or Tax Farmers, the handful of powerful financiers who managed tax collection for the French state. Jean was involved with the tax he knew best, the much-hated *gabelle* or salt tax that all French paid (or tried to avoid) to obtain a commodity that by the seventeenth century was considered an absolute

*Antoine Chevrot's marriage contract, tied with a pink bow to indicate the importance of the family into which he married.*

necessity. Marie's brother Philibert worked in the same trade as their uncle Claude, also present that day. Claude was a prosperous *marchand de salines*, a merchant who dealt in fish such as cod that could be preserved by being dried and salted. Other family members were involved in various ways with the trade in salt and salted fish. To make this advantageous match, Antoine Chevrot had relied on the Gillot family. By far the most successful of Marie Gillot's brothers, Germain, got his start on the path to immense wealth in the salt tax administration.

The salt trade had brought the Daulmays more than wealth: thanks to salt, they had also moved up the social ladder. Antoine's witnesses were a predictable lot for a Chevrot: no family members other than his mother (his father was by then deceased); a number of "friends," all employed as financial administrators or advisers to the court, to the city of Paris, to the Parisian Parlement. In the lot, one man was a true celebrity: Jacques Tubeuf, whose name was then virtually synonymous with finance in France. Tubeuf had served King Louis XIII as *contrôleur général des finances*, or finance minister; by 1665, his name was followed by a string of costly titles. (A small irony of history: Tubeuf's grand residence near the Louvre eventually became the property of John Law, who transformed it into the Banque Royale, the seat of the finance company that would help ruin both the Chevrot and Magoulet clans.)

But even Tubeuf was small fry next to those who stood up for Marie Daulmay.

Her father had parlayed the wages of salt into a new rank: he identified himself as the Sieur de Coulanges, the Lord of Coulanges. With the purchase of a small estate, he had distanced his family from their status as merchants who worked for a living.

On Paris' rue aux Greniers-Saint-Lazare, not far from the traditional market area, Les Halles, where the family had made its fortune, the Daulmay townhouse was so grand that the signing of the marriage contract took place there. And for the guest list the bride's family was able to muster, only a truly splendid residence was appropriate.

The first witness signed her name, Marie de Bourbon, in huge letters, as seems fitting for a princess of royal blood, the widow of the Prince de Carignano, the founder of the Savoy-Carignano branch of the House of Savoy. Marie de Bourbon resided in one of Paris' fabled residences, the Hôtel de Soissons or the Hôtel de la Reine, constructed in 1572 for Queen Catherine de Médicis when she decided that the Louvre was not up to her standards. The distance between the two homes was not great, but still—Marie de Bourbon did not leave her regal abode for just anyone. Her visit to the Daulmays speaks volumes about the power of salt.

She was in good company: two other Savoie princes, the Comte de Soissons, and the fabulously wealthy Louis de Rohan Chabot, Duc de Rohan. Those grand names figure on the list of signatures just before the modest pairing of Chevrot and Daulmay. Antoine signed with the assured signature typical of the Chevrots, but the "Daulmay" next to his was added by the bride's father, for unlike Antoine's mother, Marie Daulmay could not sign her name.

The financial terms were generous; they were also unusually precise: Jean Daulmay wanted to control the way in which his money was used. Of the total 4,000 livres, only half was given without strings. The Daulmays contributed 1,400 livres for the young couple's lodging and food as they got started in life, 600 toward furnishings for a new home. They covered the costs of the engagement festivities and the bride's "nuptial garments."

As these specifications made plain, life in the new social sphere into which Antoine Chevrot was moving came at a price. As an unmarried lawyer, he had had only modest living expenses. But from May 1665 on, everything—the clothes necessary to impress those he would now frequent, the apartment in a more exclusive neighborhood, as well as the trappings necessary to bring it up to the level that would be expected by his future guests—would be sumptuous.

The third Antoine Chevrot did not live up to expectations. As soon as the Daulmay funds ran out, he fell into debt.

By May 1679, the Daulmays had had enough. Marie filed for a *séparation des biens*, a separation of property. After an investigation by Police Commissioner Charles Gazon, on September 30, Antoine was ordered to return the entire 4,000 livres of Marie's dowry, and a payment plan was agreed to. But Antoine continued to disappoint. By October 11, 1692, he had repaid precisely 334 livres. He was ordered to hand over the house on the rue du Perche to his bride.

Legal proceedings such as these were not uncommon in important Parisian families. They could indicate deeper personal problems for the couple, but in the vast majority of cases they functioned as they did in the case of *Chevrot v. Daulmay*: as a way for the bride and her family to protect the property she had brought into the marriage and to ensure that her husband's creditors could not come after her estate.

In the 1680s, Marie Daulmay would have been a tempting target for those angry creditors. Her family's fortunes were booming, because salt was surging: at this moment, the salt tax was the most onerous imposition of all. This was particularly true in Paris: in 1680, salt sold there for 10 sous, a half livre, per pound—then the daily wage of a farm laborer—whereas its real cost was only 4 deniers, or one third of a sou. That government levy multiplied the cost of salt by 30.

Such financial separations were also designed to preserve property for the next generation. The 1692 proviso sheltered the rue du Perche house and guaranteed that it could be passed on to future Chevrots, first of all to the couple's sole heir, another son named Antoine.

By 1698, the wisdom of that separation became clear when a document of a kind new to both families was signed at Versailles. The fourth Antoine Chevrot would henceforth move in what every Frenchman of the day saw as the ultimate corridors of power, those of Louis XIV's château at Versailles. On February 3, Antoine received his appointment to an official court function: he was to serve as one of the sixteen valets de chambre of the court's most beloved figure, the Duchesse de Bourgogne, wife of the king's grandson and subsequently mother of three sons, one of whom later ruled France as King Louis XV. A valet de chambre (the French term was used at the English court as well) took up residence at court and performed a variety of functions, ranging from holding up mirrors to "protecting" the royal personage's bed during his or her absence by standing guard next to it. There were sixteen valets who served in rotation, four at a time. Antoine was on call during the second quarter, from April to June.

In centuries past, valets de chambre had been chosen from the ranks of young noblemen, but by 1698 there were no longer enough aristocratic families able to afford the honor, for royal appointments were business arrangements, just like posts in administrations such as the tax authority. His parents invested 7,000 livres, and in return Antoine would receive "wages" and various "rewards" for loyal service (about 300 per annum). For that price, he became part of one of the fastest-growing administrations of the day: as Louis XIV's ambitions ballooned, so did his court. The king also allowed others—his wife, his brother, his eldest son and his wife—to create their own courts. More court functions meant more positions and therefore more revenue for the royal coffers.

To secure this costly honor for their son, Antoine's parents had counted on the head of the Duchesse de Bourgogne's household, her *dame d'honneur*, Marguerite Louise de Béthune, Duchesse Du Lude, among the wealthiest and most powerful women in France, who personally signed Antoine's letter of appointment. And this was not the only arrangement made on Antoine's behalf in 1698 with help from the powerful duchess: on November 23, another marriage contract was signed. Antoine, "of age" but still living with his parents, was taking a far younger bride: Marie Françoise Boulanger was then only about fifteen.

This contract was also ribbon-bound: it sports a bow in a royal color, blue. And its signing took place in the grandest French residence of all, the palace of Versailles, in the private apartment of the woman Antoine had just begun serving as a valet de chambre, the Duchesse de Bourgogne.

Marie-Adélaïde de Savoie would certainly have been sympathetic to this union: she was a newlywed herself, married for less than a year; and, at two weeks shy of thirteen, she was even younger than her valet de chambre's bride. The famously high-spirited duchess seems to have viewed the occasion as a sort of party to which she and the Duchesse Du Lude had invited a most distinguished guest list indeed.

To save time for the château's inhabitants, the notaries had prepared the document in advance: all that remained was for the signatures to be added. The notaries had left the amount of space they had considered necessary, but so many came forward to stand for the young couple that great nobles were obliged to squeeze their names in wherever they could so that there would be room for all the signatures, as well as the many, many titles of all those who had assembled in the Duchesse de Bourgogne's suite.

Marie-Adélaïde signed first, followed by the Duchesse Du Lude. Then came the Duchesse de Sully, the Duchesse de Verneuil, the Duchesse de Guiche, the Duc de Sully, the Duc de Cardonne, the Chevalier de Sully—a veritable who's who of Versailles' most splendid denizens.

Only close family members were in attendance that day, among them the mother of the groom. Marie Daulmay had never learned to sign her name, but she was surely proud of what she had been able to accomplish for Antoine with her family's revenue from salt.

This fourth Antoine Chevrot's many honorifics were intended to prove how far his family had come in the course of a century: he was a valet de chambre, and also a *conseiller du roi*, or royal counselor, a title automatically conferred with the purchase of his principal claim to status, his position in a corps of financial officers, the *contrôleurs généraux des rentes de l'Hôtel de Ville*, who oversaw payments on a prominent type of investment, the *rentes* or royal annuities administered by Paris' city government.

The work of three generations of an upwardly mobile Parisian family had culminated in a rich array of honorifics, all of which had been for sale. Due to the ever higher cost of waging war, the French monarchy, like so many of its subjects, was increasingly dependent on credit.

In England, to finance the Nine Years' War, the Bank of England was established: in 1694, when the bank opened subscriptions, many signed up to take on a share in the war debt because their government was willing to pay high interest, 8 percent, in order to raise funds quickly. Across the Channel in France, Louis XIV financed his armies instead by selling more and more positions of all kinds. The practice, which had begun in the mid-sixteenth century, knew its heyday beginning in 1689. Antoine Chevrot's family had taken full advantage of the Sun King's broadscale marketing of signs of distinction.

By the end of the seventeenth century, some forty-five thousand posts great and small were up for grabs. Officeholders could treat their positions as property and sell them; they could buy the right to bequeath them to their heirs. Their sale was in fact a long-term loan to the crown. The officeholder received what were called wages but were actually interest on the sum invested in his office. Since the government paid interest at a low rate, the wages were never high, but the positions brought with them other kinds of value: the exemption from certain taxes, for example. Above all, as the marriage made by the fourth Antoine Chevrot made evident, the titles added after one's name promised distinction, social standing, and authority.

The positions were often less distinguished than their names implied. Antoine, for example, loved to refer to himself as a royal counselor, a title that at one time had had true significance. By the turn of the eighteenth century, however, so many people had acquired this alleged distinction that insiders began to quip that anyone and everyone, even those with the position of livestock inspector, could call themselves royal counselors. Still, Antoine's list of titles remained impressive.

It was also fraudulent, for Antoine had no right to the first title he listed on his marriage contract, *écuyer*—literally a gentleman, but a word that had become a synonym for "noble," which Antoine was not. When he made this claim to aristocratic status, Antoine ran the risk of exposure for usurpation, a crime punishable with a fine of roughly 2,000 livres, as well as public embarrassment. But Antoine knew that this contract would be treasured and passed on to future generations; he was thus eager to cast the best light possible on his status. And Antoine's desire to appear eminent both for his bride-to-be and for future Chevrots was so strong that he was prepared to be reckless. This was the first example of the risky behavior Antoine would consistently demonstrate, always in the name of social advancement.

The bride's family had long had court connections: her uncle had served in the household of Louis XIV's wife, Marie-Thérèse. Her father, Barthélemy Boulanger, was the Duchesse Du Lude's chief officer, and her mother, Marie Charlotte Perrin, spent most of her life in the duchess's service as well. The status conferred by connections like those were the bride's attraction, for the dowry she provided was not up to the usual Chevrot standards: it included only 500 livres in cash.

The Boulangers recognized that this sum was meager, so her father handed over the deed to Courcelles, a property near the city of Orléans that had been in his family since 1629. As estates went, Courcelles was a modest affair, but its farms brought in rental income and its owner had the right to add an honorific after his name. And sure enough: Antoine would soon identify himself in the corridors of Versailles as *le Sieur de Courcelles*, the Lord of Courcelles.

Barthélemy Boulanger also turned over the papers for the final part of his daughter's inheritance, surely the oddest part of any Chevrot marriage contract, a two-page enumeration of the possessions recently bequeathed to her by a Boulanger aunt. Some of these were basic goods reminiscent of Marie Gillot's household furnishings in 1604: a bed and bedding worth 50 livres, household linen and dishes valued at 130. But all the big-ticket items were of a very different ilk: the aunt's personal wardrobe of high-fashion garments.

There was a complete formal outfit in rose damask, another in lilac satin, with an extra skirt in the textile of the moment at Versailles, Chinese silk. There was a more casual outfit in the other fabric favored by ladies of the French court, hand-painted cotton imported from India, in a green and white pattern, lined with crimson satin. All this was valued at 570 livres, more than the cash Marie Françoise Boulanger brought into the marriage. And topping the list was an accessory truly of the moment: a Bourgogne, a type of bodice named for the duchess, who upon her arrival at the French court had at once become a fashion trendsetter. This Bourgogne was adorned with lace overembroidered in silver, the kind of ornate work produced by court embroiderers such as Jean Magoulet.

In all, women's high fashion clothing accounted for more than two thirds of the 1,450 livres in personal property included in the dowry. Marie Françoise began her married life decked out in finery more suitable for a court personage than for the wife of a young man embarking on a career in financial administration.

The document ends in a most bizarre fashion. On September 1, 1703, Antoine and Marie Françoise, by then the parents of Louis as well as a second son, Antoine Charles, returned to the office of the notary who had drawn up their marriage contract, along with her parents. They were there to sign an addendum to the original contract: it specified that the clothing that had been an essential part of her dowry was in reality worth 300 livres less than the listing included with the contract had stated. To make up the difference in the dowry promised in 1698, in 1703 Barthélemy Boulanger and Marie Charlotte Perrin were obliged to add 300 livres in cash.

Nearly five years after their wedding, who could possibly have come up with a more accurate evaluation of the worth of what had been at the start used clothing? What could have provoked Antoine to bring such humiliation on his in-laws and his wife? However, by 1703, it was not difficult at all for Marie Françoise Boulanger's parents to believe that their son-in-law was capable of petty conduct such as this.

That addendum stands as a clear warning of what was ahead. The seemingly limitless financial greed that caused Antoine to reevaluate the price of vintage high fashion would in due course wipe out everything the first three Antoine Chevrots had worked to accomplish.

CHAPTER FOUR

# Upward Mobility 2:
# Purveyors to the Crown
# The Magoulets: 1638–1678

T HE MAGOULET ASSAULT on France's capital began on October 24, 1638 with the contract that made official the forthcoming marriage between Jacques Magoulet and Marie Lescrivain. The agreement laid out the terms for a kind of union that had long been traditional among Parisian merchant families. This was as typical a marriage among artisans as the Chevrots' ambitious forays into the merchant class had been atypical.

The groom and the bride's father shared a profession: they were *gainiers*. They enjoyed elite status in the corporation that governed the exercise of their trade in Paris: both were *maîtres*, masters, a rank to which an artisan was named after extensive training in the workshop of a master and once his chef d'oeuvre, or masterpiece, had been accepted by guild authorities.

*Gainiers* created cases to protect precious objects so that they could be safely carried about. The objects for which they invented containers varied immensely over time. As new objects came into fashion or use, *gainiers* learned to make leather sheaths or leather-covered boxes to address their specifications. In the first half of the seventeenth century, when the Magoulets' story began, French *gainiers* were enjoying a moment of great prosperity.

Their dream clients lived, as great nobles had for centuries, an often nomadic existence. The French court was housed in multiple royal castles, and members of the court traveled regularly from one château to another—to avoid war or disease or to spend the hunting season in a region known for its well-stocked woods. Every time the court moved, its belongings went along with it. This created the need for leather cases, trunks, and containers to protect fragile possessions, each constructed to the precise dimensions of a precious object.

*Seventeenth-century leather case designed by a Parisian* gainier *for the safe transport of a fragile object.*

*Seventeenth-century leather case open to display the jeweled coffer it was crafted to protect.*

In the 1850s, when a young *malletier,* or trunk maker, named Louis Vuitton launched his workshop, his success was founded on his pledge to create cases that could "securely pack the most fragile objects." Vuitton's seventeenth-century Parisian precursors designed the same cases on which the Vuitton empire was built, and they designed them with the same goal of safely transporting delicate possessions. *Gainiers* constructed a wood frame, shaped and proportioned to the object's exact dimensions. They padded the wooden core with fleece and lined it with fabric. They then covered the substructure with fine hide such as Morocco leather. The seventeenth-century French case shown here was crafted specifically to protect this jewel-encrusted casket.

Master *gainiers* were true artists. The leather covering for a case might be dyed; it was lavishly decorated, at times with elaborate designs traced with tiny gold and silver nails. At others, heated tools were impressed on the leather, and rollers and stamps were used to create a recessed pattern, subsequently filled with gold leaf and polished to a glow, creating a surface that gleamed in candlelight.

Theirs was among the smallest of the luxury guilds: in the decades when the Magoulets practiced this craft, there were only about thirty-five master *gainiers* in Paris but nearly three hundred master embroiderers, a fact that indicates that embroidery was by far the more prominent and more lucrative trade. The group that gathered in the notary's office in October 1638 to celebrate Jacques Magoulet's upcoming marriage included a large percentage of the master *gainiers* in the city. Two "friends" stood up for the bridegroom: Pierre Prigay and Gabriel Grandin, both masters. Most of the bride's witnesses were identified in the same way. *Gainiers* were such a tight-knit bunch that in the guild's records all through the century, the same family names recur.

Literacy tended to be high among master artisans in the luxury goods trade, especially among craftsmen who worked for the French court and engaged in complex business dealings with those in the top ranks of French society. The ability to write facilitated their work and lent social prestige. It's hardly surprising, therefore, that virtually every one of those *gainiers* from different generations present to celebrate the Magoulet marriage, including the bride's father, was able to sign his name—all but one, that is. In this company of his professional peers and competitors, the bridegroom declared that he "could neither read nor write."

A signature was not the only form of identification missing from Jacques Magoulet's marriage agreement. No family members were present; like the first Antoine Chevrot in 1604, he made no mention whatsoever of his origins. Although this once again means that Jacques was not a native Parisian, there is no indication of his place of birth, no hint as to his place in the French social hierarchy. The Magoulet dynasty of Parisian master craftsmen, a force to be reckoned with for well over a century, was founded by another young man from nowhere, someone who chose to obscure his origins.

But the similarity between the agreement that began the Chevrot family's story in Paris in 1604 and the contract from 1638 that inaugurated the Magoulet saga ends there.

The Chevrots and the Magoulets were all *bourgeois de Paris*, literally residents of the city of Paris. They inhabited a vast and ill-defined sphere: bourgeois clearly stood beneath aristocrats, and just as clearly above simple working-class Parisians such as manual laborers, shopworkers, and servants.

But within the middle ranks there were many shadings. The Chevrots and the families with which they forged alliances considered themselves positioned at the middle sphere's upper limit. That conviction, as well as the distinction between professionals and those who practiced a trade, convinced them of their evident superiority to craftsmen such as the Magoulets. In reality, as the story of their two families indicates, at many junctures, the distance separating them was infinitesimal.

Upon his marriage, Jacques Magoulet displayed no indication of discontent with his lot. In economic and professional terms, he and Marie Lescrivain were equals. The bridegroom and his bride's father were following a logic traditional to Paris' merchant class: a union between the families of artisans from the same guild provided a secure foundation for a stable future.

Every aspect of the Magoulet-Lescrivain union was anchored in this sensible mercantile thinking. While all four Antoine Chevrots favored Paris' Right Bank, Jacques Magoulet chose a less elegant Left Bank life. His marriage contract was signed without frills—there was no colored bow on this document—at the notary's establishment on the Place Maubert, the Left Bank square that was the epicenter of bourgeois Paris.

The family into which he married lived on one of Paris' oldest streets, the rue Mouffetard, in another classic Left Bank neighborhood located to the southwest of the Place Maubert, the Faubourg Saint-Marcel. Beginning in the Middle Ages, leather workers of various stripes had settled there, near the banks of Paris' other river, the Bièvre: they had used its waters for preparing, tanning, and dyeing skins. Many *gainiers* lived there as well, close to the raw material needed for their craft.

The marriage was an economically modest affair. The bride's dowry came to a total of 300 livres, and of that only 100 were paid in cash; the remaining 200 took the form of household possessions. This was nothing in terms of the dowries sought after by the Chevrot men, but it was fairly standard for artisans during a decade when France's finances were badly strained due to its involvement in the Thirty Years' War. In June 1640, when Marie Lescrivain's sister Catherine married, she received an identical dowry.

Catherine's husband, twenty-eight-year-old Jean Danonné, was a *maître passementier, tissutier, rubanier*, a master artisan who confected ribbons, laces, braids, buttons, and fringes—every variety of the many textile-based trims that were abundantly applied to high fashion garments. Other members of the extended Lescrivain family were masters in the same guild; two uncles were master *savetiers*, specialists in the art of redesigning old shoes and boots, and two were wine merchants. Still another uncle was a mason. All of them lived either in or in close proximity to the Faubourg Saint-Marcel. The Lescrivain clan stayed among its own kind.

Jacques Magoulet was present for the June 1640 marriage of his wife's sister; his name leads the list of witnesses, proof of the close relations between the two young couples that would continue through the decades ahead. He may not have had his own family nearby to support him, but he knew how to forge family ties.

Neither of the Lescrivain sisters was literate, nor was their mother, Catherine Sahult. In contrast, the numerous male relatives, including Danonné, could sign their names—all but the lead witness, Jacques Magoulet.

The Magoulet-Lescrivain union was a long and prosperous one. Five sons and three daughters reached adulthood. Most went on to get married and have children of their own. And Jacques and Marie were both examples of a longevity striking for the period. When their son Jacques married in 1685, his parents, in their seventies by then, were there to stand up for him.

At the time of Marie's death in May 1699, at the then almost inconceivable age of about eighty-five, the Nine Years' War had brought the French economy virtually to a standstill. Yet to honor her memory, their eldest son Hubert, a master *gainier* like his father and his maternal grandfather, staged what was for their milieu and for the time a funeral intended to remain memorable within the tight-knit community of Parisian *gainiers*.

Hubert paid 73 livres to print the announcements of the funeral, known as *billets*, or tickets. These were lavishly printed sheets 13 by 19 inches. They listed the name of the deceased, the place of death, the church where the funeral mass would be held, and the date and time of the ceremony. They could be distributed and also posted in prominent places to turn out as large a crowd as possible. Hubert paid an additional 35 livres to have *crieurs*, town criers, broadcast the news even more widely. He paid for candles, and even 137 livres so that "the grand choir" of Saint-Barthélemy, his parents' parish church, would sing at his mother's funeral mass. At a time when the average cost of a master artisan's funeral was 145 livres, Hubert's expenditure ran to nearly 300 livres, the amount of his mother's 1638 dowry.

The church where the ceremony took place, Saint-Barthélemy, was among the oldest in the city; it was situated on the Île de la Cité, between Notre-Dame and the Sainte-Chapelle. (Saint-Barthélemy was demolished shortly after the Revolution of 1789.) From about 1650 on, as the luxury goods industry took shape, *gainiers* began to move north in close proximity to Paris' better-known river, the Seine: Saint-Barthélemy became their parish church.

*Gainiers* took up residence in the small streets of the Île de la Cité surrounding Saint-Barthélemy. They chose one address above all, the embankment that runs along the Seine between the Pont Neuf and the Pont-au-Change, the Quai de l'Horloge, the Quay of the Clock, constructed in the early seventeenth century and named for the huge clock positioned on the façade of the nearby Palais de Justice, or Law Courts. That address, convenient to the Louvre and the neighborhoods adjacent to the royal palace, home to the city's most elegant clientele, created a more upmarket image for their trade. Jacques moved his family to the quay in the late 1650s; from then on, he and Marie Lescrivain never left that address.

The Quai de l'Horloge was also in close proximity to what long remained the center for upmarket commerce in Paris, the Galerie du Palais, the Palace Gallery, the city's original high-end shopping arcade. Both sides of the walkway leading to the Great Room of Paris' Law Courts were lined with small shops in which artisans presented their wares. The Palace Gallery was the

*A 1640 view of the Palace Gallery, Paris' first luxury shopping arcade.*

place where fashionable Parisians went to see and be seen. By 1700, 180 merchants maintained shops there.

On February 9, 1661, Jacques signed a lease on one of those coveted spaces. The document situates its location with great precision: it was "backed by the wall of the Palace and looking out onto the great waterway [the Seine]." The lease further makes clear the shop's exact situation on the embankment by giving the equivalent in today's terms of its street number: "formerly its shop-sign depicted Saint Nicolas; now the sign represents a Golden Acorn." Subsequent leases mention a Golden Apple rather than a Golden Acorn, so the round gilded object depicted on the sign did not have the same specificity for every viewer. As far as the Magoulet family was concerned, that golden shopsign long signified home. For the next seventy-two years, a Magoulet could always be found at the sign of the Golden Apple.

Faithful to another trend in his profession, Jacques was also diversifying: he now called himself a *gainier cassetier*, advertising a subspecialty in the production of a recently redesigned and highly desirable object: *cassettes. Cassettes* were small coffers or strongboxes outfitted with tiny locks: they provided security for valued possessions and sensitive documents. By the second half of the seventeenth century, all important Parisians owned *cassettes*.

Shortly after the move across the river from the Louvre, Jacques advanced to a pinnacle of his profession, an appointment that required frequent contact with that palace's inhabitants: he was named *maître gainier cassetier privilégié suivant la cour*, a privileged master coffermaker following the court, an official purveyor to the crown.

This was another French royal honor acquired through a combination of talent and cash. Selected merchants and artisans were given the possibility of purchasing letters of privilege that allowed them to add after their name this designation, "following the court," that offered a royal endorsement and thus attracted commissions from outside the court. The positions also exempted these artisans from various fees and taxes such as the salt tax. In the early 1660s, when Jacques joined this club, there were in all 594 who "followed the court," but that number included representatives from 101 professions—butchers and bakers and pastry chefs, jewelers and tailors and glove makers. Their total was limited, as was the number allowed from any given field: there could be no more than twenty butchers, sixteen tailors, eight pastry chefs, six embroiderers.

For centuries, there had been no *gainiers* in their ranks. When the first cohort was finally named in 1651, this was a tribute to the craft's increased visibility and status in France. Even then, only two *gainiers* were admitted to the elite corps. The two serving in the mid-1660s when Louis XIV's court was still young, Jacques and his closest associate from the early 1650s on, Louis Daubancour, were thus among the very first of their corporation ever to enjoy this privileged status.

These several hundred men at the top of their professions literally followed the court: when the court left the Louvre for another location, they were obliged to close their shops in Paris and travel with it, thereby guaranteeing that lords and ladies would never go a day without their favorite pastries—or a leather case for a new acquisition.

In classic master artisan fashion, Jacques intended to found a dynasty, to train his sons in the craft that allowed him to make a good life for his family. In the case of two of those sons, his strategy worked brilliantly, or nearly so.

On January 16, 1662, Jacques signed a compact placing sixteen-year-old Claude Magoulet in the workshop of another master *gainier*, Jean Le Jeune, for two years of additional on-the-job experience. Claude was soon a master in his own right and in 1689 was elected *juré*, an official of his guild. This was a fine career indeed, but it fell far short of the outstanding professional trajectory of the oldest Magoulet son, Hubert. But then Hubert was clearly the family's favored son; it would have been hard to match his accomplishments.

Hubert was named master directly after an apprenticeship with his father. Already on February 23, 1664—three years before Jacques began to work for the court—Hubert attained the rank of court artisan, higher still than purveyor to the crown. On that day, Hubert was named a "domestic officer" in the court of Queen Marie-Thérèse.

In 1664, the queen was at the height of her power: married not yet four years, she had already performed her most important function and had given Louis XIV a male heir, and she was pregnant for the third time. She was young—just twenty-five—and she loved all the beautiful clothes and beautiful things with which she had been surrounded during her childhood as an infanta of Spain at the court of her father, King Philip IV.

A portrait dating from the moment of Hubert's appointment advertised Queen Marie-Thérèse's status as mother of the heir to the throne: the tiny hand of her young son is tightly attached to her elegantly black-gloved hand. Both their outfits take opulence to the limit: they are intricately and densely embroidered in silver thread; dozens of huge pearls, fat diamonds, and colored gemstones have been applied with truly royal abandon.

The woman in that portrait was not yet the Queen Marie-Thérèse more familiar today, the woman neglected by her husband in favor of more glamorous royal mistresses. In the mid-1660s, Marie-Thérèse was a vibrant and confident queen of France, still the brilliant infanta featured in Velázquez's portraits of her at the Habsburg court.

In 1664, the queen appointed as her first official *gainier* a young man her own age, a rare mark of distinction for an artisan so early in his career. It was proof not only that Jacques Magoulet's business was successful enough that he was able to pay the roughly 5,000 livres necessary to purchase the office for

*A portrait of France's Queen Marie-Thérèse
and her son, the Dauphin of France. Both are
wearing garments elaborately embroidered
with precious stones and pearls.*

his son, but also that Hubert's talent was distinctive enough to have quickly singled him out. The terms of Hubert's appointment are unusually precise: he was to be the queen's personal *gainier* and to create for her all the *écritoires, petits coffres et cabinets* that she could possibly require—all her portable cases with compartments to contain every piece of equipment required for writing; all her small coffers and cabinets, every one of them with an intricate internal design, often featuring multiple drawers and lift-out trays.

Hubert had been selected to play the role of Louis Vuitton to the most powerful queen in Europe.

Hubert's long career proves that Marie-Thérèse had an eye for talent: he went on to dominate his trade. Like his brother Claude but well before him, he was elected to his guild's governing body. By 1676, he, like his father, had a shop on the Quai de l'Horloge, also at the sign of the Golden Apple. Hubert ran a shop at that address until his death on December 16, 1706.

Hubert was proof of the success of Jacques and Marie's parenting. The closest thing to a black spot on Hubert's record was the complaint made to the police in 1676 by Elizabeth Baillard, a neighbor on the embankment: in Hubert's absence, his apprentice Charles Lutteau had insulted her niece Jeanne with "atrocious abuse." Hubert got Lutteau to apologize, and the charges were dropped.

All in all, Hubert was the kind of firstborn son of every parent's dreams. He waited until he was well established to marry, and when he did so, on October 10, 1672, Hubert married well. Of all the marriages in the Magoulet and Chevrot clans over two centuries, this is the only union that can truly be called a marriage of equals.

Anne Goujon was also "of age," and like Hubert she was an established professional. A *maîtresse lingère*, she ran her own shop selling the wide variety of high-end linen goods—from collars and cuffs to tablecloths and napkins—found in abundance in prosperous seventeenth-century households. She, rather than her father, was responsible for her dowry, a very handsome one indeed: 2,500 livres.

Hubert's witnesses were the two younger brothers who shared his trade: Claude and Jean. Jean was the son Jacques surely then believed would carry on his legacy at least as brilliantly as Hubert. Jean may in fact have been the prodigy of them all: on January 20, 1667, Jacques had presided over a ceremony at which Jean was named simultaneously a master *gainier* and to the rank of artisan "following the court." The elected officials of their corporation were present to ratify this highly unusual joint appointment.

Only someone exceptionally gifted could have come so far so fast. And yes, Jean Magoulet, the man whose very identity later became inseparable from the title "The Queen's Embroiderer," received his professional training in high-end leather goods.

At the time of Hubert's marriage, there were no clouds in the Magoulet sky. The family had flourished during fifteen years on the Quai de l'Horloge. Jacques and Madeleine's sons were becoming successful on their own; Jacques' business had proved so prosperous that he was able to give all his children a good start in life. In 1669, when their eldest daughter, Jeanne, married Eustache Girardié, a master candle maker, her dowry was three times what her mother's had been: 1,000 livres.

Jacques had invested considerable financial resources and professional clout to have his son Jean so quickly named to the elite ranks of the purveyors to the crown. However, in 1674, Jean abruptly left the *gainier* profession in which he had attained mastery, not only squandering family capital but causing his father personal embarrassment.

Had Jean remained in the same corporation as his father and brothers, he would have come in for close scrutiny and would have been under pressure to follow established practice and be a model artisan. Throughout his life, Jean worked hard to find and to create environments that left him room to play fast and loose with the rules. He learned the rules well—in order to break them.

Jean had been awarded a mastership as a *gainier*; he simply acted as if it were natural to transfer it to another craft, embroidery, an art requiring a thoroughly different skill set. There is no record of how he received his training (or, truth be told, whether he was formally trained), but by early 1674—seven years after he had been proclaimed a master *gainier*—Jean was nevertheless employed as an embroiderer. He did not yet call himself a master, but he was already doing work for the greatest nobles in the land—notably Louis II de Bourbon-Condé, Prince de Condé, Louis XIV's first cousin, among the most celebrated generals in the history of France. And his work in 1675 for the prince must have been memorable, for it began an association between his family and the prince's court at Chantilly that would be continued by both Jean's son and grandson.

In 1674, when Jean left the leather goods enclave on the Quai de l'Horloge, he remained on the Île de la Cité. But even the short distance that separated his family home from the Priory of Saint-Denis de la Chartre transported him into a radically different world.

Today nothing remains of either the church dedicated to the first bishop of Paris, Saint Denis, or the area that surrounded it: all was swept away during Baron Georges-Eugène Haussmann's redesign. In the seventeenth century, Saint-Denis de la Chartre was one of several spots in the shadow of Notre-Dame cathedral in which centuries-old private ecclesiastical jurisdictions still flourished. Because of this independent status, its prior was able to rent out work and housing space in the church's former cloister: the roughly eighty artisans who lived there enjoyed freedom from guild restrictions, from the authority of the Parisian police, even from certain taxes. In this privileged environment, Jean Magoulet officially became an embroiderer. He also observed a new way of working as an artisan.

His father and brothers operated in a community dedicated to a single craft. At Saint-Denis de la Chartre, Jean was surrounded by a highly diverse group— shoemakers and tailors as well as fellow embroiderers: he learned the advantages, economic as well as artistic, of diversification and collaboration. In subsequent decades, Jean's finest work and his most lucrative contracts resulted from his tendency to function as a miniature luxury goods conglomerate.

And only two years after he began working as an embroiderer, Jean was elevated once again to the elite cadre of privileged royal artisans. In 1676, Jean was designated *brodeur ordinaire du roi*, one of four embroiderers appointed to serve Louis XIV on a quarterly basis.

But he wanted something else, and on December 24, 1677, he got it. That day, Jean Magoulet was named all at once master embroiderer, valet de chambre, and *brodeur de la reine*. In the letter that made his appointment official, Marie-Thérèse announced her intention of "rewarding his faithfulness in our service." Jean then became known by the title with which first he and then his eldest son would be identified for the next century, long after the queen who had appointed him had died: The Queen's Embroiderer. He was no longer a part of a team of four; from then on, he worked alone and made all decisions on his own.

Not even a year later, he was already behaving recklessly.

Court artisans enjoyed great privilege: Jean ran an independent workshop, supervising embroiderers who realized his designs. If the queen wanted something quickly, Jean had the authority to commandeer other master embroiderers to help him complete the job on schedule, but guild officials did not have the right to inspect his workshop. Even so, that did not mean no one was watching.

One key aspect of the production of luxury goods by court artisans concerned their use of the costliest raw materials of all, precious metals. The king's economic advisers always feared that artisans might be tempted to employ gold and silver allotted to a royal commission in work for their private clients.

Not even a year after Jean Magoulet became the Queen's Embroiderer, in mid-December 1678, a moment when for the first time since the 1640s, the value of precious metals was sharply on the rise, Nicolas de La Reynie, newly appointed lieutenant general of the Parisian police, ordered an inspection of his workshop. The findings? "Even though his workers were producing designs that required only silk thread," Jean stocked gold and silver on the premises. La Reynie confiscated "twenty-six g." (grains, the equivalent of the weight of twenty-six barley kernels) of precious metal and informed the Marquis de Seignelay, eldest son and close confidant of Louis XIV's finance minister, Jean-Baptiste Colbert. Seignelay was concerned enough about the anomaly to report it to the king himself. After consultation, Louis XIV decided to return the grains of gold to Jean but requested that La Reynie keep a close eye on him.

At Saint-Denis de la Chartre, Jean met Jean Inselin, another young embroiderer living in the enclave. Jean Inselin introduced Jean to his sister Simone.

When he married Simone Inselin, Jean allied himself with a powerful clan of court artisans whose members were active in a diverse range of guilds. Earlier in the century, the Inselins had been known exclusively as *maîtres fondeurs en terre et en sable*, founders who sculpted small objects of cast metal by shaping them inside molds of sand and clay. By the 1670s, some Inselins were master embroiders; others were master shoemakers; there was even a goldsmith in their ranks. Jean and Simone's mother, Peronne Bastard, came from another family of master founders.

The Inselins and the Bastards had something else in common, and this may well have been what attracted Jean Magoulet's attention. Both families moved in court circles at ranks far beyond that of royal artisan. A Bastard had served as *garde du corps* to Louis XIV's mother, Queen Anne d'Autriche, one of the elite officers who marched in processions ahead of the queen. And Jean and Simone's deceased father, Adrien Inselin, was always referred to as "valet de chambre of the Queen of England." Queen Henrietta Maria of France, the youngest daughter of France's King Henri IV, later wife and then widow of England's King Charles I, spent decades as a refugee in France, living with the court of Anne d'Autriche: it was then that Adrien Inselin served her. Jean Magoulet's new in-laws were at least the social equals of those with whom Antoine Chevrot allied himself in 1698.

Simone Inselin helped her husband reach his goals in another significant but far less traditional way.

His father, Jacques Magoulet, had risen high in the ranks of elite Parisian artisans despite the glaring obstacle of his illiteracy. But every important occasion in his professional as well as his personal life had involved the signing of a document, and each of those documents had ended with the statement "Jacques Magoulet declares that he can neither read nor write." Jacques had been determined that his children would never know moments like these, so he had paid particular attention to their education, daughters as well as sons. All of Jacques' children were literate and possessed exceptionally sophisticated signatures—all except his son Jean.

In 1674, when Jean received his first important contracts in his chosen field of embroidery, each ended with the statement his father, Jacques, knew all too well: "Jean Magoulet declared that he could neither read nor write."

On June 9, 1679, when the Inselin clan gathered to celebrate the marriage of Simone's brother Jean, Jean and Simone made their initial important appearance as a couple, and on this occasion the document did not end with that embarrassing formula: for the first time, Jean Magoulet was able to write his name.

*In 1679, the Queen's Embroiderer, Jean I Magoulet, learned to sign his name.*

The signature he produced in 1679 was hardly polished. Only the initial letters *mag* have a touch of the flow and connectedness of cursive writing. The remaining characters are all quite distinct, and the final *et* appear to have caused particular difficulty. They are composed of a series of short, rigid, almost brutal strokes. The signature seems the work of someone who handled a quill only awkwardly; in all the decades that followed, its quality never improved.

Like all the Bastards and Inselins, Simone wrote firmly and fluently. With her husband, she had achieved a result that paternal determination, a parish parochial school education, and sibling peer pressure had been unable to produce: at home and in private, she had taught Jean Magoulet to shape the letters that formed his name.

The patterns with which *gainiers* ornamented their cases and containers could be sketched out by a reasonably talented draftsman, but embroiderers were far more dependent on the ability to manipulate a pencil or quill or other penlike instrument with great dexterity. The foundation of the art of embroidery was the ability to produce designs both exceptionally accurate and exceptionally intricate and original.

How could someone long unable to recreate the letters in his own name and, under pressure, capable only of the extremely crude strokes that composed one of Jean Magoulet's signatures conceivably have created the complicated designs he was required to submit to Queen Marie-Thérèse for her approval and then to his workers to be executed?

Today the relation between brain development and the ability to form letters on the page is well documented. We know that a particular region of the brain controls children's ability to see letters and to reproduce them. Children who do not yet know how to write don't distinguish letters: they respond to them as they would to shapes such as triangles. This may well have been how Jean Magoulet conceived of his signature: as a series of forms to be reproduced on the page.

Did the Queen's Embroiderer have a condition that might now be diagnosed as an extreme form of dyslexia? The condition would have hampered his education in reading and writing without interfering in any way with his drawing skills—it perhaps even enhanced them as a form of compensation.

Because he was clearly the most gifted of Jacques' children—almost outrageously so—it's otherwise hard to imagine why Jean alone emerged illiterate from the childhood education he shared with his siblings. By the time he was named the Queen's Embroiderer, he had come to recognize that if he wanted to find custom among the most exalted personages in the realm, every trip to a notary's office to sign a contract could not end with that humiliating but legally obligatory statement of his illiteracy.

The Marie-Thérèse whom Jean was named to serve was no longer the same queen who had chosen his brother Hubert. The fourteen intervening years and the deaths of five of the six children she had given the king had considerably altered her status at court. In 1677, the real queen of Versailles was Louis XIV's longest-reigning mistress, the Marquise de Montespan, by then the mother of five of his children.

Ultimately more important still from Jean's perspective was something no one could have guessed at the moment when he invested 6,000 livres for a chance to serve in the queen's court: Marie-Thérèse, born the same year as her husband, was not destined to equal his longevity. Whereas Louis XIV reigned until 1715, when Jean was appointed in 1677 the queen had less than six years to live. If all Jean's royal wages had been paid in full—and this was hardly a given for court artisans—he might just have made back his investment.

No doubt Jean would have made this calculation down to the last sou. Penmanship did not come naturally to him, but another skill essential for a successful career in the luxury goods trade did: accounting. He did not initially see the value of letters, but the worth of figures was evident to him from the start.

Calculation was also the name of the game for the sibling with whom Jean was closest: his younger brother Jacques. All their lives, Jean and Jacques Magoulet looked out for each other: they gave each other business tips; they introduced each other to individuals able to help them in various ways; they encouraged each other in various forms of financial risk taking.

At the very moment when Jean reached the pinnacle of his success as an embroiderer with his royal appointment, his brother Jacques was just embarking on his chosen path, service to the crown in a succession of royal financial administrations. Jacques became the first Magoulet to make money from money rather than from making things.

This choice of career by a master artisan's son had surely also proved controversial in the Magoulet clan. In his father's generation, the worlds of high finance and high craft rarely if ever intersected, and this remained true for many artisans in the late seventeenth century, Hubert Magoulet among them.

But all his life, Jacques moved in circles very close to those frequented by the various Antoine Chevrots. When Jacques wanted people to stand up for him, he looked to the most influential and wealthiest financiers he could muster. Simple master artisans had no importance in Jacques Magoulet's eyes.

In the late seventeenth century, the traditional epithet *bourgeois de Paris* no longer designated simply a resident of Paris. Merchants and artisans more and more often no longer referred to themselves as master jewelers or master embroiderers. Instead they called themselves *bourgeois de Paris*, using the phrase as a cover-up that distanced them from any association with manual labor and merchandising. The expression also began to be used in a second new way: to designate Parisians whose income was the result of their financial acumen. In such usage, *bourgeois de Paris* became a synonym for those who made money exclusively by trading in money: financiers.

These were the connotations that the younger Jacques Magoulet had in mind when he identified himself, as he always did, as a *bourgeois de Paris*. Jacques' choice is emblematic of the powerful lure that finance exercised over many gifted young Frenchmen in the decades that marked the transition between the seventeenth and eighteenth centuries.

# CHAPTER FIVE

# Salad Days
## The Magoulets: 1679–1698

HUBERT MAGOULET, THE reliable older brother who realized their father's dreams, never became a role model for Jean. Another brother played that part: Jacques, the only son to choose a profession unrelated to the luxury goods trade. Among all the Magoulets and Chevrots born in the seventeenth century, Jacques constitutes a unique case: his career was launched without a substantial economic investment on the part of his parents, the sum necessary for the purchase of a position. Jacques made his way in the world solely on the basis of personal initiative and merit.

His sudden and spectacular rise to influence and affluence was made possible because of a behavior of which he, and Jean in his wake, provide textbook examples: the ability to size up a previously unencountered set of circumstances and see potential new prospects and quickly act to profit financially from those opportunities.

Jacques became a particular kind of fiscal officer. Rather than receive a fixed wage in return for an initial outlay, he worked as a kind of financial bounty hunter. He led complex investigations concerning taxes potentially due the French state; if money was owed, he supervised its collection, and in exchange he was allowed to keep a percentage of the funds recovered.

The moment when Jacques' star was on the rise, the late 1670s, was widely perceived in France as the best of times. Louis XIV seemed unstoppable on the battlefield: his victories, above all in Flanders, had redesigned his country's northern and eastern frontiers and brought under French control significant new territory and prize border cities such as Cambrai and Valenciennes.

Prosperity was widespread in France. A temperate climate guaranteed good harvests; this translated into stable prices for basic commodities all over the kingdom. France's currency was sound, its economy booming. Many Parisians had money to spend on themselves and their homes, and this meant solid profits for the city's merchants. In those best of times, Jacques was—as Shakespeare had Cleopatra describe the woman she had been in her "salad days"— "green in judgment, cold in blood." Young and inexperienced he might have been, but he was bright—the son who had best profited from his father's desire to give his children the kind of education he himself had not known—possessed of a keen head for business and the kind of ruthlessness that allowed him to go toe to toe with the scions of families far above his station and the biggest financiers in the land.

Jacques caught the eye of none other than Louis XIV's most trusted finance minister, Jean-Baptiste Colbert, who ruled over virtually every nook and cranny of the French economy. Colbert soon found a very attractive niche for his protégé.

In the 1660s and 1670s, Colbert engaged in a major overhaul of the kingdom's taxation system to improve its efficiency and increase revenue from the royal domain. One area ripe for reform was a kind of property tax or right, the percentage of the sale price due the king in his capacity as ruler over the royal domain each time land changed hands. The business of investigating property transactions and determining when this mutation fee had not been paid and then recovering the sums due became Jacques' specialty and an area in which he seems to have had no rivals.

By the mid-1670s, when his brothers were becoming established artisans, Jacques was already a visible presence on the French fiscal scene. In partnership with someone with whom his career intersected for decades, François Gallois, Jacques had been doing business with a future director of the French Indies Company, René Chaperon. By 1678, Chaperon owed them a tidy sum, nearly 45,000 livres.

From the start, Jacques was playing for high stakes and with men at least as ruthless as he. In addition, his business partners were individuals who by the century's end would have become among the most powerful financiers in the country, men who presided over vast fortunes. And Jacques was living this life when his father and brothers, while preeminent in their own fields, were dealing in sums that were paltry next to those obligatory in his world.

In the 1670s, Hubert's and Jean's court positions cost 5,000 and 6,000 livres respectively, for a combined total that came to barely half of what Jacques was then owed for a single deal gone wrong. At that moment, Jean, too, was trying to collect a debt, the amount he was owed by the estate of another embroiderer—66 livres.

To someone as fiercely financially ambitious as Jean, such invidious comparisons with his brother's achievements surely caused him to wonder whether his path to success had been the right choice.

Jacques' salad days began in 1678 along with those of the Sun King. Over the next two years and in dizzying succession, Finance Minister Colbert gave Jacques fiscal authority over one French province after another. By 1680, Jacques controlled the recovery of the royal domanial sales fees in Brittany, Burgundy, Champagne, La Marche (a considerable share of the region we now know as Nouvelle-Aquitaine, or in other words, a huge swath of central France), assorted bits of territory here and there, and even the vast region in southern France known as Languedoc.

Then on June 30, 1681, he got it all. Louis XIV announced his intentions of "following Colbert's advice": he put Jacques in charge of recovering the seigneurial due in "the full expanse of my kingdom." The last word on all the lands and fiefdoms of every great French noble, on every corner of the kingdom of France, would henceforth be pronounced by one man: Jacques Magoulet. In one fell swoop, Jacques had become someone the most influential Frenchmen would be eager to cultivate.

In every region, Jacques worked with its farmer general. These were private individuals responsible for the collection of many taxes due the crown (on salt, on wine, and so forth). Each made an annual estimate of the sum he would raise (or "farm"), a sum that he paid the king in advance. If a tax farmer was not able to raise the declared sum, he was obliged to make up the difference, whereas anything above and beyond it was his to keep.

Jacques consulted with the farmers general, but he was an independent contractor, in charge of his own autonomous administration: he had subcontractors in place all over France. They would move in, set up offices in provincial cities, and issue summonses to nobles under investigation. The nobles were then required to travel, often long distances, bringing with them the titles that established their ownership of each parcel under review, as well as all documents concerning their sale.

In theory, Jacques' administration was charged with recovery on sales that had taken place only during a fixed period—in most cases, 1650 to 1673. But Jacques often dealt with venerable aristocratic houses, and proof of ownership might date from many centuries in the past: the land a noble had sold in 1650 might well have become part of his family's estate in, say, the twelfth century.

If documents proving their right to the land did survive—and this was often a big *if*—their retrieval was rarely easy. It's hardly surprising that many families claimed to have no idea where such documents might be.

Then there was the issue of "exchanges." On every occasion when a piece of property in the royal domain was transferred to an individual in exchange for equivalent property transferred to the royal domain, the arrangement became subject to taxation. Since a royal fee had traditionally not been imposed, such transactions had rarely been documented. When Colbert decided to take advantage of this untapped source of revenue, he made exchanges part of Jacques' purview.

A cottage industry quickly sprang up to cater to nobles in need of deeds from the distant past. Genealogists either searched archives or relied on forgers to help them come up with the needed proof. Complex machinery was invented to convince Jacques Magoulet that a given property transfer had been properly documented and that all due tax had been paid.

For several years, Jacques was assured a fine income indeed, and an additional profit came in the form of long-term benefits: Jacques forged bonds with individuals involved in various aspects of tax collection, individuals on whom he relied in the decades to come. He also gained firsthand knowledge of the underhanded techniques needed to fabricate claims to land and titles. These were lessons that neither he nor Jean would forget.

Jacques' presence on the French fiscal scene was outsized in yet another way: the sheer volume of protests lodged against his administration. No one would have expected a tax recovery specialist to be completely aboveboard: the possibilities for extortion and bribery were too numerous to resist. But literally hundreds of complaints have survived, both in manuscript and in print, all denouncing in strident terms Jacques Magoulet's personal greed and the corruption that characterized his administration. Their authors invariably stress that this was corruption more generalized than anything previously known.

The first complaints were registered as soon as Jacques' power became absolute. In late 1681, Jacques' administration in Burgundy was accused of fraud and accepting bribes. A virtually identical affair began in Brittany at the same moment. And no region was more up in arms than Languedoc, where many nobles claimed that they had paid taxes for a second time just to get Jacques off their back. The Comte de Limoux explained that he had produced receipts for twenty-two of the required twenty-six years; receipts for the remaining years had been destroyed in a fire, "but Magoulet was still demanding them."

Through it all, Colbert's support was unwavering. In May 1682, when Nicolas Joseph Foucault, among the most trusted provincial administrators of the day, took up some of the complaints with him, Colbert professed his belief that sums collected by Magoulet were all "legitimately owed." And on August 23, 1683, Jacques was even given the authority to have the furniture and personal effects belonging to nobles who were refusing to pay back taxes seized by officers of the law and held until they paid up.

With the unswerving approval of such a formidable protector, Jacques did not hesitate to face off against the most entrenched bastions of power. In March 1682, the highest jurisdiction in the land, the Conseil d'État, responded to a petition by Jacques by declaring that henceforth royal secretaries would have to pay all taxes just like everyone else.

The title *secrétaire du roi* was purely honorific: the nearly 250 men who in the 1670s were known as royal secretaries had each paid at least 60,000 livres for that right. They had no duties, only extensive and valuable privileges, one of the most cherished of which was the exemption from paying taxes on any property they acquired. (It was rumored that many acquired the title just before they planned extensive investments in real estate, solely to avoid the tax.)

Naturally, men of great influence did not give up a right acquired at such expense without a fight. One royal secretary named Viton began a long legal battle to avoid paying the sums for which Jacques was billing him.

It might have gone on like this for many years, but—just weeks after the queen on whom Jean's status was founded had passed away—on September 6, 1683, Finance Minister Colbert died. The best of times were over.

Barely two months later, Jacques' complex web of influence was unraveling. On November 27, the members of the Conseil d'État who during Colbert's lifetime had always taken Jacques' side turned against him for the first time. Jacques was ordered to provide a formal accounting of his activities, and he was given only two weeks to provide full documentation. If he failed to comply, he would be imprisoned. Officers of the law personally delivered a copy of this decision to him so that he couldn't pretend to be unaware of the court order. To guarantee that no one could fail to notice the way the wind was now blowing, the council's decision was circulating in print before 1683 was out.

By early 1684, formal inquiries into allegations of fraud made against Jacques' administration had been opened in several provinces. At first, it was business as usual, and Jacques continued collecting back taxes. But without Colbert to stand up for him, the taxman who for years could do no wrong soon could do no right. On January 14, 1684, he crossed swords publicly with Jean Thevenin, among the most powerful financiers in the kingdom. You have to admire the daring necessary to demand money from someone so influential at that particular moment. Thevenin paid up—the 1,500-livre tax bill was, after all, small change to him—but a decade later he was still demanding that the money be returned to him and that Jacques be penalized.

On February 19, 1684, Jacques' meteoric rise came to an end as abrupt as its beginning. That day, the Conseil d'État ordered Jacques to cease all activity before the end of the month.

But just at the moment when he seemed to run out of options, Jacques suddenly shifted course: he married. This turned out to be the best business decision of his life.

The guardian of Marie Freslin, the young woman on whom he set his sights, had been, like Jean, a longtime member of Queen Marie-Thérèse's household. Marie was descended from merchants active in various sectors of the luxury goods trade (cloth manufacturers, hosiers), though her antecedents were more prosperous and upwardly mobile than Jacques'. When her parents married in 1656, her mother had brought into the marriage a dowry twelve times larger than that of Jacques' mother.

Marie Freslin was an orphan and of age, living on her own in the apartment in which she had grown up, on the Saint Michel Bridge, in a house that was adorned with the shopsign of the Golden Sun.

On February 21, 1685, when the Magoulet-Freslin marriage contract was signed, the bride had her financial ducks neatly lined up. Upon her mother's death one year earlier, Freslin had had an inventory of her possessions drawn up. By November 16, 1684, the executor of her mother's will, Nicolas Mascon, her cousin and yet another luxury goods merchant, formally settled the estate. The following week, Mascon handed over her inheritance. The scene was set for her marriage three months later.

At the notary's office that February day, many Magoulets stood up for the groom: his parents and three brothers—Hubert, Claude, and Jean. Only Jean is identified through reference to his profession. All the others are described solely as *bourgeois de Paris*, as are the bride's father and her cousin Mascon. The Magoulets, who normally called themselves master *gainiers*, surely used this uncharacteristic phrase in deference to Jacques' aspirations. Indeed everything about his marriage contract makes it plain that Jacques continued to view himself as very much part of the community of French financiers, in a world apart from those who worked with their hands. Also there to stand up for the bridegroom were several men he described as "friends," all active in the royal financial administration. His chief witness, François Legendre, identified himself as an all-powerful royal secretary.

Whereas Anne Goujon had brought his older brother Hubert a dowry of 2,500 livres, a handsome sum in the *gainier* community, Marie Freslin tallied up over 9,000 livres invested in annuities and furniture plus an additional 1,000 livres in cash, for a total of between 10,000 and 11,000 livres. In his heyday, Jacques could have held out for considerably more lucrative terms. In the 1680s, midlevel financiers expected a dowry of at least 50,000 livres; only those on the lowest rungs of the administration settled for dowries in the 10,000 range. Jacques evaluated his personal contribution to their finances at 4,000 livres, but unlike Marie Freslin, he gave no specifics, indicating that he had neither cash nor secure investments of any kind. By then, Jacques' self-image as a financier was largely an affair of smoke and mirrors.

All through 1685, additional judgments against Jacques were pronounced by courts of law all over the kingdom. No other member of Colbert's tax administration was the object of anything like the same volume of investigations; no one else was so often condemned, or in such stringent terms. Because of what one provincial governor termed his outsized "appetite for profit," Jacques made the name Magoulet synonymous with fiscal corruption.

On December 22, 1685, only months after his marriage, the Conseil d'État handed down the harshest of all condemnations of Jacques' tax recovery work. And they made sure that the decree convicting him on charges of fiscal fraud and embezzlement was quickly printed in a pamphlet that advertised Jacques' fall from grace to the world at large.

Jacques' marriage contract also contains the record of an unimaginable occurrence. On October 7, 1685, the chief witness, François Legendre, returned to the notary's office to declare that he "didn't know what he could have been thinking" when he said he was a royal secretary; in reality he "had no right to that title." Another financier on the move had surely threatened to expose Legendre for the criminal offense of usurpation of identity.

In the long run, Legendre became all he dreamed of and more. In June 1685, he signed an agreement with four colleagues to raise money for the construction of a new canal, the Canal Royal d'Orléans, designed to connect the Loire River to a network of already existing waterways. Among those who invested in the deal was Antoine Crozat, among the very wealthiest and most powerful of all French financiers: Crozat long held the monopoly on trade with the entire Louisiana Territory. When the canal was completed in 1692, it proved essential to the transportation of merchandise in central France—and it turned a very handsome profit for its original investors.

With his share in his pocket, in the 1690s Legendre joined the ranks of the country's principal tax farmers, so wealthy that his daughter became Crozat's wife. When Legendre died in 1696, he left an estate worth well over 900,000 livres. Legendre's story proves that in the volatile economic climate of the late 1680s and early 1690s, a meteoric rise to riches was indeed possible.

By the end of 1685, Jacques Magoulet's only position was a modest one, as a *commis*, or clerk, in the employ of François Legendre.

In 1686 and 1687, through Legendre's patronage, Jacques was once again briefly active in tax recovery, this time in Flanders. But another wave of virtually identical complaints soon followed, as well as new corruption charges. By December 1692, Jacques was so deeply in debt that he was forced to turn to his brother Jean as an intermediary to help deal with his creditors. Years of nonstop legal battles had taken their toll: Jacques was seeing a physician for "severe neck pain," and he couldn't pay his bill. Jean, by then far wealthier than the brother who had encouraged him to think like a financier rather than the artisan he was, called both parties to his home and negotiated a settlement.

By April 1698, Jacques' finances were in tatters: his wife, Marie Freslin, initiated a separation of property so that she could not be held responsible for Jacques' debts and his creditors would be unable to touch property held in her name.

By then, they were the parents of four sons, two of whom were destined to amass the kinds of fortunes their father had only dreamed of. Jacques lived until 1710, Marie Freslin until 1714. From 1698 on, Marie Freslin's firm control over their finances was everywhere visible: thanks to her choices, her heirs lived in ever greater prosperity.

After 1698, Jacques tried his hand at various ventures. Often in partnership with Hubert's oldest son, Antoine, he traded the commodities, grain in particular, that were in shortest supply during the nonstop wars of the turn of the eighteenth century. (He might well have been up to his old ways: many commodities traders then stockpiled grain so that when famine struck and prices soared, so did their profits.) But Jacques never again regained firm financial footing: at the time of his death, numerous creditors went after his estate.

During the second half of their marriage, their property was held in Marie's name, and her influence was never merely nominal. In their final years, the couple chose only the kinds of investments—real estate, relatively secure annuities—that Marie had brought into their marriage but that were looked down upon by financiers because they never brought windfall profits. After Jacques' death, when she planned for their children's futures, her choices were also conservative. In 1712, Marie acquired for her oldest son, Jacques François, just the kind of expensive post in a fiscal administration that Finance Minister Colbert had considered a poor use of disposable income.

When she died, Marie was living in an apartment whose walls were covered with fine paintings she obviously treasured. Her estate was worth well over 60,000 livres, a sum fully worthy of a financier, and the only creditor who came forward was one of Jacques' former associates. The old ways had paid off handsomely for this woman who had always kept her eye on the bottom line.

But the new financial ways and the high-risk dreams to which Jacques introduced the Magoulet clan were kept alive by his brother Jean. Jean began by abandoning the art of embroidery. Soon he abandoned his wife and children as well. From then on, there seems to have been no limit to what Jean Magoulet was willing to do, always in the hope of turning a fast profit.

# CHAPTER SIX

# *Annual Income, Annual Expenditure*
## The Magoulets: 1677–1691

TODAY, THE LUXURY goods industry is a life force of the French economy. On May 3, 2017, LVMH (Moët Hennessey Louis Vuitton) became the top performer on the CAC 40, the benchmark French stock market index, bypassing the petrochemical giant, Total. This was the first time since the creation of the index in 1987 that a powerhouse of the luxury goods industry had outperformed the mainstays of heavy industry. Over the past ten years, LVMH's stock has risen nearly 60 percent, and in 2016, the group recorded profits of 37.6 billion euros—10 billion of which resulted from sales by the most famous *gainier* of all time, Louis Vuitton.

Luxury goods and renowned artisans are an essential part of the French heritage and the brand name France. High fashion and fabulously crafted objects of many kinds are woven, stitched, laced, and embroidered into the very fabric of the French nation.

All this first became true during the period when Jean Magoulet served as the Queen's Embroiderer.

In the 1670s, state sponsorship of the luxury crafts began in earnest. When the Gobelins Tapestry Works became a royal manufactory and the official supplier of all furnishings for every royal château, it welcomed artisans representing a variety of specialties into its enclave: they were soon collaborating on the production of high-end decorative objects, everything from fine furniture to fine carpets. In 1672, Colbert launched an expansion of the guild system that more than doubled the number of trade corporations active in Paris. In 1677, Louis XIV personally authorized a major enlargement of the Royal

Household, the institution that employed the finest artisans in the land: in 1677, 160 craftsmen worked for the court; by 1683, they numbered 230.

When he purchased his appointment in 1677, Jean Magoulet was getting in at the start of perhaps the most crucial growth spurt in the history of the French luxury goods industry. The decade that followed (1678–1688) was a golden age for France's craftsmen. Work was plentiful; standards were high; numerous exacting clients wanted only the best, and they had the money to pay for it. French and foreigners alike longed to bask in the reflected glow of Versailles. They counted on court artisans such as the Queen's Embroiderer to make sure that their outfits and their possessions were fully up to royal standards.

During his first two years at court, Jean kept his head down and his nose to the grindstone, pleasing the queen and his private clients while quietly amassing capital. In September 1680 came an initial modest sign of success. Jean and Simone Inselin moved from the Saint-Denis de la Chartre enclave to a nearby address. The rue des Hauts Moulins, or High Windmills, later wiped off the map by Haussmann in 1866, was situated on the Île de la Cité a bit closer to Notre-Dame than to Saint-Barthélemy.

Meanwhile, his brother Jacques' high-rolling days as a taxman were also just beginning. By 1681, when Jacques' ship came in and he was put in charge of tax recovery for the entire kingdom, Jean began a rapid transformation of his own: he would soon be living large, well beyond the means of artisans of his rank. Jean Magoulet's true character first became visible in his investment strategies.

Among the many collateral benefits of a position as a royal artisan was the possibility of chance encounters in the corridors of power. A craftsman able to engage great nobles in casual conversation had a great deal to gain from insider information, and Jean Magoulet was just the man for this job. It's easy to imagine him spotting a prince or a count wearing one of his lavish creations and rushing over to ask if the client was perfectly satisfied, taking advantage of that moment also to explain that he had a bit of money put aside and to inquire about potential tips.

On March 21, 1681, Jean purchased a small property, just over an acre, in the Vexin, a lush agricultural region not far from Paris. The parcel's owner, Jean-Baptiste Briçonnet, was an important figure in the Parisian Parlement and the owner of a splendid château. In the years ahead, Jean signed contract after contract with individuals at least as prominent as Briçonnet. The son of a self-made man of humble birth, a mere artisan who could barely scratch out his signature, there was Jean Magoulet doing business with the finest lords in the land.

By 1681, financiers had tired of that allegedly dead safe choice, real estate, and were turning instead to ventures with potential for quick returns. Only months after what was to be the one and only land deal of his life, Jean was following their example. And he never looked back.

On August 11, 1681, Magoulet concluded a pact with the scion of an old Breton family. Jacques Du Marchy, Chevalier de Catuelan—his family's handsome château still survives today—was a colonel in the royal cavalry. Magoulet had embroidered items guaranteed to make the officers in Catuelan's regiment and their mounts stand out in military processions, but the dashing cavalry officer couldn't pay the 300 livres still outstanding, so he offered Jean what would now be called a debt-to-equity swap. A second high-living young officer in Catuelan's regiment (he claimed to be the king of Poland's son) had long owed the chevalier 3,000 livres, and Catuelan had been unable to recoup his money: he proposed that Jean take over the process. If Jean succeeded in collecting the funds, they would share the profits, and Catuelan's debt with Jean would be canceled.

Six weeks later, on October 4, 1681, Jean and Simone displaced their household once again, and this time they were really on the move. They abandoned the artisans' quarter on the Île de la Cité and migrated across the Seine to the political heart of the city, the neighborhood adjacent to the Louvre. Their new location, at the spot where the Pont Neuf intersected with the Quai de l'École (today's Quai du Louvre), laid bare Jean's latest vision for his life.

In terms of distance, he did not move far from his family's headquarters: a walk of a minute or two just halfway across the Pont Neuf will take you from the Quai de l'Horloge to the Quai de l'École. But in terms of status, the two embankments were worlds apart. The Quai de l'Horloge drew its identity from the merchants and artisans whose shops lined its expanse, whereas the Quai de l'École derived its character from the royal palace, the Louvre.

The Queen's Embroiderer's new address had everything going for it. The building faced onto the Seine: from its windows, inhabitants could take in the panorama of the river. Its proximity to the Pont Neuf, Paris' principal north-south connector, made it highly convenient for someone often crisscrossing Paris. But it was above all a power address, just steps from the Louvre: the most fashionable individuals in Paris could easily drop by the establishment of the Queen's Embroiderer. Henceforth, Jean would not only be in business with the finest French families—he would be living alongside them.

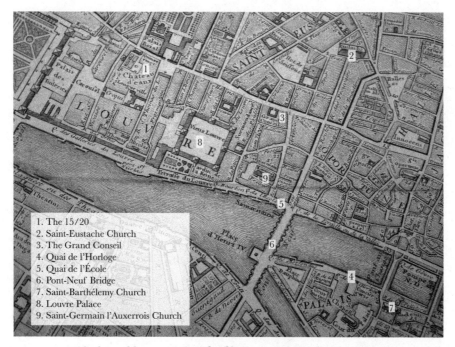

1. The 15/20
2. Saint-Eustache Church
3. The Grand Conseil
4. Quai de l'Horloge
5. Quai de l'École
6. Pont-Neuf Bridge
7. Saint-Barthélemy Church
8. Louvre Palace
9. Saint-Germain l'Auxerrois Church

*The key addresses in the life of both Queen's Embroiderers and the Magoulet family in general.*

Even the highest-end artisans on the Île de la Cité rented apartments or what leases described as "small houses." A small house, usually situated above the artisan's shop, was truly small: a kitchen plus at most two rooms. For their living quarters plus their shops, craftsmen typically paid 150 to 250 livres a year.

Jean Magoulet's new home, however, rented from a nobleman, was a residence fully worthy of an aristocrat. The lease calls the house "large," and it certainly was that: three floors, with several rooms to a floor. In seventeenth-century terms, the house was positively pharaonic, particularly for artisans. And its rent was every bit as colossal: 1,600 livres, among the most expensive rents in Paris, a sum so far beyond anything paid by anyone in Jean's entourage that it surely seemed inconceivable to family members that one of their own would live so lavishly. This was the first incontrovertible indication of Jean's megalomania.

On November 20, 1681, Jean signed another lease, on the shop located on the ground floor of his new home: it rented for 150 livres, or as much as Jean's father and mother were then paying for a shop and the "small house" in which they had raised a large family. He also agreed to pay for remodeling, and those expenses alone would have been staggering. Magoulet explained that he planned to install a storefront "appropriate for his profession": the changes he had in mind were truly visionary.

The remodeled shop on the Quai de l'École is the elegant space seen here in Magoulet's publicity image. The depiction highlights a lavish use in the super-sized windows and the invitingly half-open door of what was then an extravagantly costly luxury commodity, large panes of glass. And what this view of the interior couldn't represent was in fact Magoulet's most significant innovation of all: the shopfront he added was made up entirely of panes of glass, a concept so revolutionary that the merchant who took over the lease in 1695 still considered it too daring and insisted that it be removed.

Magoulet's façade is the earliest recorded instance of a glass storefront, what we know as a shop window. With it, the Queen's Embroiderer single-handedly invented modern shop display and the phenomenon of window shopping.

Magoulet owed his inspiration once again to Louis XIV's court. In 1681 and 1682, thirty-six thousand workers were frantically putting the finishing touches on Versailles. On December 1, 1682, the foremost of its grand parade spaces was formally inaugurated: the Hall of Mirrors. The huge mirrors installed in the Galerie des Glaces were composed of 357 individual panes of glass, each measuring 26 by 34 inches, roughly the size of those Magoulet installed. Magoulet's shopfront brought the Galerie des Glaces to town and gave ordinary Parisians a preview of the glittering expanse that all would have heard about but that almost no one would have had occasion to see. The Queen's Embroiderer had decided to beat the Sun King at his own game.

*The entrance added to the Louvre Palace in the 1670s, facing*
*Saint-Germain-l'Auxerrois Church and the Quai de l'École.*

The lease on the apartment was to start in early 1682, but the young couple were so eager to celebrate Christmas 1681 in their new home that they paid an extra 100 livres to move in sooner. Simone was expecting their first child, and Jean was about to become a family man.

On Thursday, February 26, 1682, a son was born: they named him Jean. Their recent move guaranteed that his baptism on Wednesday, March 4 could take place in the most prestigious Parisian church, Saint-Germain-l'Auxerrois. The Magoulets now shared a parish church with the kings of France.

Saint-Germain-l'Auxerrois is not much changed from its seventeenth-century incarnation: it remains an intimate church in a quiet corner of the city now just steps away from the bustle of the rue de Rivoli. The church itself is a medieval and Renaissance construction, but when Jean Magoulet was setting up his little palace just around the corner, its interior was being refurbished for the Sun King's use. Charles Le Brun and other royal artists responsible for Versailles' magnificence designed the monumental carved pulpit completed in 1684. Those who exited the Louvre via architect Claude Perrault's newly completed colonnade and walked the few steps that separated the palace from its parish church found themselves in a setting that recalled the splendors of Versailles.

Two other Magoulet children soon followed: Charlotte in June 1683 and François in November 1684. Contrary to standard practice among craftsmen, the children's godparents were not family members but business connections of their father, mostly financiers. The only family member ever chosen was Jean's mentor, Jacques, who signed the church register as François' godfather. François' godmother was fifteen-year-old Marguerite Legendre, daughter of François Legendre (for whom the baby was surely named) and future bride of the all-powerful financier Antoine Crozat. This choice of godmother stands as the ultimate indication that Jean's allegiance lay no longer with the

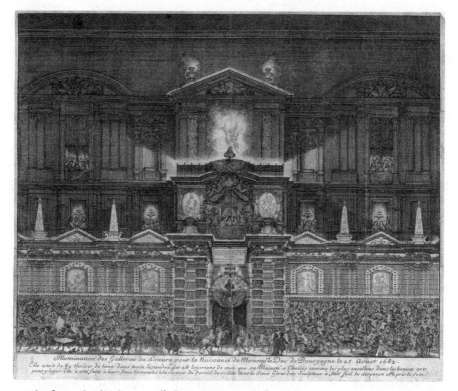

*The fireworks display set off above the Louvre's façade in August 1682 to celebrate the birth of Louis XIV's first grandson, the Duc de Bourgogne.*

community of artisans but in the realm of high finance. The clearly upwardly financially mobile baptisms of Jean's children might just as well have taken place in the Chevrot family.

The year 1682—marked by the birth of a son, the move to a glamorous address, and the inauguration of what was surely the most spectacular shop in all Paris—was Jean's finest hour. The same could be said of Louis XIV.

On May 6, 1682, the French court moved definitively to Versailles, the palace to end all palaces. On August 6, the royal family also celebrated the birth of a son, Louis XIV's first grandson, the Duc de Bourgogne—the future husband of the woman at the center of Antoine Chevrot's Versailles career. The news of the birth of another heir to the throne set off a celebratory frenzy all over France. From their new windows, the Magoulets had a front row seat as the Louvre's east façade was illuminated by a spectacular display of fireworks.

In the summer of 1682, Jean was flush with profits from important commissions: a single contract for "gold and silver tapestries" brought him 14,000 livres. As the money built up, his personal biology of risk kicked in. Jean began to consort with hustlers and devotees of the high life, individuals with considerable revenue but so addicted to credit that they shared among them an ability to run up phenomenal amounts of debt. In 1682, Jean was already involved with the Lescots: Raymond, a lawyer for the Parisian Parlement, and his son François, both of whom consistently lived far beyond their means. In September 1683, to settle multiple lawsuits, the Parlement ordered them to repay over 200,000 livres to creditors, including Jean.

In January 1682, Jean was negotiating with the Lescots to buy, at what they called "a very low price," the harvest of 30 acres of wheat and rye, which the Lescots promised to deliver to him in Paris. Jean was using surplus real estate on the Quai de l'École as a storehouse and getting in on the ground floor of a new financial gamble.

Earlier in the century, when speculators realized that grain prices invariably shot up in the months that followed a particularly bad harvest, they began to stockpile grain and wait for the shortage to provoke a spike in prices. During Louis XIV's reign, speculators started to hoard grain even before a crisis began in order to be able to create an insufficient supply, the earliest man-made food shortages in French history.

This wasn't the only novel use Jean made of his vast space. He rented out a large apartment, elaborately furnished right down to the silver salt cellars and the Flemish tapestries on the walls, for a rent so handsome—800 livres—that it went a long way toward justifying what he was paying for the house. Or would have gone a long way, had he not rented it to Raymond Lescot and his wife. The Lescots being the Lescots, they lived there for eighteen months without paying a penny. Jean was still fighting to recover this debt in 1687.

Deals such as these prove how quickly Jean Magoulet expanded his business model well beyond activities traditional for embroiderers. He was eager to diversify, quick to spot a potential market, just as quick to step in.

As work was heating up at Versailles in 1681, money flowed freely at the court and in Paris. From that moment on, credit swaps similar to the one Jean signed with Catuelan and the king of Poland's son became second nature to him. Beginning in 1681, the Queen's Embroiderer was running simultaneously a luxury goods workshop and a one-man credit and loan operation, in which he extended credit for interest (generally 4 to 5 percent).

The scale of his parallel commerce indicates that it was hardly a sideline. The Lescots, for example, ran up a bill with Jean for 14,000 livres' worth of embroidery; at the same moment, he lent them 23,000 livres. An agreement on the Lescots' loans was negotiated only on October 4, 1687, and only after

Jean had had Raymond confined to debtors' prison. Jean consented to a settlement of 12,000 livres plus interest: four times a year, Jean was to receive 600 livres, paid to him directly by the occupants of rental properties owned by the Lescots. In circumstances such as these, no merchant could have accurately predicted his cash flow. Small wonder that Jean incurred many debts of his own and was constantly negotiating settlements with suppliers for his workshop or embroiderers who had worked there.

And lest anyone think that this should have been risk enough for any one man, 1682 also witnessed a final multilayered credit arrangement, the most bizarre of them all. And this one opens a rare window onto still another of his parallel lives, one he fought obsessively to shroud in secrecy: Jean Magoulet, womanizer.

On December 23, 1682, just before Christmas in the year of his first child's birth, Jean was summoned to a lawyer's office for a most unusual "confrontation": 5,000 livres of high fashion apparel was to be compared with a preexisting inventory to make sure that the garments corresponded to the description it contained. Jean himself had drawn up the inventory and had offered the attire it listed as collateral to Jacques Broust, a master carpenter in his new neighborhood, to whom he owed 1,100 livres—surely for work done on his fancy shop's amazing new façade.

At that price—more than three times the value of the high fashion clothing in the dowry of Antoine Chevrot's bride in 1698—the garments were luxurious indeed. They could even have been taken for the creations of the Queen's Embroiderer: a man's scarlet cloak with gold embroidery, a *justaucorps* in violet satin embellished with three columns of embroidery in gold and silver, a woman's skirt richly adorned with gold flowers. But Jean had played no role in their confection—indeed, they were in no way his property.

Also present that December day was a thirty-year-old woman going by the name of Barbe de Ville. She had hired a lawyer to stage the "confrontation": once she recognized the clothing as belonging to her, she was allowed to take it away. It's astonishing that she could have laid claim to such expensive apparel.

Her real name was Barbe Briet. The child of an impoverished jeweler from the tiny Burgundian village of Semur-en-Auxois, she had arrived in Paris penniless in early 1682 and had soon taken up with Jean. Soon after that "confrontation" at her lawyer's office, she married a much younger man, Nicolas Forbi, the son of a well-to-do merchant. In their marriage contract, she included in her dowry the identical list of high fashion garments that Jean had recently claimed as his personal property.

Barbe Briet became notorious in French legal history as the perfect example of why it was dangerous for young men to marry without parental consent. The

suit her husband, Forbi, and his father later brought against her for embezzlement was judged by none other than Henri François d'Aguesseau, chief
lawyer of the Parisian Parlement and the most celebrated legal mind of the age.
D'Aguesseau's deliberations on *Forbi v. Briet* became a classic of law textbooks,
reprinted well into the nineteenth century. Of Barbe Briet, d'Aguesseau's opinion was clear: once she moved to Paris, "her conduct became less strict than it
had been in the place where she was born"; he refers to her as a prostitute.

This was the woman with whom Jean Magoulet was involved at the moment
of his first son's birth. Was she conning him, or was the opposite the case?
They seem two peas in a pod, two grifters trying to take any and all for
everything they were worth. And Barbe de Ville—Barbe Briet's identity
after she came to the big city—is but the best known of the other women in
Jean's life.

François was the last of his children with Simone, but he was hardly the last
of Jean Magoulet's children.

By the time his involvement with Barbe de Ville ended, Jean was embroidering for a new clientele: high-ranking officers in the royal army, particularly young nobles who led a cavalry regiment. Each one of the contracts he
began signing in March 1684 opens on the phrase *haut et puissant seigneur*, "high
and powerful lord," words used exclusively for those possessing both a title
(from *chevalier* up to *duc*) and at least one landed estate. Jean's contracts feature a panoply of marquis and dukes and counts from the finest families in the
land including the Duc de La Feuillade and the Marquis Du Chastelet, each of
whom was there to deck out the cavalry regiment under his command.

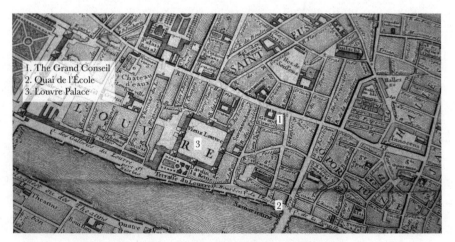

1. The Grand Conseil
2. Quai de l'École
3. Louvre Palace

*The key addresses in Jean I Magoulet's life in 1688.*

On June 11, 1687, Jean signed still another lease, on a property on the rue Saint-Honoré "directly facing the Grand Conseil," almost equidistant from the Louvre and his shop. He now had a second home for his secret life. He also occupied a front row seat in a theater of power very different from the fashion world: politics.

The Grand Council, or King's Council, was a superior court, a type of supreme court; its magistrates, members of eminent families that had served the crown for generations in the highest functions, were privy to the most important news of the day and advised the king on complex legal matters. From his perch directly opposite, Jean could keep track of their comings and goings; in a flash, he could pop over and make small talk about developments looming on the political front.

In March 1688, when Jean first used his new address, the insider information of the moment would have been talk of an upcoming war. In the summer of 1686, the League of Augsburg—an alliance of the Holy Roman Emperor, William III of the Netherlands, Charles II of Spain, and various German princes (England was drawn in in 1689 when William III became king)—had been created to oppose France's overwhelming power in Europe. Observers soon warned that this move made a new war inevitable. In March 1687, a respected periodical, the *Historical and Political Mercury*, published in The Hague, cautioned that because Louis XIV considered their so-called Grand Alliance illegal, "everything indicates that we'll soon be at war with France." "The king of France is in such a flourishing state," the periodical added, that "if he has the slightest opportunity he will use it to extend the limits of his prosperity," by annexing new territory "beyond the Rhine."

When Jean signed that lease just three months later, the periodical's prognostications were already coming true: French generals were laying out strategy for the next year's campaign. The following June, the French military occupation of Cologne marked the beginning of the devastating conflict known as the War of the Grand Alliance, the Nine Years' War, or the War of the League of Augsburg. On September 24, Louis XIV published a manifesto listing his grievances with the coalition: on September 25, the king in person led the French army in a triumphant crossing of the Rhine. He proceeded to do just what the Dutch press had feared: lay siege to major Rhineland cities and seize new territory.

The Nine Years' War, fought simultaneously against multiple adversaries on virtually all French frontiers, made unprecedented demands on France's forces. Louis XIV and his secretary of state for war, François Michel Le Tellier, Marquis de Louvois, expanded the nation's army to a scale previously unimaginable. At the end of Louis XIII's reign in 1643, France had but 33 infantry regiments; by the late seventeenth century, that total had grown to 260. During the Thirty Years' War (1618–1648), the French army was never more than 125,000 strong; in the Dutch wars of the early 1670s, Louis XIV relied on 280,000 troops. For the Nine Years' War, 420,000 men fought in the French army: these were the largest land forces assembled in Europe since Roman times.

The Bourbon monarchy of Louis XIV was vastly wealthy, with annual revenue four times greater than that of the king of England and nearly three times greater than that of the Dutch state, but even these resources were not enough to wage war on such a scale. The monarch created and sold positions of all kinds. The French state borrowed colossal sums from wealthy financiers whose ranks included several of those who had stood up for Jacques at his marriage. Those deals made them fabulously rich.

Louis XIV also sacrificed prized possessions. In December 1689, he shipped off to the Paris mint the magnificent silver furnishings and adornments in Versailles' Hall of Mirrors. Twenty tons of silver were melted down and exchanged for newly minted coins.

Jean's new address afforded him easy access to those making war plans: knowing a year in advance which regiments would be on the move allowed him to get a jump on the most lucrative deals. Thus over one active two-month period in the spring of 1689, he signed contracts with six "high and powerful" young lords due to lead their regiments into battle in 1690. Jean promised to deliver embroidered gloves, pistol holders, and ammunition pouches for each regiment's officers, plus, since a nobleman's horse was adorned with the same richness as its rider, hundreds of saddle cloths—all to the tune of 19,719 livres. Thousands of the horses that trampled the fields of Flanders during devastating campaigns arrived there glittering with embroidery from the workshop of the Queen's Embroiderer.

Jean quickly began to diversify his services. Dispatched regiments, he learned, needed spare mounts as well as mules to carry their rations. So there was the Queen's Embroiderer on February 25, 1690, signing a contract directly with Louis de Crevant, Duc d'Humières, grand master of artillery for the French armies and head of operations in Flanders. Jean promised to deliver directly to the battle lines twenty-four horses, fully equipped with saddles and bridles, the first of many such deals. Jean was soon subcontracting—with an artillery captain who had eighty horses left over from the last campaign, with a harness maker on the rue Saint-Honoré, with an officer in the French postal system experienced in moving horses from one relay to the next.

Jean's operation never rivaled those of major players such as Adrien Révillon, who supplied 2,800 horses and mules and arranged for their rations as well as those of troops: Révillon signed contracts worth over 4 million livres. As usual, Jean imitated big fish on a modest scale.

He also continued his credit and loan activities. As soon as war preparations were under way, he began lending money out at least as fast as he signed embroidery contracts that brought funds in.

At times, the risk involved seems minimal. In April 1688, Nicolas Darnolfiny from the illustrious Arnolfini dynasty of textile merchants, premier brigadier general of Louis XIV's army, was in need of a small sum: 1,200 livres.

Then there was the Comte de Gadagne. He was descended from a long line of distinguished military men, all richly endowed with noble titles. But the young count, like many with whom Jean did business, was a classic second son. He wouldn't inherit the estate anyway, so why not fritter some of it away? Gadagne was in Paris relishing the freedom from family protocol that army life provided. In March 1691, his colonel, the Comte de Bouzoles, entrusted Captain Gadagne with a promissory note for 6,000 livres (this would have functioned like a check) to purchase sheets for the regiment. That day, Gadagne admitted, he "unfortunately was a bit confused." The money "was lost"—in a card game perhaps?—and he turned to Jean.

This loan brought with it numerous red flags, but Jean nonetheless took it on, and he lived to regret his bet. By July 23, 1692, Jean had initiated a lawsuit. On November 26, he had the count locked up in debtors' prison in Paris' Petit Châtelet. And in this ignominious setting the young aristocrat remained until February 1693, when his widowed mother made the long journey from the family estate in the far southeastern corner of France to promise Jean repayment— by then, Gadagne's debts totaled 15,000 livres—and thus won her son's release.

The five-year period that began in March 1688 proved the most profitable in Jean's life. At its start, Jean was clearly feeling invulnerable, a master of the new universe then being designed. But in mid-1688, that fearlessness caused him to make the biggest mistakes of his life.

On the surface, the document Jean signed on May 29, 1688 was unexceptional: he paid Jean Dupré, a merchant on the Île de la Cité with whom he occasionally collaborated, to take on his son as an apprentice. Dupré described himself as a "wholesale jeweler," someone who sold ornaments made by others rather than objects of his own creation. (He furnished, for example, gold braid to trim regimental horse cloths.) The apprenticeship seems a surprising choice: the most visible member of a family of royal artisans wanted his son to learn a business, merchandising, rather than a craft.

But the document's real stunner is the identity of the child whose career path Jean was charting: "My son Nicolas Magoulet." The document was official recognition of a son born out of wedlock. Jean thereby entitled Nicolas to use the name Magoulet, agreed to take financial and legal responsibility for him, and gave Nicolas the right to claim a share of his estate. In addition, the document indicated that this was hardly the beginning of the education Jean had given this son: the boy signed with the kind of signature that his father had never mastered, the result of careful training. Jean was, moreover, planning a future for this illegitimate son before he provided for his firstborn, Jean II. Magoulet lied about Nicolas' age, describing the boy who, subsequent documents make clear, was younger than Jean II, born in early 1682, as "about 15." In 1688, Dupré was in deep financial trouble; the 150 livres Magoulet paid up front for his son Nicolas' apprenticeship would have inclined the merchant to ignore the glaring discrepancy.

The document served a final purpose: it deprived Jean Magoulet's legitimate child Jean II of his birthright and signed away his place as the Queen's Embroiderer's eldest son. And the Queen's Embroiderer's plans for removing Jean II from his life were far from complete.

Only two weeks later, on June 12, when the first French troops were invading the Rhineland, Magoulet signed a document known as a *traité*, a business agreement. These typically involved goods and services, but this was no typical arrangement: Jean was dealing in human goods, the services of his legitimate eldest son.

That June morning, Charles de Joissy, Baron de Vérac and major of the French possession he described as "Sainte Croix in America," was stopping over briefly in Paris, lining up personnel to run his plantation on the island in the Caribbean now called Saint Croix. The baron belonged to an aristocratic family from the region in west central France known as Poitou; in the seventeenth century, the Véracs did not yet maintain a Parisian townhouse. Those who signed contracts with him all had close ties to the chief administrator of France's island colonies, Colbert's son, the Marquis de Seignelay, for whom Jean was just then embroidering fabulously expensive jackets.

Among those the Baron de Vérac added to his staff was Louis Constantin-Mandolly, the nineteen-year-old son of the maître d'hôtel of Colbert's brother, the Comte de Maulévrier. The young man wanted to follow in his father's footsteps: the baron promised to take him on his return trip to the island of Sainte Croix where he was to spend "at least three years." Louis was present to sign the "consent form," proving "that he agreed to make the trip."

The agreement Magoulet had signed earlier the same morning was alto-gether a different kettle of fish. Magoulet alone did the "consenting"; the person he referred to as "his son Jean Magoulet" was not present. The baron was to take Jean II along on his return trip to the island, where the boy would spend three years "working as his clerk and keeping his business register." The arrangement was virtually cost free for the baron; he agreed merely to feed Magoulet's son and pay his return passage to France—a cost of about 50 livres.

For the Queen's Embroiderer, the deal was a stupendous bargain. He had one fewer mouth to feed, and he was spared the expense of an apprenticeship, an outlay of some 150 livres a year.

In one fell swoop, a child not even six and a half years old, who had lived until then in one of Paris' most elegant neighborhoods, became an indentured servant and was shipped halfway around the globe. His father's business arrangement set the course for his eldest son's life. It also launched the chain of events that sealed the fate of his dynasty and that of the Chevrots as well.

The document makes no mention of the son's precise age: the baron had had a surprise when he reached the port of Dieppe for his voyage back to the Carib-bean. But under no circumstances could he have refused to fulfill his end of the bargain: Magoulet required the baron "to promise to return to the islands imme-diately and directly." The baron further agreed that if he failed to comply with the contract's terms, he "would be responsible for damages"—in other words, he would bear the cost of any legal action Magoulet brought against him.

Childhood had very different parameters in earlier centuries: a boy of six to seven in 1690 was much older than in today's terms. Boys could and did, for example, become apprentices at that age. They moved away from home and into a context in which they were expected to work hard and to follow rigor-ous discipline. But other boys were not shipped halfway around the globe for their entry into the workforce.

At age nine, Alexander Hamilton was employed as a clerk and on the same island, though the Saint Croix Hamilton knew in the 1760s was a thriving pivot of the Danish West Indies. When Jean II arrived there in 1689 at age seven, he found instead a failed experiment in French colonial policy, a lonely outpost poised on the brink of disaster.

In the first years after the French Indies Company purchased the island of Sainte Croix from the Knights of Malta in 1665, the colony had grown rapidly; soon well over a hundred plantations dotted its 83 square miles. The island's economy centered on two crops: tobacco and sugar. It was a hardscrabble place: there were no great houses, only modest dwellings, no high life, no

Parisian luxuries. Most settlers had been forced to move there because they were deeply in debt to the Indies Company.

By 1681, the island's population had known modest growth, to 1,126. From then on, it stagnated, so that in 1695, there were still but 1,235 inhabitants, while during the same period nearby Saint-Domingue (today's Haiti) saw a 40 percent population spurt.

One crop, tobacco, proved a fiasco when its price declined sharply. Sugar production didn't rise fast enough to keep the economy afloat. A bit of cotton was planted; some exotic wood was exported for use in marquetry designs on Versailles' floors and furniture. The island was too remote to attract much trade: while under French rule, it had no regular transatlantic traffic. Add to this a corrupt local administration given to illegal commerce and demanding kickbacks at every turn, and it's easy to see why prices on such staples as cloth and candles remained sky high and settlers found it impossible to make ends meet. As if all this were not enough, time and again yellow fever decimated the population.

By 1690, when deaths from hunger were common, many simply gave up and moved to Saint-Domingue. In late 1695, the remaining colonists were evacuated, and one small French outpost was officially put out of its misery.

On the island, the second Jean Magoulet experienced a class system completely unlike the one he had grown up in, though at least as rigid. There were a few true aristocrats among the planters, lured there by the dream of finding quick riches in the islands and returning to France with the cash necessary to rebuild the family estate; any landowner was a world apart from a simple indentured worker. But Magoulet stood just as far above those who made Sainte Croix's economy run, the slaves. In 1688, there were 631 free residents on the island and 559 slaves. Slavery was thus a basic fact of the boy's daily life.

The boy also occupied a particularly odd position on the social scale, truly in a class by himself. In 1681, there had been 94 indentured servants on Sainte Croix. Whereas the practice continued to be common on other French islands, as the colony on Sainte Croix ground to a halt, so did this labor force. By 1688, when the Baron de Vérac signed up his new servants in Paris, only two indentured workers were left on the island. In 1695, after Jean II had returned to France, there were none. In this way, too, the Magoulet child stood at the end of a line.

Jean II endured a miniature version of the military conflict that his father hoped would make his fortune. By October 1688, when the boy was crossing the Atlantic, Louis XIV wrote the island's governor to warn that war was imminent. In early 1689, the French captured Saint Eustache (now known as Statia) from the Dutch; in June 1689, the Dutch retaliated by landing on Sainte Croix in the dead of night. During Jean II's years there, all the European powers at war with France repeatedly invaded Sainte Croix, trying, just as their armies in Europe were doing, to grab land. All the while, the island was completely cut off from France. Not a single trading ship docked there in 1690; inhabitants were forced to buy from other islands at vastly inflated prices. The outpost's brush with the Nine Years' War ended its years as a French colony.

Jean II shared his father's gift for sums and calculation, and his years in the baron's employ, a total immersion in the world of maritime trade and fluctuating commodity markets, added financial maturity. Alexander Hamilton subsequently put the experience he gained on the same island to work creating capitalism in the United States, but his predecessor clerk had no such lofty ambitions.

The Magoulet boy returned to France three years later, at age nine or perhaps ten, with one burning desire: for revenge on the man who had sent him on a miserable and dangerous journey to a war-torn colony on its last legs. He carried his hatred for his father with him all his days.

Two long sea voyages made alone and at such a young age, the struggle to survive a form of white slavery and to do so in an environment crippled by poverty and corruption—these traumatic experiences endured by Jean II with no adult to protect or care for him would have been enough to create a morally depraved individual. It's impossible to know when Jean II first exhibited the cold-blooded ruthlessness with which he later dealt with those nearest to him. From the minute he returned to France, one thing became evident: he made history repeat itself. Every major turning point in his existence, every moment when his violent behavior escalated, all of them reenacted his father's life. Everything his father had done, Jean II pulled off in turn—and on a grander scale. Every swindle and every crime his father had gotten away with he recreated—and he did him one better.

Never was this clearer than in June 1719, exactly thirty-one years after his father had signed the agreement to ship his son to a French possession across the ocean. On June 12, 1719, Jean II made plans to have his eldest child, Louise, follow in his footsteps, to send her on a sea voyage to America as arduous as the one he had endured. That June day, Jean II truly became *his* father's son.

# CHAPTER SEVEN

# Secrets and Lies

## The Magoulets: 1692–1704

M ANY LIES ARE nurtured within families.

In 1688, as soon as the Queen's Embroiderer made those arrangements for Nicolas and for Jean II, a new era began for the Magoulet clan. No family member could have ignored that one boy had suddenly disappeared, and this just when another boy had officially become a member of their ranks. From then on, Jean Magoulet's secrets—both these and many others of which I found traces but no definitive proof—festered, until they became a central part of the Magoulets' collective identity as a family.

Family members are always reluctant to denounce one of their own; they instinctively seek to avoid the scandal that would bring shame on their name. *Omertà*, the code of silence and noninterference in the legal activities of others that reigns within close-knit communities, was certainly as strong three centuries ago as it is today. Just such a collective silence sheltered Jean Magoulet's secrets and his illicit activities and allowed him to manipulate both the law and human beings with impunity.

Beginning in 1688, none of the Magoulets had clean hands, but there were two circles of knowledge. The outer circle was composed of those who, while aware of what was going on, did not enable it in any way. There was also a small inner circle: these family members took turns witnessing the official documents that allowed Jean to redesign his family history at will.

With their complicity, Jean Magoulet's criminal behavior long went off without a hitch. And the years when he was acting as if there were no bottom line were also those when Louis XIV and his army knew some of their finest hours.

The ever larger French army realized its most memorable victories of the Nine Years' War. Fortress after fortress was captured by Sébastien Le Prestre de Vauban, the greatest master of the art of siege warfare of all time. Three of Vauban's most critical victories carved out for France a new frontier in Flanders: the fortress at Mons fell to French forces on April 8, 1691; the key citadel of Namur on June 30, 1692; and Charleroi on October 10, 1693. But by the time Vauban had secured this new border, crisis was looming, and French military strategy was being curtailed to reflect a new financial reality.

The economic model put in place at the pinnacle of Louis XIV's reign— wild overspending funded by massive short-term loans—kept both the splendors of Versailles and the gargantuan war efforts afloat for nearly fifteen years, just as long as nothing unforeseen came along to alter the foundations on which the model had been constructed. But in the early 1690s, the unexpected came to pass.

The crushing military defeats then suffered by the French army and the crisis that paralyzed France's economy by the middle of the decade both had their origin in an episode of sudden climate change.

During the most successful period of Louis XIV's reign (1678–1690), his country was blessed with excellent weather and abundant harvests. In an agricultural society such as France, the grain harvest was the determining factor for the population's well-being: bread was the staple at the center of all dietary regimes. A five-year-old French child consumed a pound of bread a day, a woman a pound and a half, and an adult male manual laborer up to three pounds per day. Much of the bread was eaten in soups along with dried beans and root vegetables; wealthier households added lard or a bit of beef. It was during the years of nutritional prosperity that the country became increasingly dependent on credit and the ability it afforded to live wildly beyond one's means.

The tide turned suddenly in 1692, an exceptionally cold year and one that saw an unusually high rainfall. Those who lived through it described 1692 as a year "with no warm period, not a single summer's day." Such conditions naturally resulted in disastrous harvests all over the country—though, since many regions still had reserves of grain, prices did not spike right away. In the great market of Paris, Les Halles, in July 1691 a *setier* (a measure of grain equivalent to roughly twelve bushels) of wheat was worth 10 livres; a year later the price had risen to 15.

But then in 1693 "the rain never let up"—nor did the cold. When the harvest of 1693 proved even more disastrous than that of 1692, prices soared. By July 1693, the *setier* of wheat was up to 28 livres—by September to 42. In just two years, the price of bread had more than quadrupled. And for the first time in more than thirty years, famine became widespread in France.

All over Paris, hordes of women roamed the streets, pillaging bakeries in order to feed their children.

In October, thirty ovens were constructed in one of the Louvre's courtyards. In them, 100,000 loaves were baked daily. Known as "the king's bread," the loaves were sold, right there at the entrance to the Louvre, at what was then a

*Starving Parisians in 1693, fighting for a loaf of "the King's bread."*

bargain price: two sous a pound. Even though soldiers were present to try to keep the process orderly, starving masses rushed the gates every day, as this engraving from 1693 shows.

In 1688, when Louis XIV provoked what he intended as a short conflict on a single front, stocks of wheat were uncommonly high and prices rock bottom. These were the ideal conditions for feeding soldiers and their mounts in an army of unprecedented size. Just as soon as the record cold began, in February 1691, the *intendants*, officials in charge of supplying the troops, began to make massive purchases of grain. During the campaign of 1692, the rain made it so difficult to get supplies to the front that hundreds of horses died pulling carts of grain. The size of the French army peaked in 1693, just as food shortages were most critical. On May 30, 1693, the Parisian Parlement published an ordinance forbidding anyone from "constituting a stock of grain larger than that necessary to feed their family."

On May 18, Louis XIV had left Versailles, bound for the front in Flanders. Torrential rains and illness slowed the progress of his journey. In early June, he reviewed the troops and planned strategy for that summer's campaign with his generals. Then, on June 13, the fifty-four-year-old monarch who loved combat and who had always led his armies into battle suddenly decided to return to Versailles. His early departure left his generals in disarray and contemporary observers perplexed—and caused widespread rejoicing in the enemy camp. Many saw it as a dire omen. This was the last time that the king—whose reign continued for another twenty-two years—ever saw a battleground.

Jean Magoulet's fortunes had risen in a spectacular fashion with the onset of the war in Flanders. As the war strategy fell apart, his fortunes knew an equally spectacular reversal.

On May 20, 1693, Jean had drawn up the last document in which the rue Saint-Honoré address appeared; from then on, he worked exclusively from the Quai de l'École. Because of the looming economic crisis, plans were on hold for the campaign of 1694. Rather than riding proudly into battle in eye-catching outfits, "high and powerful" young lords were left bogged down in mud-clogged fields. Besides, none of them could have afforded to add sparkle to their outfits: in the years between 1690 and 1700, the cost of precious metal rose by 26 percent. In the tough economic times of that decade, Jean Magoulet could never have charged enough for his work to make up for such a spike.

Jean never again found work as an embroiderer; he never again dealt in credit and loans. From 1693 on, his only business dealings were increasingly desperate attempts to recover some of the vast sums still owed him by "high and powerful" cavalry officers.

The arrangement Jean accepted in the final agreement signed on the rue
Saint-Honoré only weeks before Louis XIV fled the battlefields of Flanders
was a clear indication of the state of France in mid-1693. Antoine, Marquis Du
Chastelet, a brigadier general of the noblest blood who by then owed Magoulet over 10,000 livres for embroidery completed for his regiment, announced
that "all he could offer at the moment by way of payment" was "the fruit" of
one of his properties. The Queen's Embroiderer was obliged to accept the produce of a farm—such as it could have been after the pitiful harvests of recent
years—in lieu of money.

By mid-1693, the marquis' situation was typical: no one in France had any
coin left. The Hague's *Historical and Political Mercury* chronicled the critical
shortage of precious metal that originated that year: "Throughout the kingdom, the scarcity of money, like the scarcity of food, could not be greater." To
deal with the looming monetary crisis, in 1693 the French government printed
for the first time *billets de monnaie*, mint bills, a paper substitute for coin
intended to keep supplies and pay flowing to its armies.

In the 1690s, these notes circulated in such limited quantities that very few
Frenchmen encountered them. But between 1693 and 1720, every time that
war, famine, and pestilence joined forces to devastate France, forms of paper
money came into ever wider use.

Militarily, 1693 was the last good year for the French army. At that point, as
the nation plunged ever deeper into misery, Louis XIV's fabled luck finally
ran out. The 1694 campaign got off to a late start, for even though the army
had requisitioned vast amounts of grain and thereby increased famine among
the civilian population, stores remained insufficient. And because enemy troops
were stationed on all the country's frontiers, supplies could not be brought in
from abroad, as had been done in the past when France's own harvests proved
inadequate.

That year, for the first time, there was no major siege in Flanders; from then
on, the French army increasingly fought a war of defense. And soon it was
failing at defense as well. On September 5, 1695, the French forfeited their
prize acquisition when Namur fell after a long siege, with heavy casualties on
both sides and at a colossal economic cost as well. The Peace of Ryswick signed
in 1697 was widely viewed as a defeat for the French. Before the century was
out, France had returned to its 1668 borders: all the conquests won through
decades of combat had been lost.

A war machine of unprecedented size had been brought to a grinding halt by
the price of bread. The same could be said of Louis XIV's kingdom as a
whole.

As the cost of grain skyrocketed and famine became ever more widespread, all over France people began to leave their villages to roam the countryside in search of food. The number of beggars rose sharply in 1693. And then came the winter of 1693–1694.

Record cold that year made an already dire situation far bleaker still. By the summer of 1694, in some parts of the country grain was six times more expensive than before the crisis. Priests reported that their parishioners had been reduced to eating grass. Cities began locking their gates against ever larger mobs of starving paupers; the homeless would then try to dig their way under the walls. Typhoid—its spread facilitated by wandering crowds—broke out and killed many already weakened by famine. In 1693–1694, some cities lost as much as 12 percent of their population. In May 1694, The Hague's *Historical and Political Mercury* reported that bodies of those dead from hunger had become a common sight in the streets of Paris. In 1694, child abandonment quadrupled because so many parents simply couldn't afford to feed their offspring.

The demographic crisis of 1693–1694 far exceeded those caused by the Revolution of 1789 or by either of the twentieth century's world wars. Out of a population of roughly 22 million, more than 2.8 million Frenchmen died from famine and poverty. Between January 1693 and January 1695, France lost nearly 7 percent of its population.

Jean's wife, Simone Inselin, was among the casualties of the winter of 1694–1695. Though it's likely that her death took place in late 1694 or early 1695, it's impossible to pinpoint the date of her demise, because her husband kept it a secret—naturally, for financial reasons.

Upon a wife's death, a father with children under the age of legal majority, twenty-five, was required by law to have an inventory of the family's possessions drawn up, since at that moment, the couple's property was divided into two equal parts: one remained his, while the other belonged to the couple's children. In addition, the wife's dowry became upon her death the property of her children. Until they were of age, their father managed the funds for them, but as each of them turned twenty-five or married, their father had an obligation to turn over their share of the dowry and to provide an accounting of how the funds had been managed. By the time of Simone's death, Jean Magoulet's risky investments had wiped out the vast profits from his embroidery workshop. He dispensed with his legal obligation to have a probate inventory established. His decision would come back to haunt him.

In the 1690s, as the French army ballooned to an unprecedented size, the war administration knew equally spectacular growth. There was a central bureaucracy, headed by the secretary of war, whose officials were in charge of every aspect of the complex business of feeding and clothing and providing for soldiers and their horses. Each province had its own administration, and there were also private contractors. Soldiers were promised a pound and a half of bread daily. An army of sixty thousand required forty thousand horses, which meant that a thousand tons of fresh forage had to be found locally every day. The army sometimes changed the city targeted for a siege due to insufficient nearby fodder.

These operations were complex under normal circumstances, but in the 1690s, that complexity reached epic proportions. And along with every new complication, new possibilities for graft were introduced into a bloated system known to be positively riddled with fraud all down the line. Jacques Magoulet had key contacts in this corrupt administration.

The chief witness at Jacques' wedding, François Legendre, was second in command in Flanders during the Nine Years' War. Another witness, Louis Cauchon, also held a high administrative post. Both got rich during the war years; they also helped various Magoulets find work in the army bureaucracy, first of all Guillaume Morel.

Morel was the foremost of the small number of men on whom both Jean I and Jean II Magoulet could rely to back up every one of their lies. Morel first played this role in 1695 for Jean I, and he was still fulfilling the same function in 1719, when he helped Jean II ship his eldest child off to "the islands."

Morel was an in-law, a member of the Magoulet clan by virtue of his marriage to Jean's older sister Marie. In 1695, he was employed as treasurer for supplies for the army in Flanders, a position from which he clearly realized considerable personal profit: whereas in 1689, he had been obliged to borrow money from his wife and her mother, after the war he was able to lend sizable sums to his other Magoulet ally, Jacques. And during the war years, Morel was using his windfall profits to finance his lifelong proclivity for philandering.

In January 1695, there were at least three women in Morel's life—his wife; the widow of the noted luxury goods merchant Pierre Thomire (in 1725, Morel died of a heart attack in her bed); and Jeanne Gombault, the wife of one of his employees, Louis Prévot. The Prévots lived in the very building where Jean had maintained an office. Even though Morel's official address was on the Place des Victoires, he kept a second apartment on the rue Saint-Honoré. He had either taken over Jean's quarters, or all along the Saint-Honoré space had doubled as a love nest shared by both men.

On January 18, 1695, Morel's long-suffering spouse finally caught up with him there. His employee had been conveniently sent away for six weeks to figure out how they could possibly find food for the troops during the upcoming summer's campaign, and in his absence Morel had taken up full-time residence on the rue Saint-Honoré. Morel's wife, Marie Magoulet, questioned people all over the neighborhood until she managed to track him down. Once she learned the truth, Marie began to harass the other woman. If she spotted her at her window, she would cry out that Gombault was a whore. Marie showed up at her door, slapped Gombault several times, and tore her gown.

At that point, Jeanne Gombault turned to the police, and the officer assigned to this district, Inspector Jean Regnault, opened an investigation. He interviewed not only the principals but also neighbors, servants, and the well-known haberdasher Lesgu, whose shop was on the ground floor. He learned that Morel was forty years old and that he favored a dove-gray suit, that everyone knew "Magoulet the embroiderer," and that Marie Magoulet was so tall, of "such imposing stature," that she was unforgettable. Marie, "obviously suffering," explained that her husband was trying to lock her up in a convent for the rest of her days.

As for Morel, his defense was simple: just deny everything. He denied living on the rue Saint-Honoré (even though Regnault had been to his apartment there and had interviewed his servants), denied knowing Gombault, even denied knowing his own wife. His defense worked: Marie's complaint went nowhere.

This was the man who took Jean II under his wing when he returned from the Americas sometime in 1692 or 1693. Guillaume Morel taught him the ways of the French world.

The Saint-Honoré scandal was but the first time that the Magoulet name was dragged through the mud in 1695. On August 11, just as the French army was suffering brutal defeats in Flanders, the opening arguments in *Forbi v. Briet* were pronounced, and Jean's involvement with Barbe de Ville was revealed. Then, on August 25, a warrant was issued for the arrest of thirteen-year-old Jean II; five days later, he turned himself in and was promptly locked up in one of Paris' most notorious and toughest prisons, the Grand Châtelet. (It was destroyed in the nineteenth century and replaced by today's Place du Châtelet.)

The young prisoner identified himself as a junior member of Morel's administration, one of roughly 150 agents who used notes drawn on the treasurer general to pay agents in the field for food and supplies. Jean II was thus a small cog in the vast machinery trying with increasing difficulty to feed the royal army. His incarceration lasted nearly three weeks, but the charges that inspired it remain unclear: the first half of the document describing his interrogations has not survived.

To justify immediate internment in the Grand Châtelet, the crime of which the thirteen-year-old stood accused must have been serious indeed. Jean II Magoulet may well have been born a violent child, and all he had lived through in his first thirteen years had surely made him capable of anything, as his adult life would make clear. But we'll never know what he did to deserve this, only the first of the many periods of confinement in virtually all of Paris' prisons that from then on punctuated his life at regular intervals.

The remaining portion of his prison interrogation makes this much plain: Jean II's incarceration was somehow bound up with his hatred for his father and with Jean I Magoulet's refusal to give his children an accounting of Simone Inselin's estate.

The legal irregularities that surrounded Simone's death came to light only when, during his imprisonment, her son Jean II defended himself by accusing his father of abuse. His complaint produced a significant result.

Upon the death of a parent with minor children, those under the legal age of twenty-five, French law also required the surviving parent to organize a formal gathering: in the presence of a representative of the state, family members and close friends met in order to elect a guardian and coguardian to manage the children's financial affairs. Long after Simone Inselin's death, on October 4, 1695, just as D'Aguesseau was making public his judgment in *Forbi v. Briet* as well as Jean's involvement with Briet, that assembly finally took place. The official account followed standard format by listing the names of children identified as those of Jean and Simone, beginning with the eldest, their first son, Jean.

The process of naming guardians was under the control of the civil lieutenant, or head of the civil branch of the Parisian police. The state, however, almost always simply followed the family's recommendations and contacted those on a list submitted by the surviving parent. The assembly organized after Simone's death included various Magoulets: brothers, including Jacques, by then also employed by the Flanders war administration; François Moustrel, a brother-in-law, husband of their sister Marguerite. In contrast, given that the maternal inheritance was at stake and that Simone Inselin was part of an extended family, all of whom lived in Paris, it's odd that only two people represented Inselin family interests: one a distant relative, an otherwise unknown cousin-in-law; the other the only dodgy Inselin, Simone's brother, Adrien, a shoemaker. This imbalance could have alerted authorities that something was off-kilter.

Those assembled named Jean guardian and Adrien, the only possible Inselin relative, subrogate guardian, with the duty of looking out for the children's

financial interests. Neither Charlotte nor François was included on the list of
their children; they had presumably died young. But other names did appear:
Nicolas, Antoinette, Alexandre, Angélique. Jean had taken advantage of this
legal ceremony in the presence solely of members of his inner circle to slip
four illegitimate children, including Nicolas, officially into the Magoulet clan.
(The three youngest children were never mentioned again and can also be
assumed to have died at an early age.)

   Any satisfaction Jean felt at having pulled this off was short-lived, for his
eldest son, Jean II, still not even fourteen but hardened by his years on Sainte
Croix, quickly contested the document. This obliged the Parisian police to
interrogate both father and son. Jean painted a picture of a rebellious and profligate child. His son had run away from home, he claimed; he had frequented
tramps and migrants—"of one and the other sex"—and in that company had
led "a degenerate and immoral way of life." In other words, since his return
from the island, Jean II, his father contended, had been living on the streets,
along with so many other homeless individuals in 1694 and 1695, and as a
result he had contracted, his father further maintained, "venereal disease."

   In his defense, the son painted a picture of paternal cruelty. And the fact that
he dared do so is early evidence of the boldness that would characterize his
adult life. All forms of intimate violence have always been underreported
crimes: in seventeenth-century France, abuse against minors was the most
underreported abuse of all, far less often recorded than domestic violence.
The accusations made by thirteen-year-old Jean II Magoulet constitute the
only contemporaneous case I've encountered of a child well under the age of
legal responsibility willing to denounce his own father's abusive behavior and
willing and able to present himself as a victim of intimate violence.

   As long as his mother had been alive, Jean II explained, she had helped him
in any way possible—but "always without his father's knowledge." As soon as
she had died, his father "had stopped at nothing" to force him and his brother
Nicolas to leave home—and this was but the most recent manifestation of
"the hatred and complete lack of paternal instinct" that had always characterized their father's dealings with them. His father's most recent accusations had
all begun when his son had demanded an accounting of his mother's estate, an
inventory that his son was sure would expose his father's wrongdoing, his
"dissipation" of his children's inheritance. Jean II ended with two requests:
that the inventory become mandatory and that he be released from his father's
guardianship.

   The police response was predictable: they rebuked the son for "insolence"
toward his father. They decreed that because of his conduct and because no

one on either side of his family would substantiate his claims, the guardianship should continue even after he was of age.

Faced with a wall of opposition, Jean II simply took matters into his own
hands.

How did he do it? Blackmail seems the obvious answer. He knew so many of
his father's secrets; he had watched him tell so many lies. He surely threatened
some sort of revelation so explosive that he terrified the Queen's Embroiderer.
It took a bit of time, but before the decade was out, the son had brought his
father to his knees.

Already in June 1695, the Queen's Embroiderer had been obliged to give up
the lease on his once marvelous shop—to a merchant who asked that that
revolutionary façade for which Jean had paid dearly be replaced with an ordinary one. And he had been borrowing heavily for some time. Only two days
after he was appointed guardian to his children, one creditor, a widow named
La Roche who had taken over her husband's engraving workshop, initiated a
lawsuit to recover the 3,000-livre loan Jean had taken out the preceding April,
during the period when he was refusing to account for his wife's estate. To get
her off his back, in November, Jean turned over the title to all his personal
effects, including his furniture, as security on a new loan, which he used to
pay off the old one.

Henceforth, the Queen's Embroiderer had neither a place of business nor
possessions—and soon this didn't matter, since he no longer had a home in
which to house his effects: the following February he gave up the lease on his
grandiose lodgings on the Quai de l'École. And even the ragtag income that
could be extracted from the many cavalry officers still in his debt became
increasingly elusive. One after another, "high and powerful" lords such as the
Marquis Du Chastelet were "condemned" by the army's top brass to pay their
debts to Jean, but in a time of monetary crisis so dire that almost no one in
France had any specie still on hand, these condemnations were meaningless.

By the end of 1696, all Jean had left was the title "the Queen's Embroiderer"
that harked back to the glory days when he and Versailles were in their prime.
When all was lost, he began to identify himself with a series of honorifics to
which he had no legal right whatsoever.

First came *gendarme* in the *garde du roi*. This title identified him as an officer
in an elite military unit whose some two hundred members, most from the
high nobility and all with considerable and noteworthy experience on the
battlefield, formed an honor guard for the king when he rode in public ceremonies. Next, appropriating the name of an estate that he had never owned,
Jean called himself *Sieur de Toulongeon*. In January 1698, he even referred to

himself as an *écuyer*—a noble, just as Antoine Chevrot began to do that same year.

In the document in which he called himself a noble, Jean assumed legal responsibility for any problem that might occur if Nicolas obtained a position in the service of a major financier, M. de La Bonardière. The post involved the management of considerable sums, and Nicolas' prospective employer was naturally concerned about his trustworthiness, so Jean once again stood up for his illegitimate son.

He underestimated the influence of his legitimate son. During the events of 1695, Nicolas and Jean II had formed a bond that was never to be broken. They soon joined forces to fleece their father.

Before long, Nicolas had taken over Jean's bogus aristocratic title, which his father never again used, and was referring to himself as Magoulet de Toulongeon. Nicholas soon found new employment, clerking for still another of Jacques' cronies, François Gallois, who had also become immensely wealthy during the Nine Years' War. And Nicolas parlayed that position into the kind of life that had remained beyond his father's reach.

Nicolas had obviously inherited the Magoulet charm: he soon acquired an enormously wealthy wife. (By 1716, Nicolas was being pursued by the French fiscal authorities for the nearly 40,000 livres in back taxes owed by the estate of his recently deceased spouse.)

After his marriage, Nicolas' attacks on their father were over. But driven by a hatred as patient as it was fierce, Jean II proceeded systemically to reduce the Queen's Embroiderer to the status of an official nonentity. Before beginning, he bided his time for a bit, waiting for the right occasion.

In 1699, Jean's negotiations with the family of the Comte de Gadagne finally came to an end. At this point, the head of the household, the count's uncle, Camille d'Hostun, Comte de Tallard and Marquis de La Baume, lieutenant general of the Royal Army, took over the deliberations. D'Hostun drew up a settlement with the long list of his nephew's creditors: he forced them to agree to greatly reduced sums, and even those he didn't pay outright. Thus, rather than the 12,000 livres Jean was still owed, he had to be content with 5,500, to be paid as an annuity that gave him 270 livres annually.

But when eight years of negotiations with the La Baume family finally ended, they concluded with a devilish twist.

In the final accounting on September 7, 1699, Jean identified himself merely as "formerly an embroiderer," while Jean II, who was also there to agree to the terms of their settlement, described himself as "the king's official embroiderer"—in other words, the original position in the royal household that his father had occupied in 1676 before being named the Queen's Embroiderer. This sudden reversal of status signaled the onset of Jean II's campaign for revenge. The son had no right to call himself "the King's Embroiderer." Unlike his father, he had never been in Louis XIV's employ. But he did have the right to share in the monetary benefits from his father's court service, and the Gadagne settlement gave him his part, along with all he had requested in his official denunciation to the police. In the legally binding agreement he signed with the Gadagne estate, Jean formally identified Jean II as "my eldest son and of age" (even though he was then but seventeen and a half)—thereby both officially returning his son's birthright and freeing him from the constraints of a guardianship. In addition, Jean declared that he and Jean II were Simone Inselin's sole heirs, thereby eliminating the four other children, including Nicolas, whom he had recognized in 1695. Jean concluded his declaration by handing over to his eldest son and heir the annuity he had been awarded in the settlement of the Comte de Gadagne's debts—"with no possibility of restitution."

Now 270 livres a year was not a fortune, and the sum hardly made up for three lost years in Jean II's life, but taking control over the annuity did deprive his father of his only sure source of income. It also obliged him to recant in an official context the lies he had concocted about his offspring.

And all this was just for starters. Jean II next obliged Jean to set him up in life—both personally and professionally.

On June 6, 1701, a marriage contract was signed in Paris. The bride was young, underage, and still living with her parents; the groom was nineteen, though he claimed, as his father had given him the right to do in 1699, to be over twenty-five. Jean II had been well trained and by two of the best, his father and Guillaume Morel, so he knew that as long as you had a family member willing to back you up, and as long as there was no reason for those for whom you were concocting the fiction to doubt you, you could swear to anything, even in the presence of officers of the law.

The marriage was far more prominent than this bridegroom had any right to expect. Noel Poisson, the bride's father, had held a modest position in the court of Marie Anne de Bavière, the wife of Louis XIV and Marie-Thérèse's firstborn: he was among the many who carried dishes from the kitchen to her table. In 1701, Poisson was *directeur de la ferme des suifs*, financial administrator of the Tallow Farm, the organization that oversaw the taxation of tallow, the animal fat that was the principal component of the most commonly used and least expensive type of candle. The dowry he and his wife, Marie Anne Duchesne, gave their daughter Louise was more than respectable—2,500 livres, plus an additional 500 in household effects. The parents promised 1,800 up front, with the remaining 700 livres to be paid over the next five years.

French marriage contracts also contained a financial promise made by the husband-to-be, the dower: it stipulated the sum to be reserved from his estate and settled on his wife for her support in the event that she survived him. The dower remained a theoretical sum, since it was not paid up front, but its amount served nonetheless as a measure of the groom's worth. The oldest Magoulet brother, Hubert, had promised 800 livres; Jacques had pledged 4,000. Jean II offered a dower of 2,000 livres, followed by the longest explanation of anyone's financial situation I have ever encountered in such a document, all to arrive at the conclusion that he had a net worth of 6,000 livres. It was at that moment that the bride's parents should have grabbed their daughter Louise and run for their lives.

In France today, the name Magoulet has disappeared. But anyone who hears it thinks automatically of the words *magouille*, *magouiller*, and *magouillage*. The terms are modern, created only in the 1960s or '70s; their origin is unknown. A *magouilleur* is an individual who habitually acts in a dishonest or illegal fashion, who will say or do anything it takes to pull the wool over someone's eyes, while a *magouille* is chicanery, unscrupulous behavior. The vocabulary could have been invented to characterize Jean II.

Juridical documents such as marriage contracts always contain legal formulas, an official language that varies from country to country and from one period to another—a sort of legal jargon or legalese. But once the code is cracked and you know the commonly used formulas, such documents are easy to follow. Beginning with the settlement for his first marriage, Jean II invented a variant of legalese: *magouillese*. It hews close to the legalese of his day, but it is so full of overly complex, empty formulas that it's close to gibberish. Every time Jean II had recourse to such language, he was up to something, some sort of *magouille*, or duplicitous operation.

In 1701, he was striving to create an illusion of prosperity for himself and his family—and given the recent past, he didn't have much to build upon. This explains his decision to identify himself in his marriage contract as a *bourgeois de Paris*—in his case, a complete cover-up—and to review his financial situation in such detail. This also explains his choice of the only witness there to stand up for him, Jean Voigny. When Voigny had married only months before, he had offered an identical dower. He was a young man primed for success in the world of high finance, and he went on to fulfill that early promise. When he died in 1762, he had become *de* Voigny, truly an *écuyer*, ennobled by the king, and he lived in a grand residence with a private entrance for carriages.

This was exactly the kind of future Jean II hoped to conjure up for those present in 1701.

Also there to stand up for the groom was his father: this was, after all, to be still another day of reckoning for him. Jean II returned his past to him just for the moment when he signed the contract as "the Queen's Embroiderer": it was the last time he would ever allow his father to use that title. Much of the *magouillese* explaining Jean II's balance sheet was clearly included expressly to get under his father's skin. Jean II announced most notably that he would be paid 3,000 livres from his mother's estate, a sum that his father had promised to give him "just as soon as sir his father will have found the time to have the inventory of his mother's possessions drawn up."

The *magouillese* could have distracted attention from a remarkable absence: other than the two Jean Magoulets, there was no one by that surname present. And for such an extended family, all of whom lived in Paris, this says it all: no other Magoulet was willing to step into the inner circle and enable Jean II to trick the Poissons into this alliance.

There was a good reason why Jean Magoulet wanted to marry in 1701: France was once again going to war, and still another gigantic army was being assembled to fight a Europe-wide coalition. Young men were selected for conscription by means of a lottery, but the names of married men were removed from the list. Between 1701 and 1703, 623,000 Frenchmen took a wife: then, as soon as the monarchy eliminated the automatic exemption from military service for young married men, the number of weddings fell dramatically.

After the signing, the Magoulets father and son stayed on at the notary's for another ceremony. With the bride's family safely out of the room, Jean I admitted that he didn't have the money owed to his son by his mother's estate—the same funds the son had just listed as the foundation of his personal wealth. Instead, Jean was turning over "the prerogative that was his to embroider and to run an embroidery workshop under the title the Queen's Embroiderer." He further pledged "to provide him with a privilege that would guarantee that his son would be in no way interfered with in the exercise of his profession."

In 1701, eighteen years after Queen Marie-Thérèse's death, her last official embroiderer was finally ending his association with her court.

Some royal positions, particularly those in financial administrations, could be passed on to one's offspring; there was an extra charge for this privilege. Artisans were not in this category, particularly those who had worked for a court that no longer existed. Jean thus had no right to hand over his title.

He did have the right to bestow "a privilege," to pronounce his son a master embroiderer. Sons of master artisans were routinely allowed to skip over the apprenticeship on the assumption that they had already done their training under their father's supervision. But to be sure that the embroiderers' guild would not "interfere in the exercise of his profession"—that is, to guarantee that they would accept the legitimacy of this privilege and not try to put his son out of business—Jean should have convoked at least one guild official to witness the document, as his own father had done in 1667 when Jean was admitted to the ranks of master *gainiers*.

The legal status of his new privilege wouldn't have much concerned Jean II. He may even have enjoyed the hint of irregularity: his father, after all, had entered the ranks of master embroiderers only because of his court position rather than by following official procedure, and the son more than shared his father's appetite for risk.

How much systematic training did Jean II really have? He could and probably did begin an informal apprenticeship in his father's workshop before he was shipped off to Sainte Croix; most children of royal artisans did learn the family craft. When Jean II began to run a workshop, it was a family affair: his wife worked with him, as did her younger sister Catherine, and later his three oldest children. He may also have mastered the profession in which he made a name for himself on the fly, much as his father had done during the years he spent in the Saint-Denis de la Chartre enclave.

Jean II's years on Sainte Croix keeping the baron's books would have prepared him well for the financial side of the business. And he had a significant edge over his father, a diametrically opposed relation to writing and writing instruments. The original Queen's Embroiderer had lived with the specter of his illiteracy hanging over him, but his son was a master of the quill: his signatures are polished, his handwriting as fluent and elegant as any in Paris at the time. Even his spelling and his syntax were perfect; I encountered not a single deviation from the norm in any document in his hand. And this was far from a given at a time when all but a handful of the most highly literate Frenchmen spelled in a more or less idiosyncratic fashion. It's hard to imagine how the original Queen's Embroiderer was able to overcome his clumsiness with writing instruments in order to produce master designs to be recreated in needlework, but it's easy to see his son as the expert draftsman he clearly became.

Jean II's proficiency with the quill was so absolute that he also turned into a master forger, able to produce counterfeit signatures, even entire documents that he could then allege to have been written by someone else. His capacity for forgery put him at a particularly cruel advantage over his wife and children. He was able to make any allegation about their behavior that he liked to

*Signature of the second Queen's Embroiderer, Jean II Magoulet, in 1701.*

the authorities and then produce the evidence needed to back them up—all with a few strokes of a pen.

On the 1701 documents, the father listed as his address the rue des Petits-Champs, a street not greatly distant from his former location but far less prestigious. The son, on the other hand, gave "parish Saint-Germain-l'Auxerrois at the tip of the Pont Neuf"—that is, the location of his parents' fabulously expensive apartment. To anyone in the know, this would have served as still more proof of his intended take-over of his father's identity.

On February 4, 1704, Jean II at last fulfilled that dream. That day, he signed a lease on a house virtually next door to the one his parents had begun renting just weeks before his birth. The property belonged to the Marquise de Dauaray, and its rent indicates that it must have been an aristocratic affair indeed. The 1,600 livres his father had paid was already a princely sum for an artisan, but his son easily went him one better when he agreed to 2,440 livres—this at a time when artisans paid between 250 and 500 for their shops and living quarters combined, when Antoine Chevrot and Marie Boulanger were renting a spacious apartment in a less elegant but still excellent neighborhood for 400 livres, and when only 2 percent of Parisian apartments rented for more than 2,000 livres.

These new quarters were vast beyond the wildest imagination: four floors of rooms, an independent wing, cellars and attics, plus two shops, all facing onto the Quai de l'École and the Seine. The young couple rented out one of the shops for 450 livres, but still. . . . The price was so clearly a stretch for an artisan, even one with alleged court connections, that the marquise insisted on additional security: not only Louise Poisson but both her parents cosigned the lease to guarantee payment of the rent. This was yet another financial arrangement with Jean II Magoulet they would live to regret.

With the lease on that Quai de l'École real estate, Jean II's revenge was complete. He now had it all: the title, the earnings, the privilege to work as an embroiderer, even at the same location.

His father had nothing: from then on, he was practically invisible, with no title, no source of revenue, and no fixed address. He seems to have moved often, surely running from creditors. The formerly proud Queen's Embroiderer surfaced only when his son needed a family member's signature on a legal document—for during the early years of his marriage, all other Magoulets, even those who had stood by his father at his worst moments, kept their distance from his vengeful son.

# CHAPTER EIGHT

# A Person of Consequence
## The Chevrots: 1692–1708

A T THE DAWN of the seventeenth century, the first Antoine Chevrot had arrived in Paris determined to rise above his origins, and each successive Antoine Chevrot more than matched his ambition. Each of them married money, even though not one of them was given to the acquisition of fine possessions or elegant clothing, and none lived in a showy fashion or in one of the capital's best neighborhoods. There were no attempts to acquire real estate beyond the property part of each bride's dowry. Instead, the Chevrot men wanted funds for one reason alone: they were seeking the means necessary to purchase titles that guaranteed social advancement.

With each successive Chevrot heir, this quest for higher standing became more imperative. By the century's end, the individual who turned out to be the final Antoine Chevrot was striving with overt desperation to become, in his own words, someone "who has a certain name in the world."

Antoine's parameters were clear: the only name worth having was a noble title. In France by 1700, non-nobles were able to join the ranks of the aristocracy in various ways. Marriage provided an obvious path for women: all that was required was a dowry of gargantuan proportions. Even the most powerful houses often had such socially dubious alliances buried somewhere in their past. The Du Lude dynasty, the family of the all-powerful duchess who masterminded Antoine's career, was no exception. In 1622, a moment when women from solvent aristocratic families received dowries in the neighborhood of 40,000 livres, a Du Lude son chose a bride with no "name in the world" whatsoever. Instead of social standing, Marie Feydeau, the daughter of one of the country's principal tax farmers, brought into the marriage a dowry of 500,000 livres—in cash. This would have translated into nearly 10,000 pounds of silver or 750 pounds of gold.

As for men, by 1700, those with an income similar to that of Marie Feydeau's father could acquire a title—Antoine Crozat was named Marquis Du Chastel in exchange for massive loans to the crown. But the Chevrots had nothing like the wealth of a Crozat. The best they had ever been able to come up with were insignificant domains such as Coulanges (part of the Daulmay dowry) or Courcelles (part of the Boulanger inheritance). Even Antoine, for all his often ludicrous pretensions, surely realized that such paltry "estates" did not significantly enhance his station. His only real hope came from the administrative positions that could be so freely acquired whenever the monarchy needed quick money. After all, as a 1723 guide to the intricacies of the French social structure put it, "the only way to determine someone's exact degree of superiority is to know the *charge* [the position] that the person occupies."

Just as the guidebook suggested, Antoine Chevrot was constantly both evaluating the "degree of superiority" of all those around him and trying to make sure that everyone he encountered had an exact appreciation of every nuance of his own eminence. This obsession with distinction was the single trait that defined him best.

If only his own family had had the means to satisfy his rapacious craving for social status, all might have been well.

The previous Antoine Chevrot had certainly never achieved true financial stability. Antoine's mother was determined that her husband's financial difficulties would not hinder their only son's advancement. When in December 1692 the crown created many new positions, among them additional *payeurs* and *contrôleurs des rentes* at Paris' City Hall, she jumped at the chance. Antoine was among the new *contrôleurs des rentes* then named. Marie Daulmay Chevrot was able to finance this purchase with the backing of her family's income from the salt trade.

In the early sixteenth century, *rentes*, or annuities, were developed as still another of the monarchy's tools for obtaining funds expeditiously in periods of crisis. The annuities offered by Paris' City Hall became particularly popular: by the late seventeenth century, they were a basic investment strategy for more than one hundred thousand Parisians. Investors paid a sum up front and in return were given a certificate that entitled them to quarterly interest payments at a rate of about 5 percent. An administration was established to oversee the payment process, made up of *payeurs* (payers) and *contrôleurs* (controllers). By the turn of the eighteenth century, there were roughly seventy payers and as many controllers overseeing the millions invested in these annuities.

In 1692, the Daulmays did not go all out and invest the 150,000 livres necessary to obtain one of the top positions as a payer in the annuity administration, but only 20,000 for a controller's post. That huge difference in price was naturally reflected in the income generated by each type of position: a payer received well over 6,000 livres a year in legal wages, a controller not even 900. The differential might not have been crucial for a young man still living with his parents, but it proved telling once Antoine had a family of his own.

The disparity in cost was paralleled by an equally significant disparity in responsibility. In theory, controllers were to verify that payers were doing their job properly and that those who came forward to collect interest payments were the legal titleholders of the annuities. In reality, however, the controllers served mainly as bookkeepers and to rubber-stamp the decisions of those they allegedly controlled. Payers were highly respected and extremely important officials, men of real distinction, while controllers were much less significant players.

In December 1698, just a month after Antoine married Marie Françoise Boulanger, a new government edict suppressed all the positions in the annuities administration that had been created in 1692. Controllers could accept a refund on their original investment; officeholders who wished to continue in their functions had to come up with an additional 10,000 livres.

By 1698, the Daulmays had washed their hands of Antoine. Thus it was that on December 23, one month to the day after their marriage contract had been formalized at Versailles, Antoine and his new bride were signing a contract of a very different kind in the presence of a notary. Antoine so desperately wanted to hold on to his position that he had agreed to borrow the additional sum now required. The loan marked the beginning of his adult financial life; this was the first arrangement he had ever made on his own. Since his resources alone were not a sufficient guarantee, Marie Françoise Boulanger was there to cosign his loan: they had no sooner been married than Antoine forced his new wife to join him as a partner in the downward spiral of credit and debt that would govern all his future life.

This contract was a business arrangement that the bride's family would long regret. In March 1719, a decade after their daughter Marie Françoise had died, her parents finally forced Antoine to settle his obligation with them. Because of their daughter's signature on that loan, they had been obliged to pay off

Antoine's debt when he had defaulted on it. Even in 1719, Antoine could not pay cash; instead, he offered the Boulangers only a promise to pay interest on what he owed them, thereby creating still another encumbrance that would not be settled in his lifetime but would be left as a burden for his heirs.

The new and more expensive controller's position was an improvement over the 1692 arrangement in one key way: the post had been made hereditary. That fact was so important to Antoine that on the official document naming him controller for the second time he obliged the bureaucrat handing it over to add in the margin a note affirming that the post was indeed "hereditary." He then held on to the document with that magic word; it was among the family papers that his notary turned over to his eldest son upon Antoine's death in 1729.

By then, that son, Louis Chevrot, would have spent twenty-eight years with the specter of the position that his father was determined to hand down to him hanging over his head. Almost three years before his son's birth, Antoine had resolved that his future heir would follow in his footsteps and spend his life rubber-stamping the decisions made by more significant government officials.

The year that followed that loan agreement, the first year of the Chevrot-Boulanger union, was a brief period of calm, perhaps the only moment when Marie Françoise could have felt that all would turn out well in her marriage. On January 3, 1699, Louis XIV officially granted Antoine the revised hereditary post. On January 10, a ceremony at the *chambre des comptes*, or audit chamber, welcomed its freshly appointed members. The year was rounded out on November 26, when a final welcoming reception was held by the governing officers of the municipality.

Even though such ceremonies might have seemed relatively minor occasions when viewed in the context of the full span of a life, Antoine meticulously preserved every document and every invitation: they, too, were part of the thick stack of family papers presented to Louis after his father's death. In retrospect, they must have stood out for Antoine as reminders of the one shining moment when his rise to a position of real distinction could have seemed inevitable, when an outsider would have perceived the newlyweds, with their contacts at Versailles and in Paris' financial administration, as a power couple in the making. By the time of the celebration for new officeholders at City Hall in December 1699, Marie Françoise was pregnant. But by then, Antoine was already coming apart at the seams.

The young couple had incurred expenses during the first year of their marriage, notably when they moved from their first address near Antoine's parents to a more fashionable one, an apartment in the shadow of Saint

Paul's church in Paris' Marais neighborhood. And Antoine's first independent business decision had not been a wise one: he had been unable to meet the payments on the loan. In order to get one man off his back, he took out a second loan, once again cosigned by his wife. As collateral on the new loan, he offered the wages on his position as annuities controller. This time, Antoine borrowed from a formidable businessman: Jean Alexis Loir, a wealthy goldsmith who was enormously successful at the kind of credit and loan ventures that brought about Jean I Magoulet's downfall. Antoine now had a debt whose payments he couldn't manage and an administrative post with little real clout, the income from which he was legally obliged to hand over to someone else. From then on, the wages he received from his post as the Duchesse de Bourgogne's valet de chambre were his principal source of income.

He became desperate—understandably so. Antoine's bride was a fashionable young woman who moved in circles where fashion mattered, notably the court of one of the age's great tastemakers, the Duchesse de Bourgogne. All her life, Marie Françoise kept her wardrobe up to date, and she turned to fine purveyors to do so. High fashion has never been an inexpensive affair.

In early 1700, Antoine initiated a series of lawsuits in an attempt to recover money owed him by a number of individuals with court positions similar to his own, for example, the 140-livre debt of the man who had formerly guarded the entrance to Queen Marie-Thérèse's apartment at Versailles. The sums were all small; lawsuits meant lawyer's fees, and even if a case was decided in Antoine's favor, it usually took years to collect a debt. It must soon have been clear that all this effort could not turn things around. With a child on the way and financial pressure growing, Antoine cracked. He could hardly have chosen a more public forum in which to blow a gasket.

In March 1700, a four-page pamphlet had been handsomely printed and was circulating freely in the streets of Paris. Producing such a document had been a fairly costly affair. Its author, Antoine Chevrot, obviously considered it essential that its contents become public knowledge. Readers surely wondered why anyone would want to air their dirty linen in this manner.

The pamphlet reproduces a complaint Antoine had made on March 1 to Police Commissioner Nicolas Menyer. As he made his case, Antoine maintained every step of the way an almost inconceivable level of high dudgeon.

Antoine flaunted all his claims to notable rank, calling himself "*écuyer*, valet de chambre of Madame the Duchesse de Bourgogne, and the lord of Coulanges." He was also "the accuser," and the accused were Marie Perrin and her servant Barbe Pierre. Perrin he identified only as the wife of Hugues Rimbault, a *huissier priseur*, an officer in the ranks of the Parisian police who helped draw up inventories and estimate the value of the contents of estates. (Only eighteen months earlier, when Jacques Magoulet and Marie Freslin had obtained a legal separation of their property, Rimbault had been in charge of determining its worth. This was but one of many occasions when the worlds of the Magoulets and the Chevrots intersected.) Antoine neglected to say something that would have seemed crucial to interpreting the story he was telling: Marie Perrin was his wife's cousin, a member of the family of her mother, Charlotte Perrin Boulanger.

Antoine accused Perrin of "premeditated murder," specifically of "the assassination"—a word he used repeatedly—of "the wife of lord Chevrot." Of course Antoine's wife, Marie Françoise, was still very much alive. The crime he was reporting to the police was in fact a case of assault and battery: in Antoine's telling, the servant Barbe Pierre, following the orders of her mistress, had attacked his wife, slapping her in the face and kicking her in the stomach. And since his wife was then three months pregnant (that much at least was true), the attack "had put her life, as well as that of her child, in danger."

It's easy to see why Antoine failed to mention the family tie: the picture he painted of Marie Perrin sounds more in character for a fishwife than a member of a respectable house. He claimed Perrin led a dissolute life, spending her time gambling with soldiers and inviting unsavory types to dine in her home. He also attributed language to her that would have been more than a bit shocking for a woman of her standing. In Antoine's version, the attack had been preceded by scenes during which Marie Perrin would shout insults at the Chevrots, including one that featured *bougre*, an invective then considered so coarse that the printer abbreviated it as B.: "B. Chevrot and his B. of a wife, I'll make sure that they die by my hand; I'll run them through with a sword," Antoine quotes Perrin as saying.

The view of the relations between the two couples presented by Marie Perrin and Hugues Rimbault could not have been more different. In their version, they had been friends and had often spent time in each other's company; they had even been together on the night before the alleged attack, "until about 10 in the evening." Marie Perrin further explained that in mid-1699 "while Antoine had been serving his quarter at Versailles"—his annual term as valet de chambre lasted from April to June—it was she who had stayed with her cousin to care for her when Marie Françoise had miscarried and lost her first baby.

It's hard to imagine anyone but Antoine publishing this kind of pamphlet in 1700. Parisians went to the police to accuse others of various crimes: since such accusations had legal weight, there was no reason for anyone to repackage their charges for public circulation.

Later in the eighteenth century, by the 1730s, when pamphlets similar to this one did exist, they became known as *causes célèbres*, accounts of celebrated legal cases that had aroused widespread controversy and provoked heated public debate, and they were authored by lawyers rather than by those involved in the case. Antoine may have been the only person ever to try to create a cause célèbre—to care enough about giving perfect strangers the impression that he was a person of consequence that he was willing to become celebrated in a perfectly sordid manner.

In the end, Antoine's sound and fury signified exactly nothing: the *lieutenant criminel*, the magistrate with jurisdiction over all criminal affairs judged in Paris, let the case drop. Although Antoine claimed to be "sure that the magistrate was simply fed up with the repeated solicitations made by the Rimbaults and their cabal," he offered no explanation for the case's resolution. Instead he claimed to have been too busy caring for his wife to have had the time to follow up.

If I'm inclined to believe that Antoine concocted the entire wild tale, it's because I know that this was but the first of several remarkably similar complaints he made to the police, each time accusing an alleged assailant of attempted murder. By the time I came upon the second and third cases, it became abundantly clear that lightning couldn't have struck that often. Each time, it also became clear that the real crime, the root of Antoine's rage, was a perceived slight to his sense of distinction.

After Antoine had gone to the police with his complaint, Rimbault had presented the couple's side of the story, in Antoine's words, "to several persons of quality": in short, he had turned for help to members of the social category to whose ranks Antoine aspired with every fiber of his being—the nobility. And this, in Antoine's eyes, was an unforgivable "affront to his honor," one that had brought "shame" on him and obliged him to continue the matter by initiating a lawsuit, despite the fact that, as he claimed, "lord Chevrot is not inclined to be litigious"—this from a man who all through his life went to court on every possible pretext and who at any given moment had at least a half dozen lawsuits active. It was also because of Rimbault's "affront to his honor," Antoine explained, that he had felt obliged to print the pamphlet as a "response."

As the alleged victim, Marie Françoise should have been at the center of Antoine's account. Instead, she remained a complete cipher. Readers never heard her opinions or her voice. They never even learned her name, for Antoine referred to her solely as "the spouse of sir Chevrot." And in every rehearsal of the Rimbaults' crimes, "the danger to his wife" seems far less significant than "the affront to [Antoine's] honor": "How could a mere servant dare attack the wife of an officer of the court, of someone who has a certain name in the world because of the honor that he has to serve such a great princess?"

Barely a year into his marriage, Antoine had already established a key pattern of his adult life: each time his obsessive overreliance on credit had reduced his personal value in the world, he would run to the police with still another lurid tale.

On September 9, 1700, the person who would pay most dearly in the aftermath of one of Antoine's crises of consequence, his first son, was born. According to testimony Antoine subsequently often repeated in legal documents, contrary to then standard practice, the baby was not baptized within days of his birth, but only much later. That delay was easily justified in Antoine's mind. He was waiting for the individual he was determined to have as his baby's godfather to make time for the ceremony.

Twenty years afterward, when punishing Louis for alleged disobedience, Antoine consistently defended his actions by invoking his son's particular claim to consequence. He had been named Louis in honor of his godfather, Louis de France, the dauphin, heir to the French throne. Louis Chevrot, his father explained each time, "had known the honor of being held over the baptismal font in the Royal Chapel at Versailles" by Louis XIV's eldest son. And this, in Antoine's eyes, made his son such an eminent personage that he could never be allowed to dishonor his name through an alliance with Louise Magoulet.

The only problem with the story of the Chevrot crown prince sponsored at baptism by his nation's crown prince is that it was still another figment of Antoine's imagination. The activities of members of the royal family were always carefully accounted for and made available in print, so it's easy to verify who was where and for what purpose. Thus, every time that the dauphin held a baby over the font at Versailles, this signal honor was recorded for posterity. But records of the dauphin's appearances between 1700 and his death in 1711 contain no mention of Louis Chevrot.

The question of Louis' alleged royal baptism long weighed on Antoine: in the years to come, he evoked it often in legal documents, each time mentioning a different date for the ceremony. The baby was surely baptized at some point, with a stand-in godfather, but such a ceremony would have counted for nothing in Antoine's eyes. In the case of his eldest son's baptism, Antoine once again punished those nearest to him, all in the name of an aspiration that ultimately remained unfulfilled. This time, Antoine deprived his eldest son of the protection a godfather could afford because of his desire for a baptismal rite that in his mind would have moved his son one step closer to his father's dream of possessing "a certain name in the world."

Antoine's financial difficulties only worsened in the aftermath of his first son's birth. By August 1702, Nicolas de Frémont, member of a major dynasty of French financiers from whom Antoine had taken out a loan in order to pay off one of his earlier debts, had still received none of the payments to which Antoine had agreed. Frémont had won an injunction against Antoine: all his remaining rights in the annuities administration were about to become the object of a legal seizure. By taking on still another loan, Antoine managed to come up with enough money to pacify Frémont and to reimburse his legal fees, but this was but one more temporary stopgap. And it was just at this time that Marie Françoise gave birth to a second son: Antoine Charles, the only other of the couple's children to survive both his parents.

It was in this context of increasing need and mounting debt that on September 1, 1703, Antoine humiliated his wife and her parents by obliging them to return to the office of the notary who had drawn up their marriage contract in order to declare that the clothing in Marie Françoise's dowry had in fact been overvalued by 300 livres, a sum the Boulangers were then forced to turn over to him.

Three other children followed in steady progression: Barthélemy François (named after Barthélemy Boulanger and thus the first Chevrot son ever to be identified with his maternal line), born in about September 1704; Alexandre, just one year later; and finally, in January 1708, Marie Françoise, the first daughter fathered by an Antoine Chevrot in the entire century during which four of them in succession had lived in Paris.

Antoine and Marie Françoise's five children, like the five children of Jean and Louise Magoulet, were part of a remarkable baby boom: in just eight fertile years in the early eighteenth century, France reversed all the monumental demographic losses caused by the climate crisis of the 1690s. The years between 1704 and 1707 saw the highest birth rate of all: nearly a million children a year were added to the country's population of about 22 million.

But within months of the birth of his last child, Antoine's already dire situation turned catastrophic during a terrible winter and the famine that ensued. He knew his day of reckoning in the aftermath of what quickly came to be known as the Great Winter. This was the only time in French history that a winter was considered harrowing enough to be singled out with an appellation.

# CHAPTER NINE

# *The Great Winter*
# The Chevrots: 1708–1716

IN 1701, LOUIS XIV initiated the final conflict of his long reign, the War of the Spanish Succession, in order to claim the Spanish throne for his grandson, Philippe d'Anjou. Another pan-European alliance formed to oppose him, and the war dragged on until 1714. Soon after, the French national debt was so huge that the country's desperate rulers allowed John Law to launch his financial experiments.

The war began under ideal conditions. From 1701 to 1708, the weather was warm and dry, the winters mild. Food was plentiful, so the troops were well fed. And the absence of mud-clogged terrain greatly facilitated logistics and strategic planning.

Then, between 1705 and 1707, the climate began to heat up. One contemporary said of the winter of 1707 to 1708, "we had no winter." As the summers became ever hotter, drought conditions set in.

But as of May 1708, the tide suddenly turned. Late frosts killed off summer fruits and vegetables, as well as the grapes for the wine harvest. There were extremely heavy rains all summer long and thus a meager yield of grain. Winter started early, with heavy snowfalls already in October. And the weather became increasingly frigid as the country was hit by a succession of cold waves. The Great Winter was the most significant natural disaster of Louis XIV's long reign.

January 1709 was the cruelest month of all. The sudden and brutal drops in temperature that began during the night of January 5 took a devastating toll not only on plant life, but on human life as well. All month long and all over France, people were being found dead in their beds come morning—they had frozen stiff during the night. By early February, Louis XIV's sister-in-law, the Princess Palatine, reported that "in Paris alone" twenty-five thousand had died. The cold invaded even the Sun King's gilded palace. By January 18, the *Amsterdam Gazette* reported, court life had been brought to a standstill by the winter: "All entertainment has ceased." The record low temperatures continued until late March. Elm trees all over the country died. Paris seemed a ghost town. Theaters were shuttered; shops barely functioned. "Never in the memory of man has it ever been so cold," lamented the German-born Princess Palatine.

A new financial crisis had begun in 1707, when the state was near bankruptcy because of the war and still another severe monetary shortage. French troops were once again pitted against a Europe-wide coalition: with fighting on all the country's frontiers, next to nothing could be exported, and internal commerce was weakened. As the *Amsterdam Gazette* concluded in its January 1, 1709 paper, "France went to war to uphold its glory; it has sacrificed everything in the process." By January 1709, all over the country, Frenchmen would surely have agreed that the price had been too high.

Between January 1708 and January 1709, in Paris the price of wheat jumped from 10 livres a *setier* to 20, and it doubled again between January and March 1709. In May 1709, it hit 55. The price of bread was sky high; wine and cider, the standard beverages in French households, five to ten times more expensive than normal. Famine naturally rose along with the cost of basic foodstuffs. And when that happened, just as had been the case in 1694, people fled the countryside for urban centers.

The suffering was even more acute than in 1694. Cities all over France, and Paris in particular, were overwhelmed by the hordes of homeless individuals wandering in their streets, and the situation continued all through 1709. At the same time, many residents of those cities were dying of hunger. Some municipalities estimated that 40 percent of their inhabitants were surviving thanks only to food distributed by civic and religious authorities.

Between April and October 1709, when the shortage was most critical, riots broke out in many cities almost daily. In Paris, an angry mob tried to break into the home of the Marquis d'Argenson, the head of the Parisian police. The situation in the capital was so dire that the dauphin, the crown prince whom Antoine Chevrot dreamed would become his son's godfather, no longer dared visit the city. And inside his château, Louis XIV could hear the crowds massed outside its gates screaming for bread.

In the first quarter of 1709 alone, the death toll in the country as a whole exceeded the average by more than a hundred thousand. During the year that followed that fatal January, the mortality rate in France was nearly 40 percent

higher than usual; in Paris, mortality was up by almost 50 percent. The Chevrot household contributed to both those statistics.

In the entire span of Antoine Chevrot's financial life, one period stands out:
late 1707 to early 1709. During that brief spell, it almost seemed as if Antoine
was beginning to reverse the tide that, since his marriage in 1698, had dragged
him farther and farther down the social scale.

Following his father's death in 1706, by August 13, 1707, Antoine was assuming his position as the new head of the Chevrot household. That day, he signed
arrangements with the families occupying two houses that had been part of
the inheritance that his great-aunt Geneviève Bajou had left to the Chevrot
heirs in 1665. The properties, located in Cormeilles-en-Parisis, a small rural
community not far from Paris, were occupied by a mason and a winemaker.
To pay their rents, they set up two tiny annuities with Antoine as the benefi-
ciary: 20 and 22 livres (the vintner promised "a basket of grapes from the harvest" as well).

Then, in April 1708, when France's monetary crisis had become critical,
Antoine somehow suddenly found the money to bring his payments up to date
on the loan he and his wife had taken out in December 1698. In November
1708, after the onset of the Great Winter, he paid off 181 livres on a second
loan. This despite the fact that the couple's finances had probably not stabilized: during the ten years of their married life, they changed address five
times, a pattern that usually indicates individuals on the run from creditors
and mounting debts. The last three of their moves were all within the same
neighborhood, situated in today's 2nd *arrondissement*, or division, to various
small streets in close proximity to a major artery, the rue Montorgeuil. Each
time, the couple moved just far enough to throw debt collectors off the track.
Their final relocation, to the rue Neuve Saint-Eustache (today's rue d'Aboukir),
took place in 1708, just as the situation in France was worsening dramatically.
By late 1708, Paris was in total economic crisis: there was no coin to be found;
100 million livres in mint bills, hugely devalued, were circulating.

On March 5, 1709, Antoine and Marie Françoise appeared together in a
notary's office for the last time. They were making an addendum to the loan
she had cosigned a month after they were married. Marie Françoise merely
stated that she still stood by her original decision to underwrite the loan, so
the codicil did not modify the original document in any way. But one detail
stands out: even though individuals never stated their ages on such documents,
Marie Françoise described herself as "over 26." This meant that she was of age
and therefore able to make decisions on her own. The fact that she mentioned
this might well have indicated that her parents were not in favor of this action.

In March 1709, Marie Françoise was ill; she was perhaps also pregnant once more: she had been with child virtually every other March since their marriage had begun. Pregnancy was always a dangerous moment for women, never more so than during the Great Winter. By having Marie Françoise reaffirm her guarantee on the loan, Antoine made sure that in the event of her death, he could prove to her parents that she had backed him to the end. Indeed, the young woman who identified herself as "over 26" did not live to see her twenty-seventh birthday.

On March 26, 1709, Easter Sunday, seven ships reached the French port of Port-Louis: they carried between 20 and 30 million livres of Peruvian silver. Because of the ships' cargo, France avoided economic collapse. The government was also able to purchase foreign grain and thus alleviate the suffering.

Relief arrived too late to help the Chevrots.

On April 20, Antoine and the Boulangers gathered family members to appoint guardians for the five young children who had just lost their mother, Marie Françoise. The assembly made the predictable choices: Antoine was appointed guardian, Barthélemy Boulanger subrogate.

Next, at 8 A.M. on Saturday, April 27, the newly appointed guardians were present in the young couple's last apartment, on the rue Neuve Saint-Eustache in a building located "between an upholsterer's shop and that of a wheelwright" for a lengthy appraisal of the apartment's contents. In this inventory drawn up after her death, it becomes abundantly clear that, at just over twenty-six years of age, Marie Françoise knew exactly who she was and how she wanted to live. She had made a home for her family that was both stylish enough to satisfy a woman accustomed to the ways of the grandest court in Europe and a place where young children would have felt at home. And since all of Antoine's numerous future apartments were furnished in a completely nondescript manner, it's clear that Marie Françoise had been fully responsible for the apartment's decoration.

Their home's contents were estimated at just under 3,000 livres, a sum nearly up to her husband's aspirations. (When Hubert Magoulet died in 1707, the value of his possessions totaled only 885 livres.) The couple owned a good deal of artwork and porcelain, some fancy mirrors, a card table, even a harpsichord, an instrument so large and costly that it was usually found only in royal châteaux. And Marie Françoise's originality was nowhere more evident than in the apartment's layout.

At a time when virtually no home in France had a space dedicated to dining— the first dining room at Versailles was added only in 1735—near the entrance was located "a small dining room." And near the entrance to the dining room was found "a small basin for washing one's hands," a touch of refinement that in 1709 would have been found in only a handful of the city's grandest residences.

But the most innovative idea of all was that of "a children's bedroom." Children of the bourgeoisie then normally slept together in one big bed. Very few children of any rank knew the luxury of having a room of their own. Two rooms were set aside for the Chevrot children; each child had an individual small bed. Portraits of their patron saints hung on the walls, and the room shared by sons Louis and Antoine featured a painting whose subject speaks reams about the relationship between Marie Françoise and her children: a mother hen and her baby chicks.

A tutor named Forget came to give the boys lessons; Madame Tison taught them music on that harpsichord. In an age when there is little indication that most parents were greatly preoccupied with their children's upbringing, at least until they had survived the most critical years for child mortality, the Chevrot children had lived a charmed existence. A lovely young mother who gave them the kind of education usually reserved for the offspring of great families and who was trying both to develop their artistic potential and to make individuals of them—this was a situation beyond rare in 1709.

Their mother was also a lady, with a lady's maid, Marie (who was paid 100 livres a year, more than half Antoine's annual wages from his post at Versailles), and a valet to wait on her. And she was a woman of fashion. Marie Françoise still owned the fine garments that had been part of her dowry, and she had greatly expanded her wardrobe; she had a penchant for accessories: high-heeled mules, gloves, scarves in the latest styles, even a baby bearskin muff. She left behind many debts, notably the 435 livres she owed to Louis de Nogent, the glove maker and perfumer who had supplied her with scents and gloves and fur muffs.

All this had obviously not been financed by Antoine's uncertain income alone. Marie Françoise's parents must have decided to defray the costs of maintaining the standards and the style in which their daughter had been raised, and of preparing their grandchildren for the kind of life they hoped they would lead. The inventory reveals an absolute disconnect between Chevrot and Boulanger.

That disconnect quickly turned lethal.

At the end of the day on April 27, Antoine and Barthélemy Boulanger jointly signed the inventory. But two days later, Antoine was back at the notary's office—alone. Marie Françoise's parents would thus not have been immediately aware of the codicil he added that day. And by the time they did learn of its contents, it would have been too late to do anything about the way in which it forever altered their family's history.

Most of the addendum is merely a list of expenses that Antoine claimed to be owed by the estate for debts incurred during "his wife's illness": 500 livres to a grocer, 50 more to a butcher, expenditures for laundry and medicine. He makes no mention of a doctor or a nurse, so she had clearly received no professional care. These were all expenses that would be shared by Marie Françoise's estate; half would thus be deducted from the amount due the children as her heirs.

The initial expense included, though hardly routine, is listed as though it were equivalent to the cost of baked meats or dirty laundry. It is to the Widow de La Roche: "100 livres, for the expedition of Barthélemy François Jacques and Marie Françoise, to the countryside, where they will arrive by the end of this month of April." Antoine had shipped off two of his children to a place outside the city that he either had not bothered to determine or whose name he had decided not to reveal. Given that they were to arrive before the month was out, they had surely been sent away the minute the inventory was signed and their grandparents were out of sight.

The price was right: two fewer mouths to feed, and for not even a quarter of the sum owed his deceased spouse's glove maker. The system Antoine used had been established to deal with overcrowding in the institutions designed to house children abandoned in Paris. Small children were packed upright into padded boxes strapped to the backs of "runners." Since, as Antoine's codicil indicates, the men received their fee before departure, there was no incentive to feed or care for their charges along the way: over 90 percent died during transport. The few who survived the journey were almost certain to die soon after arrival: infant mortality was particularly high among children sent to nurses in the country. And in April 1709, there was no grain left in France.

Neither Barthélemy François Jacques nor Marie Françoise returned from that "expedition" only days after their mother's death.

Antoine's choices seem coldly calculated. There was no question of picking his eldest son, whom he identified in the inventory as "L. . . . . ., not yet named": in other words, Louis had not yet had his name officially bestowed upon him in a ceremony in Versailles' Royal Chapel. His second son was also safe: no Antoine Chevrot would ever have done away with the child designated to carry the name Antoine into the next generation.

The first to go was the youngest and frailest child, also a girl, and thus not destined to carry on the Chevrot name. But the child who accompanied fifteen-month-old Marie Françoise on that fatal journey was not the boy one would have expected, the next youngest, Alexandre. Alexandre was allowed to live: he was still part of the family in March 1719. (After that, there is no further trace of him.) Instead, Antoine selected his third son, Barthélemy François Jacques. He disposed of both the baby girl named for her mother and the son named for his mother's father, thereby destroying the most evident reminders of the marriage that had united Antoine Chevrot to the Boulanger family.

And then they were three. One morning barely a week after their mother's death, the three boys marked for survival awoke to find that two of their siblings had disappeared.

By 1709, Antoine had broken off ties with the Boulangers, and the boys began to live more or less in isolation. Their family unit now had a new identity, founded on a secret they shared. By listing the price of that "expedition" in the codicil to Marie Françoise's inventory, Antoine had guaranteed that her estate would cover half of its cost: he had thus made the boys, as her heirs, unwitting accomplices in the disappearance of two of their siblings.

In the seventeenth and eighteenth centuries, widowers who found themselves with young children to raise virtually always chose to marry again within months of their spouse's demise. In the contemporary context, Antoine's decision never to remarry could only have been seen as astonishing.

One explanation for his surprising choice was economic: given his financial difficulties, Antoine could hardly have hoped to attract a bride with any dowry to speak of. And his situation continued to worsen in the years following Marie Françoise's death.

In the aftermath of the Great Winter, France saw a series of bad harvests. As a result, grain prices remained sky high until 1715. Feeding three growing boys would have been a constant concern for their father.

On October 14, 1710, an especially onerous new income tax was instituted: the *dixième*, or tenth. All income was subject to a 10 percent assessment: real estate, investments, even wages from official posts. It proved to be such a crushing burden on most Frenchmen that it was soon repealed. But the 1710 levy reduced still further whatever revenue Antoine had left. Then there were the bills from his wife's estate to settle, interest on his loans to pay off. As a result, he and the three boys were soon on the run. And they never stopped running: Antoine uprooted his family at least five times in the course of the next fifteen years.

But there was a second reason for Antoine's failure to remarry: another woman, Anne Lesage. He referred to her at first as his servant, later as his housekeeper. She was, in other words, the kind of woman with whom someone with Antoine's pretensions to social status would never have begun an official relationship.

Since Antoine dismissed Marie Françoise's servants immediately, even before the inventory was drawn up, Lesage may already have been on the scene at the start of his new life as a single parent. But the true nature of their relations became clear only in November 1712, after Antoine, and his country as well, had lived through still another momentous crisis.

This time, nothing less than the future of the Bourbon monarchy was at stake. On April 14, 1711, Versailles was shaken by its first death from small-pox, that of Louis de France, Louis XIV's eldest son and heir, the godfather Antoine had dreamed of for his eldest son. From then on, Antoine simply referred to Louis' baptism at Versailles as a fact, as though the ceremony had actually taken place.

Next, on February 12, 1712, the Duchesse de Bourgogne, the raison d'être of Antoine's existence as an honorary noble, died of measles. On February 18, her husband, the Duc de Bourgogne, was carried off by the same disease. On March 8, their eldest son, the Duc de Bretagne, became still another victim. The prince next in line for the throne, the Duc d'Anjou, also contracted the disease but survived, later becoming the next Bourbon king, Louis XV. But since in the space of not quite eleven months France had lost three heirs, and since the Duc d'Anjou was barely two years old when he became crown prince, Louis XIV, then nearing age sixty-four and the end of his very long reign, suddenly had to fear for the future of the Bourbon line.

The Duchesse de Bourgogne's death spelled the end of her court and thus, for Antoine, a personal crisis: he lost still another source of revenue and in addition his treasured position as one of her sixteen "official valets de chambre." Even though Antoine could, and did, still continue to refer to himself as "valet de chambre of the deceased Duchesse de Bourgogne," his prestige was diminished.

The solution worsened dramatically in 1712, when Antoine's right to the Bajou estate, the foundation of his only sure sources of revenue, came under attack. Nicolas Bajou, an officer of the Parisian police, suddenly contested Geneviève Bajou's 1665 will and therefore Antoine's claim to the farms in Cormeilles-en-Parisis and to the house on the rue du Perche purchased by a previous Nicolas Bajou in 1612.

Despite Antoine's continued efforts—more than 350 lawsuits initiated—to have the case dismissed, the litigation dragged on for decades, indicating that Bajou's claims had merit. As soon as this new crisis of prestige was upon him, Antoine staged a virtual reenactment of his cause célèbre of 1700.

In November 1712, Pierre Regnard had just been named *commissaire* in the Parisian police force; among his first cases was the strange affair for which Antoine, identifying himself as "valet de chambre of the deceased Duchesse de Bourgogne," appeared in Regnard's headquarters at 9 P.M. on November 3 to request an intervention. Antoine claimed to have returned home—he by then had moved to an address near Paris' traditional market area, Les Halles— shortly before, only to learn that at about five thirty that afternoon "his servant Anne Lesage" had been attacked by "an unknown man" who had "broken into his home with violence and demanded the keys to all cabinets and strongboxes" before attempting "to kick in the door to one of the rooms." The individual then proceeded "to grab Lesage by the throat, to punch her in the stomach with his fist, and finally to kick her in the stomach about twenty times," all the while cursing her and calling her a whore. Since Anne Lesage was the "about eight months pregnant, her life was in danger" because of the attack.

The next day at 8 A.M., Antoine was back to request that Regnard arrest the man, who, he contended, had reappeared earlier that morning "either to attack Lesage again or to try to rob him." The police easily caught up with the alleged assailant right where the curious incident had begun: in Antoine's apartment. When the man was interrogated, it became clear why he hadn't tried to flee. He identified himself as "Louis Dinan, about 30, from Caen in Normandy." Dinan denied all of Antoine's charges and instead gave a decid-edly different version of the previous day's events.

Dinan claimed never to have touched Anne Lesage, whom he described as his wife's sister. He had come to Paris, and to Antoine's apartment, in order to retrieve a copy of an important document; that's why he was looking for the keys to the strongboxes. He had returned to the apartment that morning, he further contended, only because Lesage had asked him to help calm Antoine down.

It was one man's word against another's, but Dinan was of no consequence next to even a vastly diminished Antoine Chevrot. When Antoine refused to let the matter drop, Dinan was arrested and spent time in Paris' Grand Châte-let prison.

In his accusations, Antoine identifies Anne Lesage as "the wife of Adrien Allou, servant of Monsieur Metaried." In all the many documents in which Lesage makes an appearance in Antoine's legal life, this is the only occasion on which he describes her as a married woman. But in 1712, Antoine surely felt obliged to offer an explanation for Lesage's advanced state of pregnancy.

The alleged husband was never mentioned again. But the baby whose arrival was imminent in November 1712 eventually became a tool of Antoine's revenge

against his son Louis. Twelve years later, in November 1724, Antoine made a
new will: in it, he provided for a girl he described as his goddaughter. The
man who had been unwilling to feed his legitimate daughter by Marie Françoise promised 2,000 livres to the daughter Anne Lesage had named, not Adri-
enne, after the man Antoine claimed was her husband, but Antoinette, after
the man quite possibly her father.

The same pattern—loss of income coupled with loss of status—played itself
out one final time in Antoine's life.

All through 1713, the winemaker renting one of the farms in Cormeilles was
unable to make his payments. Antoine chose to litigate still again, but on August
23, he was forced to settle for greatly reduced sums on both the vintner's past
debts and his future rent.

Antoine's next woe was a final forfeiture of prestige.

On September 1, 1715, a long and memorable era in French history came to
an end with Louis XIV's death. The court that had taken shape around the
Sun King left Versailles, which would remain shuttered until June 1722, when
a new court began to be established with the twelve-year-old Louis XV at its
center. In September 1715, all those who, like Antoine Chevrot and Jean Magoulet, had spent their entire professional lives in a world governed by the Sun
King and had measured their personal status in relation to his court realized
that their stature would be reevaluated.

Three months after the Sun King's death, on December 4, 1715, Antoine
showed up in Police Inspector Pierre Regnard's office with more accusations,
allegations that seem designed to prove that he remained still someone to be
reckoned with.

In the summer of 1715, Antoine had moved to a modest building on an
unpretentious street. The Chevrots were living not in the most prestigious
apartment—that was always the unit on the second level, then known as "the
noble floor"—but in accommodations on the less desirable floor above. Their
apartment faced not onto the street, as did the most highly prized quarters,
but onto an inner courtyard. And the new objects of Antoine's anger, those he
wanted the police to investigate this time, were precisely the inhabitants of his
building's "noble floor."

Antoine of course identified himself with his usual long list of titles. Oddly,
he never mentioned the status of those he was accusing; he merely listed their
names. But even the few details he did supply are enough to indicate that they
outranked him in more than real estate.

Those residing on the noble floor were people of means: they employed
numerous servants, all of whom are also named in Antoine's charges. More

significant is the fact that his downstairs neighbors were *porteurs d'épée* (sword bearers), a phrase Antoine repeats time and again, so badly did this very visible sign of their prestige irk him. This detail distinguishes them as "nobles of the sword," members of the landed aristocracy: in Old Regime France, only "nobles of the sword" had the right to carry on their person this outward symbol of their rank. And in the final years of Louis XIV's reign, many such aristocrats demonstrated particular hostility to all upstarts.

This time, Antoine's tale seems at first a familiar one to anyone who has ever lived in an apartment building: one neighbor makes so much noise that the other has trouble sleeping. In his telling, the Gresset family "beat on the floors of their apartment all night long, so violently that he [Antoine] can get no rest." And when Antoine complained to his neighbors about the racket they were making, "Gresset had insulted and made fun of him."

That appears to have been the heart of the matter: a perceived slight, Antoine's sense that these true nobles would not take him seriously and thus validate his status as a person of consequence.

The crisis had come to a head on the evening of December 4, 1715, and all because at about 8 P.M., Antoine's eight-year-old son—this would have been Alexandre—had felt the need to go to the bathroom. In early eighteenth-century Paris, indoor facilities of various kinds were becoming common: the grandest apartments in the newest and finest buildings were equipped with their own private conveniences, while in other residences, inhabitants shared facilities located in common areas, generally near the stairwell.

At eight on a December evening, all would of course have been dark in the hallways: residents lit their way to the communal toilet facility—then known euphemistically as *le lieu*, "the place"—with candles. On December 4, Alexandre was alone as he exited "the place," and he was armed with accoutrements that only Antoine could have imagined to be appropriate for a small boy of his rank and means. He was wearing a plumed hat, another accessory reserved for the nobility, and carrying not a simple candle, but a grand "silver torch." His getup was straight out of Antoine's fantasy life, perhaps appropriate for a valet in the Duchesse de Bourgogne's court striding along the corridors of Versailles, but not for a middle-class boy walking to the bathroom in the halls of a Parisian apartment building.

And the Gressets, it seems, could not resist taking advantage of the situation to mock their monumentally pretentious neighbor. According to Antoine, they set upon Alexandre "as he was leaving the place," took his silver torch away from him, and proceeded to fill his grand hat with "fecal matter."

Alexandre, Antoine reported to the police, "called for their servant," and Anne Lesage arrived on the scene. The Gressets, Antoine alleged, then "threatened to kill Lesage with their swords, and they would have done so, had she not managed to escape to his apartment along with Alexandre." His neighbors proceeded "to break down the door and, once inside, to call Lesage a whore." Finally, the Gressets took on Antoine himself "by insulting his honor and his reputation": "with one voice they proclaimed him to be a good-for-nothing, a beggar, and a dishonest man, whom they hoped to run out of their home."

Antoine was not satisfied with Inspector Regnard's response, so by January 8, 1716, he hired a lawyer and was in court again. Witnesses were called; two people, who declared that they had just happened to stop by that evening, testified that they had heard a commotion in the stairwell. Neither corroborated the more dramatic details of Antoine's story about swordplay and a death threat, but both did confirm two of his accusations: the bit about Alexandre and the hat full of "fecal matter" and the insults to Antoine's reputation, in particular, that his neighbors had called him "a beggar and a dishonest man."

A subpoena was issued ordering the Gressets to appear in court, but they didn't bother to show up. And in the end, despite multiple lawsuits, another of Antoine's protracted legal affairs came to nothing.

After an early childhood that as time went by must have seemed increasingly like a magical fairy tale, this was the life that Antoine and Marie Françoise's three surviving sons knew during the seven years that followed their mother's death: an existence spent on the run from creditors, with their upbringing confided largely to a "servant" of whose ambiguous role in their father's life they could hardly have been unaware. Their father would have been a rigorous authority figure with inflexible notions about the standards of dress and deportment they had to maintain at all times, even when slipping off to the bathroom before bedtime. But he would also have been largely an absentee parent, devoting much of his time and energy to endless litigation, with nearly all the lawsuits inspired by his obsessive need for public validation of what he presented as crimes against his honor, offenses the criminal justice system seems never to have taken very seriously.

In the spring of 1716, just when Antoine's suit against the Gressets fell apart, John Law was given the right to create France's original national banking institution, the Banque Générale, the General Bank. The wild ride culminating in the original stock market boom and bust was about to begin.

# CHAPTER TEN

# The Deadly Years
## The Magoulets: 1705–1718

W ITH HIS MARRIAGE, Jean II managed to dodge firsthand participation in the War of the Spanish Succession, but no Frenchman could have avoided the shadow of the conflict that darkened the final years of the Sun King's once splendid reign.

During the first seven years of the eighteenth century, Louis XIV appeared to be on the path to victory. The conflict truly began to turn against the French only once the climate did. By the end of 1708, the French had known some of their most stinging defeats in the protracted struggle that would bring their country to its knees: notably on October 22, when the city of Lille fell to enemy forces. By the year's close, the French had lost their hold on Flanders. And by 1709, their allies, recognizing that the Great Winter had seriously weakened Louis XIV's hand, were trying to force him to surrender significant territory.

In economic terms, the final years of the seventeenth century and the years between the Great Winter and Louis XIV's death in 1715 were two of the most harrowing periods in the history of Old Regime France. All necessities were in short supply; there was a virtually uninterrupted monetary shortage.

Sandwiched in between these moments of crisis were the early years of the eighteenth century, when the French population suddenly and quickly rebounded. All but one of the Magoulet children were part of that population boom.

Those years of fertility were also a time of relative prosperity for the Parisian luxury goods industry. There was still a court at Versailles, and its habitués were expected to keep up appearances and follow the latest fashions—many of which originated in the entourage of the period's ultimate trendsetter, the

Duchesse de Bourgogne. Because of this, at the moment when the younger Jean Magoulet's family was growing, he continued to find steady work as an embroiderer, and always in the same areas in which his father had specialized. For one client alone, the master tailor Nicolas Thuvin, for example, he ornamented men's high fashion garments—to the tune of 7,882 livres. Early in his marriage, Jean could have been seen as following in his father's professional footsteps, as well as building the kind of career as a luxury goods craftsman for which the Magoulets had been known for the past two generations.

But his work never added up to the kind of financial success that would have made it possible to care for his growing family and to pay the astronomical rent on the vast Quai de l'École property they began to call home in early 1704. His failure as a businessman can be explained in two ways. To begin with, Jean II more than shared his despised father's love of credit.

All those doing business in Paris' luxury goods industry were frequently obliged to extend credit, and never more so than in economically trying times. But as Louise Poisson argued in court when she succeeded in obtaining a financial separation from her husband a decade after they had rented that gigantic apartment, there was credit and there was credit: the second Queen's Embroiderer, his wife claimed, was far too willing to extend credit to any and all, without a thought as to whether those in his debt might one day be able to pay the sums owed.

Jean had nothing to do with the second reason for his business' failure: he first attempted to earn a living in the luxury goods trade at a moment characterized by virtually uncontrolled economic experimentation.

In September 1701, the monarchy once again began printing mint bills and encouraging its subjects to exchange coin for the new bills. The state planned to reissue the coins thus obtained at a new value; it also planned during the minting process to cut small pieces of each coin, thereby constituting a stock of precious metal.

Until 1702, bills were issued only to the amount of gold and silver on reserve; subsequently, the mints were authorized to print without regard for deposit. By December 1703, 7 million of the notes were in circulation; by February 1708, that number had grown to 136 million. An edict from September 27, 1703 was designed to reassure shopkeepers about the validity of the new legal tender: they were told that "His Majesty promises to exchange [bills] promptly for gold and silver"; shopkeepers were encouraged to accept the notes "just as if they were cash."

But this radical fiscal experiment was founded on empty promises, for His Majesty could never have exchanged the new notes for precious metal. By

February 1708, even before the climate began to wreak additional economic havoc, the crown's debt stood at 482 million livres, while the royal treasury's reserves were down to 20 million. When that long-awaited convoy of bullion from Peru finally reached France in March 1709, the influx of silver kept the wolf from the door for only a matter of weeks. By 1710, the cost of precious metal was once again rising sharply.

Already by 1706, the individual who had conceived of mint bills as a bridge to keep the French economy afloat, Controller General of Finance Michel Chamillart, pronounced the brief experiment a dangerous failure: by then, there were so many notes in circulation that paper was far more common than coin, and, as Chamillart concluded, "the disorder that has resulted is extreme."

But even as Chamillart was reaching this conclusion, paper money's advocates were gearing up for a fight. In 1707, the most influential early promoter of a currency revolution, John Law, made his initial contact with the French state to promote new economic theories. He circulated a memorandum "proving that a new kind of money was superior to gold and silver" and predicting that "shares in the Indies Company could function as this new form of currency." But in 1707, French authorities were not yet quite ready to hear Law's siren song.

On October 7, 1710, the king's advisers decided that it was at last time to pull the plug on the mint bills. On February 1, 1711, all the money bills in circulation were pronounced worthless. Another royal decree informed those who not eight years earlier had been encouraged to believe that the new form of currency was an absolutely safe alternative that from that day on, "they can no longer be given or accepted as a form of payment."

On July 30, 1708—just as the climate and the war were veering off course and in the midst of the monarchy's disastrous experiment with mint bills—Jean lined up the contract that sheds the most light on these early years of his career. He organized a group of four embroiderers. Together they were to complete a project that on the surface might seem identical to the deals that were his father's bread and butter in the early 1690s: fancy ornamental trappings for regimental mounts. But the differences from his father's work were key: these were not horses destined to ride into battle but the mounts of the cavalry that protected the Louvre's gates. And by 1708, the profligate ways of the early 1690s were decidedly a thing of the past. The ceremonial guards who had come to Jean were looking for pomp and splendor on a budget.

In his father's work in the early 1690s for cavalry regiments heading off to the Nine Years' War, the richly embroidered saddle cloths had been as high-end as possible: those he designed for the mounts of each regiment's officers were made of crimson velvet and adorned in the exact manner of a great lord's most formal outfit, with embroidery in silk thread wrapped with gold and silver. The least expensive such blankets were budgeted at 60 livres each, while the most highly ornamented cost as much as 93 livres. And even those destined for the horses of the lowliest cavalrymen—made in woolen cloth rather than velvet, dyed merely scarlet instead of the more expensive crimson, and embroidered in simple wool thread—each set the regiment back from 6 to 8 livres.

Some fifteen years later, the contract Jean signed was on a completely different scale: the royal cavalry of the Louvre could afford only the humblest model, on scarlet cloth embroidered in wool, and had budgeted a mere 3 livres per blanket. Each embroiderer working on the contract would have taken home barely 300 livres for his efforts. Furthermore, the Louvre's cavalry was to make payment, their arrangement carefully specified, not in the far more desirable coin, but in mint bills, the very mint bills that would be deemed worthless by the king just two and a half years later.

Despite all this, the agreement signed in July 1708 must soon have seemed a good deal. By the following summer, when the climate shift that culminated in the Great Winter suddenly struck, few were ordering adornments of any kind. And the country did not recover quickly from the crisis of 1709. In early 1710, France was hit by yet another cold wave. From 1710 to 1714, all the harvests were poor. One of the period's most astute commentators, Versailles insider the Duc de Saint-Simon, referred to the period from 1708 to 1715 as *les années funestes*: the deadly years.

They certainly were that for Jean Magoulet's family.

As the weather and the economy worsened, at the moment when Louis and the younger Chevrot children were living out their year of trauma, Louise Magoulet and her younger siblings were obliged to witness their mother endure increasingly violent abuse and humiliation—and to suffer abuse themselves.

Domestic violence was an integral part of the Magoulet marriage almost surely even from the start. In the deposition made in June 1717 when her life was almost over, Louise Poisson Magoulet testified that "she had hidden from her family as long as she possibly could the savage behavior" that she had suffered at her husband's hand "during the sixteen years that she had had the misfortune to be his wife." Like the vast majority of those who endured spousal abuse, Louise long hid her secrets; it's thus impossible to recreate a precise timeline for this crucial phase of the Magoulet family drama. But the numerous depositions Louise made to the police from 1709 on make it clear that as the economic situation worsened, Jean's violence continued to escalate. At the drop of a hat, she testified, he would "fly into a rage against her and call her a bitch and a whore."

He began to bring "women of ill repute" into their home, giving them free rein of the quarters, and even of Louise's personal wardrobe. In one incident she reported, which "she remembered clearly," she described returning home one evening to find several women dressed in her finest outfits. Her husband was preparing to escort them to one of the premier forms of Parisian entertainment: the public ball held three times a week at the Paris opera.

When Louise protested, "he pursued her with a naked sword yelling that he would kill her—which he would have done if several people had not heard the noise and come to her rescue; they sheltered her in the basement of the building in which they were living." She described hiding out in this way for several days. And when she did dare return to their apartment, "he tried to knock her out, using a very heavy mirror—and he would have killed her this time had someone not arrived just at the moment when he was about to hit her over the head with it."

All this still did not convince Louise to turn to her family for help. But after the opera ball incident, Jean persuaded one of the women in his entourage, an embroiderer named Renouard whom he employed in his workshop, to go to the police and accuse Louise of "having insulted Renouard's honor." Renouard further took advantage of her visit to inform the police that Louise "was prostituting herself and had thus contracted venereal disease." An investigation ensued, and when Louise was called in to defend herself against Renouard's charges, she finally ended her long silence and countered with a formal complaint of her own to Police Inspector Jean-Louis Chaud.

When Jean learned that she was fighting back, he forced her to withdraw her complaint by threatening to take a knife to her face. He threw her out of the expensive apartment that he had been able to rent only because she and her parents had cosigned the lease, declaring that "if she ever dared return, he would drag her out by her hair and leave her in the gutter where she belonged."

The episode of the opera ball became the point of no return in Louise Magoulet's married life. It started her on a long road, at the end of which she achieved a goal that few battered wives ever manage to attain: she reclaimed her independence and rebuilt her life.

As soon as she had gone public, Louise went to live with her father (her mother was no longer alive); she remained there for nearly a year. She later described the period as a trial separation, saying that "she hoped all the while that her husband would come to his senses and begin treating her as a husband should."

But Jean soon proved to Louise how easily he could still manipulate her both legally and financially. He decided to leave that grand apartment in one of the premier locations in Paris—for an even grander space in the building right next door. On April 4, 1714, he signed the lease, and Louise cosigned it. (He would later admit to the police that she had done so only under duress.)

The building belonged to an aristocrat, the former director of the by then deceased Duchesse de Bourgogne's court. In his capacity as valet de chambre, Antoine Chevrot would have served under him. Indeed, everything about Jean's new home would have made Antoine green with envy: the lease described it as "the premier apartment" (that is, the one situated on "the noble floor"). And whereas Antoine's small apartment faced onto a hardly glamorous inner court-yard, visible from the windows of Jean's eight rooms and his large kitchen was a full panorama of the Seine, Notre-Dame cathedral, and the Île de la Cité.

But even this was not enough. Jean also imagined an equivalent for that glass-fronted storefront that the original Queen's Embroiderer had had built as soon as he moved to the Quai de l'École. The 1714 lease concluded with an additional commitment, to which Jean also obliged Louise to agree: "the rent-ers promise to have constructed at their own expense two balconies with orna-mental balustrades in wrought iron and French doors leading into the apartment, as well as to obtain and pay for the permissions needed for their construction."

Like his father, the second Queen's Embroiderer would have his miniature version of the Hall of Mirrors.

And he forced Louise to help defray the cost. Noel Poisson had long avoided paying the last installment of his daughter's dowry: he realized that once they were handed over to a spendthrift, those 700 livres would be forever lost to his daughter and her children. But in October 1714, Jean won a round: he com-pelled Poisson to make good on that final payment. He even obliged him to relinquish an additional 200 livres, a sum he described, with a phrase that liter-ally makes no sense, as "an augmentation of the dowry." A dowry was a dowry, its amount fixed at the signing of the marriage contract. No parent ever chose to "increase" a dowry thirteen years after the wedding, and certainly not at a time when his child's marriage was in full crisis.

Whatever Jean did or said to get Noel Poisson to agree to this outlay fright-ened Louise so badly that she realized she had to move more quickly. She started to build the dossier required by law in order to obtain a *séparation de biens*, a legal division of property.

Throughout the long judicial battle that ensued, Louise had the unwavering support of her father: in an age when it was extremely difficult and in many cases virtually impossible to challenge a husband's absolute dominion over his wife, Louise could never have made her voice heard in the legal system had she not had the backing of a male figure of some status. In such situations, fathers almost always chose to keep silent in the hope of avoiding a public scandal that would stain the family name. Noel Poisson was of a different breed. He stood by his daughter publicly and categorically. As a result, *Magoulet v. Magoulet* pitted one male authority against another.

Property separations could and did mean very different things. In the case of Antoine Chevrot's parents in 1679 and in that of Jacques Magoulet and Marie Freslin in 1698, the process had sheltered as much of the couple's wealth as possible from the husband's creditors. Louise sought a division of property in order to preserve her family's possessions and to be able to control her own assets.

On Tuesday, April 30, 1715, two verdicts were transcribed into the registers of an institution something like a modern public prosecutor's office, Paris' Civil Law Court. Both had been a long time in the making.

The first was a ruling against Jean Magoulet: some of his many longtime creditors had joined forces and were calling in numerous promissory notes signed by him. The list of those demanding their money was extended: Jean was drowning in debt. The second contained a summary of all the acts that had been pronounced in Louise Poisson Magoulet's favor during her quest for a separation of property, as well as the names of those who had agreed to testify on her behalf.

By May 9, her lawyer requested that formal proceedings be initiated: Jean and his lawyer, as well as witnesses for both parties, were convoked for 9 A.M. the following day. On May 10, the court waited in vain until 3 P.M., when the court recorded "the nonappearance of the defendant," and the hearing took place without him.

Louise had assembled an impressive lineup of witnesses, all mature men in their fifties. Each testified to having known the defendant for well over a decade, virtually since the beginning of his marriage. To a man, they portrayed Jean as deeply in debt because he had extended credit and borrowed money so freely, had signed promissory notes left and right, and had incurred huge expenses gambling, carousing, and womanizing. Each ended by affirming that from the start Jean had misused Louise's dowry and had perhaps already squandered most of it.

The testimony of Étienne Simon Du Bourg, age fifty-two and living on the rue Vieille du Temple in Paris' Marais neighborhood, is representative: he described Jean as "a madman completely addicted to his pleasures, someone who goes out drinking every night and spends huge sums because he always buys

rounds for everyone in the *cabaret*. As a result, his business is in a shambles."
The *cabaret*, where patrons gathered to imbibe inexpensive wine, was a venerable Parisian institution. But by the early eighteenth century, when polite society met to share a beverage, it was in a newer and far more upscale kind of
establishment, the café. Once cafés had proliferated in Paris, *cabarets* had been
deserted by elite Parisians and were frequented mainly by a rough clientele:
they were often the scene of violent skirmishes. For his nights on the town,
Du Bourg thus made it plain, Jean preferred low life to high.

On May 24, 1715, Louise Poisson Magoulet was awarded her financial independence. Jean was ordered to refund her dowry and to reimburse Noel Poisson for that 1714 dowry "augmentation." When he did not pay up, on July 20,
all Jean Magoulet's possessions were seized by court order: they brought in a
total of only 600 livres when they were sold a week later. On August 26, Jean
paid 1,000 livres to his wife's estate: this was the only part of all he owed that
he ever reimbursed. In 1733, when Louise Poisson Magoulet was long dead,
his surviving children were still fighting to obtain what was rightfully theirs:
the 3,000 livres of her dowry, plus 400 in interest.

On August 26, Jean also affirmed that Louise had moved out of their Quai
de l'École apartment and was therefore no longer responsible for her share of
the rent. Louise's financial independence was now complete.

In French law, a father's authority over his offspring was absolute. Jean had
no interest in his children's upbringing, but he did not turn them over to their
mother. Indeed, once Louise began her new life, Jean quickly "expedited," to
borrow Antoine's expression, their two youngest children: Marie, born in 1708,
and Dorothée, born in 1709. Years later, the surviving Magoulet children
learned that their father had sent Marie and Dorothée to Paris' most dreaded
public institution, the Hôpital Général, or General Hospital. Paris' General
Hospital, established in the mid-seventeenth century in an attempt to deal
with the growing problem of urban poverty and homelessness, was far closer
to a prison than to a medical establishment. A sprawling and unruly complex
on the city's southwestern limit, the General Hospital housed some ten to fifteen thousand unwanted or undesirable Parisians in crowded dormitories so
dilapidated that they were often on the verge of collapse and in conditions
considered grim even by the officers of the Parisian police.

The vast majority of the children living there had either been abandoned at
birth or were orphans. Only desperately poor Parisian parents condemned
their young daughters to such conditions, and even they did so only in moments
of severe crisis such as the Great Winter. When Jean banished his two girls to
a living hell, he reenacted once again his own father's behavior.

On September 1, 1715, Louis XIV died: the only regime that any Magoulet then alive had ever known was over. The court that had given so many Magoulet family members employment and status came to an end at the exact moment when Louise Poisson Magoulet set out on her own.

By the time of Louis XIV's death, Louise had already begun a far more difficult legal struggle, to obtain a second type of separation, a *séparation de corps et d'habitation*, "separation of body and domicile." Such separations, intended to protect wives from abusive behavior and defamation of character, were sought far less often and rarely granted. Louise would not live to see the end of this quest.

In Old Regime France, separated women were in social and legal limbo: they could never hope to remarry, and they enjoyed very limited freedom. Almost all returned to live with their parents or took up residence in a convent. Louise's choice was highly unusual and demonstrated an uncommon degree of independence, imagination, and determination to create the best kind of new life possible.

Her new quarters in a public institution were far more modest than the grand apartment on the Quai de l'École. The residence known as the Quinze-Vingts (the 15/20) was founded in the thirteenth century to create "a home for blind Parisians": until the late eighteenth century, when it was moved to its current location, it occupied a sizable terrain, prime real estate adjacent to the Louvre. It owed its name to the fact that it was built to house three hundred (15 times 20) of the city's blind inhabitants.

A battered wife could hardly have hoped for a more secure habitation: to guarantee the safety of the institution's principal residents, the territory

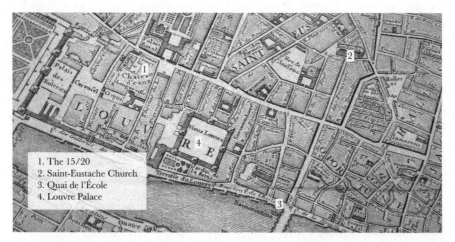

1. The 15/20
2. Saint-Eustache Church
3. Quai de l'École
4. Louvre Palace

*The key addresses in Louise Poisson Magoulet's life in 1717 and 1718.*

allotted the 15/20 was enclosed, with a porter stationed at the main entrance. In addition, even though her new home was only a short walk from the Quai de l'École address, leaving her surely too close for comfort to the man who had long been terrorizing her, it was just as near her father's residence on the rue des Deux Écus next to the church of Saint-Eustache.

Louise owed her good fortune in obtaining her new residence to by far the most prominent personage in her entourage, someone who wielded much more influence than did Noel Poisson: Claude Fontaine. After his name, Fontaine brandished the kind of title recognized by all as a mark of true consequence: *maison et couronne de France et de ses finances*, "house and crown of France and its finances," a position in the royal administration that conferred hereditary nobility on those wealthy enough to afford the several hundred thousand livres necessary for its acquisition.

Fontaine was a longtime family connection of the Magoulet couple. When Jean and Louise's third child and only son was born in 1705, the boy was named not for his father or a grandfather, as would then have been standard practice, but Claude, after his godfather, Claude Fontaine. Fontaine was also a rare kind of human being, willing to intervene publicly on behalf of a victim of abuse. A decade after Claude's baptism, he stood resolutely on Louise's side: he lent her money, and he used his position as the administrator of the 15/20 to obtain lodgings for her there.

The 15/20 was a privileged enclave, much like Saint-Denis de la Chartre: a royal decree from 1657 gave those who lived within its walls the right to practice their craft without having served the traditional apprenticeship and without belonging to a guild. These statutes made it possible for Louise to earn a living.

Louise's younger sister Catherine moved in with her, lending an air of respectability to what was after all a highly unusual and irregular situation. Like Louise, Catherine was a skilled embroiderer. Soon, Louise was running an embroidery workshop in her new apartment.

By day, five of the immense embroidery frames used by professionals were set up there; Catherine and several young embroiderers worked alongside Louise.

For the 240 livres she paid in rent, Louise had the use of three rooms and a kitchen. One room was devoted to her workshop, but since those cumbersome frames could be hung directly on the walls to free up space, it could have doubled as a second bedroom. The apartment was furnished with pieces borrowed from her father and friends.

From the inventory of the apartment's contents that Noel Poisson had drawn up after Louise's death, it's clear that the children could have lived with their mother at least some of the time: Louise had made provisions that allowed

*An embroidery workshop in eighteenth-century Paris: those huge frames
were used by professional embroiderers.*

others to share her space. Catherine slept on a daybed in the living room. That
room also contained "a large sofa," a surface expansive enough to serve as a
child's bed. Louise's room had not only a bed, which she could have shared
with one or more children, but also a *couchette*, a word that then signified "the
kind of small bed on which children usually sleep." Her dishes, though hardly
a matched set—nine plates, eight soup bowls, and two serving dishes, all porcelain, plus "two drawers full of old plates"—were clearly more than sufficient to accommodate both workers and children at mealtime.

Both Jean's work and his carousing would have kept him frequently out of
the Quai de l'École apartment, thereby giving his three remaining children
the chance to find support outside their home. Their grandfather lived close
by: in the new complaints Louise was soon registering with the police, she
stressed "the care her father always showed her children." And their mother,
who likewise lived only minutes away, took great pains to transform her three
rooms in the 15/20 into a real home for them.

The inventory of Louise's apartment is a far cry from the sketchy listing one
might have expected in the case of someone living on a shoestring and surrounded by borrowed furniture: Louise's personality and her will to live are
everywhere evident.

Louise brought together a hodgepodge of disparate items with color: red for
the living room, blue with yellow accents for the bedroom. She lined the walls
with brightly colored textiles. She couldn't afford to have her borrowed living
room furniture reupholstered, so she positioned a brightly colored cotton

handkerchief—handkerchiefs were then quite large, roughly two feet square—on the back of every chair.

The inventory even hints that Louise just might have managed somehow to rebuild her life in another way.

Every woman's closet has a tale to tell: Louise Poisson Magoulet had invested the little money she spent on herself in clothing designed for nightwear and the bedroom. She owned only two dresses—but three *manteaux de lit,* "bed coats," garments worn over sleepwear and only in the bedchamber. These were Louise's fanciest garments: one was in striped satin, another in striped taffeta, the third in cotton voile.

The accounting of her finances contains one unexpected entry: she had received an extremely generous loan, 1,250 livres, from François de Brémond. Brémond, member of a venerable noble family and captain in the royal cavalry, had been decorated with every imaginable chivalric order and was even named Chevalier de Saint-Louis, a precursor to today's Legion of Honor, an order founded by Louis XIV in 1693 to reward the services of his most

*A state bill worth 180 livres issued by the French government in November 1716.*

exceptional officers. A dashing cavalry officer thus just might have played a role in the final chapter of Louise's life.

On May 4, 1716, the French government launched still another experiment with paper money. This time, the notes were named *billets de l'état*, state bills, to stress their official state sponsorship. On May 20, a new bank, the General Bank, was established by royal decree, although its name did not appear on the notes. And on May 26, the man driving this renewed promotion of paper money, John Law, was naturalized and given all the rights enjoyed by native-born French subjects. A decade after Louis XIV had rejected Law's proposals, Philippe d'Orléans, the regent who governed France from 1715 to 1723, the years between Louis XIV's death and the beginning of Louis XV's independent reign, was ready to heed Law's advice.

The small sheets first printed in May 1716 are "blanks": preprinted forms with blank spaces so that the date and the amount could be filled in by hand at the moment when each note was attributed to an owner. The notes were numbered, and a register was kept in which all state bills were listed, along with their holders and the date of their acquisition. The bill shown on the previous page, number 4,200, was issued on November 20, 1716 for 180 livres.

That same month of May, the government initiated an extensive campaign designed to encourage the French to exchange all handwritten promissory notes for state bills. The main arguments used to persuade them to do so made good sense: first, it was easy to forge a handwritten document or to modify it in some way; second, if a promissory note was lost, you could not readily have it replaced. In contrast, because state notes had a legal life, it was a simple matter to prove their authenticity; to have a lost one replaced, you simply had to provide its serial number.

Members of the Magoulet family quickly stepped up to convert promissory notes, first among them the brother-in-law who had proved essential to Jean I's double-dealing in 1695 and would soon play a similar role in his son's life: Guillaume Morel. Jacques Magoulet's sons also switched the notes they were holding for the allegedly safer currency, including IOUs to the tune of 6,000 livres signed by Jean II and cosigned by his father. By early 1717, Jacques' oldest son was doing business exclusively in state bills, which he called "the new legal money."

Law's plans moved ahead quickly. By April 1717, a royal edict specified that state bills could now be used "just like coin" to pay one's taxes and for all official transactions. And on August 19, a new trading company was created, called the Compagnie d'Occident, the Western Company, since it was to control trade with the West Indies, and it was soon put in John Law's hands.

These developments were closely followed all over Europe. In its September
12 issue, a London paper, the *Post Man*, informed its readers about the sale of
stock in the new company. Indeed, in the ten days between September 14 and
September 24 alone, well over 28 million livres in *actions*, or shares, were purchased; they were set to begin paying interest at a rate of 4 percent by July
1718. Many international men of finance were among the first to buy shares,
and for large amounts, a minimum of 100,000 livres. After just six weeks, the
new company had raised over 40 million livres in capital.

The Western Company's shares were issued in the form of 500-livre state bills,
the tender that the *Post Man* referred to as "bills of Common Cash." The state-
backed paper money and shares in Law's trading company had become synonymous; this was a move essential to Law's pledge to his supporters that he
could make France for the first time a major power in maritime commerce. Before
1717 was out, the French were hearing all around them the news that trade
with Louisiana would provide the answer to their country's economic woes.

This image, for example, was circulating in the French capital by late 1717.
"Trade Between the Indians of Mexico and the French in the Port of the Mississippi" depicts the arrival on the shores of a clearly flourishing colony of a

*This 1717 image encouraged the French to believe that trade was already flourishing
between their countrymen and Indians in "the port of the Mississippi."*

flotilla of ships carrying elegantly dressed French businessmen. The French-men are welcomed with open arms by natives eager to share with them the produce of their land, while in the background, proof of France's past commercial success there is visible in the form of the already extensive settlement built up around the harbor in which their ships have dropped anchor. The image could have convinced anyone that "the Mississippi's" future was bright indeed.

This, then, was the backdrop against which Louise Magoulet and her children lived out a terrifying year: everyone was talking about the huge sums of money being raised in nothing flat, about the quick returns on their investments of which those able to buy into the new system were confident, in short, about the prosperity that seemed guaranteed for anyone with the means to acquire stock in Law's company. All that talk of easy money at a moment when Jean Magoulet had nothing but debt could have pushed an already angry man even closer to the edge.

In the course of 1717, Louise went to the police at least four times, and her father made at least three additional depositions, always to report her husband's abuse. They felt compelled to come forward and thus take the risk of provoking even greater rage because of the threat Jean made repeatedly that year: that he would denounce his wife Louise as a prostitute and thus obtain her internment in the General Hospital. She knew that he was fully capable of this move, and she surely knew something else as well: even as rumors of the new prosperity that Louisiana would bring were swirling, so were rumors about the many new colonists needed there.

Already in October 1716, the regent wrote to the colony's governor to urge him "to prevent as much as possible" marriages between Frenchmen and Indians: he promised to "send women from France as soon as it will be possible to do so." Many of those first sent to "the Louisiana" were mature women who found themselves in prison because their husbands had accused them of prostitution.

Louise was surely aware that her new independence put her at high risk of this particular accusation. Beginning in the late seventeenth century, the Parisian police had received orders to distinguish two types of prostitution. Any behavior, no matter how scandalous, that took place behind closed doors and stayed within the family was considered of little danger to the city and the state and was to be overlooked. But any behavior that could be considered prostitution that was negotiated in public, outside the home a woman shared with her husband and family, was to be stringently prosecuted.

On July 26, 1713, the lieutenant general of the Parisian police received a directive ordering him to prosecute "public prostitution" with new severity. Henceforth, women thus charged could be imprisoned indefinitely, with no

*Louise Poisson's signature.*

possibility of appeal. Jean began accusing Louise of prostitution shortly after those new laws were pronounced, and Louise realized that after her move into the 15/20, she could be considered guilty of "public prostitution."

When all that remains of those long dead are legal documents, most people seem mere ciphers, since individuality tends to disappear behind official formulas. But in every statement she made to the police, Louise Poisson Magoulet's voice was as forceful and purposeful as her signature was clear and firm. She expressed herself powerfully; her conviction never faltered. And her repeated depositions were truly acts of exceptional courage. In the eighteenth century's early decades, few women found the resolve to do even once what Louise Poisson Magoulet did on multiple occasions in 1717 alone: walk unaccompanied into a police inspector's office and recount the smallest details of her estranged husband's repeated attempts to terrorize her. Her strategic intelligence is also impressive. She returned always to the same inspector, Martin Marrier; she was careful not to let her emotions get the better of her: her reasons for being there and her goals were always clear.

Louise's initial appearance in Marrier's office was on Friday, February 26, 1717, at five in the afternoon. Two hours earlier, she reported, an artisan named Bégon, a master at the craft of spinning gold to produce gold-wrapped thread, had appeared at her door demanding payment of the 250 livres that Jean owed him. Since the bill dated from before their separation, she was legally responsible for half of the sum. She objected that she had already paid 110 of her share and offered to hand over two silver spoons as a pledge on the remaining 15. Bégon laughed at her and said "she had better pay Jean's full debt right away, for if she didn't, her husband had promised to have all her belongings carted off and to have her taken away to the hospital"—precisely the treatment reserved for public prostitutes under the 1713 statutes. Louise concluded her deposition by explaining that it was for this reason that she "had been advised" to go to the police.

Next, on Monday, April 18, it was her father's turn. Jean's creditors were now showing up on Noel Poisson's doorstep, so he went to discuss the situation with his son-in-law. Jean responded by insulting his father-in-law, Noel reported in his deposition, then announcing that "if Poisson didn't pay up, he would thrust his sword into his stomach." Jean reached for his sword but was prevented from using it by his brother. Jean promised that the next time he ran into Poisson in the street, he would make good on his threat, and then he yelled that Louise was "a common whore and that he was planning to have her locked up in the hospital." Noel went straightaway to the police.

On the morning of Tuesday, June 15, Louise took matters to the next level. She began an extraordinarily lengthy deposition by reminding Inspector Marrier of the dates on which she had previously testified before him. She then went over in detail the evidence of Jean's abuse that she had presented on those occasions, preparing her case for a "separation of body and domicile."

Louise concluded her deposition with evidence that Jean was now stalking her. On a recent Friday afternoon, she reported, she had decided to visit friends; her brother had come along for protection. Jean soon spotted them: he began shouting that she was a prostitute and chasing them, with his sword in one hand and a small pistol in the other. They ran into a nearby shop and took refuge in its cellar. When they emerged hours later, they learned that Jean had been all over the neighborhood, stopping and searching carriages, looking, as he said, for "his whore of a wife."

On November 5, 1717, just after Law had successfully raised 40 million livres in capital for his new company, Noel Poisson was back to testify about still another frenzy of abuse: this time, Jean's target was his twelve-year-old son Claude. Jean had, Noel reported, kept Claude "in chains for eight days and then thrown him out on the street." And Jean's abusive treatment of Claude was not a unique incident. In his deposition, Noel further contended that "his cruelty towards his children had become a daily occurrence," always with the same goal: to oblige them to run away from home and live rough, alone and fending for themselves on the streets of Paris—thereby to reenact the moment after Simone Inselin's death when Jean's own father had condemned his thirteen-year-old son to the life of a vagrant.

Louise's repeated depositions about domestic violence were unusual. But Noel Poisson's testimony on the subject of child abuse was positively off the charts. Crimes against children almost always went unreported; very rarely did anyone appeal to the state for an intervention on their behalf. Even more rarely did anyone outside the nuclear family turn to the state for assistance, and the few who did so tended to be uncles. Grandfathers simply did not figure in complaints made to the Parisian police.

That November deposition to Marrier was not even the first time that Noel Poisson had requested help on his grandchildren's behalf. Already on April 21, 1717, he had gone straight to the top: to the lieutenant general of the Parisian police himself, Marc René de Voyer de Paulmy, Marquis d'Argenson. D'Argenson had called Jean in on more than one occasion to voice his disapproval, most recently the very morning of November 5, when Noel, arriving to file his complaint, had run into Jean just as he was leaving d'Argenson's office. When he saw his father-in-law, in d'Argenson's presence, Jean had cried out that Noel's daughter "was a whore, that Noel himself had encouraged her in her behavior and had prompted her to leave her husband, and that when she left, Louise had stolen over 60,000 livres of Jean's personal effects."

The matter ended there. As Jean Magoulet well knew, Louise and Noel could give depositions until they were blue in the face, but the worst fate that a man with his status and connections risked was to be upbraided by the lieutenant general of the police. Even d'Argenson, who during his eighteen years at the head of the police became known as one of the most serious and effective of all its administrators, would have taken no action more serious than that.

Only weeks after Noel Poisson's November deposition, the climate shifted again. Several years of temperate weather were followed in 1718 by an an exceptionally dry year; the heat was excessive all that summer. The death rate rose, and all over France, authorities were concerned about the sudden spike in infectious diseases. By late 1718, the price of bread was on the rise again.

On December 4, 1718, the next milestone on the road to John Law's transformation of France's economy was reached: the institution backing the new state currency, the General Bank, became the Banque Royale, the Royal Bank, and thus officially the financial arm of the French state. The stage was now set for 1719, when Law would become a household name, synonymous with the belief in instant wealth and tales of rags to riches. That year in France, the rush for stock market gold would eclipse all other news.

By the time John Law's reign began, the resolute protector of her children Louise Poisson Magoulet was dead.

# CHAPTER ELEVEN

# The Gold Rush
## Jean Magoulet: 1718–1719

L OUISE POISSON MAGOULET died during the night of Thursday, November 10, 1718. Two prominent figures in the French medical world and among the most enlightened medical men in the country—Jacques Molin, official physician of both Louis XIV and Louis XV, and Pierre Dionis, authorized surgeon of both Queen Marie-Thérèse and the Duc de Bourgogne—had attended her at the end. Her estate included Molin's bill for ten consultations and Dionis' for twenty. Noel Poisson had spared no expense and had called on his court connections to get his daughter the best care possible.

At the time of her death by unknown causes, Louise was still young, surely not yet forty.

A week after Louise's demise, on November 18, 1718, an assembly was convoked by the branch of the Parisian police that dealt with legal matters: a group of men met to elect a guardian and a subrogate to watch over the affairs of Jean and Louise's five children. In such cases, the surviving parent typically called upon mostly close relatives from both sides of the family and perhaps a few dear friends. The company Jean assembled could hardly have been less conventional.

Noel Poisson was there to represent the maternal line. His presence would have reassured the authorities, who acted on the belief that families wanted the best for their children, encouraging them to believe that all was in order. But Noel, the only member of the Poisson family present, was so far outnumbered by those Jean trusted to follow his wishes that any attempt to speak out was pointless. In addition, recent events had indicated that Jean Magoulet's authority outweighed his.

Jean's choice of representatives for the Magoulet line was truly extraordinary, a situation that is simply never encountered in such cases. Not one of the
many Magoulet relatives then living in Paris was present, not even the most
unscrupulous of the bunch. None of them seems to have had the stomach for
this subterfuge. Instead of relatives, Jean had scraped together enough men to
avoid attracting suspicion; each professed to be his "friend." If this was indeed
the case, they were hardly close confidants. None of their names can be found
on any of the many previous documents in his legal life; only one of them
would ever be associated with him in the future, also in less than honorable
circumstances. Jean II had once again trounced Jean I at his own game: he had
managed to convene a group of men guaranteed to be even more oblivious to
the interests of his children than the lot chosen by his father in 1695 after Simone Inselin's death. With such men voting, the usual procedure was followed:
Jean was appointed guardian and Noel subrogate. There were many reasons
why Jean would have wanted to play this role. His appointment would have
been one more proof that his authority could not be challenged. Jean also had
a considerable financial stake in the decision: once he was appointed his children's guardian, Noel no longer stood a chance of recovering Louise's dowry
for her children. And then there was perhaps the most potent motivation of all:
Jean II's own father had never given his children an accounting of the maternal inheritance he had allegedly managed in their name, and the son once
again planned to reenact his childhood.

He had no sooner had his control reaffirmed and had gotten his hands on any
money that could be recovered from his wife's estate than Jean accomplished
something long planned: he drove his children definitively from their home.

In early 1719, Jean most decidedly did not want his offspring underfoot. All
he really required was a bit of money to throw around; with that plus his fancy
apartment and grand title, he had what he needed to pull off a coup: he was
planning to remarry—the sooner the better.

For a man with underage children to find himself at the altar once again
within months of his wife's death was then common practice. In most cases the
new spouse was a younger woman with the stamina to raise another woman's
children. But Jean had set his cap on an altogether different sort of bride: at age
thirty-seven, the Queen's Embroiderer had decided to turn fortune hunter.

Jean could have met Anne Legrand Chicot in the neighborhood that they
shared. She and her late husband were longtime residents of the rue de la
Heaumerie, a small street destroyed during Haussmann's demolitions that was
situated a short walk from Jean's apartment, just north of the next embankment
down from the Quai de l'École, the Quai de la Mégisserie.

Professional contacts could also have alerted him to Legrand's pending change in status. Her first husband, Pierre Chicot, was a well-respected *peaussier*, a craftsman who took already tanned animal hides and used various preparations including dyes to transform them into the kind of skins that artisans such as glove makers and *gainiers* required. By the fall of 1718, the closely knit community of Parisian leather goods artisans would already have been well informed about Chicot's terminal illness because he had prepared his death so carefully.

Jean's notary could just as well have been his source of information. Notaries were accustomed to giving their clients advice on various subjects; many marriages began with a notary's tip about an eligible partner. Jean Magoulet and Pierre Chicot shared a notary, Nicolas Duport, and it was Duport who on November 26, 1718 drew up Chicot's last will and testament. Duport would thus have been the first to be certain that a wealthy widow would soon be able to consider proposals.

On that November morning when Duport arrived at Chicot's apartment on the "noble floor" of his building, the merchant began by admitting that he knew just how serious his illness was. Though he signed his will with a trembling hand, its contents were carefully considered: he even remembered to leave money so that their faithful servant, Anne Simon, could afford to have a mourning outfit made. The couple's long marriage had produced no children, so Chicot named a favorite nephew, Joseph Hubert, his sole legatee: Hubert, however, would inherit only upon Chicot's widow's death. Finally, Chicot chose Anne Legrand to act as his executor, proof of his trust in his wife's judgment.

Chicot was not one of those who refuse to face his pending death: he had begun attentively putting his financial house in order a full year before he died. All his decisions can be seen as part of an effort to guarantee that he would leave behind no debts for his wife to deal with and that she would be provided for in every way.

On November 26, 1717, one year to the day before his will would be notarized, Chicot went to Duport's office to sign up for the type of investment considered by serious merchants such as himself to be relatively risk free: immediate fixed annuities. An investor paid a lump sum to the French government or a government organization (in this case it happened to be the Tallow Farm, the administration whose operations were overseen by Noel Poisson); in return, the investor received a semiannual income, a percentage of that sum. Government annuities were not always rock solid: the government could and did on occasion lower the rate of return. But to the conservative French investor, state annuities had traditionally seemed the safest way to make disposable income work for them.

And Chicot had a good deal of that: that month alone, 6,250 livres to be exact. He took out one annuity in his name, another in Anne Legrand's. Upon his death, his would be transferred to his wife; both would terminate with her death. Payments were to begin immediately. And the rate of return—6¼ percent—would have been highly attractive at a moment when anything over 5 percent was considered excellent.

On August 23, 1718, the Chicot couple returned to their notary's office to sign another type of contract. This time, Chicot had chosen a second strategy favored by conservative investors: real estate. They were buying, at a cost of 5,100 livres, a house, and not just any house, but a large and fine dwelling on the rue Saint-Médéric in Versailles. The property was located in the neighborhood known as the Parc-aux-cerfs, the deer park. The area was then newly developed in order to provide housing in close proximity to the château for some of the many court officers whose duties required long hours of attendance; the house's previous owner, François de La Fosse, had been the first valet of the royal wardrobe.

Since the château had been shuttered upon the death of Louis XIV and the court would return only in 1722, after Louis XV's coronation, prices for prime Versailles real estate were low in 1718. Chicot must have seen the deal as a chance to acquire rental property in an up-and-coming area at the bottom of the market, and his instincts proved right. Soon, the neighborhood had become so fashionable that the Marquise de Pompadour, mistress of Louis XV, maintained a residence just down the street from the Chicot home.

And these were but two in a long line of well-considered choices on Chicot's part that at the time of his death left his wife of nearly thirty-two years handsomely provided for indeed: Anne Legrand became a most affluent widow, with a steady income stream from rental property and numerous fixed annuities. But Chicot's was the kind of conservative investment strategy that would very shortly be made to seem completely outdated.

On December 4, 1718, the Royal Bank was established. John Law's privately owned bank had been nationalized and had become the official agency of the French government, able to issue both notes and stock. As a result, during the early months of 1719, Law's system for revolutionizing the French economy began to take shape.

Pierre Chicot did not live to see the stock market bubble that drew many of his fellow countrymen into a whirlwind of speculation. His demise at 8 A.M.

on December 9 sealed the fate of Anne Legrand, who soon became the target of one of Jean Magoulet's charm offensives.

The inventory of Chicot's estate, drawn up on December 17, makes it clear that it had been possible for a middle-class Parisian to prosper during the years of economic turmoil that had brought down Antoine Chevrot as well as both Jean Magoulets: Chicot had built his comfortable fortune from scratch in the years since his marriage in 1687. The inventory also reveals the kind of risk-averse business model that, had it been shared by any of those three, just might have saved their families.

Chicot left few outstanding debts, and small ones at that. The rent on their apartment was fully paid up. And realizing that Anne Legrand would have no need for a shop and such large quarters after his death, Chicot had even found a new tenant for the premises: Antoine Delandelle, a dealer in kidskin, was to move in as of October 1719. Would Chicot have been surprised to learn that his wife had moved on and moved in with another man well before October came around?

The inventory also reveals a fastidious man who cared about his person, a true clotheshorse actually, as well as a woman with little interest in fashion: Chicot's wardrobe was valued at three times the cost of his wife's! And whereas Anne Legrand's included mostly "old skirts" and the like, his featured the latest model of hat and the snazzy scarlet cloak that he tossed around his shoulders on a winter's day.

In addition, Chicot paid attention to the decoration of his home, or at least one room in it: the bedroom. Very nearly a third of the total value of all the couple's possessions was tied up in their bedroom's furnishings. These included eight pairs of sheets, and this at a time when most middle-class couples owned perhaps four or five random sheets and no one owned matched sets. That bedroom was so exceptional that it remained intact long after Chicot's demise: the inventory drawn up when Anne Legrand died revealed that during all the years of her marriage to Jean Magoulet, the couple had slept on the same bed and the same sheets and in the same decor she had inherited from her first husband.

Chicot had left his wife one final present: a generous amount of cash that was not declared in the inventory and therefore not considered part of the inheritance to be passed down to his legatee. His widow wasted no time disposing of a chunk of it.

On the day of his death, while his body was still lying in their bed, Anne Legrand Chicot made a trip to their notary's office to put an additional 3,000 livres into still another annuity. Then, in the five months between the inventory and the contract for her second marriage on May 27, she made purchases worth 3,000 livres more, nearly twice the appraised value of the total contents of the apartment she had shared with her first husband. Her choices were far less prudent than before: the woman who had previously owned nothing finer than "old skirts" was now decked out in diamonds and a gold pocket watch with a fancy gold-nail-studded case crafted by a master *gainier*. Her new financial adviser, Jean Magoulet, had clearly encouraged her to invest in luxury goods. He even drew up a listing of her purchases, which was included as part of their marriage contract.

How old was Anne Legrand in 1719? When she had married Pierre Chicot in July 1687, she was at least fifteen years old, and more likely between eighteen and twenty. Jean, born in February 1682, was but five years old in 1687.

And yet, when Anne Legrand became a June bride—in a ceremony held not in the less prestigious church that she and Chicot had attended, but in Jean's church, Saint-Germain-l'Auxerrois—the license issued by the priest who married them makes note of two details that are rarely seen on such documents: their ages. The bride's was listed as forty-five, and the groom's was forty-five as well. Either he had lied to her, and she had chosen to believe him, or both were adjusting their ages in an attempt to cover up the disparity in their May-December union. This was neither the first nor the last time that Jean adapted his age to suit changing circumstances. He had first claimed to be "of age," twenty-five or above, in 1696, when he was actually only fourteen. And for decades he somehow got away with it.

There is perhaps no greater proof of Jean's artistry as a con man than the turnout for the signing of their marriage contract. On the groom's side, only one Magoulet was present, his father. The original Queen's Embroiderer had been coerced once again into standing up for his son when he married under false pretenses. His signature was tremulous, that of an elderly man. This was the final appearance of the individual who had made familial abuse an integral part of the Magoulet family saga.

Anne Legrand's family demonstrated no such caution. Her sister Marguerite, widow of a royal painter, Henry Le Bicheur, was in attendance, as were two other royal painters, both nephews of the bride: Jean Le Bicheur and Pierre Nicolas Huilliot. Huilliot, married to Marguerite's daughter, was a prolific and noted still life artist, known for the lush floral bouquets that decorated many great châteaux. The king's painters may have felt that in marrying Jean, always identified as "the official embroiderer of the deceased queen," Anne was broadening the family's court connections.

Anne Legrand was savvy enough to retain complete financial autonomy. There was no community property; Anne kept control over her income and possessions. She had even added a clause specifying that "she will get all the benefits from any loans and investments and that she will be able to deal with her finances without seeking authorization from her husband."

Just as he had at the time of his first marriage, Jean once again demonstrated considerable dexterity in the presentation of his finances. Instead of the customary dowry and dower, the couple exchanged "mutual gifts." Jean promised that if he were the first to die, Anne would receive "a share of his estate equal to that of one of his children"; this is the only mention of his first marriage in the entire document. If she were to predecease him, Anne pledged 4,000 livres in cash—on one condition, that is. Jean would not inherit "if there were any surviving children from the marriage." After over three decades of a childless marriage, this woman pushing fifty thus publicly professed a desire to have children.

Children of her own, that is, for Anne Legrand had no wish to raise Jean's progeny. And by June 3, 1719, when the wedding took place, those five children were fending for themselves.

Jean, meanwhile, was living the life of Riley. His bride's generosity was most evident in a private document not part of the marriage contract and thus kept secret from her family. She agreed to pay all their living expenses—the astronomical rent on Jean's beloved apartment, food, the cost of maintaining a household—"out of her own money." And her bounty did not stop there: every quarter, Jean received "an allowance," just as though he were the owner of a fat, dependable government annuity. The amount of that allowance was never spelled out, but it was surely not insignificant.

And it kept Anne Legrand Magoulet safe. She was the only one of Jean's wives never to have gone to the police to file a report about his abuse.

The marriage brought Jean still another benefit. He had no right to the income from the house in Versailles, since that was part of the Chicot inheritance. But when a lease was signed with a new tenant, an interesting phrase was added to the usual legal boilerplate: "the owners keep for their own use a small room located just above the kitchen." What was described as "a small room" was hardly what most people would have considered a modest space: it was large enough to accommodate a bed, an armchair, several other chairs, a buffet to store dishes, and so forth. It was in other words a fully functional studio apartment. And since it also had a private entrance, no one need have known of its occupant's comings and goings.

Thanks to that "small room," Jean was able to explain away any overnight absences. A luxury goods artisan could well have been grateful not to have to make the long trip back to central Paris by public coach at night after meetings with his clients at court.

But when he left their home on the Quai de l'École, Jean Magoulet was in fact traveling a much shorter distance. The apartment he shared with Anne Legrand was located at the spot where the Pont Neuf joined the Quai de l'École. A mere hop, skip, and a jump across the first span of that bridge would have brought him to still another home away from home, the apartment on the Quai de l'Horloge that he shared with another woman, Marie Louise Desjardins, and where he assumed his identity as Clément Magoullet, neither a court artisan nor a master craftsman, but a simple run-of-the-mill *gainier*.

There was one final aspect to his new wife's bounty that, in the summer of 1719, would have been particularly attractive to someone with a taste for risk. In addition to Jean's allowance and to the considerable discretionary income that maintained a lifestyle far more lavish than that of any household he had yet known, Anne Legrand had easy access to a commodity then considered priceless: cash.

The Magoulet-Legrand wedding and the launch of the original stock market frenzy coincided precisely. The month when Jean promised to remarry marked another milestone in John Law's transformation of the French economy: the first company put under Law's control in August 1717, the Western Company, was fused in May 1719 with the two original French trading concessions, the East Indies Company and the West Indies Company. These companies had been founded in 1664 but had never been even remotely as profitable as their English and Dutch counterparts and rivals. The May 1719 fusion created a gigantic conglomerate also known as the Indies Company. The multifaceted enterprise was under Law's command: one man was responsible for everything from large colonies to tiny trading concessions, from the administration that supervised finances to the flotilla required to service outposts from Pondicherry to Martinique. From then on, this behemoth enjoyed an absolute monopoly on France's overseas trade.

On May 24, 1719, stock in the new Indies company began to shoot up; on May 27, the Magoulet-Legrand marriage contract was signed; on June 3, they were wed. In May, fifty thousand new shares were printed; they sold out in just twenty days. Anyone with 500 livres could have bought into the new stock venture at the bottom. By June 20, shares were up by nearly 300 percent since the beginning of the month. And Jean Magoulet had just come into some cold hard cash.

The Magoulet-Legrand nuptials also closely paralleled a second chronology. One year earlier, on May 7, 1718, an outpost named for the regent governing France, Philippe, Duc d'Orléans, had been founded in the New World. The original incarnation of New Orleans was quickly destroyed by a hurricane. Development then shifted to slightly higher ground nearby; grid planning was adopted; and soon a settlement close to what is today known as the city's French Quarter emerged. But to reach that goal, a quick influx of labor was required.

Jean remarried only three days before the first French vessels carrying slaves to New Orleans docked there. By then, Jean, like numbers of his fellow Parisians, was aware that a new method was available for ridding families of children they considered troublesome or undesirable: all one need do was to have them arrested and then get their name on the manifest of a ship bound for the Indies Company's latest outpost.

On July 27, a merchant named Magoulet requested that "his daughter" Louise Magoulet be arrested and transported on the next boat to Louisiana. Under his identity as Clément Magoullet, Jean set in motion the process designed to rid him permanently of the child whom he saw as the only threat to his carefully laid plans for a fresh start.

Jean's double life was about to go into high gear.

# CHAPTER TWELVE

# The Invention of Money
## Louise Magoulet and Louis Chevrot: 1719

H AD LOUISE POISSON Magoulet lived just a year longer, her eldest daughter would not have been left to fend for herself in a money-mad world.

In early 1719, when Louise Magoulet turned seventeen and the boy king Louis XV turned nine, their country was about to descend into an obsession no Frenchman could have encountered before. That fixation soon became the focal point of life in Paris. On October 6, Antoine Louis Le Fèvre de Caumartin de Boissy, great aristocrat and president of the Grand Council, characterized the compulsion as "a mania, a sickness, a delirious fever" and described its principal symptom as "the inability to think of anything but their profits, or to talk of anything but the millions they have invested." The Duc de Saint-Simon concluded: "Everyone's head was completely turned around." It was as if the French had suddenly discovered money.

Caumartin de Boissy insisted in his letters to his sister in the provinces that "people of our sort really shouldn't concern ourselves with riches of that kind." Like all those of his station, he loved to poke fun at individuals of "obscure" birth who, after having become fabulously wealthy in a matter of months, didn't know the proper way to use the fine silver and carriages they quickly began to acquire. But in the next breath he always congratulated himself on having bought his shares near the bottom and bragged about the value of his portfolio.

The old values seemed to have gone out the window in a society under the sway of a new measure of a man: net worth.

In a half year's time, France became a modern land of plenty, a country driven by finance and the market. The new France was governed no longer from the Louvre or Versailles, but from a modest street in central Paris, the rue Quincampoix. The rue Quincampoix was France's Wall Street, the place chosen by John Law as the location for Paris' original stock exchange.

Law was nothing if not a master communicator: anyone following the news from France in 1719—the French press, the official edicts and communiqués about Louisiana and the Indies Company—would never have guessed that there was a downside to the prosperity that John Law was showering on France.

Law's first propaganda campaign was centered on his new venture in Louisiana. The most widely read French periodical of the day, *Le Nouveau Mercure galant* (the *New Gallant Mercury*), published in its March 1719 issue what purported to be a letter from a Frenchman named François Duval who had landed in New Orleans just after its founding and was sending news to his wife in France for the first time.

Duval described his adopted home as "an enchanted land where every seed one sows multiplies a hundredfold," "a place laden with gold and silver mines." Everyone was safe: the natives and even the wild beasts were friendly. Everything one needed was abundant and cheap; there were no taxes to pay. Only one thing was missing: "industrious individuals willing to do the work necessary to make this the most flourishing colony in the world." Volunteers would receive free passage; the Indies Company would give them acreage and the wherewithal to farm it. Unmarried women would even get new clothes and 50 livres, the down payment on their life as a Louisiana bride.

Duval was in all likelihood as fictive as this depiction of what was then a settlement with virtually no buildings and no one in it as an earthly paradise. But the March 1719 account is noteworthy because it laid out for the first time in a completely public forum the terms in which Law had decided to promote Louisiana to the French: as a land of milk and honey where the food so often in short supply in early eighteenth-century France literally fell off the trees and sprang out of the ground and as a territory abundantly endowed with two natural resources that had been at the origin of every European nation's colonial dream: gold and silver.

Nowhere was this vision of Louisiana more flamboyantly displayed than in the building Law planned as a highly visible emblem of France's new economy: his temple of finance, the Royal Bank.

Law's original bank, the General Bank, had been housed in the Marais not far from Paris' City Hall, but as soon as the Royal Bank was established, Law set his sights on properly regal quarters. The January 1719 *New Gallant Mercury* announced that the Royal Bank would soon be relocated just north of the Louvre, in the heart of Paris' new financial neighborhood. By March, Law had acquired two grand adjacent townhouses on the rue de Richelieu: he moved the bank into one of them and reserved the other, for which he paid over a million livres, for his private residence.

Law transformed the bank into a gigantic advertisement for Louisiana. From Italian artist Giovanni Pellegrini, Law commissioned an imposing frescoed ceiling that dominated the bank's main space, known as the Mississippi Room. Pellegrini imagined a vast (130-by-27-foot) allegory of the wealth that the colony was exporting to France: the river Seine was depicted embracing the Mississippi; on the banks of the Seine, ships were unloading piles of treasure straight from Louisiana.

Every investor who entered the Royal Bank encountered in Law's design for its grand staircase the most graphic of his promotions of Louisiana's riches. The staircase's balustrade was richly decorated with gilded cornucopias. Some overflowed with traditional signs of abundance: grapes and apples, the fruits of the earth that, according to Law's propaganda, grew so easily in Louisiana's rich soil. Others were brimming over with a form of bounty never previously displayed in horns of plenty: coins, many of which can be identified as actual coins then in circulation in France, among them the livre minted in silver in December 1719. That image of silver-laden Louisiana was essential to Law's plans for French investors. Indeed, French newspapers were soon announcing that "prodigious quantities of silver" had begun to arrive in France straight from those Louisiana mines.

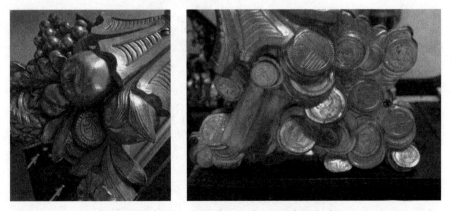

*The balustrade of John Law's Royal Bank was decorated with these cornucopias: some overflowed with the earth's bounty, others with gold coins.*

From December 1718 on, the Royal Bank began issuing ever greater quantities of a revolutionary type of banknote. The state bills printed by the General
Bank in 1717 were marked *billet*, "note" or "bill." The new ones bore no such
reminder of the fact that they were mere representations of "real" money.
Instead, they were designated simply "livres," with the amount (10 in the case
of the note shown here), as though they were now fully the coin of the realm.
Until then, the livre had been solely a money of account, so these were the
first livres that anyone in France had ever seen. The Royal Bank suddenly
made the livre real, on paper at least.

Whereas previous state bills had made no mention of how, for which currency or kind of money, the notes would be exchanged, beginning in 1719 all
notes, like the one shown here, bore this sentence: "The Bank promises to pay
the bearer a hundred [or some other sum] livres in silver coin." As soon as the
silver load in Louisiana was announced, Law's bank began to print only bills
identifying specie explicitly with silver.

In tandem with his promotion of Louisiana, Law ran a second publicity
campaign, one designed to convince the French that this new paper currency was the perfect money. On April 22, 1719, a royal edict announced
that since henceforth, banknotes would be "more useful to his Majesty's subjects than gold and silver coin, they deserve a most singular protection. The
crown thus guarantees that notes will never be devalued, as can happen with

*In April 1719, the Royal Bank issued this ten-livre banknote.*

coin, and that they will always be paid in full. Paper will never diminish in value."

From early 1719 on, Law kept the French treasury's supply of gold completely separate from its silver. In April 1719, gold coins were devalued, and this produced the desired result: Parisians descended on the bank in hordes to acquire the new bills, tied to silver and officially guaranteed to maintain their value. On May 12, so many showed up to convert gold into paper that the bank ran out of notes. By May 15, the bank had become a mob scene, and Swiss guards had to be sent over from the Louvre for crowd control. The bank stockpiled all the gold, which the state then used to pay its running expenses. In the regent's eyes, Law became ever more the man with a remedy for France's economic woes.

The year 1719 was a watershed for the French, the moment when money matters, currency in all its newfound complexity, became a central focus of life. To begin with, money was suddenly present on a formerly unimaginable scale: a far larger supply of money than ever before was in circulation; many new bills were printed in denominations such as 10,000 livres, far larger than any previously known.

In addition, monetary transactions became ever more intricate. Anyone who wanted to purchase anything or to pay any bill had to decide in which currency or currencies the transaction would be carried out. Everyone had to keep constant track of various indices: which currency had been devalued, which currency would soon no longer be accepted at the bank or as a form of payment. Individuals who previously had been concerned only with quotidian financial preoccupations such as the price of staples that one could or could not afford, or the amount of the tax bill one owed, became fixated on various manifestations of something with which they had had limited prior experience: pieces of paper, monetary instruments of various kinds. These developments took shape quickly and all at once. France was rushing into the modern financial age at breakneck speed.

It must have been simultaneously exhilarating, frightening, maddening, and confusing to the point of dizziness. English merchants doing business in Paris at the time reported in their letters home that what Parisians were referring to as Law's "system" was distracting them from all else.

Between May 1719 and January 8, 1720, stock in Law's Indies Company rose from 500 to its peak of 10,100. During those months, everyone would have been aware of its increasing value. The European periodical press—papers printed in English, in French, in Dutch, and in capitals from Paris and London to Amsterdam—covered the French market intensely. Beginning in

February 1719, the month when Law initiated serious promotion of New Orleans, all papers included stock quotes in every issue. An investor who put them all together would have been able to follow the evolution of prices virtually day by day.

French papers continued to print coverage of international politics and crucial current events, but as the year went on, other information was increasingly crowded out by what was evidently the only news that really mattered, the news from the street: the rue Quincampoix. Never before had there been such a money-mad year in Paris; the press responded by becoming money-driven in its own right.

All papers were blatantly pro-Law; their coverage would have encouraged investors to trust in the Royal Bank and to view stock in his company as a sound investment. One highly respected paper, the *Gazette d'Amsterdam* (the *Amsterdam Gazette*), for example, frequently ended its reports with remarks such as "many think that shares will continue to go up." The paper characterized the administration of the Indies Company as "admirably precise and transparent." And it never neglected to report stock purchases made by the greatest French nobles, such as the Princesse de Conti, daughter of Louis XIV and wife of a Bourbon prince, thereby encouraging potential investors to believe that Law's "system" was too big to fail.

During the dot-com bubble, the NASDAQ index rose from 500 to just over 5,000, but that spectacular climb took place over the nine-year period from April 1991 to March 2000. In just five months, Law's stock rose from 500 to over 10,000. The velocity of the original stock bubble made Parisians sick with investment fever.

The months between August and November were key. Over the course of those four months, Law's status and that of his company never ceased to burgeon. Beginning with the take-over of the Royal Mint by the Indies Company in August, what had been at the start merely a trading and banking company came to dominate the economy of France. That process culminated on January 5, 1720, when Law was named the country's superintendent general of finance.

By then, Law regulated all government finance and expenditure; he was in charge of the French national debt and the mints that struck gold and silver coins. He headed the Royal Bank; he decided how much money would be printed and how much stock would be issued. He ran the company that presided over France's overseas trade and the development of its colonies from Canada to Africa and the Caribbean, as well as collecting most taxes. France was the largest economy in Europe, and that economy was in the hands of one man. Never had a single individual enjoyed such uncontested control over a preeminent state's resources and their management.

Over the course of the four months from August to November 1719, Law's company made some of its investors extremely wealthy, and it did so at a record pace. The pages of contemporary correspondence and memoirs are packed with the tales of the nouveaux riches of Paris who were then the talk of the town. They often feature ordinary people who had struck investment gold: a banker's servant had made 50 million, a waiter 30 million. Law's coachman had walked away with many, many millions. They describe "great ladies of the Mississippi who were covered all over with diamonds," as well as rich investors who didn't hesitate to walk into a goldsmith's shop, plunk down 75,000 or even 100,000 livres in notes, and ask that the shop's entire contents be delivered to their home.

In its October issue, the earliest paper to preach Law's party line, the *New Gallant Mercury*, devoted detailed coverage to the stories that were making all Parisians share the dream of instant affluence. There was, for example, the case of a man "of humble birth" who, three months before, had converted ten thousand Royal Bank notes into shares in Law's company. The editor characterized the lucky man as "fortune's champion" and described him, with a word then freshly coined in Paris, as "a millionaire."

The first recorded use of the word "millionaire" reveals that just as soon as John Law's system had made it possible to turn an initial investment of 10,000 livres into a cool million, Parisians had come to accept the idea that anyone could become a millionaire. And that conviction explains the fever pitch of Parisian life in the fall of 1719.

The world's original millionaires owed it all to still another of Law's creations: Paris' original stock exchange, the rue Quincampoix.

In Europe, stock trading originated in Amsterdam at the beginning of the seventeenth century; the practice had spread to London by the century's end. These early exchanges, on which shares in the Dutch and the English Indies Companies were traded, were sober, professional institutions, frequented by a relatively closed circle of longtime investors. Paris had currency exchanges run mainly for the benefit of merchants with foreign clients, but prior to Law's rule, stock had not been publicly traded in the French capital.

In August 1719, just as the price of Indies Company shares was about to surge, "an exchange for the commerce in Indies Company stock" was inaugurated in a house located at number 65 rue Quincampoix. The first stock exchange

to be identified with the name of a street reinvented the previously staid practice of trading as a freewheeling street market in which stock was bought and
sold by any and all investors, a place where anyone could learn firsthand about
the heady experience of speculation. Already in its September 8 issue, the
*Amsterdam Gazette* was promoting the Paris exchange as "the place where
people best understand how banknotes work."

Number 65 was destroyed in the nineteenth century during Baron Haussmann's redesign of Paris, but the rest of the rue Quincampoix remains much
as it was in Law's day. In 1719, the houses lining the street were rented out to
traders who sold stock from their offices. Since office space was cramped,
trading often took place in the street itself.

This contemporary engraving by Antoine Humblot recorded the ways in
which the rue Quincampoix became a revolutionary trading exchange. Only
men had frequented previous exchanges, but in Paris, women joined in the
game and followed their portfolios just as avidly as male investors. The men
found at exchanges in other countries were middle-class merchants, but in
Paris in most cases the clothing worn by investors identified them as either
true blue bloods or the elite newly created by the rue Quincampoix, the men

*In 1720, Antoine Humblot depicted the frenzy created by stock trading
on the rue Quincampoix.*

real nobles dubbed *seigneurs de la rue Quincampoix*, the lords of Quincampoix. It was said that you could recognize a Quincampoix noble by his clothing— *tout brodé*, dripping with embroidery, just the kind of wildly expensive work for which both Queen's Embroiderers were known.

On the street, lords and ladies, real lords and stock market nobles, stood elbow to elbow, as class distinctions and etiquette yielded ground to a common desire to make as much money as possible as quickly as possible. Strange friendships were forged: one commentator called them "the bonds of speculation."

The specter of fast wealth transformed well-heeled Parisians into an unruly swarm: investors were jammed into every nook and cranny of the street's available space. In Humblot's depiction, armed royal guards have been stationed in the foreground to try to bring order and to prevent others from rushing in. Contemporary accounts confirm that day after day, from 8 A.M. to 9 P.M., the rue Quincampoix was a mob scene. The pandemonium stopped when darkness fell only after Lieutenant General Machault had gates installed at each end of the street and ordered them locked overnight.

Humblot also depicted the techniques devised by traders to keep the crowd at a fever pitch. If a dealer was willing to purchase stock at a price above its market value, he would ring a bell positioned on a pulley outside his office window and then send agents down into the street to buy shares from investors. If, on the other hand, a trader wanted to sell below market value, he would blow a whistle. All day long, those bells and whistles fueled the perception that those who caught the tide at just the right moment could find instant wealth by joining in the speculation game on the rue Quincampoix.

During the last five months of 1719, the rue Quincampoix was a heady, giddy place, the perfect symbol for a roaring age. Those months, when all eyes in Paris were on the stock index and the original millionaires and when the city's streets were alive to the sounds of the rue Quincampoix, determined the course of Louise Magoulet's life.

Early in 1719, Louis Chevrot and Louise Magoulet were desperately trying to identify a family member willing to support their desire to get married. And help was not easy to find.

The young couple knew better than to turn to Louise's father. In early 1719, Jean Magoulet was thinking only of his own upcoming nuptials. Besides, he would never have made it possible for his daughter to wed: as a married woman, she would have become eligible to demand her share of her mother's estate without waiting for her twenty-fifth birthday.

In 1719, Louis' father, Antoine Chevrot, knew a significant reversal of fortune when his position as a financial administrator became caught up in Law's reorganization of the French economy. With no notice, all seventy annuities controllers were informed that their posts had been "suppressed"; their offices were "to be immediately liquidated" and their income was to cease: Law planned to renegotiate the financing of these positions in order to make them more profitable for the state. Officeholders were assured that the government would reimburse their initial outlay, but even in the best of times this process was rarely expedient. Just at the moment when Antoine was obsessed with that sudden loss, his eldest son blindsided him a second time by announcing his determination to marry a young woman both penniless and already pregnant with his child.

Louis' surviving maternal grandparents would have been no more sympathetic. Their lives revolved around the court of the Duchesse Du Lude, and the duchess was among the first great aristocrats to become heavily implicated in stock market fever. They would have expected their eldest grandson to make a more lucrative match.

Noel Poisson, the only relation on whom the couple might have counted, was totally preoccupied just when they needed him most. Noel's younger daughter Catherine had kept Louise Poisson's embroidery workshop in the 15/20 going after her sister's death; she quickly learned just how perilous the world of business could be for a young woman on her own, particularly at a moment when instant wealth was bringing out the beast in many. For a fine nobleman, the sieur de Longrue, Catherine had created a richly embroidered garment. But Longrue showed up late one night and simply demanded his jacket. When Catherine refused to give it to him, he gave her a savage beating instead of payment, kicking her in the stomach and bashing her head against the ground.

In addition, at the same time as Antoine Chevrot, Noel Poisson learned that his position as administrator of the Tallow Farm had been made redundant. Law announced that all the farm's contracts were to be "immediately terminated": his Indies Company was absorbing all the smaller tax collection entities. Noel never found new employment.

Just when the young couple became desperate, so did John Law. He was no longer willing to wait for "industrious individuals" to accept his company's proposition of free passage to the New World and free land when they arrived. At the moment when he turned the Royal Bank into a promotion for Louisiana's riches, Law authorized strong-arm tactics to enable him to reach his goal of lining up colonists for the newly founded city of New Orleans at the break-neck pace with which he was transforming the French economy.

In September 1718, the *New Gallant Mercury* had published an initial brief advertisement for New Orleans; the article concluded by mentioning that "forty young women will leave on the first boats. Their trousseaux are being prepared right now." It's virtually certain that Frenchwomen were not yet being transported to New Orleans, but that article and a follow-up published in February 1719 may have been the catalyst for new behavior on the part of French parents.

Early in 1719, for the first time ever, a few Parisian families asked the lieutenant general to lock up young women in Paris' General Hospital as a prelude to deportation to "the islands." Then Law introduced his new policy and, by the second half of 1719, the lieutenant general was receiving numerous solicitations from parents eager to have their daughters swiftly exiled from French soil.

By then, a family making such an entreaty would have known that it might well be successful. In all of French history, the last six months of 1719 marked far and away the moment during which requests to exile women to the New World were most frequent; dozens of such appeals landed on the lieutenant general of the police's desk. It was also the only time during which such banishments actually took place.

In every successful petition, parents accused their daughters of *libertinage et vie débauchée*, licentious behavior and promiscuity. In theory, an inquiry into such charges was mandatory. But in order to please the increasingly powerful individual running the French economy, during the second half of 1719, dossiers were processed so quickly that such inquiries were often dispensed with. The final months of Louise's pregnancy, the moment at which it became impossible for her to conceal her situation, thus coincided with the period during which her father need only have pointed to her changing body to lend credibility to his charges.

Her pregnancy was surely the factor that tipped the scales in her father's favor. Numerous requests were made to the lieutenant general, but a mere eight or nine were approved in their entirety. In only that handful of cases was the daughter not only tracked down and locked up but also placed on a list for prompt deportation.

During the last half of 1719 and the first months of 1720, the entire period when forced deportation was possible, about 180 women were sent to Louisiana. All but twenty were set to travel on the vessel on whose manifest Louise's name was inscribed, a ship named *La Mutine*, or *Mutinous*. Jean's appeal, among the few direct requests from a parent to be granted, was accepted just at the moment when *Mutinous* still had room for another passenger. The stars were aligned against Louise Magoulet.

Just then, Marguerite Pancatalin, the warden of the Salpêtrière, the hellhole in which Louise was imprisoned, was concerned for her position, which guaranteed an income, living quarters, status, and a great deal of power. In January 1719, Pancatalin had faced perhaps the most serious threat in her thirty-six years in prison administration: conditions in the Salpêtrière were so dire that sixteen female inmates had staged a revolt and had nearly succeeded in breaking free. Pancatalin had retaliated with a letter to the lieutenant general suggesting that the women responsible for what she termed a "rebellion" be sent "to the islands."

At that moment, Law knew he had found his ally inside the prison system. Once again, May 1719, the month of the Magoulet-Legrand marriage contract, proved key: Law personally called on Pancatalin to request her help identifying women for the colony that he was making crucial to his vast program of economic reform.

Law's plan could not have moved forward quickly without another key collaborator: Louis Charles de Machault, known as a particularly uncompromising lieutenant general of the Parisian police. The men who held this position varied greatly in their approaches to matters such as familial petitions for punishment: Machault was a true hard-liner, someone who believed in cracking down on crime. He was also a career administrator who changed posts frequently; he directed the Parisian police for only two years, from January 1718 to January 1720, precisely the period during which Law was rounding up women and needed a compliant lieutenant general.

Machault assigned the dossiers of women whose families were requesting their exile to a brand-new officer of the Parisian police, Jean Bourlon. In early 1719, as soon as Law's deportation strategy had been announced, Bourlon had purchased a position as a lieutenant in the division assigned the task of tracking down undesirables who could be shipped off to New Orleans. Bourlon proved zealous in fulfilling his new duties: he was responsible for the internment in the Salpêtrière of numerous women chosen by Pancatalin for deportation. He also set about recouping his investment in his new post: Bourlon was so thoroughly corrupt that in 1722, he himself spent time in prison while numerous charges against him were being investigated. Those investigations revealed that one of Bourlon's earliest moneymaking schemes involved the Royal Bank.

When investors began arriving at the Royal Bank to convert their silver, they transported it in a money bag and with great difficulty: when carried about in coins, any significant sum at all became quite a weighty proposition. But after their transactions, they found themselves suddenly in the wonderful world of modern paper money.

Instead of lugging those old-fashioned pouches, investors could slip the trim banknotes into the compartments of an accessory so newly invented by Parisian *gainiers* that it did not yet have a name: we would call it a wallet. Since even a well-stuffed wallet was feather light, it could be carried without damaging the most expensively embroidered jacket pocket. One of the many foreigners who rushed to Paris to get in on investment fever, the Baron de Pollnitz, found the new freedom heady: "A mere hundred livres in coin was too heavy for a man to carry around, but the same man could have millions in his pocket without noticing the weight. I myself can brag that I once had in my hand a wallet containing more than 32 million in bills."

Lieutenant Bourlon may have been the first to notice a fact that contemporary observers all noted before 1719 was out: for robbers, wallets were like catnip.

Bourlon was assigned the task of patrolling the bank to protect investors; he was thus informed in advance of the arrival of important shipments of bills. He would alert the prettiest and most dexterous thieves in Paris and would point out to them those who had converted particularly hefty sums. The ladies would flirt a bit, relieve the marks of their wallets, and then disappear into the crowd that always packed the bank on such days. Bourlon demanded a percentage of their take.

As soon as the deportation of the Salpêtrière's inmates became official policy, the lieutenant simply arrested as thieves all the women who had been working for him, thereby ingratiating himself with Pancatalin, Machault, and Law himself. There was no need for an investigation: with Pancatalin's help, Bourlon had their names placed on the list of those "fit for the islands." Bourlon and Pancatalin's collaboration proved so successful that on September 1, 1719, John Law returned to the Salpêtrière and made a handsome donation to thank its warden for the good work.

Lieutenant General Machault entrusted Louise Magoulet's dossier to Officer Bourlon.

Even after they realized that no relative would come to their aid, Louise and Louis still believed they would find a sympathetic cleric willing to marry them. They turned to their parish priests first, but without parental consent, they were turned down. They tried to bribe a middle-aged merchant to pose as Antoine

Chevrot and agree to their union, but the plan fell through when Louis' father got wind of it.

By the time of Jean's wedding and the moment when Law's plan to deport Frenchwomen became a reality, Louise was five to six months pregnant, and the young couple knew their marriage would not take place before she gave birth. With a group of friends, they came up with a plan to flee the increasingly manic and cutthroat place Paris was becoming.

Today, Clignancourt is a section of Paris situated at the city's northern limit and best known as the location of its largest flea market. In 1719, Clignancourt was a bucolic village renowned for its wine and its particularly flavorful cherries: it lay well outside city limits.

It was there that Louis and Louise took refuge. She was still not eighteen; he would turn nineteen on September 9, just about the time their baby was due. They settled in as secluded a location as possible, an inn outside the village called La Maison de l'Aveugle, the Blind Man's House. In that country inn whose name seemed to promise discretion—see no evil, speak no evil—they hoped she would give birth to their child. A well-respected royal physician named Bonvalet was overseeing her pregnancy and delivery.

On July 25, gold was devalued for a second time, and the Royal Bank was once again a mad whirl of Parisians with well-stuffed wallets and pickpockets trying to lighten them. Jean Magoulet took advantage of that frenzied moment to make his move. On July 27, he became one of the growing number of parents petitioning Lieutenant General Machault with requests to deport their daughters: he signed his appeal "Clément Magoullet, merchant on the Quai de l'Horloge." He addressed a second plea directly to Lieutenant Bourlon. In that missive, he identified himself only as "Magoulet," and he didn't include a signature, indicating both that this was not the first time he had dealt with Bourlon and that he wanted to leave no trace of his identity as the Queen's Embroiderer. And the wording of his request indicates that Bourlon had been a good teacher.

Jean described Louise as "having long since given up any pretense at an honorable life," as *gâtée*—ruined, sullied, spoiled, a euphemism for pregnant—and "contaminated with venereal disease" because "she has given herself to several men who are keeping her hidden away." He also accused his daughter of having stolen 4,000 livres from home before running away. Louise thereby stood charged with both the crimes for which women were being deported: prostitution and theft.

Jean supplied one further detail: he claimed that seventeen-year-old Louise was then twenty-seven. That added decade made Louise an ideal candidate: most women marked for deportation were nearing or just over thirty.

There was only one hitch: Jean did not know where Louise was sequestered. The case might thus have stalled for a long time, probably long enough for the danger of deportation to pass. But Jean knew the name of her doctor. His accusations were thus directed as much against Bonvalet as against Louise.

Jean named three men as Louise's lovers: a wine merchant from Orléans, whose name never reappears in the case file; a currency trader named Étienne Richard; and Bonvalet. All three were married, Jean contended; all were in on the secret of her hiding place. Richard he identified as the father of her child. Bonvalet he accused of having shown up at his home at ten o'clock on the evening of July 26, along with three unknown men, all of them brandishing swords, "screaming blasphemies and insults," "intending to carry out carnage and massacre." "With considerable difficulty and despite great danger," Jean claimed to have single-handedly fought off four armed men with murder on their minds, largely by "blocking their sword thrusts by using first his hand and then a broom handle." And he added a final flourish: all the while, his daughter Louise was just outside, sitting in a carriage, cheering on those attempting to assassinate her father and "laughing wildly."

Bourlon took care of the rest, and without waiting for Machault's assent. Already on July 30, Dr. Bonvalet had been locked up in For-l'Évêque, formerly the Episcopal see of Paris' bishop but since 1674 a royal prison. Bourlon's methods of interrogation were also efficient: he got information out of Bonvalet the same day.

Thus, under cover of darkness, at 4 A.M. on August 4, Bourlon caught Louise unawares and arrested her. He took his latest prize straightaway to Marguerite Pancatalin at the Salpêtrière, where, he contended, Louise confessed that Étienne Richard was indeed the father of her child. Louise's name became the final one added to the register Warden Pancatalin had been compiling for months: she completed the list of women "fit for the islands."

Since Louise was indeed, as Bourlon testified, about eight months pregnant, she was confined to L'Ange Gardien (the Guardian Angel), the wing of the internment facility where women gave birth. When Louise delivered her baby soon thereafter, she asked that her son—baby number 58 on the list of children born in the Guardian Angel in 1719—be christened Jean Louis, thereby making the only kind of public declaration available to her of the identities of both her real father and her baby's true father.

The infants of prostitutes were taken from them and handed over to wet nurses in the Hôtel Dieu, a public institution near Notre-Dame cathedral. They received such minimal care that nearly 90 percent of them died in their first months, usually in the month that followed their birth.

Life in the Salpêtrière was consistently horrific, but the period of Louise's internment was perhaps the cruelest moment ever for inmates, because the weather during that year of stock market fever was also sizzling.

The country was in the grip of a massive heat wave and dry spell. By August, the month of Louise's confinement, the drought was so intense that the *New Gallant Mercury*, which rarely included information on the weather, was reporting on a situation so dire that it had become newsworthy. Everywhere in France, small rivers, public fountains, and all sources of water were drying up and something "never before seen" was taking place: people were obliged to travel seven or eight hours in search of water. By the summer of Louise's pregnancy, Parisians were complaining that "everything was burning" and that "the heat was like fire." What must the temperatures have been in the Guardian Angel?

And then there were true fevers, the fevers of infectious disease. The intense heat and unending drought combined to unleash on the French population epidemics of dysentery, smallpox, and the various contagious diseases then known simply as "fevers." There were seven hundred thousand deaths in France in 1718. In 1719, the death count was well over 1.1 million, higher still than in that memorably lethal year, 1709.

The epidemics took their highest toll between August and November, just as the market soared. Fully half of the year's fatalities were registered during those four months. The death count peaked between late August and early September, when Louise was waiting to give birth. In 1719, death itself seemed to dance to the rhythm of the rue Quincampoix.

In an age when, in even the best of circumstances, many women succumbed to infections in the aftermath of childbirth, to deliver at a moment when the blistering heat and dearth of water greatly aggravated the already squalid conditions in the Salpêtrière should by all rights have marked Louise for certain death, as her father would well have known. But survive she did.

Within weeks of Jean Louis' birth, on October 6, 1719, the day that stock market "fever" was officially proclaimed, Louise was forced into a chain gang and onto a straw-filled cart. With Lieutenant Bourlon in charge of the convoy, 156 women left the Salpêtrière bound for the port of Le Havre. It was the perfect time to send them on their way. When the market was creating the original millionaires, and when the press was announcing that "there's no doubt that stock will rise much further still," who would miss a few prostitutes?

All the women would have been in a weakened state: rations were always meager in the Salpêtrière, where prisoners survived on little more than bread and water. In the fall of 1719 they crossed a countryside blighted by drought. Wells had dried up and any water still in the rivers was polluted. Farmers lacked food for their families and grain for their livestock: nothing remained to sell to those who had left Paris too quickly to have planned for the trip, hoping to feed their female prisoners by buying supplies along the convoy's way.

In his voluminous memoirs, the Duc de Saint-Simon was given more to satirical wit and mockery than to pity, but even he was moved by the plight of those he called "the unfortunate ones": "at night, they were either locked up in barns without being fed or, if the property had ditches deep enough so they couldn't escape by themselves, they were tossed into them. All night long, they let out cries that awakened pity and indignation." A priest charged with burying some who had died along the way named them "slaves of Louisiana": as he remarked, "no one seemed to remember their real names."

But their real names have survived on their prison files, which can still be consulted in Paris' Arsenal Library. Those records indicate that Louise traveled in the company of women who, in comparison with Louise Magoulet, were distinctly streetwise. There was Geneviève Bara, twenty and a Parisian, in prison, Pancatalin declared, because of her "licentious behavior and public promiscuity"; Madeleine Benoît, thirty-five and born in Dieppe, accused of "theft and promiscuity"; Suzanne Lavergne, thirty and a native of southern France, charged with "receiving stolen goods," and described pithily by Pancatalin as "a dangerous adventuress"; and Marie Madeleine Bidault, twenty-five and born in Rouen, of whom the Salpêtrière's warden concluded, "she bears responsibility for the deaths of several men." All four survived their terrible journey, and they may have proved crucial to Louise's survival as well.

There was only one glitch in Jean Magoulet's seemingly foolproof plan to rid himself permanently of one of his dependents. No one—not Pancatalin, surely not Bourlon, not even her father himself—had counted on Louise's resilience and her will to remain in France with Louis.

On *La Mutine*'s manifest, Louise Magoulet had been assigned the number 102. But beside Louise's name one word appears: DESERTED. As the convoy was arriving in Le Havre, five prisoners escaped: Geneviève Bara, Madeleine Benoît, Suzanne Lavergne, Marie Madeleline Bidault, and Louise Magoulet. The seventeen-year-old, raised in a vast apartment in one of Paris' best neighborhoods on the banks of the Seine adjacent to the Louvre, managed to break free from a chain gang.

When *La Mutine* sailed on December 12, 1719, just as Law's stock was collapsing, Louise Magoulet was not on board.

And before the vessel *Mutinous* put to sea, fully 17 of the 156 women who had been chained together when they left the Salpêtrière had managed to "desert." In the course of the French experiment with deportation to Louisiana, these seventeen women are the only recorded cases of prisoners who carried off successful escapes.

Among those who "deserted" when the prisoners were already in Le Havre was Marie Antoinette Néron, a Parisian who at nineteen was close to Louise's age; like Louise, she had been incarcerated on charges of "prostitution and theft." In July 1722, Néron denounced Lieutenant Bourlon to the police and revealed that he had facilitated any escape "as long as the prisoner could come up with 1,000 livres."

In 1722, Néron had nothing more to fear from Bourlon: she, as well as a half dozen other deserters from *La Mutine*, were awaiting execution: they were members all of the best-known gang in French history, under the leadership of France's Robin Hood, Louis Dominique Garthausen, known as Cartouche. In 1719, it was widely reported that Cartouche stole only from those who had become millionaires thanks to their investments. Louise's fellow escapee Marie Antoinette Néron was none other than Cartouche's wife and the most important female member of his gang.

During the weeks when Louise and Néron and the other women were on the road to Le Havre, the initial cracks in the façade of Law's absolute power appeared. Beginning in late September, stock began to fluctuate: at first, whenever stock fell, Law would intervene with a royal decree or a well-placed article hinting that the price was about to rise again, and the market stabilized.

November 28 marked the apogee of investment madness: Law paid a visit to the rue Quincampoix to watch the market in action. Through his carriage window he tossed coins to the assembled horde, and the crowd clamored back: "Long live the king and Monseigneur [a title originally reserved for France's dauphin] Law!"

Only two days later, still another milestone in the history of finance was reached: the first ever run on a bank. That initial run was so timid that it was easily contained: no one even thought to give the new phenomenon a name. The story would be different in 1720.

In the aftermath of November 30's panic, in early December 1719, Law began manipulating stock prices so blatantly that there was really no longer a market price: for the most part, shares were worth what Law decided they were worth. But two days after the ship *Mutinous* set sail from Le Havre bound for New Orleans with those women who had not managed to escape, on December 14, just at the full moon, shares plummeted for the first time, dropping from over 9,000 to 7,430. On December 21, Law retaliated by inflating the value of banknotes. Anyone who owed the crown for taxes or any other reason was obliged to settle the debt with notes; they paid a 5 percent premium to use coin. By December 23, shares were up again: they reached what Law saw as the magic figure of 10,000.

On December 30 at 10:30 A.M., a grand ceremony was staged to cap that cornucopian year of 1719 and to commemorate the breakneck ascension of Law's new company and his new bank. The celebration took place in the Royal Bank under the ceiling depicting the confluence of the Seine and the Mississippi. The directors of the Indies Company assembled there: the group included several great aristocrats who had profited most from the company's stock and the son of Jacques Magoulet's mentor François Legendre. The nine-year-old king was seated on an improvised throne; the regent presided in his name.

The board of directors voted to create something no Frenchman had ever heard of: a dividend that awarded shareholders a portion of the company's earnings. English trading companies such as the Hudson's Bay Company had used dividends; to introduce France to the concept, Law simply Gallicized the English term. At first, no one in France could decide how the new word should be spelled: newspapers wrote *dividande*; the Chevrot family benefactress the Duchesse Du Lude spoke of a *dividant*; dictionaries eventually decided on *dividende*. But Law explained the latest financial wonder in a speech that the *Amsterdam Gazette* described as "admirably clear and precise."

The dividend that rounded off 1719 was handsome: anyone who had purchased a 500-livre share in May 1719 would be awarded 200 livres. Shareholders were given printed sheets like this one that promised that such bounty would continue for years to come.

To many, the ceremony in the Royal Bank was the ultimate sign that even the monarchy had been contaminated by the rule of money. The following month, one chronicler recorded the delivery of an anonymous painting to the Royal Academy of Art: it portrayed "the king wearing an outfit completely covered with banknotes." The painting was quickly destroyed, but the sentiment behind it would only grow in the course of 1720. That year was just as tumultuous as 1719 had been; those who had watched the rapid and apparently surefire upsurge of Law's system could bear witness to its equally sudden and unstoppable implosion.

At a time when the word "money" evoked coins, Law's 1719 decision to replace precious metal with paper, rather than to use paper as a temporary stopgap measure at moments of monetary shortage, had been nothing short of revolutionary. In the manner of what is now known as quantitative easing, whereby a central bank prints more money in order to sustain economic activity, the introduction of paper at first increased the money supply and provided a badly needed stimulus to the French economy. But Law allowed the printing to go

*An early French stock dividend coupon.*

on and on; a year after his policy had begun, he had more than doubled the volume of paper money. By May 1720, the total supply of banknotes was four times larger than the gold and silver coinage previously in circulation.

Soon after Indies Company stock had begun to plummet, Parisians woke up and revolted against a policy that had allowed the state to send young people into exile without due process. After the *Mutinous* debacle, the Indies Company never again planned a crossing with a cargo composed solely of women.

Had Louise Poisson Magoulet lived just a year longer . . .

# CHAPTER THIRTEEN

# *Personation*
# Clément Magoullet: 1669–1719

S WINDLING, FORGING, LYING—THEY were all second nature to him. He was guilty of double-dealing and constant legal and financial chicanery. He persistently falsified his credentials and lied about his past and even his present to friends and lovers as well as various and sundry civil and ecclesiastical authorities. He stiffed his friends and family. He led a double life and married a second wife while married to the first—and he planned a marriage to a third while still married to both of them. He treated his children like chess pieces, shifting their positions whenever he needed a prop for a new scam. Through everything, his behavior was amazingly brazen in all its larcenous and deceitful glory.

And since virtually everything about him was fraudulent, right down to his death certificate, little can be known for certain about Clément Magoullet—not even how many of his lives were actually lived by the person who was baptized Clément Magoulet, Jacques Magoulet's fifth son.

Anyone who wonders how all that I will describe in this chapter could have been possible need only consider the management of death in the United States today. On the one hand, every year nine thousand Americans are killed off prematurely by their government when the names and Social Security numbers of individuals still very much alive are erroneously added to the Death Master File. And on the other, no one knows how many of those actually dead have not yet been officially listed there. If such a large gray area can still exist despite the sophisticated information gathering techniques now at our disposal, just think how easy it would have been to prolong the life of a deceased family member and thereby take over his identity at a time when only diplomats and those obliged to travel in wartime possessed a passport or any official papers.

In France, the turn of the eighteenth century was a crucial moment in both the history of identity and the history of forgery. The need for a universally trusted proof of identity had become widely recognized, particularly in tricky cases such as foreigners journeying in a country not their own, or indigents and vagrants seeking food or employment far from home.

Traditionally, the Catholic Church's baptismal records had been the only accepted documentation, but many felt that in a world of increased mobility, church archives had become inadequate. By the early eighteenth century, authorities in France were becoming ever more aware of the fact that no reliable means of determining identity was in place.

Technological advances always provoke crises in identity. At the turn of the eighteenth century, the new technology centered on improved techniques for falsifying documents. In 1707, the Duc de Saint-Simon, the ultimate court insider whose finger was consistently on the pulse of his age, had a revelation: Could there be fads or trends in the history of crime just as in the history of fashion? he wondered. The idea had come to him when he realized that in France in recent years a "rich vein or mother lode of forgers" had been discovered: "there are more and more of them every day." Saint-Simon concluded that the turn of the eighteenth century in France would go down in the annals of crime as one of forgery's finest hours, a moment when counterfeiting became widely recognized as an art form.

Saint-Simon had in mind a certain kind of high-profile forgery. Networks of extremely talented counterfeiters were fabricating documents to help clients pull off a usurpation of nobility. So many instances of forgery were coming to light that a special tribunal specifically constituted to adjudicate identity claims met on a regular basis: among its members was an Intendant in the royal financial administration, Heudebert Du Buisson, who had gained experience in this area through his work with Jacques Magoulet in the early 1680s. This may have been how the Magoulets became aware of the techniques and schemes devised by professionals that could prove useful to any Frenchman seeking to establish a new identity.

The period also knew many less prominent investigations of the crime of counterfeiting. In the course of the eighteenth century, in Paris alone there were a thousand forgery convictions, mostly for fraud involving such basic notarial acts as marriage contracts, with a majority of the frauds concentrated in the early part of the century and almost always with the intent of creating a new identity. In many cases, notaries, the legal representatives of the French state, had cooperated with their clients to allow them to defraud others. And for every fraudulent act reported and prosecuted, we must wonder how many others went undetected.

Until the late eighteenth century, the most widely recognized proof of self-hood was an individual's name as it appeared on his baptismal record, and therefore that person's name written in that person's handwriting: his signature. Thus when a court was asked to make a determination of someone's identity, signatures by the person on documents from different moments in his life were collected and studied by handwriting experts in order to determine whether all had been produced by the same individual.

At a time when a signature served as a priceless proof of one's identity, but when by no means everyone could write his or her name, those who could sign almost always quickly developed a recognizable signature and stuck to it. The courts were right to assume that an individual's signature did not change in any pronounced way over time.

This was particularly true of merchants and other businessmen, of lawyers and other professional men whose signatures represented their persons on documents used in legal and financial transactions. A businessman closing a deal with someone he had never met but who claimed to be, for instance, Jacques Magoulet might have wanted to be sure that he was in fact dealing with the real Jacques Magoulet. He had two ways of checking: acquaintances could have vouched for Jacques' identity, or the man could have compared Jacques' signatures on papers of various kinds.

In Jacques' case, if someone had gone to this trouble, he would have been immediately reassured. From his business dealings in the late 1670s and early 1680s to his marriage contract in 1685 to the final document he signed only days before his death in November 1710, Jacques was always recognizably Jacques. At the start of his professional life, he developed a signature quite distinct from those of his brothers, and from then on he never varied it. He wrote only "Magoulet," never adding his first name, but when I saw his mark on any document, even one that had been signed by many, including numerous Magoulets, I always knew instantly which signature was his. His signature was so carefully personalized that it functioned as a marker of his identity.

This was also the case with the Chevrot men: from the Antoine Chevrot who settled in Paris in 1604 all through the line, each signed only "Chevrot," but in a distinctive manner, as well as in a manner somehow uniquely Chevrot. Noel Poisson, Louise Poisson, Louise Magoulet—each had an easily identifiable and highly consistent signature. Even Jean I Magoulet's awkward, almost carved-out signature, once painfully acquired, varied little over the

*Jacques Magoulet's signature, 1685.*

decades. (Since he was illiterate, he would occasionally forget a letter without noticing it.)

Indeed, there is only one exception: "Clément Magoullet." Clément's was a true chameleon of a signature. No two were identical; indeed, two signatures from the same year or even the same week were often wildly dissimilar. Sometimes he capitalized the initial *m*; often he did not. And when the *m* was capitalized, it was shaped in very different ways. When I was looking for Clément's mark on a document signed by several Magoulets, I had to eliminate the known signatures before I could determine which signature was his.

Either more than one person took turns signing "Clément Magoullet," or the person who did so was consciously trying to remain elusive.

There are only two constants in Clément's signature. First, he consistently spelled his family name with two *l*s: Magoullet. Jacques Magoulet, the brothers' father, had often used two *l*s, and initially all his sons had followed suit, but eventually all but Clément settled on one *l*. Second, with rare exceptions, in dozens of his signatures dating from 1695 to 1730, Clément formed those two *l*s in a highly distinctive manner, a style so mannered that it catches the eye. Since everything else about his signature was inconstant, those carefully studied *l*s can be called the signature of Clément's identity.

Only one other Magoulet fashioned such a singular *l*: Jean II. Beginning with his 1701 marriage contract, the second Queen's Embroiderer made the sole *l* in his name similarly dramatic.

At the start, there was a real Clément Magoullet—like all the best scams, this one had a foundation in reality. On June 11, 1669, when Jeanne Magoulet married Eustache Girardié, a master in the art of making tallow candles, two of her five brothers stood up for her: Jacques and Clément. Clément signed with a confident hand, with the skill of someone who had received a good

*Clément Magoullet's childhood signature, 1669.*

*Clément Magoullet's signature, 1708.*

*Jean II Magoullet's signature, 1724.*

education. His signature indicates that he was younger than Hubert, Jacques, and Jean I, probably about twelve or so in 1669.

But after 1669, for nearly two decades there was no further trace of him. When Hubert was married in 1672, there was no sign of Clément among the brothers who served as his witnesses. The same thing was true for the major gathering of the clan that took place in 1685 when Jacques and Marie Freslin married. That day, all the other brothers and sisters were present. Only one thing can be established with certainty from Clément's long absence from notarial records: alone among Jacques Magoulet's five sons, during his adolescence and early manhood he was not positioning himself for a successful career as a master artisan or in financial administration. In either of these cases, he would have left behind a paper trail, as did the other brothers. He might have become an ordinary worker of some kind, but it's safe to assume that he had died. Clément's identity, however, lived on.

Eighteen years after his sister Jeanne's marriage, Clément began to make periodic reappearances. Whenever he did, there was a common denominator: a Magoulet was perpetrating fraud of some kind.

On March 24, 1687, a baby girl was baptized in Paris' Saint-Barthélemy Church: she was christened Marie Louise. Her father was listed on her baptismal certificate: Clément Magoullet, identified in Jacques' preferred manner as a *bourgeois de Paris*. Of her mother, no mention was made. Had she been Clément's wife, her name would have been given, even had she been deceased. The odd silence was almost certainly an indication that Marie Louise was an illegitimate child and that the ceremony had been designed to endow the baby with an official identity.

Her godfather was Jean I Magoulet, referred to as the Queen's Embroiderer; the godmother, Marie Freslin, Jacques' wife. For all the other baptisms of the various brothers' children, at least one quite socially prominent godparent from outside the family was chosen, but Marie Louise's baptism was different: the Magoulets kept this matter all in the family.

The ceremony took place just over two years after the christening of the last of Jean's children with Simone Inselin, at the moment when another woman or women were giving birth to Jean's illegitimate children. Barely two months after that baptism, Jean signed the lease on his second home on the rue Saint-Honoré.

Clément's signature next appeared at the 1695 convocation after Simone Inselin's death, when Jean pronounced his illegitimate offspring Simone's children and therefore legitimate. This time, when called upon to identify himself, Clément responded: master *gainier*. This is hard to imagine: the registers of the guild of *gainiers*, in which Jacques I Magoulet, Hubert, and Claude all figure often and prominently, contain no mention of Clément.

Clément signed the 1695 document "C. Magoullet"—the only time he ever used an initial. His signature was sophisticated, made by someone who handled a quill with true expertise. Like Jacques', this was a carefully studied signature: it could never have developed spontaneously from the 1669 writing with which it had nothing in common but a high level of fluidity. It was instead the product of a conscious decision to create a new mark of identity.

From then on, frequent changes of professional identity and that always unstable signature were part and parcel of the identity crafted for Clément Magoullet. Clément was a human shape-shifter, someone who, each time he presented himself, took on a different persona.

Clément became a consistent rather than an episodic presence in the Magoulet family only after 1701 and Jean's marriage with Louise Poisson, the moment at which the vindictive son stripped his father of both his title the Queen's Embroiderer and his privilege to work as a master of his art. From then on, Clément seems to have been at the command no longer of the original Queen's Embroiderer but of his son and successor. From then on, Clément's many roles became more interesting.

Clément's first big part began upon Hubert Magoulet's death. On December 16, 1706, when the police arrived at 1:30 A.M. to fix the seals, Hubert's second wife, Catherine Lemaigre, described the deceased as having two brothers: Jean and Jacques. Days later, when an inventory of the couple's possessions was drawn up, Lemaigre personally named an expert to determine their value: Clément Magoullet. She made no mention of any family tie, and Clément identified himself not as a master but as a simple *gainier* working in the courtyard of Paris' Law Courts, a merchant with a small stand from which he would have sold a limited selection of goods. He provided an estimated value of 1,325 livres for the contents of Hubert's shop on the Quai de l'Horloge.

The document seems routine, at least until the end of the police file in which it is included. After the inventory's completion, Hubert's two sons, absent at the time of his death, returned to Paris and declared that two diamond rings and a diamond-studded watch "that they had often seen their father's wife wearing and that should have been included as part of the couple's possessions" were nowhere to be found. An investigation was opened, but when the widow failed to respond to numerous summonses, the case was closed.

Soon after Clément provided that estimate, on February 18, 1707, he and Lemaigre met again, this time to finalize a deal: Clément had agreed to buy Hubert's stock, which he himself had evaluated at over 1,300 livres, for just over

1,000. Even though he had already taken possession of the goods, Clément paid only 500 up front, and even that he paid in *billets de monnaie*, mint bills. By early 1707, the French financial market was so flooded with these notes that their value had vastly depreciated and no savvy merchant was willing to accept them.

Clément promised to return "within six months" with the remaining 500 "in *espèces sonnantes*"—cold, hard cash—although there is no indication that he did so. As a result of the unsavory deal with Hubert's widow, he had acquired everything an aspiring *gainier* needed to found a workshop.

Clément also walked away with the deed to a new life. Effective April 1, 1707, he took over from Hubert's widow the lease on both the shop in which Hubert's business had been housed since 1676 and the upstairs apartment in which he had lived with each of his wives. At that moment, Clément shed his murky past and gained the wherewithal to take on the identity upon which he relied when he denounced Louise to the authorities in 1719: that of a respectable merchant, a *gainier* long established on the Quai de l'Horloge at the sign of the Golden Apple.

On January 5, 1709, it became clear why Hubert's widow would have agreed to such terms. On that day, Catherine Lemaigre signed the contract that set the stage for her next marriage, to the master sculptor Louis Herpin. Only one person from her previous life as a Magoulet stood up for her: Clément. She wouldn't have wanted any of the others to see the document on the table that day.

The contract ended with an enumeration of the possessions that the bride-to-be insisted should not become part of the couple's community property. Upon seeing it, any other Magoulet would have realized that, with Clément's help, Lemaigre had indeed absconded with the jewelry Hubert's sons had reported missing, as well as a number of valuable items that had long been part of Hubert's life, including the large portrait of Louis XIV in a gilded frame that had always hung in his bedroom.

January 1709, the deadliest month of the Great Winter, would not have seemed an auspicious time for nuptials. Prices for staples of the French diet, from bread to wine, were ten times higher than usual—and by then so little coin was left in circulation that few had the ability to pay for anything. During the months that followed, thousands of homeless roamed the streets of Paris in search of shelter and food. And this was only the beginning.

The decade after that January 1709 contract was a dire one for the French in general and for the second Queen's Embroiderer in particular. Economically, it was a time of stagnation. Because of the war, nothing could be exported.

Internal commerce was anemic because of monetary shortages. And another sharp cost increase was beginning for the precious metals essential to a master embroiderer's work: between 1710 and 1723, gold and silver went up by 142 percent.

In the aftermath of the Great Winter, the country failed to shake off crisis mode. As a result, France was demographically stagnant as well, largely due to a huge national drop in the birth rate. After 1709, no more children were born in the marriage of Jean Magoulet and Louise Poisson, and the period of recorded domestic violence began.

In 1710, rainfall in France was massive, provoking widespread flooding. The excessive rainfall continued over the following two years; as a result, until 1715, harvests were poor and the cost of food remained sky high. Not until 1717, when grain once more became abundant, did prices fall.

Still another casualty of the Great Winter was Jean I's favorite brother, Jacques Magoulet; he died on December 5, 1710, just as the death toll was winding down. On December 15, an assembly was convoked to plan for the future of his four children. Once again, it was an odd lot.

The big surprise is that Jacques' oldest surviving brother as well as his closest ally in the family, the Queen's Embroiderer, though still very much alive, was not there. There was only one unscrupulous brother-in-law, plus Clément, who identified himself as the children's paternal uncle and as a merchant. He then added one further word but thought better of it and asked that it be struck from the official record. But underneath the notary's black ink, that deleted word is still legible: *gainier*. In December 1710, Clément had not yet decided to let the authorities in on this part of his new identity.

Jacques' firstborn, Jacques François, was newly of age, having turned twenty-five earlier that year. The young man, who would become the most successful businessman and by far the most successful honest businessman in the clan's history, always heeded the guidance of his mother, with whom he was still living on the rue Traversine (today the rue Molière) near the Louvre. The children's lawyer was present, and Marie Freslin's cousins packed the room. Clément did not get the nod that he had clearly expected and that would have been an obvious choice: he was elected only to the relatively powerless position of associate guardian. And rather than appoint a guardian at all, the assembly came to an uncommon decision and named the still inexperienced Jacques François to be trustee for his younger brothers. That vote kept their family's estate firmly under Marie Freslin's control.

The following day, papers came through that Jacques' family had applied for several days earlier, before they could have been sure of blocking Clément's

Queen Marie-Thérèse and her son the Dauphin shortly before Jean Magoulet served as her embroiderer.

*Facing page:* The type of embroidered panel that surrounded Louis XIV's silver throne in Versailles' Hall of Mirrors, the kind of embroidery Jean I Magoulet created.

*This page:* Intricate embroidery like this decorated grand Parisian residences in the early eighteenth century.

ABOVE: A detail from a man's waistcoat from the 1730s, so fully embroidered in metallic thread that not a speck of fabric shows.

LEFT: A man's waistcoat from the 1730s embroidered in the exotic Asian style for which Jean II Magoulet was known.

*Facing page:*
TOP: A detail from a 1740s woman's court outfit, embroidered by a French Huguenot embroidress in London.

BOTTOM: The lavish dress, for which ten pounds of silver and fourteen different types of silver thread were used.

A French leather case from the period when Hubert Magoulet served as the Queen's *gainier*.

The jeweled coffer the case was designed to protect.

The painting that decorated the ceiling of John Law's Royal Bank.

An early French wallet, crafted in 1719, when the Royal Bank began issuing banknotes.

The type of "Asian" textile imagined at Chantilly in the 1730s in the workshop of Claude Magoulet.

A porcelain jar from Chantilly in the 1730s, its design copied from *The Book of Chinese Designs*.

bid to be elected guardian: Jacques' three underage children were officially "emancipated." In other words, had they had a state-appointed guardian, they would now have been liberated from his governance. This uncustomary request was one to which families had recourse primarily when they suspected a guardian of embezzlement. Marie Freslin had thus successfully headed Clément off at the pass.

But Clément was not so easily dissuaded.

On May 29, 1714, Marie Freslin died, leaving no loose ends. On March 12, she had had a will drawn up that named Jacques François executor of a substantial estate. The standard police inventory of possessions was well under way when, nearly ten days after her death, on June 7, a bombshell hit: Clément strolled in to voice his opposition to the proceedings, a recourse available to anyone owed money by an estate. Clément claimed to be there in an official capacity, "because he had been elected associate guardian for the children of Jacques Magoulet and Marie Freslin."

A brouhaha surely ensued, for when Clément returned the next day, he was accompanied by an attorney. This time, he announced that "he hadn't been appointed to the position of associate guardian." And with that final odd twist, Clément disappeared forever from the lives of Jacques' children.

Marie Freslin had hidden the fact of her children's emancipation from Clément for the final three and a half years of her life. She had given him no chance to come up with another strategy for getting his hands on their money. And in June 1714, Clément needed funds.

On June 2, after Marie Freslin's death and before he tried to meddle in her estate, Clément signed a new lease on Hubert's former shop and apartment on the Quai de l'Horloge. It was a routine document, nearly identical to the one passed on to him by Catherine Lemaigre in 1707. Even the rent remained unchanged: 320 livres. However, two things were different. Whereas he had taken out the original lease for a *gainier*'s workshop, Clément now called himself a "jewelry merchant," someone who sold retail and wholesale jewelry but who created nothing at all, a curious profession for a member of the Magoulet dynasty of craftsmen. In addition, Clément now officially had company in the apartment.

When a married man rented an apartment, it was customary for his wife to cosign the lease; this guaranteed the property's owner that she shared responsibility for the rent. But Clément had always signed alone and had never before made mention of a wife. Among all the Magoulets, only Jean I had ever taken out a lease on his own, and he had done so only on property necessary to enable his double life.

The woman Clément identified on the lease as his wife added her signature just under his: Marie Louise Desjardins, written in the painstaking, crude script of someone at most barely literate. Her handwriting was worlds apart from the assured, polished signatures of women such as Louise Poisson and Louise Magoulet.

Clément's then current lease didn't expire until April 1, 1715, so it was premature to renew it on June 2, 1714. It's hard not to see the document as a sort of official recognition of his union with Desjardins, a public acknowledgment of her role in his life that had been made possible by the death only four days earlier of Marie Freslin, witness to the ceremony that had marked Clément's first appearance as an adult: the baptism in March 1687 of baby Marie Louise. Henceforth, there was only one eyewitness left to differentiate Louise Magoulet, born in 1701 to Louise Poisson and Jean Magoulet, from Marie Louise Magoulet, born in 1687 to Clément Magoullet. This man was Marie Louise's godfather and Louise's grandfather: the original Queen's Embroiderer. And Jean I's lips were sealed.

Marie Louise Desjardins, who in 1719 would be identified by Clément as the mother of his daughter Marie Louise, was roughly the age of Louise Poisson and thus too young to have been a mother in 1687. But it's not clear how much she could have understood about the role Clément had her play in Louise Magoulet's imprisonment.

When Marie Louise Desjardins' older sister Marie Geneviève married in 1702, their father, Nicolas Desjardins, a cabinetmaker, could sign his name, but only barely: he misspelled it, leaving off the final *s*. Both his wife and his daughter Marie Geneviève declared that they could neither read nor write. Theirs was for the time a rare situation: a completely illiterate family of Parisian artisans. Clément Magoullet, a character born from a mastery of handwriting and forgery, could thus have run circles around Marie Louise Desjardins.

By 1714, Louise Poisson had made reports about the "women of ill repute" to whom her husband was giving free rein of their home, even allowing them to wear her clothing. Marie Louise Desjardins may have been among them, and she may have been singled out because of her given name.

The child born to Jean II Magoulet and Louise Poisson in March 1702, exactly fifteen years after the baby baptized in 1687, was surely christened Marie Louise: most girls in Catholic France were traditionally given Marie as a first name and in later life often used only their second name. When she ratified any official document, Louise always signed "Marie Louise."

Were Jean II and Marie Louise Desjardins legally married? If so, they did not follow custom and sign a contract in the office of her family's notary.

Another man might have been put off by the idea of bigamy, but Clément did not scare easily. After all, bigamy was but one more infraction to add to an already long list, and actually one that the French state prosecuted rather less ferociously than the particular range of crimes on which Clément's being was founded.

In the golden age of forgery, the French judicial system punished with particular severity all aspects of the category referred to in contemporary legal treatises as *du faux*: the counterfeit, the fraudulent, the fake. Clément's existence was a textbook case of every subset of "the fraudulent" found in those treatises: forged signatures, false testimony, fallacious witnesses—the list goes on and on. All Clément's counterfeiting went to the heart of a problem of which the French state was keenly aware: he provided living, breathing proof that no reliable means of establishing identity existed.

At the turn of the eighteenth century, the most frequently encountered category of falsification of all was *supposition de personne*, the substitution of one person for another with the intent to commit fraud, or what we know as identity theft. No type of fraud was considered more dangerous than identity theft, which was punishable by death. And even Clément's raison d'être was characteristic of his age: the then most frequently encountered brand of identity theft involved the substitution of a fraudulent father or mother for a child's real parents.

The existence of a bogus Clément Magoullet could be seen as the perfect crime at a moment when the ersatz seemed to be gaining territory across France.

Indeed, he blended into his surroundings so flawlessly that I would never have detected the anomalies had I not begun to investigate the problem of Clément from an angle none of the Magoulet men would ever have considered important enough to merit camouflage: Jean II's daughter, Louise Magoulet, in particular the identity of the young woman marked for deportation under the name Marie Louise Magoulet.

The reality of someone named Clément Magoullet as a person distinct from Jean II Magoulet was possible only for those willing to accept the proposition that in 1719 two young women were both denounced to the Parisian police for public prostitution: Louise Magoulet and Marie Louise Magoulet. Both were imprisoned; both gave birth to a son in the Salpêtrière; both were included on the manifest of the ship *Mutinous*. Since this could not have been the case, I soon realized that there was no Clément Magoullet.

By 1723, if any officers of the Parisian police had been paying serious attention to the plight of the five children of Jean Magoulet and Louise Poisson, they could no longer have avoided confronting just this dilemma and realizing that they were dealing with a fraudulent "Clément Magoullet." The police would then have caught on to Jean's decision in 1719 to identify his daughter as twenty-seven rather than seventeen. (He should of course have said thirty-two, since that would have been the correct age of the baby baptized in 1687, but he surely decided that Louise didn't appear to be over thirty.) By modifying that basic component of his daughter's identity, her age, Jean was able to reenact the moment in his own life when, in the aftermath of his mother's death, in order to deal with his son's claims to his mother's estate, his father had officially declared him older than he in fact was and thus made him legally of age.

In 1719, Louise's marriage to Louis and their baby Jean Louis became collateral damage in the second Queen's Embroiderer's war with his past.

# CHAPTER FOURTEEN

# "The Incredible Madness of the 20th Year of the Eighteenth Century"

## Louise Magoulet and Louis Chevrot: 1720

THE CEREMONY WITH the young king in attendance that Law orchestrated in the Royal Bank on December 30, 1719 was intended to convince French and foreign investors that all was well and that France would long remain a land of economic prosperity. Bounty from the Mississippi would continue to flow into the Seine; the fruits of the earth and all forms of money would always be abundant in France, just as the cornucopias featured on the Royal Bank's staircase promised.

On January 3, Parisians awakened to the news that the Royal Bank would no longer redeem its bills for silver. Caumartin de Boissy, the individual who had announced the arrival of stock market fever, now reported that "confidence has been shaken."

To prove that his faith had not faltered, on January 5, the regent appointed Law France's minister of finance: this was the final jewel in his crown. On Monday, January 8, Indies Company stock hit its all-time high: 10,100.

But Law no longer controlled the market, and shares began to fall. Already that same month, the English ambassador, the Earl of Stair, reported that the foreign investors who had rushed to Paris in droves in late 1719 had now "deserted" the French capital. Stair added that many were facing bankruptcy because they had invested heavily in Law's system.

As of August 1719, inflation had first begun to weigh on all those who were not becoming rich quickly. It averaged 4 percent a month from then on and peaked in January 1720, when it soared to 23 percent. As a result, the cost of basic commodities went through the roof. Before the crisis brought on by Law's system, a Parisian worker earned four livres a day; by early 1720, workers were holding out for six livres to make up for that spike in prices. Edmond Jean Barbier, a lawyer for the Parisian Parlement whose diary chronicles Paris under Law's rule, stressed that "everyone is suffering infinitely, except for a tiny handful of those who made great fortunes, and their excessive wealth is only driving everyone else ever deeper into ruin." Caumartin de Boissy warned his sister that "Paris is no longer the city you once knew."

On Thursday, February 22, without warning the Royal Bank shut its doors while Law attempted to deal with rising inflation and the excess of paper in circulation. That abrupt closure put an end to a spectacle for which Ambassador Stair had just coined a name: the February 1720 panic-driven withdrawals from the Royal Bank were the first "runs" on a bank to be referred to by that term.

Only five days after the bank closed, on February 27, a royal edict made it a crime to possess more than 500 livres in coinage, punishable by a 10,000-livre fine and the confiscation of all coin. That same day, after one of the most rapid crossings ever recorded, *Mutinous* reached Louisiana with its cargo of women "fit for the islands."

When the bank reopened on Tuesday, March 5, the price of a share of Indies Company stock had been fixed at 9,000 livres, payable only in banknotes. France's national currency had been converted into shares in the private company controlled by Law. This was the beginning of the end.

The months that followed the bank's closing became known as the Scarlet Spring: the contrast between penury and excess ignited a savage crime wave that transformed Paris into a city of mean streets and roaming predators. Bourlon's little secret had become public knowledge, and all over town, pickpockets stopped at nothing to get their hands on a wallet fat with banknotes, so everyone walked the capital's streets in fear. In March, Parisians were horrified by a spate of murders carried out on or near the rue Quincampoix. And by then, the assassins came from all ranks of society.

On March 22, Parisians learned that a young noble, the Comte de Horn, had knifed a successful speculator to death before absconding with his wallet containing 150,000 livres, all in broad daylight in a cabaret adjacent to the rue Quincampoix. The authorities shut the market down: the rue Quincampoix was closed off, and people were forbidden to gather there. On March 26, a complete ban on "all trading in any form of paper" was issued. State-sponsored speculation had lasted a mere seven months.

The Scarlet Spring became ever bloodier. In early April, lawyer Barbier chronicled the latest horrors: "For the past week, the police have been fishing out of the river a great quantity of arms, legs, and various sawed-off slices of the corpses of those who have been assassinated and cut into pieces. Everyone blames the violence on the despicable speculation in paper."

At that critical juncture, Law attempted to revive interest in "the Mississippi." An article in April's *New Gallant Mercury* informed readers about the "prodigious quantities of silver" that the colony was sending back to France and added that after testing at the Paris mint, Louisiana silver had been pronounced purer than any previously known. The article predicted that French mines would prove more productive than the fabled Potosi silver lode from Bolivia that had been a foundation of Spain's colonial wealth.

On April 24, Law took advantage of the state of turmoil in the capital to reactivate forced deportation. He created a special branch of the Parisian police force; its officers were known as *bandouliers* because of the blue-and-white bandoliers across their chests. Armed with swords and pistols, the *bandouliers* were in reality bounty hunters. They patrolled the capital's streets and had the power to arrest on the spot any young man or woman who could be described as *sans aveu*, vagrants with no one to stand up for them. In addition to their daily wage of a livre, *bandouliers* were promised a bonus of 15 livres for every colonist they brought in.

But this time Law did not get his way. Newspapers quickly began to warn of false arrests, honest workers accused of vagrancy and spirited away. Soon, whenever *bandouliers* were spotted, an angry mob would attack the bounty hunters and prevent arrests: one uprising left eight officers dead. On Sunday, May 12, by royal decree the second French experiment with permanent exile came to an end. The last chain gang sent to Louisiana, 212 men, arrived at the port of Lorient on May 29.

Instead, to make up for the lack of French deportees, in the spring of 1720 the Indies Company began to increase dramatically the number of slaves sent to Louisiana from Africa.

Investors remained jittery all that spring. After March 5, when Law first set the price of shares, he had planned a phased reduction, with a goal of 5,500 by the end of the year. But shares soon fell below the new threshold. After the March 5 decree, many professional investors moved their money to London. Law sought to calm the waters with a long letter in the April issue of the *New Gallant Mercury* assuring investors that shares were both robust and vastly undervalued, a sounder investment than real estate. But merchants were increasingly suspicious of banknotes: in late April, when a customer in Paris' Les Halles market tried to pay with a ten-livre note, the fishmonger "trampled it into the mud."

On Monday, May 20, stock stood at just over 8,000, but the next day a royal decree was pronounced: both banknotes and shares were to be devalued by 20 percent, effective May 22. Investors with insider information unloaded their shares on the 20th and 21st, at 8,000.

Ambassador Stair described Paris on May 22 as "a city taken by storm": the combination of the May 21 decree and early rumors that no silver had been found in Louisiana provoked a major sell-off. The Royal Bank was shut all morning; when it opened in the afternoon, the new decree was in effect. On May 25, a mob stoned the bank and shattered most of its windows. From then on, ordinary investors worried not only about which type of currency was still accepted and up to what amount, but about which kind might be soon devalued, or even phased out. As Barbier remarked, "terror had begun to inhabit investors." The party was over.

Stock declined precipitously by more than the planned 20 percent, to 6,000. By May 27, the price had fallen to 4,000. And between May 28 and May 30 alone, stock declined by 44 percent. On May 29, Law lost his position as finance minister.

On May 31, the *Amsterdam Gazette* published its first negative assessment of Law's policies. By then, Mathieu Marais, a lawyer for the Parisian Parlement who chronicled the madness of 1720, had concluded: "There is no longer any honor, any word of honor, any good faith." Marais cited the Duc de La Force, peer of the realm and scion of one of France's oldest families. The duke had made more than 40 million livres from his investments but was nonetheless cutting deals that obliged his brother and his closest friends to accept reduced payments on debts he had long owed them. "French nobility has never been less noble than it is now," Marais lamented.

Only a year after speculation mania had begun, at even the pinnacle of French society, behavior typical of Jean Magoulet had become the norm.

Louise had returned to Paris' mean streets just in time to witness the Scarlet Spring and the arrival of the *bandouliers*. Had she been recognized as a deserter from *Mutinous*, she would have been shipped off again, instantly and without recourse. But on May 20, she came briefly out of hiding. That day, Marie Geneviève, Clément's child with Desjardins, was married, and Louise was present to stand up for her younger half sister. Her loyalty to Geneviève, like Jean's to Nicolas, was unwavering.

Many things are odd about the contract for Geneviève's marriage to the master shoemaker Nicolas Peradin. It was not drawn up, as was traditional, by the notary of the bride's family, but by someone who had never seen Clément Magoullet before: the notary of the groom's family. The bombshell, however, was the dowry bestowed on Geneviève by her parents. Jean had had insider information, probably from his crony Jean-Jacques de Mesmes, close confidant of both Law and the regent in the spring of 1720, that devaluation was imminent.

Nothing about Jean's life as Clément was high end: he paid a mere 320 livres a year rent for the shop and apartment on the Quai de l'Horloge; when Desjardins died in 1725, the contents of their home totaled barely 600 livres. And yet on May 20, 1720, Clément promised Geneviève 1,500 livres, a extraordinarily handsome dowry for the daughter of a run-of-the-mill artisan at a moment when Parisians of this rank were living in full crisis mode, unable to afford even basic necessities. In addition, whereas most dowries were paid at best only after the marriage ceremony in a church and often over a period of years, Clément handed over the full payment that very afternoon. He demanded that the young couple agree that by accepting the dowry, Geneviève renounced any future claims to the estates of her parents. Those 1,500 livres were all she would ever see from her father. And she did not enjoy them for long.

The young couple had surely been thrilled with that princely sum, but reality would have quickly set in. The compact carefully stipulated that the dowry was paid in *billets de la banque royale*, the very banknotes that were officially devalued the day after the marriage contract was signed and notarized.

On May 25, a ship docked in the French Mediterranean port of Marseille, bringing from the Levant a cargo of cotton cloth. This textile was deadly: it carried fleas infected with the bubonic plague. The disease spread rapidly through the city, killing nearly half its inhabitants, and then throughout southern France, where a quarter of the population succumbed to the infection. The Great Plague of Marseille was the last significant European outbreak of the bubonic plague.

For months, Parisians were terrified that the plague would devastate their city. The disease was successfully contained in the south, but the specter of the plague lent an apocalyptic air to the summer of 1720. Religious leaders warned that the pestilence was a divine punishment for the greed that had overtaken the country.

By June 2, the runs on the Royal Bank had assumed monumental proportions: "Today was a bloodbath," Marais reported. The bank was open only in the morning, and each client could obtain a maximum of 100 livres. Barbier summed it up: "Everything is topsy-turvy and constantly changing. The only thing certain is that we all continue to lose money and that we will all be ruined."

By June 3, no merchant would accept payment in banknotes, but on June 11, still another edict decreed that anyone making a payment over 100 livres was obliged to use only banknotes or face a 3,000-livre fine. Soon, on the rare days when the Royal Bank did open its doors, investors trying to redeem the increasingly worthless notes in their possession obtained only pennies on the dollar.

From then on, the crowds that began to gather at 3 A.M. in the hope of getting into the bank to redeem notes before the limited daily supply of money ran out were so huge and so feverish that people were dying in the crush. On June 5 alone, one observer noted that two women and three men had been trampled to death.

There was precious little coinage left in the city, and prices were skyrocketing: virtually overnight, the price of a yard of cloth jumped from 12 to 80 livres. Already by 3 A.M. on June 17, more than fifteen thousand people had gathered in the street in front of the bank. By then, riots had begun to break out all over the city.

After that, it only went downhill. One day, notes would lose 75 percent of their value; the next, a royal proclamation would assure the population that there was nothing to worry about. Sometimes you could get only 10 livres in silver for a 1,000-livre banknote. On June 14, Marais lamented: "No one has a coin left to their name. Never before in modern memory or in history have Parisians been reduced to this state."

On July 3, Marais reported that the Scarlet Spring was bleeding into a scarlet summer: a jeweler named Capel had been robbed and brutally murdered; his corpse had been left lying exposed, virtually under Clément's windows on the Quai de l'Horloge. He added that banknotes had lost another 35 percent of their value and that he had stood in line at the bank from 6 A.M. to 6 P.M. just to get a 1,000-livre note broken. The rejection of paper was so widespread that on July 17 it officially became a crime: Parisians could go to the police to report merchants who declined paper money; officers had orders to "immediately" fine them double the sum they had refused.

By Saturday, July 6, the Royal Bank was bankrupt. That same day, a card game was organized to amuse the young monarch: Louis XV had his heart set on a bit of gambling, but he ordered his guests to bring coin: "he didn't want to see any banknotes." Even the king of France refused to touch the notes issued by his nation's official bank and under his own protection.

Law later described May 27 as having marked "the end" of his system: on that day, Parisians were introduced to the ultimate proof of the failure of his reforms when it was announced that it would once again be possible to purchase annuities issued by Paris' Hôtel de Ville. The government had decided that this was the only way to absorb some of the vast quantities of banknotes still in circulation. In early June, when notaries began issuing annuity contracts, investors rushed to sign up, despite the fact that the new annuities were far less attractive than previous ones. Whereas in 1714, an investment of 10,000 livres had come with a guarantee of an annual income of 400 livres, in 1720 the same sum promised a return of only 250 per annum.

Those new annuities naturally necessitated a new administration. Indeed, the June issue of the *New Gallant Mercury* contained this announcement: twelve positions as payers and twelve as controllers were being created; even foreign papers such as the *Amsterdam Gazette* reported on this development. And when the October issues of Parisian papers published the names of those newly appointed, Antoine Chevrot was number 11 on the list of controllers. Antoine thus had the double satisfaction of having his raison d'être in the world returned to him and of seeing the news broadcast far and wide.

He paid dearly for the pleasure. Antoine's parents had invested 20,000 livres in his original post; in the climate of wild inflation that characterized the end of Law's system, the government was asking 50,000 for the new ones. In August and September 1720, Antoine was taking out loans that would have ruinous effects for years to come.

Antoine had known that Louis still intended to marry Louise well before July 1720. But somehow the matter seems not to have caused him undue concern as long as he himself remained in social limbo. The minute he felt that his life was being returned to him, however, he changed his tune.

Antoine was assuming a colossal amount of debt, far more than he could handle, and his moment was poorly chosen. In the summer of 1720, only the most successful speculators had money to lend; they knew full well that the deck was stacked in their favor, and they set their terms accordingly. Antoine perhaps told himself that he had Louis' interests at heart, even though by then he surely realized that Louis did not share his conviction that the post of annuities controller was the finest inheritance that a Chevrot could pass on to his son.

In July 1720, Paris was going down in flames: so many were being killed during the daily riots near the Royal Bank that six thousand soldiers were called away from their posts and stationed nearby; they were given orders to open fire on the "mutinous population" if anyone tried to loot elements of the bank's grand décor. What must the beleaguered Parisian police have thought when, as their city was veering out of control, on July 8 Antoine Chevrot showed up to declare his eldest son missing and to denounce a young woman for having "abducted" him?

That same month of July, Louis and Louise began for a second time to approach priests they hoped would be sympathetic to their cause. They tried first a curate in Saint-Ouen, a village near Clignancourt, someone they had known during the summer of Louise's pregnancy. He went straight to the top and addressed a request for permission to marry them to Louis Antoine de Noailles, cardinal and archbishop of Paris, but to no avail.

On August 4, banns, the official announcement of an impending marriage, were published in Paris' Saint-Eustache church. This was Louis' parish church, as well as that of Noel Poisson; its curate was the priest who knew them best. Faced with objections, surely from Antoine, he was forced to back down. They tried a third curate: still more banns were published at Saint-Barthélemy church, but with the same result. Three priests had so believed in their commitment that they had agreed to perform a marriage ceremony even without parental consent, but the young couple had not been able to wed. At this point, Louis and Louise realized that even the Catholic Church could not countermand their fathers' will.

By mid-August, France's capital had become so violent that a government official described Paris as "at present a country detested by all." Louis and Louise fled their homeland's toxic environment.

They arrived in London in late August. On September 7, they were married there. In all their years of hiding and running, none of their other exploits can begin to compare to what they pulled off in order to make that ceremony happen.

Louis and Louise could not have foreseen that London, too, would be gripped by the very madness they were fleeing.

When Law took control of the French economy, his plans were closely followed in England and Holland, the other nations carrying massive national debt after the War of the Spanish Succession. In January 1720, the English decided to float shares in their South Sea Company to help reduce that debt. At first, the scheme went very well indeed for investors: from 120 in late January, shares rose to 950 on July 12.

Louis and Louise reached London just in time to see history repeat itself. In August, the frenzied speculation that soon became known as the South Sea Bubble reached fever pitch; shortly after their arrival, the English house of cards began to collapse. On September 6, the day before Louis and Louise were wed, the *Amsterdam Gazette* warned that the situation was deteriorating rapidly. By September 24, the bubble had burst: the *Amsterdam Gazette* reported that because of their excessive risk taking, investors in all ranks of English society faced bankruptcy and financial ruin. By October 1, shares had fallen to 290; by year's end, they were down to where they had started in January.

During the final three months of 1720, the English financial system teetered precariously. The government bailout undertaken in 1721 and 1722 to stabilize it was so massive that nearly three centuries later, on December 27, 2014, Britons learned that even today they continue to pay interest on those loans.

On Saturday, September 7, just as reality was setting in and all over London investors were trying to dump rapidly falling stock, at a moment when money was scarce and prices sky high, a wedding took place. It was a quiet affair: just the bride and groom and two hastily assembled witnesses were present.

In eighteenth-century London, Catholics worshipped only in secret, in private chapels or in the chapels of ambassadors from Catholic countries. Embassy sanctuaries enjoyed diplomatic immunity; their clergymen were allowed to celebrate mass and perform the sacraments. On May 31, 1720, the *Amsterdam Gazette* reported that the Duchy of Savoy was taking control of the Kingdom of Sardinia. By September, the embassy of the Kingdom of Sardinia in the Lincoln's Inn area of the city on what is now Sardinia Street added a new sanctuary to that list.

In the mid-eighteenth century, when that chapel had become the best known and the most fashionable of all Catholic embassy shrines in London and among the most prestigious churches in the city, the Bishop of London referred to it as an "ersatz cathedral." By then, its services were open to the public at large, and seven chaplains officiated there.

But in 1720 the Sardinian Chapel was hardly London's "ersatz cathedral." In fact, since the earliest previously known records of its functioning date from 1722, Louis and Louise's marriage may well have been the first sacrament performed there.

In the midst of madding crowds feverish over stock prices, these two strangers in a land growing stranger by the moment had somehow learned that they could be wed in a chapel so new that it was completely under the radar. The Sardinian Chapel seems not yet to have been fully functional, but Louis and Louise managed to become legally united somewhere on the tiny territory under the protection of the Sardinian embassy in London.

The cleric who pronounced them man and wife was then himself in a similar sort of legal limbo.

On their license, written in Latin, the pan-European ecclesiastical language, he identified himself as Henrico (Henry) Clerek, one of many pseudonyms used by this most mysterious man of the cloth. Certainly the word "cleric"—a member of the clergy in any religion—aptly sums up his ambiguous status.

In the long campaign later launched by Antoine Chevrot to have their marriage annulled, he always referred to the man who performed the ceremony with one of the clergyman's more frequently assumed names: Moyses. Clerek alias Moyses, English and born in 1701, was an exact contemporary of Louis

*Document certifying that Louis Chevrot and Louise Magoulet were legally married in London on September 7, 1720.*

and Louise. He led a peripatetic life, coming and going between England, France, and Portugal. He was christened George Whitaker, though he preferred to be known as John Frankland or John Moyses or Moses.

"Clerek" spent much of 1719 in France, especially in Boulogne on the edge of the English Channel, where he could have encountered Louis and Louise after her escape. Their marriage license is the only indication of his associa-tion with the Sardinian Chapel—or indeed with Catholicism—prior to 1722.

As he later recorded it himself, the official history of the individual known variously as Whitaker, Clerek, Moyses, Frankland, and Franklin goes like this: He was so moved by a sermon delivered at the Sardinian Chapel in November 1722 that he converted to Catholicism. He left England for Portugal, and early in 1723 he entered Lisbon Seminary, a college where English students studied for the Catholic priesthood. He was ordained a Catholic priest in Lisbon on June 15, 1726 and returned to England on September 7, 1727, seven years to the day after he had officiated at a Catholic ceremony in London at a moment in his life when he was not yet a priest and not yet even a convert to Catholicism.

Yet somehow no authority ever contested the right of "Clerek" to marry Louis and Louise on September 7, 1720, and there were many with a legiti-mate right to do so. There were to begin with the two women who identified themselves as "representatives of the King of Sardinia" and who served as witnesses: Andrea Swaddell and Margareta Liane. There was Hercule Thomas Roero, Marquis de Cortanze, known to the French as Courtance, the diplo-mat who represented Sardinia at the English court: Clerek was described as "one of his chapelains." There was the man who on September 20 added his signature to the certificate that vouched for the ceremony's legality, the tem-porary head of the French embassy in London, chargé d'affaires Chammorel. And lest anyone wonder whether the marriage certificate had been forged by the by then desperate young lovers, Chammorel's signature perfectly matches those found on numerous contemporary documents. As a further guarantee, Chammorel also affixed the seal of his office.

Not even the two men who had first challenged the couple's right to marry, their fathers, contested the ceremony's legality. As long as Louise remained Clément's daughter and thus unable to claim a share of Louise Poisson's estate, Jean had no objections: this explains why he was careful to distinguish between Louise Magoulet, daughter of the Queen's Embroiderer, and Marie Louise Magoulet, daughter of Clément Magoullet, a simple *gainier*. In fact, on Wednes-day, October 23, 1720, Clément initiated the process of having their English marriage legalized in France by "depositing" the certificate with a Parisian notary; the document would thus have been on record so that anyone who doubted their claim could examine it. True to form, Clément chose a notary, Jean Baptiste DeJean, with whom no Magoulet had had prior dealings, still another representative of the French state who simply accepted the word of the man sitting before him that he was, as he claimed to be, "Clément Magoul-let, Parisian merchant."

A week before Clément's visit to the notary, on October 17, upon Antoine's encouragement, Louis' maternal grandparents had written to Louis II Phélypeaux, Marquis de La Vrillière, to ask that Louis be confined to Bicêtre, the correctional facility that was the equivalent of the Salpêtrière for men. The minute he learned of that English certificate, Antoine ratcheted up the pressure by many notches. Already on October 24, he made the first of innumerable requests to the Parisian Parlement to have their marriage annulled.

When they returned to Paris, Louis and Louise found that the situation had only deteriorated during the weeks they had spent in London. On the eve of their wedding, a mob had turned on Law, hurling stones and mud at his carriage. By then, the Parisian marketplace was in a state of paralysis: the stock market's failure had shut down all other commerce in the city.

On September 15, still more monetary laws had been made public. One specified that promissory notes would continue to be honored, but at only 25 percent of their stated value. Marais concluded wryly: "It was as if we were all being told that if we had agreed to pay someone 1,000 livres, we could suddenly get away with giving them 250: now panic is really setting in."

That same week, the *Amsterdam Gazette* reported that terrible storms had destroyed the harvest and even entire villages in many parts of France. Cardinal de Noailles published a pastoral letter proclaiming these natural disasters further divine punishment for stock market greed. The cardinal characterized the profits from speculation as "criminal wealth" and chastised those who had most benefited for their "lack of compassion for the misery of their brothers."

On October 9, Caumartin de Boissy recorded his latest fear: "Hundred-livre banknotes are now worth only 27; before we know it, bills will be worthless." The very next day, his prophecy came true.

On October 10, banknotes were "abolished." An October 24 decree ordered all those who "had managed in a very short time to attain a level of opulence odious to the public and contrary to the good of the state to turn over all their stock to the Indies Company." Of course, as Marais observed, "no one believes they'll ever see their stock again." On October 28, four days after Antoine first took legal action against Louise, the Royal Bank was likewise "abolished." This time, Marais concluded: "All those millions and millions of millions are now reduced to zeros."

As 1720 drew to an end and the system's unraveling became complete, staples such as coffee and candles were nine times more expensive than in pre-inflationary days. Marais estimated that Law's system had made "a thousand people fabulously rich" while it had "reduced 100,000 hard-working Parisians to poverty."

The parish priest of Saint-Sulpice, among the wealthiest churches in Paris, confronted one parishioner, a duke whose fortune had been vastly increased through speculation, to explain that his own servants, whose wages and living expenses he had paid in banknotes, were living off the parish's charity. There was a wave of suicides among artisans and small shopkeepers who had no way of feeding themselves and their children. In the end, Law's experiment had reduced the French to a state of misery identical to that created in 1694 and 1708 by the combined forces of war, winter, and pestilence.

Insider information made it possible for the 1 percent to come away from the collapse in possession of their fine new millions. They had always moved from one currency to another just ahead of devaluations. Rare were the small investors who came out well.

Marais described in detail the day he spent "suffocating" in the crush, trying to convert his stock before it lost all value: he was sent from one clerk to the next; he handed over his shares and in exchange his name, "as it appeared on his baptismal certificate," was written in a ledger, along with the information on his shares. By the end of the day, he walked away "with only a receipt, a little scrap of paper signed by an official named de La Nauze." "No one," he concluded, "has any idea about what will happen next."

Barbier opened his journal for 1721 by reflecting: "Last year I possessed 60,000 livres in paper; I knew this wealth was imaginary, but I didn't have either the intelligence or the good fortune to cash it in for silver, and it is now worthless."

At year's end, when it was clear that the game was up, decrees were published to encourage Parisians to use their banknotes to buy annuities before it was too late. First November 10, then November 30, and finally December 31 became the "ultimate" deadline for converting bills before they lost all value. Among the last to get in under the wire was Jean Magoulet. He had hoped, almost to the bitter end, to be able to avoid doing so. And it's easy to see why.

On December 20, a very unusual "meeting" took place in the presence of the same officers of the Parisian police who just over two years earlier had presided over Jean's appointment as guardian to his children. In this context, Jean was obliged to include Louise as one of the "five underage children of Louise Poisson." Once again, in an assembly gathered to make decisions regarding his children's welfare, their only blood relation present was Noel Poisson. Jean's uncle-in-law Guillaume Morel, who could always be counted on when there was dirty work to be done, was there, as well as one of the small circle of friends present at the original convocation. Once again, this was a group tailored to defend Jean's interests rather than his children's.

The most problematic aspect of all was the assembly's rationale. They were voting to give Jean a highly irregular permission: "to be able to employ the sum of 3,000 livres which belongs to the children for the acquisition of annuities." While such major investors in Law's system as the Princesse de Conti, Antoine Crozat, and the Chevrot family protector, the Duchesse Du Lude, were doing the same thing at exactly the same moment, there was a key difference in this case. They had speculated with their own funds, whereas Jean had used money from his dead wife's estate that was intended for his children's needs. He had invested Louise Poisson's dowry in some form of paper issued by the Royal Bank, and now he was taking a loss and converting the soon to be worthless paper into an annuity.

On December 19, 1720, John Law slipped out of Paris; as an ultimate favor, the regent had granted him a passport, making it possible for him to escape the country where so many saw him as the cause of their ruin. On December 21, in the dead of a moonless night, Law fled France. On January 5, 1721, the Indies Company was broken up into the smaller units. By that April, Barbier reported that a share in its stock, "for which some Parisians had paid 15,000 of their hard-earned cash, was worth 55." By then, a rumor was circulating: "a vast number" of natives had set upon colonists newly settled in New Orleans while they slept in their brand-new homes; "1,500 of both sexes had been slaughtered."

Three centuries later, the jury is still out on John Law. In an essay written two decades after Law's flight, one of his earliest defenders, Voltaire, contended that he had revolutionized the way business was done in France, bringing the country into the modern age; that it was because of Law that France had acquired a navy worthy of the name; and that if only Law hadn't pushed reform too far and too fast and raised share prices to an unsustainable level, by 1738, France would have become "the most robust and powerful economy in the universe."

Many economic theorists still share Voltaire's view that, nearly until the end, Law's system had greatly benefited the French and the French nation. They observe that Law succeeded in paying down the massive war debt run up by Louis XIV. In its September 1720 issue, the *New Gallant Mercury* ran an article with the first published estimate of that debt—2 billion 62 million livres—and explaining how, with Law's help, the regent had been able to retire it. His modern defenders also consider Law a gifted financial engineer:

*In late 1720, Bernard Picart created this vision of the "incredible madness"*
*of the year then ending.*

they point out that he modernized France's antiquated tax collection methods
and that his system produced a successful alternative to a silver-based monetary system as well as vastly increased access to credit.

But in December 1720, no one would have dared take up Law's defense.
Instead, for many Parisians, this image by the engraver Bernard Picart stood
as the only possible view of the year they had just endured. Picart's print imagining "a monument commemorating the incredible madness" of 1720 was circulating in Paris on December 7, just as investors were turning in the last of
their banknotes and shares.

The year was not yet out, but Picart was already conjuring up posterity's view
of 1720. Indians with MISSISSIPPI emblazoned on their feathered headdresses
share the street with investors carrying paper "contracts" issued by the bank
and the Indies Company. The goddess of fortune dances over it all, tossing more
bits of paper into the crowd, while people from all walks of life, women as well
as men, frantically try to catch some. A sign reading QUINQUENPOIX (*sic*) is
posted on the upper right, identifying the street that would go down to posterity as the place where the singular madness at the heart of 1720 found a home.

Women are crying; soldiers are striking people to the ground; one man is pummeling another violently with his bare hands; still another has been crushed to death under the wheels of the cart belonging to "a trading company" and driven by Folly in the guise of an eighteenth-century Frenchwoman.

The image is a faultless visual re-creation of the message found in the numerous chronicles left by Parisian eyewitnesses. The true contagious disease of 1720 was the modern world's first ever investment fever rather than its last ever bubonic plague. Greed and savage inhumanity were the twin horsemen of the apocalypse into which John Law had led the French nation.

Louis and Louise had been caught in the maelstrom of the two original stock market boom and bust cycles but had managed to turn the pandemonium to their own advantage. In 1719, Louise had been arrested and deported in the name of John Law. But in 1720, the havoc wreaked by Law's system made her marriage possible. And at the end of that incredibly mad year, Louis and Louise were at long last able to live as man and wife.

# CHAPTER FIFTEEN

# *Aftershocks*
# Everyone: 1721–1723

THE COLLECTIVE INSANITY that had gripped France did not come to
an end on December 21, 1720 when John Law slipped across the frontier
and into the obscurity in which he spent the rest of his life. By February 5,
1721, the Parisian lawyer Mathieu Marais reported, those who hadn't cashed
out early could get only 7 livres in silver for a 100-livre bill and only 63 for a
1,000-livre note. On May 15, Marais chronicled the suicide of Bergeron de La
Goupillière, among the principal counselors to the Parisian Parlement: he
shot himself in the head "out of grief at having invested all he had in banknotes.
The death toll from Law's System is mounting up." That same month, an
Amsterdam periodical, the *Lettres historiques* (*Historical Letters*), summed up a
nation's plight: "No one can see how France will ever emerge from the laby-
rinth of misery into which the entire country has been plunged."

Caumartin de Boissy explained to his relatives in the provinces that at the
French court, previously known as the place where foreigners came to spot the
latest trends in fashion, outmoded was now in: even on days when new ambassadors came to present their credentials, everyone dressed down, "wearing only
their old clothes, outfits now faded and completely out of date."

On September 30, he named the obsession that had replaced investment
fever: he called it *faute d'argent*, want of money, or poverty. "The collective
tragedy that we call poverty has reduced us all to a point of no return. Everyone to whom we owe money is demanding that we settle up, but no one will
pay us what they owe or extend any credit." France had become a society in
which everyone owed everyone, and no one was able to retire their debts.

On May 17, 1721, the guild of Parisian leather goods artisans sent bailiff Pierre Lesage to the home Jean Magoulet shared with Anne Legrand to collect the 26 livres and 8 sous still owed on her deceased husband's taxes. Pierre Chicot had settled his accounts for 1717 but not the tax due for the months of 1718 prior to his death. Jean, as usual, simply lied: he claimed that since he and Legrand were already married in 1718, she was not responsible for Chicot's debts from that year.

When the bailiff insisted on proof, Jean threatened "to throw him out the window unless he left their apartment immediately." He cursed Lesage, punched him in the nose, grabbed a sword, and promised "to run him through twenty times." Jean worked himself into such a "terrible furor" that it took the combined forces of the bailiff, the soldier who had accompanied him, Legrand, and a visitor to force him into a room where they could lock him up. Bailiff Lesage headed for a nearby café, "right at the tip of the Pont Neuf," to write a report recommending that Jean be punished for "having mistreated and rebelled against officers of the law."

And so it was that Jean spent roughly three weeks in Paris' debtors' prison, For-l'Évêque. In Jean's case, its location virtually next door to his home was convenient. In his defense to Gabriel Teschereau, Seigneur de Baudry, who would never have recognized the name Magoulet since he had taken office as lieutenant general of the Parisian police in July 1720, well after Clément Magoullet's accusations against Louise, Jean identified himself as a "master embroiderer," repeated his lie about their 1718 marriage, and argued that "the entire neighborhood would testify in his favor." Someone apparently did, for on June 9, Baudry signed an order for Jean's release.

At For-l'Évêque, Jean narrowly missed the chance of walking in the prison courtyard with France's most celebrated thief, the bandit Cartouche, whose wife had been part of Louise's chain gang. On March 2, 1721, Cartouche had pulled off the daring jailbreak that turned him into a Parisian celebrity.

The Parisians who relished Cartouche's exploits were also terrified of becoming his next victim. On June 16, Caumartin de Boissy reported that Cartouche roamed the city's rooftops freely: "Every night, he slips down to rob someone new." On October 14, officers finally succeeded in arresting Cartouche once again. The police wasted no time blaming the city's long-term crime wave on Cartouche and his accomplices. On November 27, when the twenty-eight-year-old legend was publicly executed, record crowds packed the square in front of City Hall. Before he was put to death, Cartouche professed his love for Louise's fellow escapee, Marie Antoinette Néron, swore that she knew nothing about his illegal activities, and publicly proclaimed John Law responsible for all his crimes.

In 1721, like his country, Antoine Chevrot was sinking to new depths.

During the years when most Frenchmen were struggling, the vintner Barthélemy Langlois had fallen behind on the rent for a small farm that Antoine's father had inherited from his Bajou aunt. By February 1721, Langlois owed Antoine 35 livres, barely more than Jean's tax bill. Rather than simply press him for payment, as others of his rank who found themselves in similar situations were doing, Antoine initiated legal proceedings against Langlois, suing him again and again and again: there were so many lawsuits that after Antoine's death in 1729, Louis requested that the notary inventorying his father's papers stop noting all the dates.

And on May 17, just when the Amsterdam papers were announcing that the French would never find their way back from the brink and as lawyers were putting guns to their heads, and the day when Jean was arrested for nonpayment of taxes, Antoine kicked off the longest running and most complex legal battle of his life: his struggle to make his son's marriage to Louise disappear.

Seven months had passed since Antoine's first motion in October 1720. He had used the time to bone up on the law.

Antoine never appealed to an ecclesiastical tribunal to contend that his son's marriage had been invalidly contracted: he argued instead that the Catholic Church itself was the problem. He thus transformed Louis and Louise's love story into a case study with particular resonance in 1721 because of what by then had become one of the great European battles between church and state for control over the institution of marriage. It was the French equivalent of Henry VIII's attempts to bend canon law to his will.

Antoine's appeal was directed to the Parisian Parlement: he counted on the Parlement's lawyers to agree that Louis, the grandson of someone who had served in their own ranks, could not be allowed either to disgrace his family or to ruin their and his chances for social advancement. Antoine further addressed his appeal not to the regent then governing France, but to the twelve-year-old destined to reign as Louis XV, surely hoping that someone still not of age himself would understand the dilemma of a father trying to protect his underage son from predators. And rather than identify himself through reference to his current position as a controller, Antoine chose a title from his past, and called himself valet de chambre of the king's beloved mother, the Duchesse de Bourgogne.

The document entered into the registers of the Paris Parlement on May 17, 1721 established, at Antoine's request, a tribunal constituted to judge his case against Louise Magoulet and her father. Though it's hard to believe that Antoine didn't know Louise's name, in his lengthy presentation of evidence he referred to her only as "the daughter of Clément Magoullet" or "Marie." He identified Clément not as a craftsman or someone who exercised a real profession, and not even as a true merchant, but as a simple *vendeur*, someone who merely sold things—in his case eyeglasses.

He described Clément's daughter as thirty-two and thus older than the woman described in 1719 as twenty-seven. In addition, Antoine knew about Louise's time in the Salpêtrière, for he further identified the woman he accused of "having seduced his underage son" and of "having taken him to England" in order to "trick him" into marrying her as having been "confined to the General Hospital on charges of debauchery."

The document enumerated the reasons why their marriage in London should be considered invalid: his son had been "kidnapped"; he was underage and did not have his father's consent; no banns had been published at the Sardinian Chapel to request permission to perform the ceremony; his parish priest did not officiate; there were only two witnesses. In the overall context, some of those points might seem insignificant, but all were key to Antoine's argument about distinctions between canon and civil marriage law. He had chosen to attack his son's marriage as *comme d'abus*, a French legal term that designated appeals referred to the Parisian Parlement on the grounds that, in those matters, it enjoyed jurisdictional supremacy over ecclesiastical tribunals. Antoine was claiming thereby that when the church had chosen to recognize Louis' marriage, it had interfered in judicial territory reserved for the Parlement.

Antoine's forays into the legal arena were remarkably relentless. He soon filed additional motions, on May 19 and May 29. For some reason, he took June off, but on July 7, Antoine was at it again. By then, Louis had had enough: he made a move that can only be called staggering. At a time when paternal authority was absolute, particularly in the case of underage children, Louis dared to call his father out in no uncertain terms. At 9 A.M. on Friday, July 18, Louis went to the police to submit a complaint against Antoine.

When he arrived at inspector Pierre Regnard's office, he was accompanied by Louise. Since they were living, as they explained, on the Pont-au-Change, a bridge linking the Île de la Cité to the Right Bank, rather than present their story to an inspector in their own neighborhood, they had gone out of their way to reach Regnard's office, on the rue Montmartre on the far side of the Louvre, near Saint-Eustache church. In November 1712, Regnard's first month on the job, Antoine had gone to him with his wild tale of the unknown man who had broken into his apartment and attacked his pregnant servant, Anne

*Louis Chevrot and Louise Magoulet jointly signed a complaint to the police in 1721.*

Lesage. Louis might have hoped that that experience had given Regnard a sense of his father's singular character.

Regard's account of what took place in his office on that Friday morning in July is so vivid that nearly three centuries later, a reader has a sense of eavesdropping on their conversation. On the cover of Louis' file, Regnard identified the case as *Chevrot the son v. Chevrot the father*, but the reality seems to have been *Louis and Louise Chevrot v. Antoine Chevrot*.

The complaint was signed jointly: first "Chevrot," and directly underneath "Marie Louise Magoulet." Both what they had to say and the manner in which they expressed their grievances demonstrate that they were speaking as a couple, equally caught up in a situation of Antoine's creation. They were also presenting themselves as the kind of married couple I have never otherwise encountered in an archival document: although Louis signed his name first, as the law required, the transcript of their complaint makes clear that they saw their marriage as a partnership of equals.

Since Louis was doing the talking, the body of the document is written from his perspective. But Louise was with him every step of the way, and she interjected numerous remarks: those Regnard included in the left margin; each time, Louise added her initials to indicate that her words had been correctly transcribed.

In their testimony, Louis and Louise explained the facts of "their legitimate marriage" in London; they reacted to Antoine's attempt "to have their marriage broken off." Louis detailed all that was wrong about the case that Antoine had presented to the Parlement. He had in no way been "seduced" into the marriage, as his father claimed. On the contrary, he "had always intended that Louise would be his wife." He had not been "coerced" into leaving home; it had been his idea to go to England. Antoine's actions, Louise added, were motivated solely by "hatred and malice." But the document's conclusion reveals that Louise had underestimated her own father's "hatred and malice."

Louis and Louise knew that they would get nowhere without the assistance of a parent willing to help them have a marriage considered legitimate in

England recognized in France. To agree to the fiction that Clément was Louise's father and Marie Louise Desjardins her mother must have seemed a small price to pay in exchange for her father's public consent to their union.

The second half of their joint statement to Inspector Regnard opens on an account of the ways in which Clément and Desjardins had welcomed Louis and Louise upon their return to Paris. They had accepted the legality of their union and had openly "treated Louis as a son-in-law." They had "accorded their daughter and her husband an apartment in their home."

One day, Louis continued, Desjardins had pointed out to him a chair in which she claimed to have stashed away "6,000 livres in *louis d'or de Noailles*." This was a small fortune, not a penny of it in worthless banknotes, but all in the gold coins that Adrien Maurice, Duc de Noailles, then president of the Royal Finance Counsel, had had minted in November 1716. Everything about them had been precisely specified: 22-karat gold, their exact weight; they became accepted as the most solid specie in the land. Six months after John Law's flight, six thousand of these gold coins was a treasure many would have killed for. Desjardins next produced two promissory notes for 200 livres each, made out to her and payable at any time, and explained that she had set them aside "in order to purchase a position for him." The notes had been signed by someone named Mathurine Delamare in March and April 1719, just before the onset of investment fever.

Louis explained to Regnard that when he told Antoine about Desjardins' generosity, "his father had ordered him to bring the money to him," which Louis "out of obedience and submission had done, on April 28, 1721." Antoine, Louis alleged, had kept the entire sum and used it to pay down his debts. When Louis had requested a receipt, Antoine refused and threw him out of his house, "telling him he should go on living with his wife's family." Since neither Louis nor Louise had been able to obtain any acknowledgment from Antoine, they had decided that their only recourse was a formal complaint.

To back up these allegations, they had brought along two small pieces of paper, which Regnard pasted to the sheet under their signatures. These they described as facsimiles of the promissory notes, whose originals, they claimed, were still in Antoine's hands. However, these facsimiles were written in the eminently fluid hand of Jean Magoulet.

Had Jean hoped to embarrass the man who had dismissed Clément as a mere "glasses salesman" by inventing the fiction of a small fortune in gold neatly tucked away and thus portraying Louis' father-in-law as far wealthier than his father? Had he persuaded Louis and Louise to go along with his fiction in

*Promissory notes in Jean II Magoulet's hand.*

exchange for his continued support for their marriage? Did Jean realize the full implications of their complaint for their legal future together? And were Louis and Louise so blinded by their anger at Antoine that they did not think things through?

When Louis and Louise went forward with their elaborate tale about the life led by Clément and Desjardins, they implicitly signed off on the version of her biography that was essential to the case Antoine was in the process of formulating: Clément and Desjardins were Louise's parents; Louise was more than a decade older than Louis, who was then just shy of twenty-one.

They had thus set the stage for Antoine to bring suit against them on the only charge that he could possibly have invoked as grounds for successfully terminating their marriage: an odd and short-lived aberration in French law known as *rapt de séduction*.

In eighteenth-century France, marriage was defined as both a civil contract under royal jurisdiction and a sacrament, a matter for ecclesiastical courts. For centuries, in France, canon law alone counted and only the church's tribunals had ruled on the validity of marriages. But just over two decades after Henry VIII's struggle to increase state control in England, Henri II of France initiated his own conflict with the Roman Catholic Church over the institution of marriage. It was definitively resolved only long after the monarch's death, barely a decade before the case of Louis and Louise, married in the eyes of the church but without having obtained a civil contract, came before a royal court.

In 1556, Henri II ended the centuries of the church's total control over marriage in France with an edict banning clandestine marriages, a decree explicitly designed to supersede ecclesiastical law. The edict was officially proclaimed by the Parisian Parlement, the very body that would sit in judgment on Louis and Louise's marriage. That proclamation marked the beginning of a long chapter in French legal history that culminated only in 1789, when the Revolution declared marriage an entirely secular union.

Since the twelfth century, the Catholic Church had decreed that the consent of husband and wife was the basis on which a marriage was founded; the authorization of their parents, while desirable, was not essential to a union's validity. On these grounds, many French priests had continued to perform ceremonies similar to that held for Louis and Louise in the Sardinian embassy in London in September 1720. Under French law, children who married without parental consent could be disinherited and deprived of all forms of family assistance, but at first French rulers did not contend that the state had the authority to pronounce such unions legally void.

The 1556 edict decreed twenty-five for females and thirty for males to be the minimum age for marriage without parental approval. In 1578, a new French law further specified that any officiating priest was obliged to know the ages of those for whom he pronounced the sacrament and, if they were underage, to demand proof of parental consent. The law also declared a minimum of four witnesses necessary for a valid ceremony. A failure to observe any of these conditions resulted in what French law designated *rapt*. And Article 42 of the 1578 law made *rapt* a capital offense.

The crime known as *rapt* had originally applied only to certain cases, those of men who used violence to abduct women. But gradually over the century that began in 1578, the definition was expanded. By the late seventeenth century, a completely new subcategory had been added: *rapt de séduction*; the new crime was, like *rapt*, a capital offense. Rather than violently carrying women off, those accused of "abduction by means of seduction" were alleged to have suborned their victims, to have tricked or seduced them into marriage. In such cases, two factors were considered determinate: inequality of age and inequality of social status or condition. If the person so charged was either older than the alleged victim or of inferior rank or financial circumstances, a case could be made. If both these types of inequality were present, a conviction was far more likely. Once *rapt de séduction* was declared a capital offense, these cases became the exclusive preserve of royal jurisdiction, for ecclesiastical courts could not impose the death penalty.

Some argued that the Parlement's lawyers invented the new category to be certain that they alone would have jurisdiction over such cases. After all, many of those lawyers, Antoine's father among them, came from families that owed their prominence and their wealth to advantageous matrimonial alliances. For them, marriage had long been the surest path to upward mobility, and a misalliance could compromise a family's carefully constructed standing. To allow impressionable young men and women to wed without parental consent was, in their eyes, to threaten French society with what one treatise termed "the ruin of families."

The Parlement's lawyers argued that although marriage was a sacrament, it was a sacrament premised on a civil act, the contract that established the terms for transfers of wealth and property and that was signed prior to the church ceremony. That foundational civil contract, they claimed, gave Parlement the power to determine whether a marriage was legal. And Louis and Louise of course could produce no such contract.

There was one final new twist. Whereas only men had been accused of the crime of violent abduction, women were on rare occasion presented as the perpetrators of *rapt de séduction*. In fact, the definitive word on the subject, the royal declaration on *rapt de séduction* published on November 22, 1730 by the authority to whom Antoine had appealed in 1721, Louis XV, warned that "the most dangerous cases of subornation are provoked by the weaker sex."

Had Antoine been forced to make his case to an ecclesiastical tribunal, Louis and Louise's union would almost certainly have been judged valid. Under canon law, the legality of clandestine marriages continued to be upheld long after the Parlement began to proclaim its rights over marriages contracted without parental consent, and long before the Parlement became able to claim jurisdiction. Well into the seventeenth century, treatises by scholars of canon law in which the church's authority was confirmed continued to be published. In addition, even after French law began to require a minimum of four witnesses, canon law continued to recognize marriages performed before only two witnesses. Furthermore, what became the cornerstone of the Parlement's authority, the doctrine of *rapt de séduction*, came together only slowly; the arguments on which it was based were not clearly formulated until the early decades of the eighteenth century. Finally, ecclesiastical tribunals in general were far more sympathetic to the plight of young couples and far less likely to take the father's side than were the commissions of the Parisian Parlement, whose judgments consistently revealed a strong paternalistic bias.

Indeed, it was only in 1712 that the then archbishop of Paris, the future Cardinal de Noailles, formed an ecclesiastical commission: it adopted both the recently articulated doctrine and the principle of the state's jurisdiction over clandestine marriages. Under direct order from Noailles, a Parisian priest, Jean-Laurent Le Semelier, published its conclusions and thereby reversed the French church's previous positions. Well over a century after Henri II had thrown down the gauntlet, and less than a decade before Louis and Louise's marriage was brought to judgment, the crown had at last obtained uncontested authority over marriages contracted without parental approval.

Le Semelier's treatise might well have dictated the terms in which Antoine made his case. It featured, for example, this type of reasoning: in cases when the woman was of age and the man still underage, the court sitting in judgment could simply "presume" that "seduction" had occurred and that the woman had "abducted" her husband-to-be and "coerced" him into marriage.

In addition, the essay provided the clearest definition to date of *rapt de séduction*: it was never "a crime of passion," always "a crime of ambition and cupidity or venality." Women guilty of "abduction by seduction" targeted only young men "of good family"; such a marriage "brings dishonor on the young man and on his family." Finally, the treatise painted the first clear portrait of the kind of woman who would go to such lengths: she was of decidedly inferior social status and thus a social climber; she was also a gold digger, "always after the young man's assets." Most often, she was also a *femme de mauvaise vie*, a woman of easy virtue, who had counted on her talent for *libertinage*, her licentiousness, to seduce the young man.

Le Semelier and Noailles' essay was published just as the Parisian Parlement was handing down a series of key rulings in cases of *rapt de séduction*, all of which confirmed parental authority and pronounced marriages contracted without parental consent invalid. The conjunction between the appearances of that treatise and those rulings turned the decades between 1710 and 1730, the year when Louis XV issued what became the definitive statement on the new crime, into the golden age for findings of *rapt de séduction*.

Despite all this, had their case come before the Parlement's tribunal as the marriage of Louis Chevrot, son of the annuities controller Antoine Chevrot, and Louise Magoulet, daughter of the Queen's Embroiderer, Jean Magoulet, it's doubtful that Antoine would have stood a chance of obtaining an annulment: a match between a nineteen-year-old man and a seventeen-year-old woman and a union between two families whose social and financial status, although not absolutely equal, was not significantly unequal, was in no way the kind of scenario that *rapt de séduction* had been designed to prevent.

But the combination of Clément's always vague self-portrait as a modest artisan selling jewelry or some other inexpensive commodity, translated by Antoine into "glasses salesman," and Clément's denunciation of Marie Louise to the police as a "depraved prostitute" known for her "licentious behavior" seems straight out of Noailles' treatise and would have been tailor-made for Antoine's purposes. Antoine could thereby argue, as he did incessantly over the long months that followed Louis and Louise's ill-advised complaint to Inspector Regnard, that, driven by a desire to improve her social and financial status, Marie Louise Magoulet, a significantly older woman already officially accused of "debauchery," had used all the wiles known to women of easy virtue to trick his son into marriage.

Indeed, the only amazing thing about Antoine's case is that his victory came neither easily nor quickly.

Six days after Louis and Louise's denunciation of him to the police, on July 24, 1721, Antoine made another appearance before the Parlement's tribunal. He was in court three more times that July alone, always identifying himself as an *écuyer*, a nobleman, and thereby further accentuating the gulf that separated him from the father of the bride. On one of those days, July 29, Antoine added to his original request for an annulment a demand that Marie Louise's crime be punished by forcing her to pay damages. He named a precise figure, 6,000 livres, exactly the sum his son had just accused him of stealing. At that point, the Parlement issued a summons ordering Louis to appear before their tribunal, but he failed to show up. Antoine testified that his son had been prevented from coming by the Magoulets, "who were keeping him under their absolute domination."

Between late August and the end of the year, Antoine made seven additional court appearances. In November 1721, the month when the French were riveted by Cartouche's trial and execution, Antoine was negotiating for a restraining order against Louise. His motion was denied, and in February 1722 he requested once again that she be forbidden "to frequent" his son. Antoine continued to file new motions at this pace for two and a half solid years, all during 1722 and 1723.

In 1722, most Parisians would have considered themselves lucky to have nothing more serious to worry about than a by then well-established marriage of which only one family member disapproved. The fallout from Law's system was driving more and more families into bankruptcy. By January 1722, Marais reported that all over Paris, day after day, it was "one continuous riot."

By October 17, the authorities who had made Law's system possible were trying to put it definitively to rest. A special iron cage 10 feet by 8 had been constructed; on that day, in it were burned banknotes and shares and other papers that told the story of speculation fever. The following month, the Royal Bank building was repurposed: it became the King's Library. Ever since, the edifice that housed France's original bank has served as a repository for very different types of paper.

Meanwhile, all through 1722, Parisians were agog over the stories coming to light during the trials of members of Cartouche's gang. Day after day, they were able to witness public executions. On July 11, it was the turn of the first woman on the list: Cartouche's wife and Louise's fellow deportee, Marie Antoinette Néron, was hanged, at 1 A.M. to avoid attracting a sympathetic crowd. She was after all, as lawyer Barbier pointed out, "a quite attractive brunette."

On September 18, Caumartin de Boissy reported to his correspondent in the provinces that Paris was a dog-eat-dog world, absolutely "cutthroat." "All people can talk about are the murders and the robberies. I wouldn't think of carrying a wallet anymore, and everyone warns me not to stay out at night."

Official promises to the contrary, Cartouche's arrest and execution had not even slowed, much less stopped, the city's crime wave.

All this time, in addition to accumulating lawyers' fees and fees for filing numerous motions, Antoine continued to take out big loans. By July 23, 1722, he had begged and borrowed from multiple sources and had at last obtained the 50,000 livres required to resume his post as annuities controller. Antoine completed his negotiations barely in time to control the 4 million livres of annuities created as a last-ditch attempt to convert shares in Law's company into another type of asset.

Antoine regained his professional status just before the one moment in 1722 when standing would have mattered, the only event that year that could have given the French reason to hope in their future: the coronation of a new king.

The pages of contemporary periodicals and correspondences are filled with accounts of the ceremony. All agreed that at his coronation on October 25, the thirteen-year-old king offered dazzling proof that the monarchy was still able to put on a display of wealth that, in the contemporary context, could well have seemed indecent. That proof glistened at the center of the young ruler's forehead.

Some objects featured in that October ceremony dated from Louis XIV's reign, but a new crown had been designed for the occasion by a prominent Parisian jeweler, Augustin Duflos. It featured two rows of pearls surrounding a third row of gems in which sapphires, rubies, and emeralds alternated. In all, 282 diamonds, 237 pearls, and 64 colored gemstones were used. At the diadem's midpoint was a fleur-de-lis shaped in huge diamonds.

The most fabulous jewel in the crown was a staggeringly mammoth diamond still today a star of the French crown jewels and now known as "the Regent." Duflos had placed the eye-popping stone at the center of that pivotal fleur-de-lis, right over the king's forehead.

In 1717, when John Law had approached the regent with the idea of purchasing a 547-carat Indian diamond, the regent at first recoiled from the idea on the grounds that the kingdom was then unable "to cover even the most pressing necessities or to provide for all those whose suffering was great." But Law won the day, and the crown went into debt for 2 million livres, plus 5 percent interest: the transaction became for the regent the foundation of Law's credibility as a financier. The payment was to be made in installments, the last one coming due on June 1, 1719 as France's original stock market was about to heat up.

Just over three years later, when the diamond made its inaugural appearance on the coronation crown, it was rumored to have cost 3 million, and it was nicknamed "the millionaire."

On December 1, 1722, following the death of Louis' maternal grandfather, Barthélemy Boulanger, an inventory of his estate was drawn up. Normally, these were staid affairs: a notary simply listed one possession after another and assigned a value to each. But this inventory degenerated into a veritable shouting match between Antoine and Louis' grandmother. At one point, for example, Antoine interrupted the procedure to ask why the "large" silver bowl and pitcher he "knew she had at the time of her husband's death" had not been included. The widow replied that she had sold them long ago. Next, he wondered where she had hidden the diamond rings and other diamond jewelry; she retorted that she had never owned any. It went on and on in this fashion.

Antoine did come away with a clock that chimed the hours, valued at 250 livres, the creation of Zachary Martin, official clockmaker to Louis XIV. During the last years of his life, as Antoine obsessed over the loss of status with which Louis continued to threaten his family, the clock's chimes could have reminded him of his days of glory at the court of the Sun King.

February 15, 1723 was Louis XV's birthday. Although the regent continued to make decisions in his name, because of a 1374 decree that stipulated that French kings came of age when they turned fourteen, his rule officially began that day. That royal coming-of-age had given Antoine cause for concern about his lack of progress in dealing with his underage son: on February 14, he had obtained an order from a royal minister to have Louis locked up in the correctional facility of Bicêtre. Next, he opened a new line of attack.

On May 19, Antoine convened an assembly of family and friends "to appoint a new guardian for his son Louis," on the grounds that "he himself was too busy with the trial against Marie Louise Magoulet." The true explanation for his decision soon became clear. After two years of nonstop legal procedures, Antoine had made no progress with his motion to have Louis' marriage declared a case of *rapt de séduction*. He decided that he needed to prove to the Parlement's lawyers that he was not in this alone.

To the representative of the Parisian police who was presiding over their odd meeting, Antoine explained that he "needed someone to back him up in his efforts and to demonstrate that the family was solidly behind him." But Antoine's gathering in fact resembled nothing so much as those organized by the two Queen's Embroiderers when their children's futures were at stake: a bare minimum of participants and merely two of them relatives. On the Chevrot side, Antoine had persuaded only one of his distant Coulanges cousins to attend; Marie Charlotte Perrin, Louis' grandmother, alone represented the maternal line. Otherwise, there were but a few assorted "friends" with grand-sounding titles.

For the first and only time, Antoine admitted that his lawsuit was not going well: he had already pleaded his case five times; it was scheduled to be heard twice more. Despite what would have seemed a textbook case of a type of offense that the very tribunal judging it was eager to prosecute, the Parlement's lawyers were simply not convinced that Louise was guilty of *rapt de séduction* and that Louis was but an innocent boy who had been tricked into marrying her.

The assembly appointed a new guardian: Jean Masneuf, a financier whose finest hour had come in 1699, when Paris was near bankruptcy because of the massive expenses of the Nine Years' War. City authorities had found themselves obliged to hand over to private enterprise what had been destined to be the last great state-sponsored urban work of Louis XIV's reign: we know it as the Place Vendôme. They turned over the project to Masneuf, who on behalf of the city sold the land reserved for it to a consortium. He then developed the terrain and had constructed the façades still visible today, including that of Paris' Hôtel Ritz. He also made a tidy profit on the deal.

Louis' new guardian was thus intended to add gravitas to the case against his marriage. Antoine gave Masneuf a clear mission: "to convince the Parlement's tribunal that the entire family wanted Louis' marriage annulled." Antoine gave him full power to act in his name: from then on, Masneuf's name was found on all briefs.

On July 15, 1723, one of Masneuf's early motions was a demand that the Magoulets turn over all "the promissory notes, contracts, and receipts" that, he alleged, they "had forced Louis to sign for their benefit." Two years after Louis had shown the police the promissory notes he accused his father of having stolen, Masneuf threw the ball back into Louis' court. Once again, Louis refused to respond. But Antoine's gambit worked. Within six months, ever the problem solver, Masneuf had achieved the goal that had eluded Antoine for two years.

His success just might have been due to still another stroke of the evil luck that seemed to dog Louis and Louise's every move. Soon after Masneuf's appointment, because of the self-serving lies of two adolescent boys well on the road to juvenile delinquency, the brief period of time during which Louis and Louise were able to live together as man and wife came to an abrupt end.

# CHAPTER SIXTEEN

# Total Eclipse
## Everyone: 1723–1724

Dᴿᴼᵁᴳᴴᵀ, ᴴᴱᴬᵀ, ᴾᴱˢᵀᴵᴸᴱᴺᶜᴱ.
Beginning in March 1723, something was becoming clear to those who had been faithfully keeping journals since John Law had brought out the stock market wolf in French investors: the climatic conditions of 1723 seemed to announce a repetition of that deadly year 1719.

First came the drought: no rain from February on. Already by May, Barbier fretted, "we haven't seen a dry spell like this for years." And by November, he reported that drought and excessive heat were causing "epidemics of many diseases to spread like wildfire through Paris."

When the year began, Louis and Louise were living officially as man and wife in a small apartment on the Place Baudoyer. Today, that tiny square is a peaceful spot just removed from the bustle of the rue de Rivoli. The buildings that surround their location at the corner of the rue des Barres still retain the façades that Louis and Louise would have seen every day.

One of the largest squares in the city was only steps away: the Place de Grève, site of all public executions. Louise couldn't have avoided the view of the gallows ready and waiting for Néron and the other women from Cartouche's gang with whom she had been incarcerated and traveled on the road to Le Havre.

Before Baron Haussmann added the rue de Rivoli, Baudoyer Square marked the end of the rue Saint-Antoine, now, as in the eighteenth century, a street filled with small shops of various kinds. The Chevrots' apartment was located just above that of *marchand mercier* Florent Delamotte and his wife, the widow of the master painter Pierre Grandereye or Flandereye (both spellings were used). The shopsign that hung above their door represented a *louis d'or*, one of those coveted gold coins.

*Marchands merciers* were not craftsmen; they sold a variety of goods created by others. Delamotte displayed everything from silver spoons to ornate snuff-boxes to fancy shoe buckles. And right next door was Guillaume Deseine, a master potter in pewter known for his fine pewter cutlery and dishware. Each man had a son: Deseine's, also Guillaume, was then sixteen; Delamotte's step-son, Jean-Baptiste Grandereye, fourteen.

Louis and Louise's address might have seemed too close for comfort to the residences of their fathers: it was just off the Seine, minutes from the embankment where Jean Magoulet and Anne Legrand lived still, and near the rue de la Verrerie, where Antoine Chevrot, ever on the move trying to shake his creditors, had recently moved.

But in 1723 the young couple's troubles for once did not originate with either Jean or Antoine.

Directly across Rivoli from the rue des Barres, a street so tiny that it seems a miniature connects the Place Baudoyer to the rue de la Verrerie. The street is centuries old, as is its name: the rue des Mauvais Garçons, Bad Boys' Street. In 1723, that name was fully deserved, for among Louis and Louise' next-door neighbors were two very bad boys indeed.

The first sign of trouble came on April 23 or 24, 1723. When Deseine and his wife, Madeleine Gallois, discovered that the two boys had been pilfering their parents' shops and reselling the goods, they addressed a request to the lieutenant general of the Parisian police. By 1723, still another new official occupied that position: Marc Pierre de Voyer de Paulmy, Comte d'Argenson, in office since April 1722. He could thus have remembered neither the 1719 dossier of Marie Louise Magoulet nor the 1721 arrest of Jean Magoulet.

The Deseines claimed to have done all they could to give Guillaume, the eldest of their seven children, a good education and "to put him on the right path to salvation," but despite their efforts, Guillaume had been "attacked by dreadful and incorrigible lawlessness." Concerned "about what the future might bring," they wanted him confined to Bicêtre "in order to correct his behavior." It's not clear how Guillaume Deseine and Jean-Baptiste Grandereye learned of Louise's incarceration in the Salpêtrière, but once their thievery was discovered, they revealed their neighbor's seemingly unsavory past.

At 10 A.M. on Monday, April 26, Louis and Louise made their second joint appearance before Police Commissioner Pierre Regnard. This time, Louise did most of the talking, and her signature precedes Louis' at the document's end. According to Louise's statement, for months after she and Louis had moved into their apartment, they had had virtually no interaction with the two merchants and their families: during all that time, she had never even spoken to their two sons. Then the boys were caught stealing from their parents.

On Sunday, April 25, Louise alleged, both mothers had knocked on the couple's door: they accused them of the thefts and ordered them to leave the house immediately. The two women, Louise continued, had called her out in particular and had begun screaming that she was "nothing but a shoplifter, a slut and a common whore." They had then "threatened to toss all her things out the window and into the street"—this was done to women arrested for prostitution, so that after their release they couldn't just go back to work again—and "to have her whipped while she was taken away in a straw-filled cart"—this was a form of punishment traditionally reserved for pickpockets and thieves. When Louis and Louise tried to get away, the women "chased them down the street," shouting all the while "prostitute, whore."

Louise ended her statement by explaining to Regnard that "since her honor and reputation had been publicly sullied," she had been advised to file a complaint and to ask for "reparations": she was therefore requesting that the mothers be forced to pay damages.

The boys' parents quickly upped the ante.

On April 27, a second request was sent to d'Argenson: this time, Delamotte and his wife were writing about their son Jean-Baptiste to complain of conduct identical to that of his best friend. But three days had made a world of difference: by now, both sets of parents were blaming everything on Louise.

Their troubles had all started, the Delamottes explained, when they "had the misfortune to rent an apartment to Chevrot and his wife." No sooner had their new tenants moved in when the couple, and Louise in particular, "began to corrupt the two children, their boy and the Deseine child."

Louise was clearly her mother's daughter, so fashion-conscious that she favored the latest style, the loose, voluminous gowns known as "sack dresses" that lawyer Marais reported initially having spotted in the streets of Paris in August 1720. Women loved the style's unconstrained freedom of movement: sack dresses were the equivalent for the wild Law years of flapper dresses for the Roaring Twenties.

The boys' parents claimed that Louise had used her dressing gown's ample folds to rob them blind, pinching items from their shops and smuggling them out by "tucking them under her dress." Louise next passed the goods on to the boys, after "persuading" them to sell the merchandise in exchange for a cut of the profits. D'Argenson sent Officer Dechaussepie to investigate.

Dechaussepie reported back that both sets of parents agreed that the boys had stolen only "because Louise had persuaded them to do so." On May 3, their accusations took a more serious turn. They now alleged that one of Jean-Baptiste's sisters "was merely chiding Louise for her conduct when Louise suddenly whipped out a pocketknife and tried to cut up her face."

Louis and Louise split up and went on the lam again. Louis moved around the corner to live with a doctor named Hermans on the nearby rue du Monceau Saint-Gervais. Louise relocated to the far side of the rue Saint-Antoine in Paris' traditional market area, Les Halles, a veritable rabbit warren of small streets. In the hullabaloo of commerce, no one would have paid attention to a lone newcomer. Indeed, all through May and the first half of June the police were on her trail, with no success. They were assiduous in their efforts, for d'Argenson added repeated notes to her file reminding his officers that he wanted to speak with Louise and asking "why she hadn't come to talk to him." By May 23, the lieutenant general was so exasperated that he fumed about *l'insolence rare de cette femme*, "that woman's unthinkable audacity or impertinence."

On June 11, the police finally did track Louise down, to a house on the rue des Prêcheurs, Preachers' Street, owned by a grocer named Famin. Louise had been living in the building's most modest quarters, a room in the fifth-floor apartment rented by Madame Pichon, a seamstress who specialized in women's intimate apparel, and had surely been working for Pichon as well. But by the time they got there, the officers found only bits of Louise's stuff: Louise herself was long gone.

D'Argenson had had enough; he issued a verdict: *fripponerie, jeunes enfants enduits à voler.* "Fripponerie" referred to petty theft, particularly pilfering by schoolboys, while "young children seduced into thievery" makes clear the lieutenant general's opinion: in the eighteenth century, adolescents of sixteen and fourteen were hardly seen as "young children," but in d'Argenson's view, boys would always be boys, especially when an older woman had been around to "persuade" them.

With all the commotion virtually at his front door, Antoine Chevrot got wind of the messy business. Women shouting that Louise was a whore, the police going door to door looking for his daughter-in-law, Louise accused of seducing two young boys: the sordid affair must have seemed the answer to his prayers. The thefts on the place Baudoyer may have been the event that tipped the scales in Antoine's favor in his long-running *rapt de séduction* case.

On June 20, an order was issued, signed by Louis XV, to incarcerate Louise in For-l'Évêque, the debtors' prison where Jean had spent time in 1721. By then, Antoine was maneuvering behind the scenes, for when the Delamottes and the Deseines next wrote d'Argenson, they knew everything that had occurred in 1719 and 1720.

Their sons, the parents alleged in their new petition, "would never have done any of this," had they not met "a woman who had given birth to a child before she was married and then had run off to foreign places to get married, without the consent of either her parents or her husband's parents."

Next, seemingly out of the blue, an impressive character witness came forward to testify that he knew Louise well. In his capacity as "her parish priest," he assured d'Argenson that "her behavior had long been deranged" and that the only way to deal with her was "to lock her up in Paris' General Hospital." Louise's file identified the cleric who called himself her parish priest as "the pastor of the Petite Chapelle."

"The Small Chapel" was a euphemism that described the most exclusive parish in the land: the chapel in the palace of Versailles attended by the kings of France. In 1723, the curate of Versailles' Royal Chapel was Maurice Bailly, of whom the Duc de Saint-Simon said: "He heard the confessions of all those at court who were most exacting and severe." On her deathbed, Louis XV's mother, the dauphine, had refused to see her usual confessor, a Jesuit, and had asked for Father Bailly instead. Bailly, Saint-Simon added, was held in highest esteem by all those once part of the dauphine's court. This religious hardliner who found the Jesuits too accommodating had not had an easy time as long as openly pro-Jesuit Louis XIV was alive. He remained fiercely loyal to those who had stood by him during those years.

Marie Louise Magoulet, daughter of a modest eyewear merchant who lived on the Île de la Cité, could not possibly have known or been known by the curate of Versailles' Chapelle Royale. Nor would Bailly have been acquainted with Jean's daughter Louise, whose parish church had been Saint-Germain-l'Auxerrois. But one person did know Father Bailly: a former member of the dauphine's court who never forgot the connections he had made during those years: Antoine Chevrot.

Jean, too, was soon involved. Madame Pichon admitted that Louise had gone to live with "a jeweler named Magoulet, who resided at the sign of the Golden Apple." On June 23, when Officer Duplessis arrived there, he was informed that Magoulet was not a jeweler but a *gainier*. And when Duplessis tried to make his arrest, he endured a blow-by-blow repeat of Jean's behavior in 1721: "He mistreated me and tore my uniform," Duplessis reported to d'Argenson; "he called me names so injurious that I find myself unable to repeat them. He insulted you as well and spoke about you contemptuously and with a complete lack of respect. I was obliged to call over an entire escort of the town watch in order to subdue him; this man deserves punishment for having rebelled against royal justice."

Clément's defense was still more manna for Antoine. Identifying himself as a jeweler, Clément petitioned d'Argenson; offering another variant of Louise's story. His daughter had had "the misfortune" to marry Louis Chevrot; soon after they were wed in England, "her husband had begun to mistreat her; he showed her only iniquity and bitterness and soon began to indulge in horrifying debauchery." Once his son-in-law had revealed his true colors, Clément had been obliged "to appeal to the Parlement asking that his daughter's marriage be annulled *comme d'abus.*" In order "to tarnish his daughter's reputation," Louis and his parents had made common cause with the Delamottes and were accusing his daughter of "seducing" the young boys. Clément begged d'Argenson for Louise's release "since he was old and frail and needed his daughter's help."

At this point, Antoine intervened directly. Identifying himself as "the senior valet de chambre of the dauphine, mother of the king," he accused Louise, "34 years old and the unwed mother of a child fathered by a clerk named Richard," of *rapt de séduction*, as well as of "daring to call herself the wife of Louis Chevrot." Antoine recounted both Louise's 1719 incarceration and the case he had brought before the Parlement. Now that she had struck again and seduced still other young men, he concluded, she "should be taken to the Salpêtrière and locked up for the rest of her days. If she isn't put behind bars, she will continue her seduction of [my] son and will prevent him from making a future for himself."

By this point, anyone who had been paying close attention would have been confused about the identity of the "unthinkably impertinent" woman whose case was sitting on d'Argenson's desk. What was her actual name, and how old was she? Was Louis Chevrot a victim of her seduction or an abusive husband? Since each father had suggested a line of investigation that led straight to the records of the Parisian penal system, the lieutenant general soon learned about Louis' recent stay in Bicêtre and decided that he must be "the husband about whom she had been forced to complain." About Louise he received this report: "Marie Louise Magoulet, unmarried and thirty-six years of age, was arrested and brought to the Salpêtrière on August 5, 1719 by Officer Bourlon. The following month, she gave birth to a son, who was baptized and named Jean Louis, son of Marie Louise Magoulet, which is the name of her father. Her father swore that she had always been worthless."

D'Argenson might have believed that this information would put the matter to rest. But then d'Argenson had had no prior dealings with Jean Magoulet.

Jean quickly produced a significant character reference of his own, and his easily one-upped Antoine's cleric. On July 28, 1723, d'Argenson received the kind of advice government officials never ignore: "Since I have known Sir Magoulet, who lives in our neighborhood, for a very long time, and have furthermore always known him to be an honorable man, I cannot avoid recommending him to you." The letter's author, Jean-Jacques, Bailli de Mesmes, was so important that d'Argenson answered the instant the missive reached his desk on July 29. He added a note to Louise's file: de Mesmes "has taken an interest in that woman."

De Mesmes' title, "bailiff," referred to his rank in the Sovereign Order of Malta, as whose ambassador to the French court he served. De Mesmes' residence, on Paris' Right Bank near Jean's home, had been a hot spot all during the Law years: assemblies of directors of Law's company were frequently held there, as were meetings of the Royal Bank's board. And when Louis XV officially came of age, among the very first to offer their good wishes was Ambassador de Mesmes.

The Duc de Saint-Simon left this particularly sardonic portrait of de Mesmes: "dissolute, someone who clearly had a lot to hide, a man who wasn't master of his desires, a huge spendthrift, and a disgrace to his profession." This very important person was exactly Jean's kind of fellow.

Once de Mesmes weighed in, d'Argenson issued an order "to release the woman named Chevrot." The judicial process was put on hold by one of the infectious diseases then breaking out in Paris: the lieutenant general fell ill and was forced to leave the city for weeks of what he described as "my quarantine in the country." It was only on September 27 that the regent approved the release order and only on October 8 that it was entered into the official register. But Louise remained in For-l'Évêque.

And she had had enough.

In French law, the small space between the twin guardhouses that stood at the entrance to royal prisons had a special status: if a prisoner stood in just that spot and pronounced a declaration, it was seen as legally binding.

On October 13, "in the presence of Jean Claude de la Croix and Benoît Morand, guards to the entrance of the Royal Prison of For-l'Évêque," Louise made this pronouncement: "I, Marie Louise Magoulet, wife of Louis Chevrot, hereby abandon the complaint that I made to Commissioner Regnard last April 26. I declare it null and renounce any claim to damages. This declaration was made in the space of freedom between the two guardhouses."

In Louise's prison file, her statement is followed by still another bolt from the blue, the negotiation that explained Louise's decision to renounce her request for damages: "For-l'Évêque's Ladies of Charity have offered 100 livres to the Delamottes and the Deseines as an incentive to call off their criminal case." The Dames de la Charité were groups of wealthy lay women, the first of which were organized in the seventeenth century by Father (and later Saint) Vincent de Paul; they used contributions from parishioners to improve the conditions of the poorest inmates in Paris' prisons.

The Ladies of Charity who had taken an interest in Louise represented the congregation of Saint-Germain-l'Auxerrois, the parish church of Jean Magoulet and his daughter Louise.

The Delamottes and the Deseines accepted the money and Louise's retraction and dropped their case. Even though he admitted that Father Bailly's testimony still weighed on his mind, d'Argenson was obliged to release Louise.

Had he been more concerned about the two "boys" whose word everyone had been so quick to accept, he might have spared the police and the royal prison administration considerable trouble. Not even a decade later, even though he was not yet of age, Guillaume Deseine had a rap sheet as long as his arm. On January 12, 1733, then Lieutenant General René Du Hérault made the decision to lock him up in Bicêtre for at least the fifth time.

In late October, after roughly five months in prison—once again during excessive drought and heat, once again at a moment when infectious diseases were taking a massive toll even among those such as d'Argenson who lived in the best conditions—Louise was allowed to cross over and beyond that "space of freedom" between the prison guardhouses.

Louise never again turned to her father for shelter or help of any kind: she broke off all contact with him. On January 12, 1724, by which time Louise was long gone from For-l'Évêque, Clément, obviously in the dark as to her whereabouts, was still writing to d'Argenson protesting that his daughter's "prison sojourn was ruining her reputation."

By then, far more than Louise's reputation had been ruined.

At least one individual of great influence seems to have taken Louis and Louise's side. Even with Masneuf's help, Antoine had not won his case as long as Philippe d'Orléans, regent of France, remained alive, but the longtime regent died suddenly on December 2, leaving the boy king to make his own decisions. Caumartin de Boissy speculated that "many things will change quickly now that the regent is dead." A mere eight days later, as one of the first decisions of his independent reign, Louis XV rewarded his late mother's faithful servant Antoine Chevrot and delivered Louis, described by Antoine in all his lawsuits as the godson of the king's mother and his grandfather, from a scheming woman's wiles.

Louis and Louise had barely been reunited after her release from prison when on December 10, 1723, the decree Antoine Chevrot had long awaited was at last pronounced. That day, "Louis King of France in the presence of the officers of the Parlement's court" decreed Louise guilty of *rapt de séduction* and declared her marriage to Louis Chevrot null and void.

After three years, three months, and three days during which they had lived openly as husband and wife, Louis and Louise awoke one day to learn that their marriage suddenly was no more. Louise was never again able to identify herself as "the wife of Louis Chevrot." With a few strokes of a quill, more than three years of marriage were erased from the official record.

Even though the Parlement had the right to impose the death penalty in such cases, it never did so. It did typically condemn women convicted of "abduction through seduction" to banishment, from Paris or even from France. It also habitually imposed stiff fines, thousands and even many thousands of livres. Indeed, in cases where the court found the woman guilty of "abhorrent tactics," it was obliged to mete out punishment. Antoine had always asked for punitive damages, but the Parlement chose not to inflict additional penalties.

In French legal history, *rapt de séduction* turned out to be a mere flash in the pan. Such cases were successfully prosecuted only during the brief window when the church-state quarrel over marriage law was most active and when the Parlement's magistrats were strongly invested in this peculiarly French "crime," and only when sympathetic authorities were in place. Had, for instance, a priest requested permission to marry Louis and Louise just a few years earlier or somewhat later, at a moment when Cardinal de Noailles did not dominate the French church, that request might well have been granted. Once again, a malign star had governed the lives of Louis and Louise Chevrot.

While Louise was still in prison, on September 30, 1723, Jean Magoulet and Anne Legrand went to their notary's office to sign up for some of the newly fashionable annuities that Antoine Chevrot controlled. Legrand was rolling over funds from Pierre Chicot's estate already invested in government securities. But Jean professed to have money of his own: 3,000 livres, to be precise. This was the exact sum that in December 1720 Jean had claimed to be investing on his children's behalf, but in 1723, there was no longer any talk of his offspring. While others who took out certificates the same day and at the same notary's office, including the sister and brother-in-law of Marie Louise Desjardins, listed their children as beneficiaries, on certificate number 20992 Jean named only Anne Legrand.

On January 24, 1724, two of Jean's surviving daughters attempted to transfer their portion of their mother's estate to their brother Claude. Since Jeanne and Marie were still minors, their request was refused, but the procedure caused Jean to reflect upon the fact that when his children reached majority, he faced a day of reckoning. Louise, who turned twenty-three in early 1724, would be the first to attain the magic age of twenty-five.

At 6 P.M. on May 22, 1724, lawyer Marais reported, Parisians were "struck with terror" because of a total eclipse of the sun. The eclipse was total only for roughly two minutes, but the sky remained ominously dark for two hours. Parisians were quick to interpret the phenomenon as a warning portending still more disastrous times ahead for their city.

In 1724, the French Indies Company was back in business. As soon as it began issuing new shares, speculation fever returned, and Parisians were once again watching the board and following the ups and downs of its stock. Even the president of the Grand Conseil, Caumartin de Boissy, who had been badly burned in 1720, had his eye constantly on the value of a share.

Just as had happened in 1719, once those who should have been looking out for the common good were mesmerized by the bottom line, no one noticed when a young woman suddenly disappeared.

Upon the regent's death, d'Argenson lost his position as lieutenant general of the Parisian police. On January 28, 1724, Nicolas Jean-Baptiste Ravot, Seigneur d'Ombreval, was named to succeed him. Still another new lieutenant general with no knowledge of the strange doublings of Jean and Clément and Louise and Marie Louise now held office. Jean quickly took advantage of the situation.

On this occasion, despite the fact that the lieutenant general was new at his job, somewhere in the chain of command a warning bell should have sounded: this time, the same young woman who in 1719 had been locked up as Marie Louise Magoulet, denounced as a prostitute by her father, Clément, had once more been denounced as a prostitute, and once more by her father, only this time her father was named Jean Magoulet and he was identified not a jeweler or a *gainier* but an embroiderer.

As always, Jean was absolutely sure of himself. When he wrote to the new lieutenant general to ask that his daughter be imprisoned, he brought up her previous incarceration: d'Ombreval was soon informed that she had indeed been "conducted to the place of departure for the colonies."

Jean explained that it was only because of his "paternal kindness" that Louise had not made the journey to Louisiana in 1719. He had been stunned, he claimed, when he learned that his daughter "was destined to be sent to the islands" and had quickly "begged that she be restored to him with the hope that the experience would have caused her to change her ways."

It was thus with "true sadness" that he was forced to report that no sooner back in Paris, "she had begun to prostitute herself again with every stranger she met; she has had several children because of this scandalous life." Still in 1724 she "maintains licentious relations with various individuals whose only source of revenue is from their skill as cardsharps." Most recently, she had also "participated in *fripponeries*," a clear reference to the Delamotte-Deseine case. All of this "was bringing dishonor upon her family." As a result, "Jean Magoulet, embroiderer" found himself obliged to beg the lieutenant general to put his daughter away "for a second time."

Jean's petition to d'Ombreval was among his masterpieces.

Those making such requests usually employed the services of a public writer whose ornate writing made their words seem more impressive. I'm almost certain that Jean wrote this request himself: all its special flourishes are identical to those found in documents in his hand. But even had he turned to a public writer, it would have been easy to indicate that some signatures would be added at a later moment. This explains how Jean was able to get away with his subterfuge.

On the bottom line are two signatures: to the right, the name of an unknown person never otherwise associated with the Magoulets, and to the left, "Huilliot." This would have been Pierre Huilliot, member of the Royal Academy of Painting and Anne Legrand's nephew, a witness at her marriage with Jean: this signature, nothing like Huilliot's characteristic autograph, is clearly a forgery.

The petition's top line, with three signatures lined up side by side, is the scene-stealer. To the far left is Jean's own, his standard "JMagoulet"; after his name he added *père*, father, though this should have been obvious. The middle signature, "Morel," is identified as *oncle*, uncle. This is the authentic hand of Guillaume Morel, Jean I's brother-in-law, the only Magoulet in-law willing to cosign any document. Then there is the final signature in the row, "Magoulet oncle." No first name appears, but the signature indicated as that of "uncle

*Signatures of those who supported Jean II Magoulet's request to have his daughter Louise imprisoned for prostitution and deported to Louisiana.*

Magoulet" is the autograph adopted by Jean in his role as Clément, although Clément used two *l*s, instead of the single *l* found here.

Jean called on assorted VIPs to buttress his case. Foremost among them was an individual so truly significant that he was referred to simply as Monsieur le Duc, as though he were the only duke in France, which was in a sense the case. As a grandson of Louis XIV, son of a legitimated daughter of the Sun King and the Marquise de Montespan, Louis IV de Bourbon-Condé, Prince de Condé and Duc de Bourbon, was among the most influential men in the realm, fourth in line for the throne. He was also among the wealthiest: he had made many, many millions from his investments in Law's stock; his sudden decision to redeem all his shares for gold is considered a major cause of the Royal Bank's collapse. His support for Louise's arrest was the earliest indication that Jean had traded in his title of Queen's Embroiderer for the new one that he would soon adopt: the Prince's Embroiderer.

The moment Monsieur le Duc made clear "his intention that Louise Magoulet be arrested and brought to the Hospital," the police commissioner charged with investigating Jean's claims, Jean-Baptiste de Soucy, quickly decided that "there was nothing to do but to lock her up again in the Hospital."

Monsieur le Duc made his wishes clear on June 20; by June 21, the head of the king's household, Jean Frédéric Phélypeaux, Comte de Maurepas, had signed off on Louise's arrest, as had d'Ombreval. Already on June 23, a note was added to Louise's dossier by arresting officer Malinoire announcing that he "had brought Louise to the Hospital" on June 22. Five years after she had given birth there, Louise had once again been incarcerated in the Salpêtrière.

As the 1728 map on the following page indicates, the General Hospital's location was more of a no-man's-land than an urban setting. Prisoners in Paris' other prisons such as the Bastille or For-l'Évêque could at least hear the sounds of the city from their cells, but the Salpêtrière was situated north, south, east, west, and across the Seine from nothing: there were neither busy boulevards nor residential neighborhoods nearby. The prison was bordered by a cemetery on one side, a huge garbage dump on another, and on a third by a fetid pool in which tanneries had long dumped their chemical waste: its water was so polluted that it was a breeding ground for rats and infectious diseases.

Parts of the original Salpêtrière are still standing, including the late seventeenth-century chapel constructed by order of Louis XIV, who dedicated it to his patron saint. With its central octagonal dome and side chapels radiating out from it, the church remains very much the place where Louise worshipped every day. It is stark, plain, and well-used: its stone floors have been worn down by the footsteps of countless thousands of prisoners.

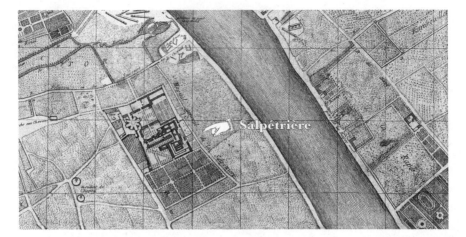

Also still standing at the heart of what is now a vast modern hospital is the dormitory to which Louise was confined, the Maison de Force, generally called simply La Force, the Workhouse. Still today, La Force, now a psychiatric ward, is somehow terrifying.

Even the political authorities who issued the orders confining women to La Force's cells considered the conditions grim. The building was dilapidated; the foul odors and humidity were notorious. There was no ventilation to speak of: each cell had a single window, only two feet wide, with bars, up next to the ceiling: prisoners might perhaps have glimpsed a fragment of sky.

La Force's overcrowding was as well documented as the nauseating smells. Up to six women shared a bed meant to sleep four, with two sleeping at the head and two at the foot. The inmates who had been confined longest automatically grabbed the spots on the bed, and those who found no room simply slept on the stone floor. The cells were just wide enough to accommodate a bed, leaving barely enough space to squeeze in two more inmates on the floor. Blankets were distributed only in winter.

Discipline, was, in the words of one lieutenant general, "severe." And the worst treatment of all was reserved for those confined by royal decree for prostitution, particularly under the regime of the uncompromising d'Ombreval. Labor was compulsory; prisoners worked at some textile trade and the Hospital sold the products of their handiwork.

In 1723, the longtime warden, Marguerite Pancatalin, had been replaced by her protégée, Mademoiselle Bailly. Bailly's corruption was well known: she sought bribes for even the few commodities that should have been freely distributed: blankets in the winter, a bit of salt at all times. But Bailly kept

La Force humming along to the precise and detailed daily rhythm her prede-cessor had decreed in 1721.

The wake-up bell sounded at five; prayers were held in the dormitory; then the prisoners had a half hour to make the beds and deal with "their personal hygiene." From six to seven, they attended mass. From seven to seven fifteen, they were allowed "to satisfy other personal needs" and given a little water to wash their hands. Work began immediately afterwards. At eight, they were authorized some wine and "a bit of bread" for breakfast; then it was back to work until eleven, when watery soup was distributed. Work continued non-stop until seven at night, at which time inmates were given their only water of the day to drink and a second "bit of bread." At eight thirty, they left the work-house for prayers in the dormitory; at nine thirty, they went to bed. Sunday was a special day: they were awakened only at six.

Another eighteenth-century Parisian, Michel Cotel, a Parisian roofer, had his eighteen-year-old daughter Françoise confined to the Salpêtrière on pros-titution charges. Three months later, he begged for her release: he had found her "in the most pitiful state conceivable." The conditions in prison were "so much worse than he ever could have imagined": he had hoped to have her behavior "corrected"; instead, "she was in danger of losing her life."

Not long after her internment, Louise's dossier started to fill up with pleas for her release. And three of them are truly memorable documents.

Noel Poisson once again had the courage to come forward: he petitioned both d'Ombreval and Maurepas with "a demand for justice for his grand-daughter Marie Louise Magoulet." In his argument, he took a clever tack.

Rather than accuse the father who had mustered such powerful support, Noel laid the blame on Louise's stepmother. Anne Legrand, he contended, "had always exercised enormous influence" over Jean. She had used that con-trol "to oblige him to force five minors out of the paternal home." And Legrand's "violence had consistently proved most extreme" against Louise.

Noel's request was followed by a petition addressed to d'Ombreval by the two of Louise's siblings who had never been confined to an institution: Jeanne and Claude. They, too, blamed their wicked stepmother "on account of the hatred she bears all of them." They attributed her malevolence to her "fear that they would seek to be emancipated from their father's guardianship and demand their mother's estate, as well as from a fear that if their father were to die, they might cause her considerable distress."

They explained that their father had obtained a royal decree ordering the "abduction" of their sister Louise, age twenty-three. They added that Jean already had in hand a second such order, which he intended to use against Jeanne, then twenty-one and employed as an embroiderer. The next oldest sister, six-teen-year-old Manon (Marie), had gone missing; they feared the same fate for her. Their youngest sister, Dorothée, had been interned in the Hospital after their mother's death and had not been heard from since. Only Claude was truly safe: he lived in the Hôtel de Bragelonne, where he was employed as a footservant. Jeanne and Claude begged that Louise be set free and that they all be protected "from their father's evil dealings and their stepmother's sinis-ter anger." The siblings promised that the parish priest of Saint-Germain-l'Auxerrois would confirm their story, and he did so.

In Louise's file, their petition was pinned together with a final one. Ten of Jeanne's neighbors had gathered in the home of the woman from whom she rented a room and in whose embroidery workshop she was employed, Madame Prunial, whom they described as "a woman of honor and integrity." Of Jeanne—to whom they referred by her nickname, Janneton (Jeanneton), just as she spoke of younger sister Marie as Manon—they offered a collective assess-ment: "Everything that any of us has ever seen or heard regarding Janneton's character confirms that her behavior has always been sensible, prudent, and judicious. We know her to be a good girl and a fine Christian."

They dated their attestation, July 13, 1724, and added their signatures. There were two wigmakers, Coquelin and Joannet. There was Des Rochers, a mounted policeman in the town watch, and his wife, Jeanne Toussaint. There was a mirror maker, Crepin; a master metal caster by the name of Robbe;

*Petition to the Director of the Parisian Police by Jeanne Magoulet's neighbors, attesting to her fine character.*

Élisabeth Collette, a young woman who identified herself simply as "of age." Madame Prunial couldn't write, so she made a large cross instead. It seems an ordinary Parisian working-class neighborhood, an urban village, taking a stand to fight for a young woman's life.

All those who wrote in the children's defense stressed that the siblings were afraid of their father's next move. That fear was well grounded: it was no longer easy to have a wayward child dispatched "to the islands," but in 1724 the authorities still regularly received such requests from parents, and some of them were still honored.

By July 31, those three petitions had paid off: for the first time in five years, authorities were questioning the word of a Magoulet and officers were investigating Jean's numerous slanders and lies. Soon, Commissioner de Soucy remained the lone holdout. Under pressure to reverse his decision, he grudgingly conceded that "even though the younger girl [Jeanne] had strayed in earlier years, she now appeared to be living wisely," but on Louise's score he refused to budge. He maintained that all his informants had confirmed "that her conduct has always been disgraceful." At July's end, Louise remained in the Salpêtrière.

But Noel's instinct to trust Maurepas had been correct, as had his decision to hand over copies of both his and Louise Poisson's complaints from 1717 about Jean's abuse and his mismanagement of her dowry. The final document in Louise's file is dated August 9 and signed by Maurepas, who had reached this conclusion: "It may be presumed" that Magoulet is afraid that "his children are reaching an age at which they will become able to demand an accounting from him of their mother's estate, and for this reason, he has been trying to eliminate them."

Maurepas seems never to have noticed two flagrant discrepancies. First, Louise Magoulet had been denounced as a prostitute by two different Magoulets, men with quite distinct signatures and identities, each of whom presented himself as her father. Second, according to the testimony of her own siblings and grandfather, in 1724 she was aged twenty-three, a far cry from the thirty-seven-year-old described by the two Magoulets who claimed to be her father and by Antoine Chevrot.

That very day, Maurepas signed an order for Louise's release. On August 4, 1719, Louise had been committed to the Salpêtrière for the first time. Nearly five years to the day later, she was released from that same prison: her third incarceration had come to an end. From the minute she passed between the Salpêtrière's two guardhouses for the last time, her presence in Paris was never again confirmed by an official document of any kind.

But Louise did not leave Paris and Louis. Antoine Chevrot's behavior confirmed this.

On July 1, 1724, barely a week after an order for Louise's arrest had been issued, Antoine had signed a contract with the financier Antoine Liare, Sieur des Noyers. He was once again borrowing a significant sum: 13,375 livres. He promised to pay Liare 243 livres, 3 sous, and 7 deniers in quarterly payments. In the event of nonpayment, he gave Liare the right to seize the rent on the rue du Perche property and the income from his position in the annuities administration.

To take on significant new debt when he was unable to meet payments on already existing loans and at a time when France was still dealing with the economic crisis brought on by the collapse of Law's institutions was high-risk behavior. In the years to come, Liare proved the toughest of Antoine's many creditors, both for Antoine in his lifetime and for his sons after his death.

But Antoine tied this millstone around their necks willingly. He was planning Louis' life after Louise.

Antoine used Liare's money to "augment" his office. At times when the monarchy was desperate for a quick influx of funds, it offered those who held positions in various administrations the chance to increase their initial investment in exchange for higher wages. Antoine was thus preparing an even more impressive nest egg for his eldest son.

And then a month after the deal with Liare was signed, against all odds, Louise walked free once again.

On September 9, 1724 Louis turned twenty-four. In just a year, he would no longer have been under his father's complete control. As he always did in moments of crisis, Antoine took serious legal action. This time, on November 24, he composed a will. Antoine carefully concealed the document's contents, but he made sure that Louis knew of its existence and even just where it was locked away.

Maurepas had not stressed the fact in his statement ordering Louise's release from the Salpêtrière, but it was now part of the public record that Louise was not an older seductress but two years younger than Louis. Did Antoine fear that his son had been given grounds on which to contest the Parlement's decision to classify his marriage as a case of *rapt de séduction*? From the will's extraordinary wording, it is clear that Antoine knew that Louise was still very much a part of his son's life and that he had forbidden Louis ever to think of a second marriage with Louise, but his son would make no such promise.

The key sentence of Antoine's November 1724 testament is a stunner: "If ever his oldest son Louis Chevrot should have the misfortune to marry (God forbid!) the woman named Marie Louise Magoulet with whom he formerly contracted a marriage in London, England, a marriage that was broken off and annulled by a decree of the Parisian Parlement's court on December 10, 1723, the testator declares that his eldest son will be completely disinherited and wants him to understand that he will remain deprived of any portion of the estate that should have been his and that the estate in its entirety will go instead to his second son Antoine Charles and then to the children of Antoine Charles."

That exclamation—"God forbid!"—remains the clearest proof of the mad rage that Louise Magoulet inspired in Antoine all through his life's final decade.

Four days after Antoine visited a notary to have that toxic will drawn up, Louis and Louise took their revenge on her father.

All through the eighteenth century, the officials of the Parisian police were spying on criminal activity in the city in various ways; in particular, networks of paid informants regularly sent in written reports concerning suspicious individuals. On November 28, 1724, along with the usual accounts from known informants, an unexpected report landed on someone's desk: the anonymous denunciation of an individual named "Sir Magoullet" (no first name and two *l*s) and identified as "a *gainier* merchant and alleged jeweler." Magoullet was reported for the crime surest to attract the authorities' immediate attention: political subversion. "To anyone and everyone who comes into his shop he launches into a litany of insults and outrageous curses against all the government's ministers." The report ended by providing the exact address of this man who dared undermine the state's authority: "He lives on the Quai de l'Horloge at the sign of the Golden Apple."

Still officially anonymous, the denunciation quickly made its way through the hierarchy of police officials. On December 6, Maurepas signed an arrest order, and on December 8, a new prisoner was "conducted to the Bastille" by Officer Langlade. There is no sign that anyone ever connected this Magoullet, officially identified as Clément, with the Jean Magoulet who had been blamed only months before for having attempted "to eliminate" his own children.

In the end, the police concluded that Louis Chevrot had authored that anonymous report.

The individual calling himself Clément Magoullet spent Christmas 1724 in the Bastille. And by the time the holiday came around, he was becoming unraveled. His normally masterful handwriting, the foundation of all his double-dealings, clearly revealed that he was in control no longer.

# CHAPTER SEVENTEEN

# "A Diabolical Person"
## Clément Magoullet:
## December 1724–May 15, 1732

H E DIDN'T SEE it coming.

On December 8, 1724, when Officer Langlade arrived at the Golden Apple to arrest an individual identified only as "the merchant named Magoullet," the tradesman, who prided himself on setting the rules of the game and on remaining at least one step ahead, was blindsided. Every aspect of this case indicates that Clément for once was simply improvising.

Paris' Bastille prison kept a careful docket of all those confined there. A separate sheet was assigned to each new resident, a truly oversized leaf of paper, far larger even than a page in a folio volume. Categories such as name, date of lockup, and so forth were printed across the top, and lots of room was left below for handwritten information.

The sheet dedicated to prisoner "Clément Magoullet" survived some major catastrophe, most likely a fire, perhaps one of those that tore through the prison at the beginning of the 1789 revolution. As a result, the handwriting is hard to decipher: nevertheless, in faint letters it's still possible to make out that when forced to choose on the spot, the new inmate had identified himself as "a jeweler in Paris." The prisoner was in for a shock when he saw the information the police officer entered next, the reason for his incarceration: "For having spoken about the government and its ministers in a highly disrespectful fashion." After all, if you consider the many crimes for which the alleged jeweler might have been locked up, this was hardly the first that would have come to mind.

Next came the listing of the contents of the prisoner's pockets: some coins, so small a sum that the admitting officer didn't bother to add it up; "a few lottery tickets"; and finally, "the key to a drawer in his home," about which

Clément remarked that "he just happened to have it on him." The man had secrets; he needed to make certain that no one, not even his alleged wife, could ever gain access to them.

Clément of course denied the charges. They nevertheless let him stew for a bit, for over two weeks. During that time, he had no visitors, and no one wrote to the lieutenant general to beg for his release.

On December 24, when the police finally got around to interrogating Clément, every aspect of his statement was odd. When asked who he was, he began by announcing that he was sixty, providing a piece of information that in eighteenth-century Paris was rarely part of a prisoner's basic identification. Jean/Clément, born in 1682, had decided that advanced age would be crucial to his defense.

He further identified himself as Catholic. But of course he was. Not every Frenchman was a Catholic, even though the vast majority were, but at a time when all other religions were officially outlawed, no one would have dared admit to the police an adherence to another faith. For this reason no one felt the need to announce that they were Catholic, and therefore Clément's unprompted admission was highly unusual.

Clément also described himself as married, with two children, so he was still counting Louise in his family unit. He said he had run a shop on the Quai de l'École for the past thirty years, which was stretching the point quite a bit, since he had taken over Hubert's lease only in 1707. Many in the neighborhood would speak up in his defense, he added, but his suggestion of a character witness was still another unexpected choice: the curate of the Sainte-Chapelle, rather than the priest Clément had always previously invoked as willing to testify in his behalf, his parish priest at Saint-Barthélemy.

As for his defense, only someone counting on the police not to connect any dots would have tried it. He had never in any way spoken "with a lack of respect about any person of the first rank." "Only a devil would have accused him of this behavior." And he knew just such "a diabolical person: Chevrot." "Who is Chevrot?" he asked in a rhetorical flourish, then answered his own question: Chevrot was a man of about sixty, Clément responded, and he believed that he lived at the Hôtel de Ville, where he "supervised" annuities. Clément Magoullet claimed never to have seen Antoine Chevrot, but he was sure of one thing: "Chevrot wanted to ruin his life."

The explanation he offered for the "diabolical" Chevrot's hatred was classic *magoulese*. Chevrot's crusade against him had begun, Clément alleged, when Chevrot's son, whom Clément described as age twenty-four and a ne'er-do-well, had persuaded Clément's daughter to marry him in a clandestine ceremony.

Clément was against this union and had had it annulled; ever since, both father and son had sought revenge. The son (Louis) had smeared Clément's reputation with "calumnies" such as the falsehood about his antigovernment diatribes. His father (Antoine) had filed lawsuits against Clément, even taking his case to the court of the Parisian Parlement. All this has happened, Clément insisted repeatedly, because Clément had defended his daughter's and his family's honor by having this marriage broken off.

After the interrogation, Lieutenant General d'Ombreval asked longtime police commissioner Jean-Jacques Camuset, whose beat was the area near the Place de Grève, to check out Clément's story and to question the prisoner informally. And thus Clément's case was put into the hands of still another officer with no prior experience with the Magoulet clan.

Clément's dossier is suspiciously thin, particularly for someone who had been arrested for a crime that the government took seriously. There is no evidence that much energy was wasted over the holiday season investigating the case. Indeed, the only testimony heard came from the prisoner's wife: about the time of Clément's interrogation, and well over two weeks after his arrest, Desjardins at last addressed several petitions to d'Ombreval: had she just noticed that he was missing from the home they allegedly shared? She portrayed both herself and her husband as "weak" and in poor health. Describing her husband as sixty-five rather than the sixty he had claimed, she begged that he be allowed to return home quickly: otherwise, "both his family and his business would be totally ruined."

The prisoner seems to have been completely forgotten over Christmas. On December 29, Clément finally had his first visitor when Desjardins showed up with fresh clothing. The list of what the woman who called herself "wife Magoullet" brought speaks volumes about the straitened circumstances in which Clément lived.

In the eighteenth century, only the wealthy changed outerwear often, and no one had outer garments cleaned with any frequency. But only those living at or below the poverty line dressed as Clément did, without regularly changing the first item of clothing men and women alike slipped on, the only clothing they wore next to the skin, the *chemise* or shift that covered their bodies from the neck to the knees. There were separate ones for day and night; a clean chemise was the foundation of personal hygiene, and they were washed frequently. Pierre Chicot, for instance, owned twelve of them, in order to be sure of always having clean ones on hand. But Clément had worn the same shift for three weeks, and when Desjardins finally visited, she brought but two more. The entire list of items for whose reception the prisoner signed was

*Clément Magoullet's signature in the Bastille's prison register*
*on December 24, 1724.*

meager indeed: two pairs of cuffs, two handkerchiefs, a tiny bit of money. His wife promised to return with something she had forgotten: a fresh pair of stockings.

Between December 24 and December 29, something had changed radically, either in the prisoner's true state of mind or in his self-presentation to the police. When he signed his interrogation on December 24, Clément was a master of the quill who produced an autograph thoroughly self-assured, one in which two letters in particular were distinctive and carefully formed: the initial *M* and the two *l*s. In contrast, the signature he affixed five days later to the list of clothing seems to indicate profound destabilization, whether actual or feigned. On December 29, Clément wrote in a decidedly primitive manner, with hardly more skill than Jean I, and without either of those characteristic letters.

Had the prisoner decided to rethink his signature so that his writing appeared as shaky and fragile as the state of his health as he described it? Or did Clément's crude signature on December 29 signal his fear that the game of his double life might soon be up? If that were indeed the case, he needn't have worried.

Camuset never tried to track down the Chevrots. The report on his investigation simply repeated, almost verbatim, Clément's accusations against those he referred to as "his son-in-law" and his father, as well as the prisoner's pleas for mercy on account of his physical "frailty." Camuset concluded that the

*Clément Magoullet's signature on the*
*list of clothing brought to him in*
*the Bastille on December 29, 1724.*

allegations made against Clément were "the invention of a man who had married his daughter without her father's permission, causing him to have their
union annulled" and suggested that "he couldn't imagine what disadvantage
there would be to releasing the prisoner." D'Ombreval agreed that surely "a
few weeks in the Bastille had been enough."

Then, suddenly, on January 17, 1725, Monsieur le Duc, Condé himself,
made known "his intention that the individual named Magoulet be released."
Somehow, Jean had managed to alert Condé to his plight without revealing
his alter ego. The next day, Jean/Clément was allowed to walk away from the
closest brush with exposure of his double life that he would ever know.

In her December 1724 petitions, Marie Louise Desjardins described both
herself and her husband as "weak and ill." But whereas Clément would go on
to enjoy years of apparently excellent health, his wife did not fare as well. Six
months after her husband's release from the Bastille, she was dead.

The young woman who may have been Desjardins' biological child, Marie
Geneviève, had not forgiven Clément for tricking her into accepting a soon to
be devalued dowry in 1720. Determined to expose as many of his secrets as
possible, as soon as her mother died on July 13, she called the police to the

scene to put seals on any furniture that could have contained important documents or valuables. And at 8 A.M. on July 14, an inventory of the contents of the apartment and the shop on the Quai de l'Horloge began; this was a process Clément would have fought tooth and nail to avoid, just as Jean I had resisted all attempts to have his belongings investigated and itemized. The July 14, 1725 evaluation marked the first time that the belongings of either Jean Magoulet were inventoried.

Geneviève had gone to great lengths to make the process happen. She had obtained a court order obliging Clément to allow the notaries in to do their job and giving her the right to be present, accompanied by a lawyer. A second attorney also followed the proceedings: he represented someone who chose not to be there but who gave Geneviève her full legal support, Louise Magoulet. The document that records the process contains not a clue as to her whereabouts, and that silence is unusual. But Louise's address was far from the most significant information missing from the official tally.

Not all French families maintained their records as compulsively as did the Chevrots, but all eighteenth-century inventories listed at least a few key documents of which the family held copies: most notably the marriage contract of the deceased, a convention whose terms were essential to the estate's settlement. The Magoullet-Desjardins couple was a most singular case, a simply inconceivable instance: they had accumulated no paper trail whatsoever. The notary responsible for the inventory turned up nothing more significant than a few receipts for rent.

In the years since they had cosigned their original lease in June 1714—years that marked the end of Jean's marriage with Louise Poisson and the first half of his union with Anne Legrand—the Magoullet-Desjardins couple had lived completely under the radar. Clément's was a family without a past.

Their tiny apartment had been located on their building's highest and least expensive floor, the fifth. To describe its rooms, the notary frequently used the adjective "small," and when notaries of the period had recourse to "small," they sought to call attention to something truly undersized. The kitchen was characterized as "small," as was the bedroom. It's just as well that the spaces were not commodious: the couple had accumulated virtually no possessions with which to furnish them.

The kitchen contained little beyond a half dozen pewter plates, a couple of frying pans, a salad bowl, a fruit bowl, and two candleholders, one of which was described as "broken." Total value of all their dishes and cooking implements combined: 20 livres. Their furniture was limited to two armchairs and three chairs. They owned four nearly worthless paintings, all religious scenes:

two represented the Virgin Mary, one Mary Magdalene, and the last the cru-
cifixion. Otherwise, the only items intended to make the place more attractive
were lined up above the fireplace: three porcelain cups, seven marble balls,
and two "small" plaster lions. Total value: 6 livres. And even that minimal decorative expense had not come out of Clément's pocket: the set had already
figured in Hubert Magoulet's 1707 inventory. His widow had simply left the
pieces in the apartment for Clément, and there they had remained ever since.
All the other Magoulets owned a certain amount of silver cutlery; this couple
didn't have a single piece.

There was almost no linen: no sheets whatsoever and only two towels, and
even they were described as "old." In contrast, Louise Poisson Magoulet owned
eighteen towels, all in good condition. There was one handkerchief, two
women's chemises ("in bad shape"), one pair of men's stockings (the pair
Desjardins had forgotten to bring to the Bastille), and finally two "old" men's
shifts, a tally that indicates that the clothing Clément had used in prison had
constituted his entire wardrobe. Clément had an explanation for this shortage,
which he knew would seem odd. During his wife's illness, "he had been obliged
to sell his clothing in order to pay for her care."

In the entire inventory, only one category stands in sharp contrast to the
ambient paucity: women's garments. Desjardins hadn't owned many, essentially
one outfit for everyday and one for special occasions, but the fabrics (damask,
silk) were of good quality. And then there was the pine box packed to the gills
with ladies' shoes, four pairs of high fashion shoes, all made from fine textiles:
one pair in white damask with silver braid, another in yellow damask embroidered with silver thread. So much elegant footwear in the wardrobe of a woman
who otherwise owned next to nothing: it doesn't make sense.

When I reflected on that part of Desjardins' inventory, I thought of Louise
Poisson Magoulet and her account of returning home one evening to find that
Jean was ready to leave for the opera ball in the company of "women of ill
repute" dressed in her clothes. The touches of women's high fashion found
amid the forlorn remains of Desjardins' life could have been outfits that Desjardins had removed from Louise's closet a decade before.

The total value of the apartment's contents, 619 livres, sums it all up. Even
Louise Poisson, living alone and struggling to make ends meet, died surrounded
by possessions worth a thousand. Jean had plenty of finery in his official existence with Anne Legrand; he had wasted no funds on his second life but had
kept it as low-rent as possible.

The workshop's contents offered still more surprises. No one could have
practiced there the craft that Clément most often named when asked to identify

himself: jeweler. There were no tools, no jewelry, not a stone, not a scrap of precious metal. Louis had been correct to denounce Clément to the police as an "alleged jeweler."

There were, on the other hand, objects crafted by a *gainier*—a couple of dozen cases for knives, a few wig boxes—but there were none of the exotic skins and fancy nails so prevalent in the inventory of Hubert's workshop. By far the dominant part of the stock was actually related in various ways to glasses: there were eyeglasses, as well as lenses for telescopes and other uses. Clément had described his trade in various ways, but in actuality, just as Antoine Chevrot had alleged when he began his *rapt de séduction* case, he had indeed for the most part "sold glasses." None of the objects were high-end: the total value of the shop's contents was a mere 574 livres, a marked difference from the 1,300 appraisal of the reduced stock that Hubert maintained still at his life's end.

That low valuation was wildly out of sync with the bills that Clément soon began to present to the estate for payment. There was to begin with what he claimed to have spent for his wife's care during her last illness. Whereas it was usual to itemize such expenses, as Noel Poisson had done for Louise Poisson's inventory, Clément merely gave a total with no breakdown, the exact total that Noel had listed in 1718. He also claimed to owe thousands to merchants in cities from London to Amsterdam, debts of up to 1,300 livres explained only vaguely as "for merchandise." Once again, it didn't add up: Why would a low-rent businessman invest many times the value of his current ragtag stock in unspecified new merchandise? And why would he have imported that merchandise from far-flung capitals?

The picture that he thereby presented, however, was clear: Marie Louise Desjardins' estate had no assets to speak of, only massive debts. There was no inheritance for anyone to fight over.

On August 11, the conclusions of the inventory were recorded and accepted as correct by "Clément Magoullet, jeweler" and by the lawyers representing his daughters, Marie Geneviève and Marie Louise. That indirect encounter was the last recorded appearance of Clément's name in conjunction with Magoulet family affairs.

Clément's signature appeared numerous times on the 1725 inventory; no two were alike. Some signatures were relatively sophisticated, others relatively crude. He shaped key letters differently each time; he didn't even spell "Magoulet" consistently. It was as if he had given up on the role.

The summer of Desjardins' death was still another moment of national crisis: France endured the most devastating famine since the Great Winter. Nowhere were the shortages as dire as in Paris. All through the summer of

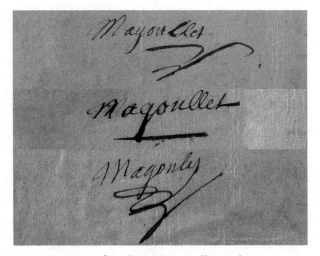

*Signatures by Clément Magoullet on the same*
*1725 document.*

1725, during the last months before flour from the new harvest could reach the city, Parisians were rioting to protest the price of bread. Because of those bread riots, d'Ombreval was forced to step down as lieutenant general.

By the time the new lieutenant general, René Hérault, took up his position, Clément was making a fresh start. Exactly four months after Desjardins' death—and at a moment when Anne Legrand was still very much alive—he took a new wife. This was the kind of speedy remarriage favored, and understandably so, by men with young children to care for after a spouse's death.

The man who at the beginning of 1725 had been described as "frail" and "suffering" from various ailments had been rejuvenated during the months when most Parisians in his economic category were fighting for their lives. On November 16, 1725, Clément signed a contract: this marriage was a matter of public record. Two in-laws, Jean Megret and Pierre Moustrel, were his witnesses.

His bride, Jeanne Nicolle Masson, belonged to a family of Parisian potters in pewter, though not a prosperous one. The meager household effects that were her only dowry were all acquired "with her own savings." Her parents gave her nothing, but they were people of very modest means. When her father died in 1730, he left his four children only an annuity worth 150 livres a year to divide among themselves. Jean had always been an extremely seductive man, and even Jean in the role of Clément would have been a big step up for Jeanne Nicolle.

Nothing more was heard from the couple for the six and a half years of their marriage. And then, in 1732, a series of seemingly unrelated events coincided.

On May 11, 1732, Jean Magoulet laid the foundation for a new phase of his official life when he signed the papers for an annuity contract. He accepted money from a young unmarried woman with a great deal of disposable income that was hers to use as she liked; the woman had chosen to entrust 4,000 livres to Jean. In return, he promised her an annual lifetime payment of 200 livres.

Not quite four months after that annuity agreement was reached, on September 9, Anne Legrand died. Nothing indicates that she had been ill or that she had known that her time was limited. No evidence of suspicious circumstances can be found, but the fact that a wealthy, much younger woman had recently come into Jean's life does render the timing of Legrand's death suspect. Legrand's effects were inventoried within days of her demise, and the formalities surrounding her estate were quickly dealt with. The stage was now set.

On October 5, 1732, not even a month after the death of his wife of thirteen and a half years and only three days after her estate had been settled, Jean remarried. This was an extraordinarily quick turnaround, even in an age when men often remarried promptly.

His bride was the young woman with whom Jean Magoulet had signed an annuity contract on May 11: Anne Tabary.

On May 14, three days after Jean's annuity contract with Tabary was notarized, the fictitious Clément Magoullet's life ended in the apartment at the sign of the Golden Apple where it had officially begun. His widow would soon make a fresh start of her own.

Clément's burial on May 15 took place not in the church he had so often described as his parish church, Saint-Barthélemy, but at Saint-Jacques-de-la-Boucherie. That edifice was destroyed during the Revolution; all that remains today is the early sixteenth-century belfry now known as the Saint-Jacques tower. Positioned on the Right Bank across the Seine from the Quai de l'Horloge, Saint-Jacques was not hugely distant from Clément's home, but still: burials did tend to take place in the deceased's own parish.

Two Magoulets signed the church record after the ceremony: both claimed to be the dead man's nephews. There was Martin Magoulet, who had helped Jacques and Marie Freslin whenever they needed a straw man to shelter their identity in questionable financial deals. The second witness to Clément's burial? Jean Magoulet, who identified himself as a *peaussier*, a practitioner of the same trade as Pierre Chicot, his soon-to-be-deceased second wife's first husband.

Was the coffin empty? Did they bury someone else in Clément's place? Did they choose Saint-Jacques because its curate, Father Grillon, was willing to go along with their subterfuge? In eighteenth-century Paris, no remotely reliable system for the identification of dead bodies existed, so the scam would not have been hard to pull off.

Jeanne Nicolle Masson did not sign the register on May 15, but there was no bad blood between her and Jean. When Jean married Anne Tabary a few months later, among those who stood up for him was someone who signed "Jeanne Nicolle" and identified herself as "a friend."

Besides, Clément's elimination was beneficial to Jeanne Nicolle. On November 29, 1732, she remarried, and this time her husband, Charles Mercier, a wine dealer, was younger than she. They had two daughters before she died on July 27, 1740.

The events of 1732 indicate that the partnership between Clément and Jeanne Nicolle Masson as well as the character "Clément Magoullet" had both run their course. The reshuffling of the cards that took place was advantageous for everyone but Anne Legrand.

# CHAPTER EIGHTEEN

# The Remains of the Day
## The Chevrots: 1725–1736

O N SEPTEMBER 9, 1725, Louis Chevrot turned twenty-five. His coming-of-age was more symbolic than real, for he remained still very much under his father's control. But by then, the times were changing. It was the end of an era: the last of the old guard—those faithful servants at the court of Louis XIV, the monarch to whom many of their generation still referred as "the king," as though there would ever be only one—were finally dying out.

On January 25, 1726, a monstrously long probate inventory was begun: notaries were evaluating the property of the fabulously wealthy Duchesse Du Lude, principal lady-in-waiting of the Duchesse de Bourgogne (Madame la Dauphine). Marie Charlotte Perrin, Louis' maternal grandmother and the head of the duchess's own court, who since her husband's death had lived in the Du Lude mansion on the rue Saint-Dominique, witnessed the entire process. She explained to the notaries that everything in her rooms had been given to her by the duchess: Perrin's possessions thus had an almost royal provenance.

Not even three months later, on April 14, 1726, still another estate was tallied up: Louis' grandmother had died. This time, her son-in-law Antoine was a witness. Since he was there in his capacity as guardian for his own two sons, who together would inherit half the estate, he was asked to identify those he represented, and Antoine Chevrot did: Louis, age twenty-four; Antoine Charles, age twenty-three. Antoine Charles was indeed twenty-three at the time, whereas Louis had in fact crossed the long-traditional line into majority seven months earlier. This was surely not an honest mistake on Antoine's part.

There was no wealth to speak of for the heirs to share. Rather than bother with an expensive detailed inventory, they simply divided up her belongings. At the time of Antoine's death, he still clung to some of these vestiges of the golden age of Versailles.

Later that year, Antoine made it clear that his position toward the son who refused to share his father's vision of upward mobility had not softened in the two years since he had made his will. On December 6, 1726, he added a codicil to that document, changing his executor from a Daulmay cousin to someone he could trust to be a more rigorous executor: Barthélemy Lambert, a lawyer for the Parisian Parlement. Antoine specified that "he wished his will to remain precisely as it was written." By the end of 1726, Louis had still not given up his hope of remarriage with Louise, as Antoine was well aware.

When he reinforced the control he planned to exercise over Louis from beyond the grave, Antoine may also have been mindful of an upcoming birthday: in early 1727, Louise Magoulet was to turn twenty-five.

By then, France was at last showing signs of emerging from the long period of turbulence that had slowed its economy since the collapse of Law's system. All agreed that Michel Le Peletier des Forts, named controller general of finance in June 1726 and who exercised that function until March 1730, had been brilliantly successful in stabilizing the country's currency.

In late 1728, the French had reason to fear that the climate would once again stymie their chances for recovery. All that December and throughout January 1729, the country was in the grip of what lawyer Barbier described as "an extraordinary cold wave, virtually identical to that of the Great Winter of 1709." Conditions in Paris were so alarming that, in an effort to avoid a repetition of the catastrophic death toll of the winter that no one could forget, municipal authorities distributed wood to the poorest households and ordered public fires built and maintained at the city's major intersections.

When many feared a repetition of the events twenty years earlier when Antoine's wife had died, his thoughts turned, just as they had in the month before Marie Françoise's death, to his estate. On February 15, Antoine borrowed still another large sum: 8,000 livres, once again "to augment" his position as annuities controller. The money was a loan from a magnate of Parisian finance: Jean François Jessaume, Sieur de Vallière, who listed the most exclusive address in the city: the Place Vendôme. Jessaume was a cutthroat businessman, hardly someone to wait patiently for late payments. This new loan tied the heaviest millstone of all around the necks of Antoine's future heirs.

By then, Antoine had a total of 71,375 livres invested in the annuities post. With the combination of this package and the provisions in his will, he surely believed that Louis would be forced to adopt the life traditional for a firstborn Chevrot: 71,375 livres was a steep price, but getting rid of Louise Magoulet was worth any sum.

This was the last time Antoine would have the chance to increase the value of his post as annuities controller. In the early hours of Sunday, August 21, 1729, he died.

Sunday or no Sunday, already at 5 A.M., Louis summoned Police Commissioner Charles Ambroise Guillemot d'Alby to the rue de la Verrerie. The minute d'Alby set foot inside the family apartment, Louis presented the kind of request that might have taken the commissioner aback: he wanted him "to search the drawers of the desk in his father's office in order to find his will." Louis promised that after reading it, he would "turn the will over to the appropriate person," before adding that "he reserved the right to contest both the will and its codicil." Request denied.

Louis and Antoine Charles next asked for access to Antoine's strongbox because they had no money to pay for his funeral and for household expenses while his estate was being settled. This request was granted, and the coins in "an old leather-covered coffer" were tallied up: 414 livres. Guillemot d'Alby then had bailiffs fix the seals.

The brothers had another unusual request. They wanted to take Guillemot d'Alby for a longish walk, across the Île de la Cité and past Notre-Dame cathedral to a small street on the other bank of the Seine, the rue de la Boucherie (today's rue de la Bûcherie). Together, they visited the apartment of a merchant who prepared and sold furs, a *pelletier* named André, so that the commissioner could take stock of a second set of Antoine's possessions, which André said had been "entrusted to his care." A large wardrobe in André's apartment was crammed with household objects, all of which, the furrier explained, had been brought to the apartment by Anne Lesage, who had identified herself as Antoine's "housekeeper." There were dishes, table knives, a coffeepot, a dozen towels, sheets, a full toiletry kit, even a jam pot.

No explanation was ever offered for Antoine's beachhead on the Left Bank. Did he and Lesage go there when they wanted to get away from his sons? Or was there still another woman in his life?

A day later, Guillemot d'Alby paid a return visit to the rue de la Verrerie apartment to look into an incident that Louis had felt "obliged" to report. On the evening of Antoine's death, the brothers had been having dinner when Louis heard in their father's study "the sound of paper being torn." He rushed in to investigate and noticed that one of the sealed bands placed earlier that day had been broken, "the one around the left-hand drawers in his father's desk." He also spotted "their cat emerging from under the carpet that lies beneath the desk" and thus decided that it was "reasonable" to assume that the broken seal was the cat's doing. Louis signed a statement swearing that he had not opened any of the drawers.

If that was indeed the case, then he discovered what his father had prepared for him only in the office of the notary chosen by his guardian, Augustin Loyson. In that event, the reading of Antoine's will could hardly have been a traditionally staid legal rite.

The thick bundle of documents that Antoine had prepared for his eldest son with exquisite care can still be viewed in France's National Archives, bound together in the exact order in which Louis discovered them in 1729. If there is such a thing as killer documents, then these were meant to be lethal.

Parents keep souvenirs of their lives and of the lives of those who came before them to help their children understand the family past and the high points of its history. Eighteenth-century French parents passed on copies of significant legal documents so that their heirs would have proof, should the legitimacy of an inheritance ever be questioned. What Antoine did bears no resemblance to either of these familiar scenarios.

Antoine's will and its codicil are the topmost papers in the stack, and thus the first documents Louis saw. And had the slightest doubt remained about why his father had treated him as he had, the subsequent writings in that thick bundle made the answer clear: "Annexes to the division of property in Antoine Chevrot's estate" reads the title page. What follows is the complete record of Antoine's relentless court battle to have Louis' marriage annulled. One appeal after another, verdict after verdict, all carefully copied on parchment, legal treasures preserved with pride. Antoine's motions, the evidence he had presented to the Parlement's court, such as the birth certificate of baby Jean Louis from 1719—all were there so that Louis could never forget a single moment of his marriage's tortured legal history.

At the moment of Antoine's death, Louis and Louise could still have believed that time was on their side. When the Parisian Parlement laid the foundations for the doctrine of *rapt de séduction*, its lawyers modified the traditional age of majority, raising it to thirty for men. In August 1729, even that final hurdle was but a year away for Louis. But then he heard his father's will: should he ever contract a second marriage with Louise, he was disinherited. And there was more.

Antoine had realized that making it impossible for them ever to marry again might not be enough to drive Louise from his son's life. "As soon as all justifiable debts have been paid," Antoine's will continued, "for the legitimate reason that he has carefully explained, the testator bequeaths all his possessions to the children born to Louis and Antoine Charles from legitimate marriages. Louis and Antoine Charles cannot sell or mortgage any part of the estate. During their lifetime, they will enjoy a right of usufruct, but the estate belongs to their direct descendants."

Louis and Antoine Charles were to spend their lives as caretakers for the Chevrot family estate, which would remain invested exactly as Antoine had decided, so that they could have something to pass on to their children. And to have even this right, Louis, then twenty-nine and unmarried, having given no indication in the nine years since the clandestine ceremony in London that he ever planned to wed anyone else, had to take a bride—any woman but Louise Magoulet.

Louis could have refused the estate: individuals did reject inheritances on the grounds that they would be "more burdensome than profitable." But the two individuals who were providing legal and financial advice, Louis' notary and Barthélemy Lambert, who acted both as Louis' guardian and as Antoine's executor, surely left him no choice in the matter. But then they would have done just that. Antoine had been confident that Lambert would see to it that his wishes were carried out to the letter, which he did. And the notary had a plan, to which Lambert gave his approval: it involved notary Loyson's niece.

Four months after his father's death, on January 3, 1730, Louis Chevrot finally affixed his name to a marriage contract. The match was radically downmarket for the eldest son of a family that for two generations had had members of the royal family present when their marriage agreements were drawn up. Louis was marrying someone whose social status, while somewhat superior to that of the daughter of a "glasses salesman," was decidedly inferior to that of the daughter of the Queen's Embroiderer.

Later in his life, Marie Élizabeth Loyson's notary uncle became an influential and prosperous member of his profession. Even though in 1730 that prosperity was a long way in the future, Loyson was the bride's most distinguished relation by far. Her deceased father, Pierre, had been a hatmaker—like her uncles and other family members, a simple artisan: there wasn't a master craftsman in the lot. Marie Élizabeth lived with her mother in a modest neighborhood very near Clément's address; Saint-Barthélemy was her parish church. Louis' brother stood up for him, as well as a friend with a least a toehold in the nobility, but the bride's witness was notary Loyson's daughter. This was a match nothing like what Antoine had intended for his eldest son.

In the matter of her dowry, 4,000 livres, Louis would have done well to read the fine print. Her widowed mother was allowing her only daughter to borrow ahead, to receive her share of her father's estate while her mother was still alive. Even so, she was able to give the couple merely 1,000 up front, and even that was a combination of cash and far less desirable personal possessions. It was only on May 4, 1734 that the dowry was finally paid in full, and by 1734 those final 1,000 livres were much too little and came much too late.

The minute Antoine died, creditors had descended to put in their claims. First in line was Antoine's "servant" or "housekeeper," Anne Lesage. The day of Antoine's death, she demanded payment on 1,300 livres in promissory notes signed by Antoine. The brothers made an initial payment of 102 that very day. Lesage, who had studied Antoine's ways, took them to court at once: on November 23, 1729, they were ordered to pay the remaining 1,200, plus interest. She also began fighting to obtain the 2,000 he had promised her daughter Antoinette in his will, "to allow her to find a suitable marriage partner." The brothers contested the bequest, a better deal than they had received, but once again they lost their case.

At the time of his death, Antoine had already spent the entirety of his income from his position for 1729. He had specified that his wages would henceforth be divided among his two sons in a precise manner: Louis would get the money due in 1730, Antoine Charles in 1731, and so forth. This would have meant something between 3,500 and 5,000 per annum. However, as the brothers learned when the estate was settled, Antoine was so massively in arrears that "there was a lien against all his property." In the years to come, the brothers received no income at all; instead their notary Loyson collected all payments and automatically disbursed the funds to Antoine's creditors.

Even before their father's estate could be settled, the brothers had to deal with what Antoine had considered "legitimate expenses." These included the fee to have Antoine's punishing will registered and thus made official. Antoine's executor billed them 500 livres for having carried out Antoine's brutal dictates with lawyerly exactitude. And there was the cost of Antoine's funeral.

If ever proof was needed that Louis Chevrot was a good man, it was provided by the send-off he arranged for his father.

Antoine had a candlelit wake, as well as a grand funeral procession, for which candle bearers led the way. His sons, who otherwise didn't own a single item of decent clothing, had proper mourning dress made. It all came to a grand total of 761 livres, then the average cost of last rites for Parisians from the world of high finance. In contrast, Antoine had spent precisely 143 livres for the funeral of his deceased wife's mother.

To pay for all this, the brothers raised cash any way they could. They began by selling the contents of Antoine's apartment. The inventory for that sale exposed various Chevrot family secrets.

The brothers, for example, had shared a room, a poorly appointed space on their building's less prestigious third floor, while living on the second, noble floor below had been Antoine and, right next door to him, Lesage. A discreet passageway tucked away behind the door to Antoine's chamber connected their bedrooms. All possessions of any value were found in those spaces. The contents of Lesage's room, all of which Antoine bequeathed to her, included the only fine mirror in the house, paintings, a chandelier, and a set of six chairs.

Antoine's clothing was worthless: two suits and a cloak, both described as "old." He owned but a single pair of shoes. The sole item that was more than utilitarian spoke to his aristocratic pretensions: a chestnut-colored periwig.

Indeed, in all the apartment's contents the only objects of note were the Duchesse Du Lude's gifts to Louis' grandmother. That grand chiming clock in a marquetry case still remained, as did a few pieces of silver, kept hidden away by Antoine in a built-in closet next to the fireplace where he also stored small indulgences for his personal pleasure: tobacco, snuff, scents.

On September 23, 1729, everything Antoine Chevrot had owned went on the auction block. His sons made only 208 livres, 19 sous, and 7 deniers from the sale, not even half the fee owed the estate's executor. By then, they had already rented the space in which Antoine had been living with Lesage to an upholsterer and his wife. Antoine Charles moved to a small rental nearby, but Louis stayed on. In January 1730, Louis and Marie Élizabeth began their married life in the single room that he had formerly shared with his brother. They furnished it with some of Antoine's bedding that was in such poor shape that the brothers had not even tried to sell it, and with possessions from Marie Élizabeth's dowry. Even modest artisans or merchants such as Clément lived more comfortably than this.

The years of Louis' marriage became one long ritual of debt. Lawyer Lambert locked the brothers into a repetition of Antoine's basic strategy: robbing Peter to pay Paul. Antoine had taken out a loan with the financier Jessaume in 1727; in order to get Jessaume off their backs, the brothers borrowed 12,000 livres from the royal tailor Charles Barbery. And that was just for starters.

Antoine had never managed to break free of this cycle of debt. Louis, who shared neither his father's passion for money nor his fervor for litigation, didn't stand a chance. The copious paper trail he left from late 1729 to early 1736 is an endless account of sums owed, lawsuits lost, court-ordered repayments, and liens against property that already had so many liens on it that creditors had to line up for a share of any income that it brought in. Interest on Antoine's many loans kept mounting up; every time a suit was decided in favor of one of their creditors, as they always were, their opponent's legal fees were added on.

Year after year, the mountain of debt grew.

There remained one sure source of revenue: the house on the rue du Perche that had entered the Chevrot estate in 1665. It was rented out for 400 livres a year, and Claude Mongrolle, the vinegar and mustard merchant who lived and had his commerce there, actually paid on time. At first, Mogrolle would even hand over the entire year's rent to the brothers on January 1.

But then Louis became so desperate that he began to borrow from Mongrolle. The merchant naturally withheld his rent while waiting for repayment: Mogrolle was patient for years; he took legal action only when Louis began to owe him money for a second reason.

Sometimes the house on the rue du Perche needed repairs, as all houses do. Mogrolle paid the locksmith and the mason who did the work himself, to the tune of nearly 1,000 livres, and Louis never reimbursed him. Louis' debt to Mogrolle kept mounting.

Louis' second marriage had been contracted with a clear mission: to produce an heir. For generations, Chevrot men had had no difficulty fathering sons; this had been the case in Louis' relationship with Louise. But the son and sole child he had with Marie Élizabeth arrived only after nearly three years.

When an heir to the Chevrot estate was finally born, they named the boy not Antoine, but Louis.

The boy's early years had nothing in common with the childhood his father had known: no one was grooming Louis II Chevrot for a future in the upper ranks of French society. He didn't have his own bedroom, not even his own bed. There was no harpsichord in the apartment, and there was definitely no money for singing lessons. He didn't grow up sleeping under a painting of a mother hen watching protectively over her baby chicks: the walls of his home were bare.

But for the first three years of his life, the future Chevrot heir at least had his parents to look after his well-being.

Louis' always precarious existence took a turn for the worse in 1735. Antoine Charles had promised to take only a single obligation off Louis' hands, one of the smallest of Antoine's debts. He was to deal with a bill first presented at the time of their mother's death, by the glove maker Louis de Nogent, for 435 livres, 14 sous. But in five years, Antoine Charles had done nothing to settle the claim. Twenty-six years after the death of his client, when Nogent still hadn't seen a penny from the Chevrots, he had begun litigation against Antoine Charles and won his case. Antoine Charles decided to sign over his share of Mogrolle's rent payments to Nogent; he thus learned that Louis had already run up quite a debt with Mogrolle. From then on, in addition to their father's many creditors, Louis had to deal with litigation initiated by his own brother.

By April 22, 1735, Antoine Charles had already addressed five petitions to Jérôme d'Arouges, civil lieutenant or head of legal affairs for the Parisian police, and d'Arouges had summoned Louis to his office. Since Louis had simply ignored all these orders, Antoine Charles sent his attorney to the rue de la Verrerie to run his brother down. Lawyer Christophe knocked at Louis' door; no answer. He then tried the immediate neighbors; they said they hadn't seen Louis in some time.

On December 30, 1735, there were new problems resulting from the loan from tailor Barbery. Barbery had died, and Barbery's widow and children were less understanding than Barbery had been. This was the start of still another fierce and protracted legal battle.

But the definitive blow fell less than three months later. On March 19, 1736, Guillemot d'Alby, the very police officer who had arrived at the rue de la Verrerie apartment at five o'clock on the morning of Antoine's death, was assigned a new and important mission. Officers of the Academy of Saint-Luc had information about "an unlicensed painter who was working in the city and producing canvases."

The age-old Parisian guild of master painters and sculptors had recently been reorganized as the Academy of Saint-Luc. In 1730, the academy published new statutes intended to restructure the business of art in Paris and tighten the academy's control over the city's artists. The statutes carefully regulated matters such as the number of masters allowed in each specialization and the process obligatory for a would-be master. They were designed as well to protect the work of master artists from fraud of any kind: one particularly well-enforced rule specified that no one was allowed to reproduce in painting scenes already engraved by members of the academy "without the artist's permission." Any artist found to be working illegally or in violation of any of their statutes became subject to heavy fines, and the punishment for failure to pay those fines at once was imprisonment.

The commissioner began his investigation by questioning experts in the fields in which the outlaw artist had been producing work: painting, carving, and gilding. (The last two are the techniques necessary to produce fine gilded frames.) Guillemot d'Alby soon learned that the guild officials knew exactly whom they were after and where to find him. They thus hadn't called on the officer for his investigative skills, but only because they wanted to have him along in order to arrest the unlicensed artist on the spot.

At 3 P.M., their party set out for the Pont Marie, the bridge that still links Paris' Right Bank to the Île Saint-Louis. In the eighteenth century, the Pont Marie was lined with houses on both sides. Once on the bridge, the officials went straight to the home of a master painter named Soustre: he belonged to a well-respected dynasty of Parisian painters and gilders, artists who produced gilded wood carvings and sculpture for churches, as well as richly decorated frames that showed off great paintings to their best advantage. Soustre confirmed that "someone was using as a studio a room on the third floor that looked out onto the bridge." In that studio, Soustre added, they would find a cache of paintings and frames created by the artist they had been hoping to track down, work that, Soustre stressed, the artist "had been selling." Soustre even confirmed that artist's name for them: Louis Chevrot.

They trooped up to the third floor and knocked: no answer, and the door was locked. The wigmaker who owned the house sent for a locksmith, who was ordered to open the door "by order of the Lieutenant General of the Police." Once inside, they found all the proof they needed: numerous bottles of oil paint, brushes, a paint-covered palette, and especially "an easel on which a canvas had been set up. Several engravings were attached to the easel to serve as models for the half-completed painting on which the artist was still at work." And all around the studio were "a quantity of paintings, some framed, some unframed," as well as many other frames, "some gilded, some not."

Antoine Chevrot's son had long maintained a second life as Louis Chevrot, artist. He had escaped to his tiny room with a view and there he had managed to pursue his dreams and create beautiful objects. He had talent, and his work had met with significant success—enough to attract the attention of the academy's officials, enough to make them feel the need to stop this outlaw with the skills and the expertise necessary to make an independent career right in the heart of Paris and thus take work away from legitimate master artists.

How had Louis managed to accomplish all that he had? He was no outsider artist, untrained and unsophisticated: he was working squarely within the parameters of the established Parisian art scene. If Louis had been able to train formally and to pursue his passion openly, he would surely have lived the life of a respected master artisan. He might even have left behind a body of admired work, and today the name Louis Chevrot would still be remembered in the world of art. But Antoine would never have allowed his son to choose art over annuities administration, to give up a title in which he had invested so heavily and that he considered a guarantee of social status. He had thereby condemned Louis to the life of a clandestine painter.

As a result, all that Louis had achieved ended in a flash. Guillemot d'Alby confiscated everything in his studio; all Louis' supplies and every painting and every frame that he had crafted were to be destroyed. If the officer put two and two together and realized that the illegal artist was the same impetuous young man who had gotten him out of bed at 5 A.M., so desperate was he to see his father's will, he made no mention of it.

The officials left Guillemot d'Alby to cart away Louis' canvases and frames and went off to report to the community of painters on their successful search-and-destroy mission: because of their vigilance, an unlicensed artist had been put out of business.

In so doing, they had of course put an end to both the source of revenue that had allowed Louis to support his family and the source of dreams that had allowed him to escape the daily grind of creditors and old debts. By having confiscated the supplies that Louis could never have afforded to replace, they guaranteed that he would never paint again. They left Louis with no way of paying the rent on that studio on the Pont Marie, a place where he was surrounded by the kind of beauty so absent in his official home.

Like all illegal craftsmen, Louis would have understood full well the affair's further implications. Guild officials would quickly have him tracked down; once located, he instantly faced heavy fines for two serious infractions of the academy's laws: painting without a license and copying the images of master engravers who were academy members. Together, the two fines would have added up to hundreds of livres. Since Louis had no cash and no way of raising money, he would be arrested and locked up without further ado in the debtors' prison in which Louise had been incarcerated in 1723: For-l'Évêque.

Either late on March 19 or the following day, Louis learned of all that had transpired. Twelve days later, between 7 and 8 P.M. on Saturday, March 31, 1736, another police commissioner, Jean Jacques Camuset, was called out urgently. This time, it was not Antoine Chevrot's son begging him to come quickly, but Louis Chevrot's widow. Louis had died, and Marie Élizabeth was concerned about what had been described in Antoine's inventory as an "old leather-covered coffer" and in which Louis' father had kept his cash. Louis still had that coffer at the time of his death; like his father before him, he had kept it locked. Perhaps the brand-new widow was afraid that if Antoine Charles got there before the police, Louis' brother would abscond with it. She knew the coffer contained important documents; did she know that the bulk of them were records of Louis' life with Louise?

The most remarkable aspect of both the widow's remarks and Camuset's report is that neither alludes in any way to what seems to have been the sudden and unexplained death of this thirty-five-year-old male. Nothing indicated that he had been ill; only days before, he had been healthy enough to be working at his painting. People have always died unexpectedly; people often die young, and this probably happened more often in the eighteenth century than today. Still, to be found dead so soon after his last financial lifeline had been abruptly cut off and in the surroundings to which his widow led Officer Camuset might well have caused anyone to wonder whether, when confronted with the realization that he now faced immediate and certain financial ruin, Louis had not hastened his own end in some way.

In France in the early eighteenth century, few taboos were as absolute as that surrounding suicide. What was then known as either "self-murder" or "self-homicide" was both a mortal sin and a serious crime: in the eyes of neither church nor state did the individual have the right to take his own life. But nothing on the scene awakened enough suspicion for Camuset to feel obliged to look further into the matter, and Louis' family was thus spared a lengthy investigation, an inquiry that would have delved into all the hidden corners of his life, including his illegal work as a painter. If Camuset, who in 1724 had explored the charges against Clément Magoullet, recognized the name of Clément's "diabolical" accuser, he left no official sign that he recalled Louis' past.

Barely a week later, things might have been different. On April 9, 1736, a decree by the Parisian Parlement that had been in the works for a decade was finally proclaimed: it became obligatory for the police to open an investigation into the cause of any death that seemed "violent" or in any way "suspicious": until their inquiry had been completed, the corpse could not be buried.

When Camuset arrived on the scene with his team, they found "the dead body lying on the straw mattress of a cot." The man who had spent his first years in the earliest child's room I've seen described in a Parisian apartment left the world lying not on a proper mattress stuffed with wool or cotton or horsehair, but on a mere sack of straw.

In the case of Clément Magoullet's apartment, the police had frequently characterized its rooms and contents as "old" and "small." In their description of Louis Chevrot's last resting place, the officers were clearly at a loss for words, in part because there was so little to describe.

The room in which they found his body was "small." In it, they found only that cot, the lone "old blanket" that was the sole bedding, and some extra straw. The only other thing in the room where Louis died was a bit of "old" tapestry hanging on one wall that would have offered only minimal protection from the cold: there was no fireplace in Louis' last home. The police described the tapestry as "of no value."

In a second "tiny" room, the police found an "old" wooden table, two chairs, a lone "old" cotton curtain, a solitary candleholder made of tin, a couple of clay pots, "an old mattress" lying on the floor, and the coffer Marie Élizabeth had been after. They put seals on that, but otherwise, as they remarked, there was "nothing else within those four walls on which to attach seals."

At the time of Marie Freslin's death in 1714, the goods that she and Jacques Magoulet left their children were appraised at 7,000 livres. In 1718, Louise Poisson Magoulet's possessions totaled 948, and Pierre Chicot's 1,520. In 1722, the worldly goods of Louis' maternal grandfather, Barthélemy Boulanger, were estimated at 2,154. Total value of all Louis Chevrot's earthly possessions: 43 livres.

He had lived on an upper floor, not in a garret, but otherwise, well before the starving artist became an archetypal figure in art and literature, the painter Louis Chevrot had lived the life of one. Louis had died penniless. He seems also to have died without his legitimate family at his side.

When Marie Élizabeth made her request to the police, she spoke of "the apartment where Louis Chevrot lived"; she made no mention of herself or their son. And when Camuset ended his inspection of the place where they had found Louis' body, he remarked on how little he had found there: "absolutely no personal effects or belongings." I've never seen such a remark in any other police report about a scene of death.

Louis did not die in his room on the rue de la Verrerie. The sparsely furnished two rooms Camuset described were located instead not far from the lodgings that he and Louise had shared in 1723, on the third floor of a house owned by a master candlemaker named Rousset. Rousset's house faced onto a marketplace adjacent to a church that has since disappeared: Saint-Jean-en-Grève. In the eighteenth century, Saint-Jean-en-Grève stood cheek by jowl with Paris' City Hall, the site of Antoine's beloved annuities administration. And even the shopsign identifying Rousset's house seems evocative of Antoine: Le Mortier, the Golden Mortar, the hat worn by French magistrates. Every time Louis returned to that apartment, his Chevrot heritage would have been all around him.

The rooms were barely furnished, but Louis had been renting them for at least three years, for a sum just about equal to the total value of all he left in them: 45 livres a year. At the time of his death, he was three years behind with his rent. All that time, on all official documents Louis had continued to use the address on the rue de la Verrerie where his wife and son resided. The apartment on the Saint-Jean marketplace was the scene of Louis' secret other life, just as the studio on the Pont Marie had been the scene of his secret professional existence.

The police remarked on one final absence in the rooms: clothing. "There was no linen whatsoever, and the only item of clothing was a dressing gown." Marie Élizabeth was so destitute that she grabbed that "and had it dyed black so that she could have it made into a skirt, since all she owned were the clothes on her back."

Thus the only personal item Louis left behind him was immediately cut into pieces, just like all his artistic production.

Marie Élizabeth knew about Louis' second address; did she know about his other life as well? Louis had married someone other than Louise, just as Antoine had forced him to do; with Marie Élizabeth, he had fathered a legitimate son. But he and Louise had never ended their relationship. Had they met in that woefully underfurnished flat located at the sign of the Golden Mortar? It would not have been the first time they had managed to have time together by staying under the radar and living below the poverty line.

All through the years of Louis' marriage and until April 1736, the month after Louis Chevrot's death, Louise Magoulet had continued to live in Paris. She had earned a living as an embroiderer in an enclave outside the guilds' control, just as her mother had. Louise had found employment in the embroidery workshop run by Madame Perenoire in the Saint-Denis de la Chartre cloister where the original Queen's Embroiderer had begun his career.

*Louis Chevrot, Annuities Controller. "His burial was paid for by a charity."*

On the cover of the dossier that contains Camuset's report, the deceased is identified as "the Sieur Chevrot, Annuities Controller," a title that seems wildly inappropriate given the only other information found there, a brief phrase that offered a sad final commentary on Louis Chevrot's life: *Enterré par la charité*.

An individual named for Louis XIV's heir, whom his father had once hoped would be baptized in Versailles' Royal Chapel—this man had had the kind of pitiful interment that was funded by charitable lay people who paid the tiny sum necessary to guarantee a minimal rite for the completely destitute who died in Paris. His body was taken to the vast Cimetière des Saints-Innocents (Holy Innocents' Cemetery), adjacent to the bustle of the city's main market, Les Halles. It remained there in a mass grave until 1786, when the cemetery was closed and all remains exhumed and transported to Paris' catacombs.

Louis had paid 761 livres for his father's funeral, but no one—not his brother, not his widow, not any relatives or in-laws—chose to contribute the mere 10 livres that would have conferred a semblance of dignity on his life's end.

On April 1, 1736, Louis Chevrot, born in 1700 into a family wealthy as a result of the salt trade and influential at both the French court and Paris' most important court of law, was buried in a pauper's grave.

# CHAPTER NINETEEN

# The Prince's Embroiderer, The Prince's Designer
## The Magoulets: 1728–1761

O F JEAN MAGOULET'S five children with Louise Poisson, only their son Claude was lucky enough to find someone willing to help him make a life for himself. Claude owed his good fortune and his success to the man his mother had had the foresight to choose as his godfather, Claude Fontaine. After her separation from Jean, Fontaine remained close to Louise Poisson: he thus knew all that his godson had endured. After his mother's death, when Claude was homeless, Fontaine quickly tossed him a lifeline.

Like his mother and his older sisters, Claude had learned his father's craft. It would have been understood that the time spent by Claude under the supervision of the Queen's Embroiderer counted as his apprenticeship.

At the end of the frenzied summer that followed his mother's death, just before his sister Louise was forced from Paris to meet the ship named *Mutinous*, Claude took his first step on the road to independence. Claude Fontaine had agreed to pay 300 livres so that his godson could become an *alloué*, or journeyman. After their apprenticeship, fledgling artisans could continue their training and gain work experience under the guidance of established masters as *alloués* in their workshops. The master promised to feed and house them. This was an ideal arrangement for a fourteen-year-old in need of both a future and a temporary home.

On September 16, 1719, Fontaine signed the contract that provided for his godson for the next four years. Claude took his place that same day in the workshop run by Jean-Paul Aublé on the rue Saint-Denis at the center of Les Halles. Aublé also knew of Claude's past: Claude's new master had collaborated with Louise Poisson on embroidery projects in her workshop.

Aublé belonged to an important family of Parisian embroiderers, but in 1719 he was shifting course. In his arrangement with Fontaine, he described himself not as an embroiderer but as a *designateur*, a designer. And he promised to teach Claude an expertise he would not have learned from his father or mother: "the art of the designer." With this choice, either Fontaine or more likely fourteen-year-old Claude himself proved almost uncannily prescient about the future of the French luxury trade.

In the late seventeenth century, the word *designateur* (the spelling was later changed to *dessinateur*) was applied to painters and sculptors renowned for their draftsmanship. By the early eighteenth century, a new field was emerging. At that moment, *designateur*, "designer," was first used to refer to those whose art was not defined primarily as painting or sculpture but as the art of creating drawings and plans. Soon it was taken for granted that there were great designers in a wide range of fields: furniture design, lace design, set design, garden design. Our modern usage of "designer" in the sense of a fashion designer or couturier follows from this usage.

It was understood that all great embroiderers had to be gifted draftsmen, as both Jean Magoulets were. But when the embroiderer Aublé referred to himself as a designer, he indicated that he considered the art of the needle less important than the art of the pattern. And by describing himself not even as a "designer in embroidery" but solely as a "designer," he further indicated that the art in which he would provide instruction was one that would not be limited to the design of embroidery patterns.

In September 1719, four months after his father had driven him from his home, Claude, the only third-generation Magoulet to pursue a career as a master artisan, shifted course, as had his grandfather, the first Jean Magoulet, when he left the world of the *gainiers* for embroidery. Claude broke with his Magoulet past and moved into a world where he associated with artisans and artists who might not immediately recall his father and his grandfather when they heard his name. Rather than be confined to a single specialization, he was choosing a comprehensive and all-embracing craft, a skill set that could be applied to many different arts.

Claude's choice was in every way a brilliant move.

Claude signed their contract with a firm hand. He was surely old beyond his age, and he had already grown into his adult signature. The years to come proved him to be far more gifted than his first mentor, Aublé.

Only nine months later, Fontaine signed a second agreement on his godson's behalf. This time, Claude became a journeyman in the workshop of one of the finest early French designers, Guillaume Gabriel Androuet du Cerceau. This was a big move up for the adolescent, and the terms of this contract prove how closely and seriously his godfather was following his development.

This time, no fixed term was specified for Claude's stay: he was to work under Androuet du Cerceau's supervision "until he had reached perfection, and Fontaine would be the judge of this." The contract also laid out with precision the areas in which Claude was to receive instruction: "the design of ornaments for churches and of decorations for all types of men's and women's clothing." He was in addition to learn "all the basic principles of architecture," as well as the art of "making paper patterns for the design of silk brocades woven with gold and silver thread." This final, hyperspecific request for guidance in the design of patterns for the most luxurious fabrics then being created in France was appropriate, for this was one of Androuet du Cerceau's areas of specialization. Fontaine's directive was the earliest indication that Claude had found his calling.

His new mentor belonged to a venerable French dynasty of architects and engravers. Guillaume Gabriel was the first from the Androuet du Cerceau family to be known as a designer; in his official capacity as "the designer for the king's collections," he was positioned at the top of the fledgling field. When Claude moved into Guillaume Gabriel's home, he found himself being taken seriously by the greatest talents in France's luxury goods trade.

Claude Fontaine could easily afford the 200 livres he paid Androuet du Cerceau up front. All his life, he demonstrated great financial acumen: Fontaine was among the lucky few to make a killing during the market bubble that John Law unleashed early in 1719. In the nine months since he had first made plans for his godson, Fontaine had been using his profits to snap up prime Parisian real estate that those who had lost out when the market crashed were suddenly obliged to sell. Fontaine paid significant sums, always in cash.

This time, godfather and godson were pleased with the arrangement, for Claude stayed put. A year later, Androuet du Cerceau was after another payment; this time, Fontaine paid the fee not in banknotes but in gold.

When Claude finished his training at age eighteen, France had entered the zone of economic turbulence that bridled all commercial activity for years. Claude bided his time and kept a roof over his head by serving as the footman of Geneviève Boucher, wife of Pierre de Bragelonne. The Bragelonne residence on a tiny street in the heart of Paris' Marais neighborhood was so grand that its rooms all had names: "the blue bedroom," and so forth. In it, the would-be designer did menial work, but at least he was surrounded by extraordinary décor and fabulous objects of all kinds.

Claude was in the Bragelonnes' employ in 1724 when he wrote to the lieu-tenant general to beg for Louise's release from prison. His petition was coun-terbalanced by that of his father's supporter, Monsieur le Duc, the ruler of what was known as "the Princes' château": Chantilly, domain of the powerful Princes de Condé, Ducs de Bourbon. A few years later, Monsieur le Duc gave Claude another big break.

By late 1727 when the economy was starting to recover, for the first time since his marriage to Anne Legrand, Jean Magoulet's career as an embroi-derer was moving into high gear. He had found a source of revenue that prom-ised a degree of independence from Legrand.

On January 1, 1728, Jean celebrated the new year by leaving the Quai de l'École, where he had spent virtually all his life except for the years on Sainte Croix. That day, he and Anne Legrand signed a lease on an apartment in a part of Paris where no Magoulet had lived before, the area that had replaced the Marais as the neighborhood of choice for great aristocrats: the Faubourg Saint-Germain. Their new address was on a tiny street adjacent to the Abbey of Saint-Germain-des-Prés, the rue des Fossés Saint-Germain. They did not lease the building's "first apartment" on the noble floor. That was already occupied by the house's owner, merchant Jean Étienne Regnault. For 600 livres a year, the couple rented instead two rooms each on the less desirable third and fourth floors.

It's likely that Jean II's decision finally to abandon the address where his father had moved just prior to his birth in 1682 was directly related to his father's death. I can't determine exactly when the true Queen's Embroiderer died, since there was no inventory of Jean I's final apartment on the rue de Harlay, just around the corner from Clément's abode on the Quai de l'Horloge.

The only Magoulet to have actually embroidered for Queen Marie-Thérèse left this world sometime prior to February 8, 1729. That day, his son formally "renounced" all claims to the estate of his father, whom he identified as "the deceased queen's valet de chambre." He "swore and affirmed in his soul and his conscience that he had not taken any possessions belonging to the estate," although he had carried away at least one key object.

One year later, he and Anne Legrand moved again, only right around the corner, but now they were exactly where Jean wanted to be. Their new lease, set to begin at Easter 1730, was signed directly with the Reverend Father Claude Dupré, representing all the priests and monks of the Abbey of Saint-Germain-des-Prés. From then on, the couple occupied the kind of grand space in which both Queen's Embroiderers felt truly at home, an entire vast house, situated within the Abbey's enclosure on the rue Saint-Benoît and known as the Hôtel de Bruxelles. They rented the ground-floor shop, five rooms on the "noble" floor, four more on the third, four more still on the fourth, plus additional small rooms here and there, as well as two cellars, an attic, a terrace, and a modest space containing toilet facilities. They even had a private entrance right next to the Abbey's church. The couple inhabited their own little world.

Considering that location and size, their rent seems reasonable: 1,200 livres. By subletting two apartments, they reduced it to a modest 470, a positive bargain when you factor in the spectacular final act of vengeance against his father that the grand residence made possible.

To promote his innovative new shop on the Quai de l'École, Jean I Magoulet had had this lavish engraving designed.

The clothing, particularly the woman's outfit and her hairdo, and the type of chair in which Magoulet's clients are taking their ease date the image to about 1685, shortly after the death of Queen Marie-Thérèse. The master craftsman depicted showing off samples of his art is thus correctly identified as "Jean Magoulet, embroiderer to the deceased Queen." But the second part of the image's caption is a classic Magoulet deception, as well as still another dish of revenge served up very cold indeed.

The caption supplies the address of the shop being advertised: "on the rue St. Benoît, in the Hôtel de Bruxelles, at the entrance to the Abbey of St. Germain des Prés." The address given, however, while accurate down to the smallest detail, only became that of "the embroiderer to the deceased Queen" in the spring of 1730, by which time the stylish set of the Faubourg Saint-Germain had long since given up the fashions and the furniture depicted here.

Had Jean II run across the image while rummaging through his deceased father's affairs and found in it one last proof of his father's accomplishments that he could appropriate? It was a simple matter to have an engraver replace the Quai de l'École address with his own location.

The image of Magoulet's emporium was printed on a sheet roughly 9 by 10 inches, large enough to wrap purchases such as embroidery patterns and thus to function as a prototype for the modern shopping bag. Those who visited Jean II's new shop on the rue Saint-Benoît carried their merchandise home enveloped in an image designed to remind them of the quality of the shopping experience Magoulet had provided, as well as his boutique's address. His satisfied customers could never have realized that what seemed a tribute to Magoulet's genius as an embroiderer was in fact Jean II's final appropriation of something rightfully his father's. From then on, he no longer cared about names once so precious to both of them. The Queen's Embroiderer, the Embroiderer to the Late Queen: after fifty years of service, these titles had at last outlived their usefulness.

On January 1, 1728, when he moved to the Faubourg Saint-Germain, Jean signed the lease using for the first time his new title: Embroiderer to the Princes. Jean Magoulet was now in the employ of the Condé family and frequenting their court at Chantilly. At that moment, no artist would have wanted to be anywhere else.

Monsieur le Duc had invested 20 million in Law's Indies Company right at the start; he had cashed in his stock for gold at the perfect moment. He then poured his vast profits into Chantilly: in a few short years, he had positioned an estate already celebrated for its fabled gardens laid out by André Le Nôtre, designer of Versailles' landscape, on the cutting edge of the world of design. Just as his grandfather the Sun King had done, Condé brought together artists from many fields, created ideal conditions for them, and expected great things from them. At Chantilly, Condé established a design laboratory to which he assigned a precise mission. He gave all his artists free run of the vast collections amassed by several generations of Condés: lacquerwork, painting and porcelain, scrolls and textiles from all over Asia. Condé asked his handpicked team, in his words, to *imiter les ouvrages de la Chine*, "to copy Chinese artworks": to filter China through a French lens. Monsieur le Duc wanted to dictate the future of *chinoiserie*, the "Chinese style" that had emerged at Louis XIV's court before spreading quickly across Europe and then to Europe's colonies around the globe.

*Chinoiserie* had helped make European consumers wild for Asian exports: Japanese lacquer, Chinese silks, cotton printed and painted in India. European economies and craftsmen alike were suffering because of the craze for everything Asian. Workshops in various European countries set out to imitate Indian textiles; others wanted to create porcelain they hoped would rival Chinese production. Condé's was the first attempt to have all these luxury goods copied in the same place and to give all the European produced goods a unified style: he wanted Chantilly's textiles to share the same design DNA as its porcelain and lacquer. To make this happen at Chantilly, Monsieur le Duc made the designer king.

Condé first established in about 1725 a porcelain manufactory. Next, he hired specialists in other fields, including embroidery. Not only had Jean I worked for Monsieur le Duc's father in the 1670s, but Jean II himself had seen the Asian trend shaping up and had quickly become recognized as an outstanding Parisian practitioner of "the Chinese style" of French embroidery. By late 1727, Jean Magoulet was known as "the Prince's Embroiderer." But the Magoulet luck had finally run out: embroidery did not become a priority for Condé, and Jean never played a key role at Chantilly.

Another Magoulet came into his own on this new stage: Claude, who had entered Condé's employ by 1729. At only twenty-four, he thus found himself known as "the Designer of Son Altesse Royale," His Royal Highness' Designer. Claude owed his success to his decision to train in design, in particular, in textile design.

In the early eighteenth century, numerous manufactories were vying to be the first in Europe to master the secrets behind the brightly colored and exuberantly patterned silks produced in China or the equally bright and exuberant cottons created in India. Other manufactories tried to rival either the Chinese or the Indians, but Condé decided to take on both textile superpowers. To do so, he relied principally on the artist who became Claude's mentor and surrogate father, Jean Antoine Fraisse.

Fraisse began his career as an embroiderer; when he arrived at Chantilly, probably also in 1729, he identified himself instead as a "painter" or a "painter on cotton." Condé put Fraisse in charge of a workshop housed in the château itself. There, Fraisse acquired still another title, *compositeur*, "composer" or "compositor": he had mastered the art of composing or assembling into a design, in the manner of a compositor laying type on a printing press, the wood blocks that were the basic printing element for textiles. Wood-block printing was the technique essential to the production of Indian cottons, and cotton was Fraisse's textile of predilection.

In his work as a designer, Claude adopted the technique essential to the Chinese textile empire: he created patterns, which he then painted on silk.

*Plate from* The Book of Chinese Designs.

Condé's dream of revolutionizing the European textile industry was founded on the Fraisse-Magoulet collaboration.

Together, the two artists created wildly experimental textiles. They worked on silk, probably woven in China; their designs were rendered with a combination of Indian and Chinese techniques. Fraisse used wood blocks to print patterns on silk panels; Claude then intervened to overpaint ornamental motifs. Together, they created design elements that became basic to the decorative style developed at Chantilly: wildly fanciful flora and fauna, fragments of pseudo-Chinese architecture, tiny figures in exotic garb overshadowed by a swirl of gigantic imaginary flowers.

Textile is fragile; only a handful of existing pieces are now attributed to the Chantilly workshop. But we know a great deal about the motifs invented there as a result of the collaboration between Fraisse and Magoulet because of Fraisse's best-known work, among the greatest of the design books that fueled the eighteenth-century obsession with Asia. The magnificent 1735 folio entitled *Livre de desseins chinois* (*The Book of Chinese Designs*), preserved the Chantilly version of *chinoiserie* for posterity.

As the work's subtitle, *Modeled on Original Works from Persia, the Indies, China, and Japan*, indicated, the patterns referred to as "Chinese" were intentionally pan-Asian. The volume's more than fifty plates were all stylistic hodgepodges,

*Plate from* The Book of Chinese Designs.

pastiches in which traditional patterns from different countries were patched together as in a quilt. The designs were created primarily as patterns for textile and embroidery, but they were also copied by artists working in other media such as porcelain. As a result, the "Chinese" style that resulted from the partnership between Fraisse and His Majesty's Designer Claude Magoulet established what became for vast numbers of Western consumers in the eighteenth century their idea of an authentic Chinese look. The volume's influence over design in many fields was also long-lasting: a full century after its publication,

French textile manufacturers were still producing patterns that diligently reproduced its plates.

Fraisse had only one child, a daughter named Françoise. On July 30, 1732, she and Claude were married. "The Prince's Embroiderer" did not make the trip to Chantilly for the ceremony, but the wicked stepmother did come that day. Anne Legrand, whose "evil influence" over their father Claude and his older sister had denounced to the police eight years earlier, signed the register as a witness. It was her last appearance in an official context before her death just five weeks later.

At 7 A.M. on Tuesday, September 9, 1732, the police entered the Hôtel de Bruxelles on the rue Saint-Benoît and fixed many seals in the Magoulet-Legrand residence: unlike Louis Chevrot's final resting place, Anne Legrand's apartment was chock-full of coffers and furniture with drawers. When Jean Magoulet showed the officers around, he did something that I've never otherwise seen mentioned by those who directed such procedures: he offered to open numerous drawers. Amazingly, each of those Jean opened was empty! There had been no community of property, so Jean could not inherit, but many heirs quickly laid claim to a share. The widower did assert that "the estate owed him money."

Jean told the officers that his wife Anne had died "right at midnight." Oddly, when Jean showed them her body lying in what he described as "her room," it was in a small, isolated space on the fifth floor rather than the spacious formal bedroom two floors down. That third-floor bedchamber was a time capsule of sorts: all its furnishings and decoration remained exactly as they had been at the moment of her husband Pierre Chicot's death fourteen years earlier. The same bedspreads and decorative curtains, even the same sheets: not a change had been made.

One thing had been added: facing the marital bed paid for by her first husband was a portrait Legrand's inventory characterized as "large." In any other bedroom of the day, this would inevitably have been an oversized image of "the king," the Sun King. But in this case, directly facing his bed, Jean Magoulet had hung a giant canvas that he described to the police as "representing his father." The vogue for family portraits was then still new and had only recently begun to touch merchant families: no other Magoulet ever sat for a likeness. But through the years when he was systematically reenacting all his father's evil deeds, "the Prince's Embroiderer" slept in a bedroom dominated by an outsized portrait of the Queen's Embroiderer, the man he so reviled. That primal hatred had literally dominated his life.

Legrand's inventory revealed that in 1732, Jean was working actively as an embroiderer. In a workshop well equipped with the tools of his profession, the police found a very expensive suit being prepared for the Magoulets' preferred type of client: Louis, Marquis de Conflans, a wealthy and powerful military man. They also listed numerous engravings and paintings that Jean was in the process of translating into embroidery patterns, as well as boxes full of patterns ready to be displayed to clients, just as in the scene depicted on his shop's wrapping paper.

Throughout the apartment, there was much to be noted: Legrand had spared no expense in maintaining her husband in the style to which she had accustomed him. Her heirs, however, quickly went after things that weren't included on the inventory and that couldn't be located.

Legrand hadn't been expecting to die: she had just received from her dressmaker, Mademoiselle Gallot, a brand-new outfit, richly adorned with costly gold and silver thread. Her heirs wanted to know what had happened to it, as well as the whereabouts of the numerous big-ticket items that had been listed on the contract for her marriage to Jean: 2,860 livres' worth of diamond jewelry, gold watches, and fine lace. Jean never mentioned the new outfit, but he did declare that "he didn't own a single piece of silverware" and explained that "in the days just prior to their marriage, his wife had sold her diamond cross to Mademoiselle Foin, an embroiderer who worked in the 15/20."

The inventory revealed that Legrand had left nary a debt: the rent on their home was paid up, as was the yearly tax on Jean's business. She had even paid in full for 1732 the allowance that she gave him on a quarterly basis. Jean nonetheless owed money right and left: to those who embroidered in his workshop, to those who had supplied him with costly gold-wrapped thread.

The notaries completed the inventory at 8 P.M. on Friday, October 2: on the following business day, Monday, October 5, Jean's next marriage contract was drawn up. If his new bride, Anne Tabary, had pressed him for the sum she had invested with him the previous May, the bridegroom would have had no cause for concern. "In the event that she predeceased him," Anne Legrand had specified that Jean was to receive 4,000 livres from her estate: this was the exact amount on his annuity contract with Tabary.

He also retained another crucial benefit that had come with the marriage to Legrand: that apartment with a private entrance in her house in Versailles. In September 1732, Jean promised to have its abundant furnishings moved to Paris so that the objects could be sold for the benefit of her estate, but no one got rid of Jean Magoulet that easily. He simply held on to the apartment and its contents; he continued to lease out the house and collect the rent. In April 1734, Joseph Hubert, a candle merchant from Orléans and the nephew named "sole legatee" by Pierre Chicot just before his death in 1718, was still fighting to have Jean evicted and to force him to turn over the documents necessary for the property's sale. Hubert even instructed his lawyer not to hold out for the best possible price, but to accept any offer that seemed "fair": he was that desperate to end his dealings with Jean Magoulet.

His third marriage was in many ways Jean's masterpiece. His bride was young, still under twenty-five, but her father was deceased, so there could be no scrutiny from the head of her family. Her father's name, Tabary, Sieur Desdemaine, indicates a position more socially prominent than that occupied by Jean's previous in-laws. Tabary's widow had continued to uphold the family standing: she resided near the parish church of the Quai de l'École, Saint-Germain-l'Auxerrois, where the couple were married.

The October 5 formalities unfolded in the manner Jean always preferred: with utmost discretion. The bride's only witnesses were her mother and sister, her sister's husband, and her father's brother. Not a single Magoulet was present; in fact, the only person to stand up for the groom was Jacques Havel, who described himself as a "merchant and a *bourgeois de Paris*." Havel's name was never before and never again found among those Jean characterized as his "friends."

The last to sign was a woman who counted herself among the bride's friends, although she might just as well have been included on the groom's side of the equation: her signature had long appeared alongside that of her recently deceased husband, Clément Magoullet. Had Jeanne Nicolle Masson served in some way as go-between for the Magoulet-Tabary match?

Tabary brought the Prince's Embroiderer the richest dowry he had seen: 7,000 in all. The annuity was included, and there was a further 3,000 in silverware and a great deal of serious jewelry: a diamond ring described as "important," a diamond bracelet, a diamond-studded cross, a gold pocket watch. There was in addition cash, which the bridegroom "declared was already in his possession."

The contract mentioned in passing Jean's "children with Louise Magoulet," but they were a problem Jean surely believed to be consigned to the past. Only eight months later, he was in for a rude awakening. The next phase in Jean's relations with his children began just before Jean's wedding to Tabary, at the moment when Claude married Françoise Fraisse.

In July 1732, Claude acquired a new family along with a bride. In the years that followed, probably for the first time in his life, Claude knew what it was like to be a part of a functional family.

Those years, the golden age of productivity for all Chantilly workshops, as well as those when the *Book of Chinese Designs* was in production, were also the moment when Claude's own family was taking shape. On July 25, 1733, the priest who had officiated at his wedding, Father Gérard Billet, longtime curate of the chapel at Chantilly, baptized the young couple's first child, a daughter they named Julie. Claude's mother-in-law, Geneviève Silvestre, was her god-mother. But Julie's godfather, although another Chantilly insider, was hardly the person one would have expected Claude to choose as sponsor for his first child: "Jean Magoulet, Embroiderer to His Royal Highness."

By 1733, Jean had initiated a process of reconciliation with the son he had so badly abused. And Claude had decided to trust him.

It had begun when Claude's sisters, excited that one of Louise Poisson's children was about to have a child of his own, decided to help their brother financially in the only way that they could. In 1733, as soon as Marie turned twenty-five, she and her older sister finally took the legal action that Jean had long feared would be initiated by his eldest daughter, Louise: they made an official request for an inquiry into the history of their mother's dowry. They had decided to settle their share of the inheritance on Claude.

In response to their summons, Jean was obliged to account formally for the five children who should have shared their mother's estate equally. On June 26, 1733, he called together three men prepared to swear to the veracity of his deposition. Two of them, as usual, were names never encountered elsewhere in his papers. But the third was a surprise: Nicolas. Jean I's legitimated son and Jean II's half brother and faithful ally was back in the life of the Magoulet family after an absolute silence that had lasted some seventeen years.

Nicolas was still using the grand title he had forced his father to hand over to him shortly after Jean II had made a grab for "the Queen's Embroiderer": he signed "Magoulet de Toulongeon." He threw the authority conveyed by it behind his confirmation of Jean's assertion that the two of Louise Poisson's children not present that day, the baby of the family, Dorothée, and her eldest, Louise, were both dead.

Dorothée had indeed died, as Jean solemnly affirmed on June 26, 1733, "in this city of Paris." She had been but eight or nine when her father confined her to the General Hospital in late 1718, upon her mother's death. She had not been heard from since, and her life had surely ended within those terrible walls, probably very quickly, perhaps even before her sister Louise gave birth in the Guardian Angel in the early fall of 1719.

But Louise? Jean presented a classic bit of *magoulese* as a final accounting for the child he had unsuccessfully tried to eliminate for years: his deposition was intended as a death certificate for Louise, a bureaucratic finale to her life.

Jean and his witnesses "attested and certified in their soul and their con-science that Mademoiselle Louise Magoulet died suddenly about ten years ago in the city of Amsterdam, in Holland, where she had gone to locate one of her Catholic relatives." "It would be impossible," they added, "to obtain any type of death certificate for her because the relative she went to find had herself died suddenly, shortly before Louise's arrival in that city, and also because of the difference of religion and customs practiced in Holland."

"About ten years ago." Jean left the date of Louise's demise vague, but even so. . . . His surviving children knew that their sister had been very much alive in the summer of 1723; in July 1724, they themselves had signed a petition protesting their father's attempts to have her deported. Were they simply pretending to go along with their father's story in an attempt to protect Louise's whereabouts? Had Louise perhaps even encouraged them to consent to the subterfuge in order to throw their father off her track?

On June 26, 1733, representatives of the French state removed Jean Magoulet's daughter Louise from the ranks of the living. Three years before Louis Chevrot died, Louise Magoulet Chevrot's father had had her ceremoniously killed off. From then on, only Clément's daughter Marie Louise had a legal existence.

The same day, Jeanne and Marie obliged their father to report on his management of their inheritance. The story he gave under oath, a tale of enormous complexity that included many details about investments made, along with specific dates and interest rates, ended with this result: Jean promised his three surviving children an annuity with an annual income of 26 livres, 13 sous, and 4 deniers. He also calculated that the investments had accumulated 180 livres in interest; that sum he turned over to the sisters in cash. In exchange, he obliged his surviving children to promise that their agreement put an end to all financial relations between them. They could never again ask their father for anything.

The 3,000 livres that the court had ordered Jean to return to Louise Poisson in 1715, the money that he claimed to have invested on behalf of his children in 1720 and that he did invest in 1723 but with no mention of their names on the contract—the same sum because of which he had had Marie and Dorothée confined to the General Hospital and for which he had declared Louise a prostitute, the accusation that condemned her baby to a quick death and her marriage to Louis to a slow one—the 3,000 livres that for eighteen years had set the course for all these lives, had at last been accounted for in the presence of an officer of the French state.

Fifteen years after Louise Poisson's death, a price was finally put on all their suffering: their father settled 60 livres on each surviving child. That Nicolas reappeared that day, so that the ceremony took place in the presence of Jean I's two sons, seems fitting. In June 1733, the saga that began in 1688 when Jean II sent his firstborn to "the islands of America" came to some sort of closure.

The sisters handed their share over to Claude without further ado. Nothing suggests that Jeanne and Marie were after anything but that payback: their father's name never again appeared in any document associated with their future lives. But Claude was a different matter. The power of hope. The following month, when Claude's first child was born, their father was back in his life, and for the next five years, Claude and his father remained close.

During that time, Claude and Françoise's family grew quickly. On September 1, 1734, a son was born. They named him for his maternal grandfather, whom they chose to be his godfather: Jean Antoine; the godmother was once again Geneviève Silvestre, the baby's maternal grandmother. On September 30, 1736, the couple had a second daughter; she was baptized on October 1, again, as always, by the priest who had married them. It must have seemed the perfect family story, all harmony and continuity. But by September 30, the peace and prosperity of Claude's new life had been shattered, and this baby's baptismal certificate clearly reflects the trouble that now reigned in Chantilly's design community.

For the first time at a baptism of one of Claude's children, her maternal grandparents were not present. Instead, the ceremony more closely resembled those organized by Jean I and his brother Jacques: wealth rather than family ties dictated the choice of sponsors. The godmother was the wife of a man of means; the godfather, who described himself as occupying a position in the financial administration of the War Office, was none other than Nicolas Magoulet de Toulongeon.

Claude named his new daughter Louise, for the mother who had died too young. Claude surely also knew of Louis Chevrot's death six months before and of his oldest sister's subsequent decision to leave Paris, and Louise Magoulet Chevrot might have been on his mind as well on the afternoon of October 1, when he watched the ceremony that admitted another Louise Magoulet into the Christian community.

One more daughter followed in quick succession: on November 24, 1737, Marie Françoise was born. By then, her parents no longer lived in Chantilly. They had moved to Paris, where they resided on the rue Dauphine, on the Left Bank just across the Pont Neuf from the Quai de l'Horloge. Theirs was still another neighborhood full of small craftsmen: this time, the baby's godparents worked as bonnet makers.

On the baptismal records of both Louise and Marie Françoise, their father was described as a mere "designer," no longer as "the designer of His Royal

Highness." The story of how Claude came to leave Condé's employ and Chantilly had begun on June 16, 1736, three months before baby Louise was born. That day, Monsieur le Duc had invited an eminent English visitor to lunch. Charles Lennox, Duke of Richmond and of Aubigny, was the illegitimate grandson of King Charles II and the woman known as his "French mistress," Louise de Keroual, Duchess of Portsmouth. At the end of their meal, the duke couldn't find his gold-headed cane. A search was begun, and the cane was discovered, "at the bottom of a vat of blue dye in the laboratory" of Jean Antoine Fraisse.

At the time of the second Louise Magoulet's birth, Fraisse was thus in disgrace. He was soon imprisoned: the police interrogated him on numerous occasions all during 1737. And on February 8, 1738, Fraisse went on trial for theft. Thus, from mid-1736 on, Claude was without his closest collaborator and surrogate father. Claude's own departure from Chantilly was surely related to Fraisse's downfall.

Jean took advantage of the situation to reel Claude in. Without Anne Legrand's management and the generous allowance that she bestowed on him, Jean was soon in financial trouble as deep as during his marriage to Louise Poisson. On May 11, 1735, he was obliged to give up his quarters at the Hôtel de Bruxelles. By then, his wife, Anne Tabary, had initiated legal proceedings against him.

On November 24, 1735, Police Commissioner Robert Germain Pinard opened a formal investigation: Anne Tabary Desdemaine wished to separate her property from her husband's. The evidence presented at the hearings held over the next two weeks uncannily echoed that of the witnesses called by Louise Poisson in 1715. The three men who testified in support of Tabary's case were all very much of the Faubourg Saint-Germain set, or at least a certain segment of it.

Jean was by then fifty-three; two of Tabary's witnesses were twenty-nine, the other thirty. Tabary's witnesses included Ignace Dumont, in the service of the Cardinal de Polignac, noted diplomat and former curate of the Chapelle Royale; Joseph Peyre, in that of the Marquis de Tréleau, a significant military man; and Antoine Terrasse, in the household of Louis de Bernage, chief representative of the French government in the province of Languedoc. Important names and functions, but the three witnesses called to testify against Jean Magoulet had a quite different claim to fame: they were mere *chefs de cuisine*, responsible for keeping the great men's kitchens running. Jean had been spending his midnight hours drinking and carousing with the Faubourg Saint-Germain's top chefs. Even during the years immediately following Clément Magoullet's burial, the time in Jean's life when his existence was apparently most exclusively centered on the finer things in life, the Queen's Embroiderer had never lost the urge to slum it.

Peyre said he had known Magoulet for four years, Terrasse for three, and Dumont nine. Each told a similar story, the same narrative Louise Poisson's witnesses had put on record twenty years before: Jean had "a very big heart"; he spared no expense in showing a good time to all he met "in even the most public of *cabarets*"; in every bar, "he picked up the tab for everyone he was with." He gambled, and for big sums, and he frequently lost. He had been forced to take out large loans and "had thus accumulated debt on all sides." Only "his pleasures" counted for him: his business was "in disarray" because he had extended credit too freely and "to all sorts of people."

Jean received a summons to confront the witnesses, but, as in 1715, he failed to show up.

On December 16, 1735, Anne Tabary was granted a legal division of property. Jean was directed to repay her 3,000-livre dowry. He was also mandated to return the 4,000 livres she had invested with him in May 1732, and finally to pay interest on her dowry, as well as the missed quarterly payments on the annuity.

Two years later, Jean had made no progress in making good on any of this, so on December 8, 1737, Tabary put a lien on Jean's property, or on income that Jean represented to her as rightly his. That day, he signed over to her "all the monies that might be owed him by Joseph Hubert, sole legatee of Pierre Chicot's estate, up to and including the sum of 3,000 livres." Tabary had no way of knowing that it was Jean who owed Hubert money, rather than the other way around.

On that December document, Jean identified himself as a "master embroiderer" and no longer referred to any ties with the Condé family. Indeed, as 1737 came to an end, he owed vast sums and was no longer employed at Chantilly, and his third wife had no intention of helping him through the bad patch. It was then that he thought of Claude, and then that thirty-three-year-old Claude was persuaded to forget the events of twenty years before.

In early 1738, father and son went into business together. Claude was so trusting that he didn't oblige his father to have the contract that bound them together drawn up by a notary: the agreement they signed was written in Jean's distinct hand and bears no trace of any official seal. It was not even dated, although Jean subsequently claimed that it had been signed on April 10, 1738.

The contract specified that their association had begun on January 1, 1738 and that it was to last until the end of 1744. During that time, both promised "to work exclusively for their company," to undertake "work in embroidery and design in general," and to share all profits and losses equally. If either chose to dissolve their partnership, six months' notice was necessary; the remaining partner "would be allowed to retain all profits, as well as all designs, patterns, and inventions that had been created while the company had been active." The partners even promised to attempt to locate apartments in the same building or, failing this, "to move into lodgings as near as possible to each other."

Trouble seems to have first broken out in October 1738. Jean had still not begun repaying Tabary, so she simply pilfered anything of value she could lay her hands on and refused to return the stolen goods. However, the objects that Tabary had snatched belonged not to her husband or even to Claude, but to Claude's mother-in-law. And Claude was having none of it.

In 1738, the Fraisse family was in complete disarray. Jean Antoine's trial for cane theft began on February 4 and went on for months; before the year was out, he died in prison. His wife, Geneviève Silvestre Fraisse, was already ill when the trial began; she had not long to live. It was then that Jean Magoulet and Anne Tabary invaded their lives.

Just around the time of Fraisse's death, Tabary absconded with the Fraisse valuables, the last possessions of any worth that the widow had left. That theft brought the brief professional association between Jean and Claude to an end.

When Claude reported the missing goods to the police, Commissioner Michel Martin Grimperel issued a summons, but Tabary refused to come to his office. The matter might have ended there but for Condé's direct intervention.

On April 10, 1739, Monsieur le Duc wrote a personal letter to Lieutenant General René du Hérault, signing with the one name in France sure to get immediate attention: "de Bourbon." Soon the entire Condé clan had weighed in. Every missive from Chantilly voiced unequivocal and unwavering support for Geneviève Fraisse and Claude Magoulet. The police noted on several occasions that "Monsieur le Duc has taken a personal interest in this affair." Such an unhesitating defense of the recently widowed wife of Jean Antoine Fraisse in the aftermath of Fraisse's trial would seem to indicate that Monsieur le Duc had believed in Fraisse's innocence—and in the guilt of another artist he had sponsored: his former embroiderer, Jean Magoulet.

Condé surely encouraged Claude to take action: a week after Monsieur le Duc directed his appeal to the lieutenant general, on April 18, Claude brought formal charges. He took the same tack he had already chosen in 1724—perhaps this was what he in fact believed—and blamed a wicked stepmother rather than his father. He explained that "his mother-in-law [Tabary] had come to him saying that she needed to borrow some silver that was absolutely essential to her because his father was seriously ill." She went off with a bowl and its cover, a plate, and a dish, all in silver, and when Claude asked for their return, Tabary explained that she had a lien on her husband's property and that Jean therefore "had no right to make any arrangements without her consent." She asked Claude to swear in writing that "he had received 300 livres that his father had promised Claude's mother at the time of their marriage," money that had nothing to do with the dowry settlement reached in 1733. Until Claude did so, Tabary would hold on to the silver.

On April 19, 1739, the police opened a file on the individual they referred to as "Père Magoulet," Magoulet the father, in order to distinguish him from Claude, his son who was bringing charges.

That same day Jean weighed in with a lengthy petition of his own to the lieutenant general in which he provided a very different account of what had transpired. Jean claimed to have fallen gravely ill, so ill that he had received the last rites. He had had no money for medication, and he had begged his son for help, but Claude had refused his request. Jean had therefore "been obliged to retain a silver soup spoon and a small dish that his son had lent him." And since, Jean further contended, he had "been desperate to deal with the expenses brought on by his illness, he had been forced to pawn the silver." The petition was written in Jean's characteristic hand; his writing was firm and confident and showed no trace of infirmity.

Jean next explained why he felt entitled to the silver. Claude had announced that he wanted out of their partnership agreement, but Jean contended that his son owed their company money—378 livres, 3 sous to be exact—and accused Claude of having "stolen all of his father's embroidery patterns and all of the tools that he had lent the company." Jean later changed his tune and asked Claude to confirm having received 300 livres that had been owed his mother.

Thus, even though each explained the debt in an entirely different manner, both Jean and Tabary had decided that Claude owed roughly the same sum of 300 livres; in view of this debt, they felt entitled to hold on to the Fraisse silver. Without Condé's intervention, the case of the purloined silver might have continued in this "he said, she said" manner until it fizzled out.

But when Monsieur le Duc took a stand, others paid attention. There was clearly a real investigation, rather than the sort of haphazard follow-up that had so often allowed Jean to get off scot-free. In the end, Hérault concluded that Tabary "had just wanted to get her hands on the silver in order to extort money" from Claude. After all, the lieutenant general concluded, "if one thinks about it for a bit, is it possible to imagine that a woman whose husband was on his deathbed could have been busy trying to seem more opulent than she really was?" Even though Hérault seemed to put the blame on Tabary, it was Jean who was punished. On April 24, Jean was ordered to hand over the silver or be arrested. The police made many attempts to recover the Fraisse family's property, all to no avail.

On June 26, 1739, Jean was confined to For-l'Évêque prison, the same facility where he had briefly done time in 1721 and where Louise had spent the summer of 1723. That very day, Condé was notified of the arrest. Jean was held for some time, until September 9. The file on his case ends with that date, but with no resolution. It's likely that Jean was released only because in late 1739, virtually all his accusers were at death's door.

On December 16, 1739, Geneviève Silvestre Fraisse died and was buried at Chantilly.

And on January 27, 1740, it was the turn of Monsieur le Duc himself. By then, Condé had run through all the millions that his investments had brought him, and more as well: he left 2 million livres in debt. Even though the porcelain manufactory he had established continued to function for about a decade, the glory days of design at Chantilly were over. The textile workshop run by Fraisse in collaboration with Claude never reopened.

In his verdict against Jean and Tabary, Hérault did not allude to Claude's second allegation. On February 1, 1739, Françoise Fraisse had died and was buried in Chantilly's chapel, once again by Father Gérard Billet. Claude's wife had died in childbirth, he explained in his April letter to Lieutenant General Hérault, after giving birth to a stillborn baby. Claude blamed his father and Tabary for both deaths: their constant "harassment," he contended, had left his wife "completely distraught."

In just over a year, Claude's wife, a new baby, his wife's father and his collaborator, his wife's mother, and then his protector Condé: all these key figures had died. Claude was left with four children in his care, the oldest of whom was only seven. Claude had remained close to the sister with whom he had always had a special bond, Marie. Marie was by then married; Claude took up residence near her home on the rue Dauphine. On May 11, 1745, when the first of her three sons was baptized at the parish church of her husband's family, Saint-André-des-Arts, Marie named him Claude Jacques: serving as his godfather was his uncle, "Claude Magoulet, designer."

By then, Claude had known serious financial difficulties. When he returned to Paris after Condé's death, he moved into an apartment on the rue des Cordeliers (today's rue de l'École-de-Médecine) that rented for 180 livres a year. But by February 11, 1743, Claude was far behind on his rent. When he skipped out, his landlord commented to the police: "No one knows where he's gone."

Claude never again got the kind of breaks his talent merited. By the 1740s, Versailles had become once again the center of French artistic life. After Condé's death, Louis XV issued appointments to some of those who had created under Condé's aegis at Chantilly. But Claude was passed over, and those granted

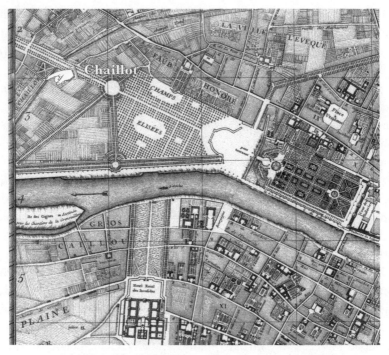

*The last address of the last male in the Magoulet line.*

COMMERCE.

*Industrie.*

Le goût des deſſeins des Indes, tout irrégu-
lier qu'il eſt, a un genre de beauté qui lui fait
donner la préférence pour les meubles, habille-
ments & autres choſes de caprice. Le ſieur Magoulet demeurant *au Bas-Chaillot, en-deçà de
la Savonnerie*, peint des ameublements ſur toi-
les neuves ou vieilles qu'on lui fournit, & aux-
quelles il donne un certain apprêt, & cela à très-
bon compte. Ses deſſeins imitent ceux des plus
beaux Pekins & font un grand effet par le ton
& la vivacité des couleurs; les plus beaux coû-
tent 9 livres l'aune quarrée. Il peint auſſi des
ſatins & autres meubles plus riches, ainſi que
des robes. On trouvera chez lui de quoi varier;
ſes deſſeins font bien traités & l'aſſortiment en
eſt complet.

*Praise for Claude Magoulet's hand-painted silks in
the July 27, 1761 issue of the* Avant-Coureur.

the title "the King's Designer" had more traditional training: Jean Baptiste Massé as an engraver, Charles Germain de Saint-Aubin as an embroiderer.

All the while, the particular Chinese-inspired art form that Claude had worked to recreate in France flourished at Versailles and in Paris. The greatest ladies in the land dreamed of dresses covered with motifs "in the Chinese style" or "in the Indian style"—patterns hand-painted onto the many yards of textile required for the voluminous fashions of the mid-eighteenth century.

By the early 1760s, Claude had moved well away from the old Paris filled with memories of his family and of generations of Magoulet artisans and had become the first Magoulet ever to live in the Paris of the future, in a part of the city that had not existed when the Queen's Embroiderer chose his home. He set up shop in Chaillot, an area on the city's fringe not yet taken over by urbanization. His address "just beyond the Savonnerie," the manufactory producing fine woven carpets located in what is now the 16th arrondissement near the site of today's Palais de Tokyo, Paris' palace of modern art, indicates that to the end, Claude worked best in a design collective. The final traces of his life are advertisements in a Parisian weekly that prided itself on announcing the latest developments in the arts, *L'Avant-Coureur* (the *Front-Runner* or the *Avant-Garde*).

In its Monday, July 27, 1761 issue, the periodical praised the designs executed on silks both old and new by "the best-known artist on textile" in the city, "the sieur Magoulet." Claude's patterns and finishes "imitated perfectly those of the finest Chinese silks." In his shop, one found a "wide assortment of patterns to choose from." The journalist praised in particular a "striped moiré silk with a pattern of leaves and flowers painted between the bands." Claude, then fifty-one, sold his most expensive designs for 9 livres a yard.

Claude's son, Jean Antoine, was the only son of the only son of Jean II Magoulet. Jean Antoine does not appear to have had children of his own. With him, the line of Magoulets directly descended from the Queen's Embroiderer died out.

As for Claude's father, it's as if he simply disappeared once he had done all he could to blight his children's futures. His known life ended at age fifty-seven, when the case of the pilfered silver fizzled out. From September 9, 1739 on, there is no further trace in the legal record of the man known as the Queen's Embroiderer and the Prince's Embroiderer.

I have no idea when the second Jean Magoulet died.

# CHAPTER TWENTY

# The King's Prosecutors
## Louise Magoulet: 1729–?

L OUIS CHEVROT DIED on March 31, 1736.
Early the following month, Louise Magoulet left Paris.

In the years between her release from the Salpêtrière on August 9, 1724 and April 1736, Louise had been cautious in the extreme. The single trace of her whereabouts places her not in Paris but once again in London. Her bonds with friends in the city where she and Louis were wed must have been tight indeed, or she would never have ventured across the English Channel again, even for a brief visit.

Nearly a decade after their marriage, on May 31, 1729, she signed another register in London: this time, it was a baptismal record, the christening of Jean La Vigne. Born on April 15, the baby was already more than six weeks old. This was a long wait for a baptism; most christenings in the same church that spring took place a day or two after birth. Jean's parents, Daniel and Ester La Vigne, had delayed the ceremony until the person they had chosen to be his godmother was able to reach the city.

When Louise Magoulet signed that register, the woman her own father would soon swear under oath had died in "about 1723" proved that she was still very much alive and well six years later. Her gesture, moreover, was another sign of her independent spirit, for Jean La Vigne was born in London because his parents, like their fellow parishioners as well as the curate who performed the ceremony, were members of the French Protestant community in exile.

In 1685, when he revoked the Edict of Nantes, Louis XIV rescinded a law in effect since 1598 and thereby ended a century during which Protestants in France had been allowed to practice their faith with considerable freedom. In 1685,

French Protestants were faced with a harsh choice: they could renounce their faith and convert to Catholicism, or they could leave France immediately. Hundreds of thousands fled.

The French luxury goods industry was particularly hard hit since many master artisans were Protestants. The greatest number settled in London: by the early eighteenth century, the city's French-speaking Protestant community was so large that thirty-five churches in London and the city's immediate surroundings were known as "French churches," with services held in French to accommodate the influx of new worshippers.

Louise had every reason to make herself as inconspicuous as possible: she was well aware that for someone with her past, to come out of hiding was hardly a safe choice. In principle, Louise's presence at the baptism entailed no real risk: after all, the ceremony was not taking place on French soil. But it was imprudent to call attention to any connection whatsoever to Protestantism. This explains why Jean, when he announced in an official context that Louise had died in a Protestant country, was careful to say that she had journeyed to Amsterdam to visit "a Catholic relative." Louise's decision to travel to London to play the role of godmother for the child of exiled French Protestants indicates that in the years since her marriage had been annulled, she had lost none of the "audacity" that had so irritated Lieutenant General d'Argenson in 1723.

Louise could hardly have chosen a more impressive setting for her show of independent thinking.

The baptismal certificate that Louise signed was written in French, in the registers of the most celebrated of the many French churches of London. The Église de la Savoie, the Savoy Church or Savoy Chapel, opened about 1640. By 1729, the chapel had moved to the address where it can still be found, in West London, just off Savoy Street and just south of the Strand. Of the edifice Louise saw, today only the outer walls dating from the sixteenth century remain.

In 1729, the Savoy Church was the most fashionable French church in town. The chapel was the place of worship preferred by the French Protestant nobility, including Catherine Mittault de Coudray, wife of the Reverend Thomas Hervé, who officiated at Jean La Vigne's baptism. Both Hervé and Mittault de Coudray were members of old French Protestant families, those who had fled France in 1685.

Thus, as Louise stepped outside the borders of the country where her father's accusation of prostitution had ruined her reputation, the woman whom Antoine Chevrot had pronounced a threat to his family's status moved in the highest circles of French society. Had Louis and Louise decided to live their lives outside France, they would soon have put the events of 1719 firmly in the past.

But in 1729, the couple had not yet given up on the future they hoped would be theirs in their homeland upon Antoine's death.

During her stay across the Channel, Louise might have met up with a defrocked French priest, the Abbé Antoine François Prévost. In 1729, Prévost was living in exile in London, where he was writing the novel that won him fame. In it, he brought to life one of the best known heroines in French literature, Manon Lescaut. Prévost's incendiary novel about a woman imprisoned on prostitution charges and shipped to Louisiana was clearly based on the story of *Mutinous*: Louise Magoulet could well have been his source for information that was then most decidedly not part of the public record.

Barely four months after Jean La Vigne's baptism in London, Antoine Chevrot died. He so feared that Louis still intended to remarry Louise that he had in no way altered the brutal will drawn up in 1724, shortly after having their English marriage pronounced invalid. When Louis accepted the provisions of that will, the chain of events that led to his death at the end of March 1736 was set in motion.

Upon Louis' death, Louise left Paris, her birthplace and the capital of France, and, with a population of roughly 750,000, the city virtually tied with London as Europe's largest. She moved to another city in France, though hardly a comparable one. In 1736, the population of Auxerre, situated near the northern limit of the French historical territory of Burgundy, would have stood only between eleven and twelve thousand strong. And Auxerre had none of the attractions that made Paris Paris: no avenues or promenade spaces, no grand residential architecture, not even street lighting.

But Louise's new home nonetheless had its own kind of energy: the small port city was bustling with trade. Auxerre's river, the Yonne, among the principal tributaries of the Seine and the main water supply for its river basin, had long been one of Paris' lifelines: to reach the Yonne's juncture with the Seine, boats loaded with such necessities as wood and grain traveled for roughly four days; from there, they quickly reached the capital.

In the eighteenth century, the fate of Auxerre and its inhabitants was centered on one commodity: wine. Auxerre's proximity to Paris through inexpensive river transport made it the commercial hub of Burgundy's wine industry, the center for the conveyance to France's capital and the world beyond of wines such as Chablis, whose vineyards were only eleven miles away. Consumer demand for Burgundy's wines both in France and all over Europe made the city and its merchant community prosperous. Auxerre's economy was so massively bound up with Burgundy's wines that leaders in this trade often identified themselves simply as "merchants," as though there were only one possible type of commerce: the wine business.

It was in Auxerre, in a mercantile setting a world apart from the luxury commerce and the neighborhoods filled with master artisans and their shops that had defined her Parisian childhood, that the second, and wildly different, chapter of Louise Magoulet's life began.

Louise joined the congregation of one of Auxerre's oldest churches, Saint-Eusèbe. Soon after, she met and very quickly married another parishioner of Saint-Eusèbe, Guillaume Billout. Billout was thirty-nine, recently widowed—and the father of seven surviving children from his 1722 marriage to Françoise Miné. He had spent the years of his marriage in the place where his family had long resided, Vermenton, a village of roughly a thousand souls some fifteen miles from Auxerre. Upon his wife's death, Billout had moved his offspring—the oldest of whom was eleven, while the youngest had just turned three—to Auxerre, the largest nearby city, where his older brother Edme, also a parishioner of Saint-Eusèbe, was a well-established merchant.

Edme stood up for Guillaume when he married Louise, as did two of his first cousins, Nicolas and Edme Chapelain, also merchants, though they dealt in grain rather than wine. The groom's choice of witnesses was indicative of a family in which the sense of tradition was alive and well. That gathering of the Billout clan was thus the polar opposite of the seemingly random groupings of so-called friends, with the occasional distant relative thrown in, consistently assembled by Jean Magoulet whenever he had been obliged to muster a show of public support.

The bride's case could not have been more different from the groom's. The woman identified in Saint-Eusèbe's parish register as Louise Marie Magoulet had not a single person to stand up for her—not a neighbor, not a fellow parishioner. After leaving Paris, Louise had continued to keep to herself.

On November 20, 1736, the date of their formal engagement, Louise's signature in the parish record book was firm and confident, every stroke identical to those found on her attempts, some fifteen years earlier, to proclaim her innocence to the Parisian police. Even as she embarked on this radically new life, Louise Magoulet was not attempting to erase her past: it's hard not to wonder whether she let Guillaume Billout in on all her secrets.

On November 20, Father Robert Gagne, vicar of Saint-Eusèbe, announced that banns had been published, both in Auxerre and in Paris, and that "no opposition had been voiced and no obstacles had been found." When Gagne questioned the engaged couple, the groom described himself as a widower, while

*Louise Magoulet and Guillaume Billout's signatures after their 1736 marriage.*

the bride identified herself with the only legal identity left to her, as "the daughter of Clément Magoullet, a merchant in Paris, deceased; and Marie-Louise
Desjardins, also deceased." She made no mention of her previous marriage,
long since stricken from all record books.

That disparity in family circumstances was echoed in the bride and bridegroom's finances. Guillaume's extensive holdings had been inventoried at the
time of his wife's death, so he didn't bother listing them all again. Louise's side
of the equation was quickly dealt with and hardly up to the Billouts' standards:
when Guillaume's younger brother Edme married Barbe Cassin, her dowry
totaled 2,000 livres in cash. In contrast, Louise brought into the marriage only
200 livres in personal effects and an annuity that guaranteed her an annual
income of 100 livres. Louise explained that this investment contract had been
established in November 1724, just when many Parisians, including Jean and
Anne Legrand, were converting the last of their banknotes from the failed Royal
Bank into annuities. She added that the annuity had been set up by an engineer named Duplessis and that it was transferable, which explained why she was
able to collect on it, though not how it came to be in her possession.

When she accepted Guillaume Billout's proposal, Louise chose a life unlike
any she had previously known. Her husband belonged to an extended family
that stayed in close touch; he lived in economic ease. She was also marrying into
the establishment, in many senses of the word. Guillaume's late father, also
Edme Billout, had served as longtime mayor of the family's home village, Vermenton. Edme was not born noble but had received letters of nobility in 1689,
as had his wife, Nicole Chapelain. Edme Billout owed that new status, which
he passed on to his children, to the fact that he was the third generation of Billouts to serve as *procureurs du roi*, royal prosecutors. Royal prosecutors were
assigned a jurisdiction; in it, they defended the monarch's and the government's interests in court, dealing with both civil and criminal cases.

At age thirty-four, Louise had married into law and order.

Last but surely not least, Louise Magoulet was finally becoming a mother, to
Guillaume Billout's seven children. At sixteen, she had found herself pregnant

virtually the moment her mother died and her father left her to her own devices. But after her baby Jean Louis was taken from her, Louise never again had a child. It seems likely that whatever brutal procedures were followed when she gave birth in the Salpêtrière had left her sterile.

On November 21, 1736, she and Guillaume married at Saint-Eusèbe only one day after they became formally engaged, whereas other couples who wed in Auxerre that year had waited at least several weeks between engagement and marriage.

In some ways, her large new family could have reminded Louise of her own early years. Guillaume's oldest child shared a name, Jeanne, with Louise's next-younger sister, while after Jeanne, as in Louise's family, came a boy named Claude. Jeanne and Claude Billout were only slightly younger than Louise's brother and sister had been at the moment when their father had broken up their family unit forever.

The family into which Louise married was hardly cut off from the world of Parisian artists. In 1728, Guillaume's older sister Laurence had married Jean Soufflot, a member of another extended family whose members lived, just like the Billouts, both in Vermenton and in Auxerre. One of Guillaume's Soufflot cousins-in-law, François, was then mayor of Vermenton. A second, Hubert Claude, served as Claude Billout's godfather when Guillaume's son was baptized in Vermenton in 1726. A third, also François, spent most of his life in Vermenton and Auxerre along with Guillaume Billout but in later years became an important Parisian architect. And a fourth, Jacques Germain Soufflot, was among the most influential French architects of all time, the most visible promoter of the new neoclassical style whose influence was evident all over Paris in the second half of the eighteenth century. Work on his best-known project, a church dedicated to the patron saint of Paris, Sainte Geneviève, started in 1757 and went on until 1790.

In the final decades of the eighteenth century, the straight lines and rigid geometry that characterized the neoclassical style gradually displaced the curving, sinuous lines that had dominated French design in the mid-eighteenth century, the style that was later named rococo and that had been inspired by patterns devised at Chantilly. Neoclassicism's biggest promoter, Jacques Germain Soufflot, was the director of the Savonnerie carpet manufactory in the years when one of the last great proponents of Chantilly's Franco-Chinese style, Louise's brother Claude Magoulet, maintained his workshop in its vicinity. Two masters of eighteenth-century French design could thus have crossed paths on a regular basis on the streets of their Chaillot neighborhood. Did they ever meet, and if so, did they connect the two halves of Louise Magoulet Chevrot Billout's life?

Guillaume Billout was no longer alive on September 25, 1753, when his son Claude married Agathe Élisabeth Malguiche in Vermenton. Louise's stepson Claude was by then still another in the Billout family's long line of royal prosecutors. The boy raised largely by Louise became a high official in the same royal judicial system that on three occasions had imprisoned his stepmother on trumped-up charges. In this capacity, Claude Billout defended the interests of Louis XV, the monarch who, in one of his reign's first official acts, had personally pronounced Louise's marriage to Louis Chevrot null and void.

Louise was not buried in Auxerre. I uncovered no trace of where or when Louise Magoulet Chevrot Billout's life came to an end.

*Aftermath*

# CHAPTER TWENTY-ONE

# To the Islands
## Marie Magoulet: Early 1740s–1848

A SECOND DAUGHTER OF Louise Poisson and Jean Magoulet was, like her older sister Louise, a consummate survivor: their fourth child, Marie, born in 1708. Thanks to Marie, the Magoulet bloodline, if not the Magoulet name, would live on.

Marie was baptized Marie Madeleine, but her siblings called her Manon. Along with the baby of the family, Dorothée, Manon was sent away to the General Hospital upon their mother's death. But, unlike Dorothée, Marie was among the lucky few children detained there to leave the Salpêtrière alive.

In 1724, when Jeanne and Claude joined forces to beg the lieutenant general to intervene on Louise's behalf, they were frightened for sixteen-year-old Manon's safety as well: she was missing and they wrote to express their fear "that she, too, has been taken away," in other words, locked up once again in the Salpêtrière. If that did indeed happen, Marie beat the odds still once more.

And Marie grew up to become, like Louise, an exceptionally resourceful and courageous woman. On June 26, 1733, she had barely turned twenty-five and was still unmarried when she took the lead in forcing her father finally to provide an official accounting of his handling of their mother's finances.

Manon married late, not before 1740, and certainly after she had turned thirty—an extremely advanced age for a woman of the day. The marriage she made was so extraordinarily fine that it almost defies belief.

Her husband, Jacques Mathieu Beauvillain, belonged to an extended family, most of whom lived in close proximity to one another near their parish church on Paris' Left Bank, Saint-André-des-Arts. Jacques' older brother Charles was a highly respected master clockmaker who spent his life on or near the rue Dauphine. When Charles married in 1733, his bride had a handsome dowry: 2,000 livres. Their witnesses had included Jules Depas, Comte de Feuquières, a major government official and military man, and his wife, Catherine Mignard, daughter of Pierre Mignard, Louis XIV's premier painter, known for his many portraits of the royal family, Queen Marie-Thérèse in particular. A second brother, Jean-Jacques, later wed a noblewoman, Marie Françoise Bernard d'Hérouville. Such were the aspirations of the family into which Manon married.

The brothers' late father, Jacques Beauvillain, had been a high officer, a controller, in the financial administration of Louis XIV's palace. Their mother, Marie Angélique Fillion, chose to remain in Versailles after his death. Charles was the only Beauvillain to pursue a career as a master artisan; otherwise, family members oversaw the finances of the country's most important men. Jean-Jacques Beauvillain, for instance, lived near Saint-André-des-Arts in the years when his children were born. But Jean-Jacques later moved to Versailles to take up employment as the chief financial officer of the man who was the chief financial officer of the entire land, Philibert Orry, Comte de Vignory, Controller General of France. The Orry family's vast wealth had originated with their brilliant success in an area where the original Queen's Embroiderer had failed to make his fortune: its ability to supply Louis XIV's armies with horses.

Manon had no dowry worthy of a Beauvillain, nor did she have significant family connections to increase her social worth. Rather than a great aristocrat who would stand up for her, the best she had to offer was her brother Claude, merely an important designer. Her sister Louise, now pronounced officially dead, she could never again mention. And with her father, Manon no longer maintained contact.

Instead, Marie won the hand of Jacques Beauvillain in a thoroughly modern way, in a manner that would become the way of the world in the following century but that in France in the 1740s and in the Beauvillains' world was still radically new: on her own merits and because of her character and personal charm.

This unlikely bride, the abandoned child who had seen her mother beaten, her brother in chains, and her younger sister's death, did the Beauvillains proud.

Manon had three sons. Two of them, Jean-Jacques and Hilarion, followed the tried and true Beauvillain path and supervised the finances of important men. They forged exemplary careers and enjoyed the privileges and the prosperity to which Antoine Chevrot had always aspired for his sons. Hilarion lived for the most part in Versailles, where he acted as the right-hand man of César Marie, Marquis de Talaru, brigadier in the royal armies and a man to be reckoned with at the courts of both Louis XV and Louis XVI. In 1787, on the eve of the Revolution, Hilarion's home in Versailles was on the rue Saint-Honoré, a stone's throw from the house once owned by Anne Legrand and Pierre Chicot.

Marie's grandson, Hilarion's son Hilarion Marie, died in 1838, in his home near the Invalides, on the rue d'Estrées, number 9. By then, street numbering had been adopted in the city and its inhabitants no longer needed to identify their addresses by mentioning notable shopsigns, such as the Golden Apple. Hilarion Marie had adapted to the world ushered in by the Revolution: he had trained as an architect and worked as a building inspector. By the time of his death, he had accumulated a most impressive fortune, which he left to his second wife and his children from his first marriage, a son, Jean Baptiste Jacques, and a daughter, Marie Thérèse. Hilarion owned two houses on the rue d'Estrées alone and had extensive real estate holdings elsewhere in Paris as well. Hilarion Marie's balance sheet indicates that in the new century, "safe as houses" had once again become a rule of thumb.

Manon's other son, Claude Magoulet's godson, Claude Jacques, was the Beauvillain who truly brought the family into the new age that began with the Revolution of 1789.

Claude Jacques married Marie Pierre Bénard; their children were baptized, as Claude Jacques himself had been, at Saint-André-des-Arts. Manon's choice of godfather for Claude Jacques helped shape his destiny: he became the only Beauvillain, as well as the last Magoulet, to win renown as a designer, proving that Magoulet blood did flow in his veins.

Claude Magoulet's godfather, Claude Fontaine, had requested for his godson training in "all the basic principles of architecture," and Claude Magoulet in turn passed on this knowledge to his namesake. Marie's son became a major contributor to another art of design: architecture.

Jean I Magoulet, the embroiderer who couldn't write but proved a genius at drafting patterns; his son Jean II, a leading embroiderer, a master of handwriting and of forgery as well; Claude, a noted designer and painter of textile patterns; and finally Claude Jacques Magoulet Beauvillain, an architect also known as a designer. For four generations, from the 1660s to the 1780s, Magoulets lived by the pencil, the pen, and the quill, masters all of patterns and designs.

Claude Jacques' career revolved around the church dedicated to Paris' fifth-century patron saint, Sainte-Geneviève. In 1744, in gratitude for having survived a critical illness, Louis XV decided to add one more church to the landscape of Paris. He chose a highly visible spot, the hill known as the Montagne Sainte-Geneviève, Sainte Geneviève Mountain, the highest peak on the Left Bank. The grandiose, immensely costly, and just as protracted process of the monument's construction was initiated in 1744 but completed only after the Bourbon monarchy had been abolished.

In the original history of Louis XV's church, composed in 1791, Claude Jacques was featured as among the few to have been part of the project's design team "from the start." When the first stone was laid in 1764 under the direction of its chief architect, Jacques Germain Soufflot, Manon's son was nineteen. He began collaborating on the new church as soon as his training was complete; he remained at Sainte-Geneviève from then on.

In 1791, Claude Jacques was forty-six, living directly opposite the church and still employed at Sainte-Geneviève as an architect, designer, and inspector (someone who made sure that all the stonework and masonry required for the construction of this vast church complied with standards). By then, Manon's son represented the last link with the original conception of a project that had never ceased to evolve. He was the living memory of Sainte-Geneviève.

Claude Jacques had a highly unusual career: he had only ever worked on one building. But then, the edifice to which he had devoted his life was special, seen from the start by its chief architect and major figures in the world of design as emblematic, a radical departure for ecclesiastical architecture and for architecture in general.

It's conceivable that Claude Magoulet had encountered its chief architect, Soufflot, in their Chaillot neighborhood and had recommended Claude Jacques; it is also possible that the connection that had brought Marie's son to Sainte-Geneviève had originated with Soufflot's Billout cousins in Auxerre, and thus with Louise Magoulet Billout, who, long after she had been declared legally dead, continued to watch over her younger siblings and their children.

Soufflot died in 1780, not living to see his church dedicated to Paris' patron saint transformed by the leaders of the Revolution into a radically different kind of monument. As proof of that metamorphosis, over its entrance and directly above those famous columns, a new inscription was soon seen on its pediment: AUX GRANDS HOMMES LA PATRIE RECONNAISSANTE, "to great men [from] a grateful homeland." In April 1791, the Revolution's governing body decided that the Church of Sainte-Geneviève would become the Panthéon, a mausoleum where the most notable Frenchmen could be buried. Among those soon interred there were Voltaire, Rousseau, and Soufflot himself. It was in 1791 that Antoine Quatremère de Quincy, charged with overseeing the transformation from church to mausoleum, wrote the history that gave Claude Jacques credit for his role. Also in 1791, the architect Pierre L'Enfant conceived the project that resulted in the best-known evidence of Sainte-Geneviève's widespread influence over the world of design: the U.S. Capitol.

*Jacques Germain Soufflot's Sainte-Geneviève Church.*

By 1791, Claude Jacques was no longer able to personally oversee the considerable stonework required by the new chief architect, François Soufflot, cousin of Jacques Germain Soufflot and son of a successor to Guillaume Billout's father as mayor of Vermenton. In 1786, Quatremère de Quincy explained, Claude Jacques had suffered "an attack of paralysis" that had "reduced him to infirmity." He had been allowed to keep his title and his annual salary of 3,500 livres.

That position and its income made it possible for Claude Jacques and his family to survive during the years when the Revolution was rewriting French history and the history of many French families, the Beauvillains among them. As part of that rewriting, in the Revolution's aftermath, a descendant of the Queen's Embroiderers made the trip "to the islands"—by choice.

By then, Louisiana was no longer a major destination for French immigration: the riches promised by Law's propaganda machine had never materialized for the colonists who had settled there. But other islands under French control now beckoned to those hoping for a new start, among them one far more distant, the Île Bourbon, today the Île de la Réunion (Reunion Island), the European Union's remotest district.

The Île Bourbon had been colonized immediately after the French Indies Company's formation in 1664, but well into the eighteenth century the number of French settlers remained infinitesimal. In 1767, when the Indies Company went into its final bankruptcy, there were only three thousand white settlers (and twenty-five thousand black slaves). At that moment, Louis XV decided to purchase both the Île Bourbon and the nearby Île de France (today's Mauritius) from the company for 7.5 million livres, roughly half of what, according to Quatremère de Quincy's estimate, had been spent on the still unfinished church of Sainte-Geneviève by 1790.

On November 1, 1767, when a new governor, Guillaume de Bellecombe, reached the Île Bourbon, he found a tiny island, a mere speck in the Indian Ocean 39 miles long and 28 wide, but a majestic speck, dotted with astonishing waterfalls, towering mountains, lush jungles, and a variety of plant life that has never ceased to fascinate botanists. He also found a community in dire straits. The paper money issued by the Indies Company had become worthless, and commerce was at a standstill. Among those who arrived with the new governor was a first cousin of Claude Jacques, Charles François Beauvillain, a much-decorated infantry officer. To encourage colonization, in 1770, Louis XV promulgated a law promising the most favorable conditions to those who "took wives in the islands," and that same year, Charles François did just that. He remained on the Île Bourbon, where he and his wife, Marie Thérèse Bouyer, had four children; their offspring in turn had numerous children of their own.

One advantage his government may have bestowed upon Charles François was a title: some archival documents identify him as Beauvillain de Montreuil, although others consider the designation illegitimate. No one contests the status of the title attached to the name of the second Beauvillain to reach the most distant of France's island colonies: Jean Charles Beauvillain de La Morinière.

Claude Jacques' son reached the Île Bourbon in late 1791. Had the Revolution's decision to turn Sainte-Geneviève into the Panthéon convinced the last surviving member of its original architectural team that it was time to encourage his heir to leave his homeland? The baby baptized Jean Charles at Saint-André-des-Arts in 1767 surely chose his destination because Charles François Beauvillain had prospered on the Indian Ocean colony. In 1794, Claude Jacques' son, twenty-seven years old and a long way from Paris, married twenty-two-year-old Marie Gertrude Bachelier, a member of one of the island's oldest families. They wed in the town of Sainte-Suzanne, founded in 1667 and soon to become the center of the island's sugar industry. Of their eight children, two were girls and six were boys and thus able to pass on the Beauvillain name.

And on the Île Bourbon, renamed Île de la Réunion in 1793 by the Revolution, Manon's great-grandchildren were fruitful indeed. Many of Marie's descendants were alive in 1848, when slavery was abolished. In 1848, a chapter in the Magoulet family saga that had begun when the first slave ships reached New Orleans, the place the French in 1719 had called "the islands," came to an end on a true island.

On June 16, 1839, when he was seventy-two, Manon's grandson Jean Charles died: at the end, he had lived in Saint-Benoît, a newer settlement whose economy was focused on coffee. By then, the island's population, just over 60,000 at the time he arrived there, had grown to 87,000. Before he died, Manon's grandson had acquired the right to call himself Beauvillain de La Morinière. The dream of nobility that Claude Jacques' great-grandfather, the Queen's Embroiderer, had realized by simply appropriating the title "de Toulongeon," which his son soon wrested from him, had now come true, even as the Bourbon monarchy that had long conferred and policed French noble status had ceased to exist.

And Manon, the little girl her father had hoped would simply be lost among the countless homeless, indigent, and virtually nameless faces who transited through Paris' General Hospital, had founded a dynasty almost six thousand miles from the land of the Magoulets.

# CHAPTER TWENTY-TWO

# A Royal Wedding
## The Magoulets: 1717–1792

I N LATE 1792, a carriage was rushing toward the French border with a family desperate to escape the Revolution before it was too late. Its passengers were among the lucky ones: they managed to make it safely out of the country, thereby becoming part of a recently created official category: *émigrés*, proponents of the monarchy who had chosen to flee France to save their lives. The Revolution soon sent representatives to the family's château in Brittany. They were armed with a search warrant, and they proceeded to confiscate the stacks of documents that the family's head, the Marquis de Penhouët, had carefully preserved for future generations.

That stash of family papers was in turn carefully preserved by those who seized it. As a result, the records that tell the Penhouët family history today fill five large boxes in France's National Archives. And those five cartons are part of a vast collection officially designated "the archives of *émigrés* and individuals condemned to death during the Revolution." The archive's index reads like the social register of France in the 1780s: there are counts and duchesses galore, high government officials, and then a name that in that august company sticks out like a sore thumb because of its absolute ordinariness and total lack of aristocratic resonance: Magoulet.

The saga that linked the Magoulets to great French aristocrats began in 1717 with still another trip "to the islands" and concluded with a royal wedding.

In 1710, Jacques Magoulet died; in 1714, Marie Freslin in turn passed away. They left four sons ranging in age from seventeen to twenty-five. The second son, Jacques Gabriel, was destined for the priesthood, while the others were to follow in their father's footsteps and deal in finance. Already in 1712, the eldest, Jacques François, entered the ranks of France's vast royal financial administration: his decades-long career was exemplary. In all Jacques François' complex business dealings, never once did a hint of underhanded activity emerge. Before he died in 1761, he had amassed a substantial fortune.

Like his father, Jacques François chose a wife who became a true partner. By the time he married Catherine Roncellet, the couple had known each other for a long time. On August 5, 1712, when Marie Freslin cosigned with Jacques François on the purchase of his administrative position for the hefty sum of 53,000 livres, the contract specified that the deal had been "partly financed by Mademoiselle Roncellet." Their wedding finally took place six years later: that long wait can be explained by the groom's urgent need to deal with his two youngest brothers, Hubert and Marie Anne, before settling down himself.

Every set of Magoulet children but the offspring of Louise Poisson and Jean II seems to have contained a bad seed. In this case, there were two of them, those two youngest boys. The third son, Hubert, seems to have inherited the genes responsible for the behavior of his father's favorite brother, the Queen's Embroiderer. Hubert was constantly lending and borrowing, then borrowing and lending some more, dealing in what were, particularly for one so young, very large sums. As long as their mother was alive, she had been able to keep a lid on things, but in November 1715, barely a year after Marie Freslin's death, Hubert was involved in the kind of dustup worthy of his first cousin Jean II.

Hubert had turned over notes worth thousands of livres to someone who had promised to cash them in for him by early 1715. But when Hubert pressed him for his money, the "banker" offered to pay half up front, and the rest in due time, a deal Hubert refused. The next thing he knew, or so he claimed, thirty men armed with guns had arrived at Hubert's door, chased him around, and led him off to prison. Hubert did what he always did: persuaded his older brother the priest to intervene on his behalf, both with the police and with Jacques François.

The fix did not last long. By the spring of 1716, Hubert owed Jacques François well over 7,000 livres and roughly 2,000 more to Jacques Gabriel, and his debts to individuals outside the family totaled over 38,000. Jacques François decided that a permanent solution was essential.

While eighteenth-century English families had a long history of shipping younger sons off to become merchants on the Caribbean's sugar islands, French families did not often have recourse to such solutions. Had Hubert waited three years to show his true stripes, he might well have ended up in Louisiana, where his chances of making his fortune would have been slim to nil. But in 1716, another French island was in the news: Saint-Domingue, today's Haiti.

In the decades that followed, Saint-Domingue was destined to become the biggest success story of all France's colonies, and all because of one crop: sugar.

In December 1721, when Parisians were wallowing in the misery provoked by Law's machinations, the Marquise de Balleroy received a letter that discussed the fates of various young Frenchmen who had crossed the ocean in search of a new start. Those who had listened to Law's siren song and gone "to the Mississippi" now found themselves "in financial ruin." But, her correspondent claimed, "all those who go to Saint-Domingue come home with millions in their pockets." Many also returned, he added, having become "great lords." He described the case of one young man whose family had sent him away "without a penny to his name"; he had just returned "with 50,000 a year in income from sugar." He might have been telling Hubert's story.

Jacques François' timing could not have been better. The French Indies Company had established a settlement on Saint-Domingue in 1698 with the intention of developing a new sugar island, but the colony's expansion went into high gear only at the very end of Louis XIV's reign. In 1713, the island was given an administration of its own; in June 1716, at the moment when the severity of Hubert's situation had just become evident, new statutes for its governance were promulgated. The following month, Jacques François revealed his intentions for his youngest brothers.

It was easy for him to arrange their passage to the New World. François Legendre, eldest son of their father's lifelong closest ally, the François Legendre who had witnessed Jacques' marriage contract, was then director of the French Indies Company; Legendre's younger son, Joseph Legendre d'Arminy, was named head of the Royal Company of Saint-Domingue as soon as its new statutes were promulgated.

Thus, three years before their Magoulet cousin Louise was signed up for forced deportation, Hubert's departure was decreed; his younger brother, Marie Anne, the family's true ne'er-do-well, was going with him. But Jacques François' methods were worlds apart from the tactics chosen by his first cousin Jean II. Whereas Louise was treated as a common criminal, Jacques François' brothers were sent off in style.

Their passage had been paid in advance. They had new outfits, right down to new boots. And Jacques François had devoted a considerable sum—3,600 livres for Marie Anne, nearly 5,500 for Hubert—to getting them started in business on Saint-Domingue. He had already purchased for them what he described, using a brand-new word, as *pacotille*, the merchandise that a businessman traveling to a French overseas colony was allowed to bring aboard ship at no extra cost. Jacques François had invested those thousands of livres in the fanciest trimmings possible for high-fashion garments: gold and silver braid, gold and silver buttons. Gold and silver were being returned to the New World.

Jacques François clearly imagined that his brothers' future on the distant island would be closely related to the luxury goods industry that had long been the source of his family's status in Paris. But fate had other plans for Hubert. On Saint-Domingue, the bad seed became a brilliant success, virtually overnight.

Hubert arrived on Saint-Domingue at the perfect time to profit from the expansion of John Law's Compagnie d'Occident in the years following the big influx of capital in 1717 and 1718. By 1720, Hubert was comfortably settled in the island's capital, Cap Français, a city of some fifteen thousand. He was soon wealthy enough to append to his name the kind of titles that were sure to impress: the King's Counselor, member of Cap Français' Superior Council. Hubert owed his new lease on life to sugar.

In the seventeenth century, salt had made the difference for the Chevrot clan. By the early decades of the eighteenth century, a new star commodity was playing salt's role, and nowhere was sugar more successful at putting those who invested wisely in it on a fast track to success than in Saint-Domingue. From 1720 on, the island was the largest producer of sugarcane in the world. By the mid-eighteenth century, Saint-Domingue alone was exporting more sugar than all the English islands combined. In the 1760s, four hundred ships from Saint-Domingue reached French ports every year, bearing 200 million livres' worth of the island's precious commodities, and that figure never stopped rising. By 1789, exports from the French sugar islands totaled 9 million English pounds, whereas those from the British West Indies were valued at only 5 million.

Eighteenth-century Europeans were sugar-mad, and Saint-Domingue fed their appetite for the sweet commodity. Throughout most of the eighteenth century, the income from this one colony propped up the French economy. Hubert reached "the islands" just in time to profit from the boom: he sold his remnants of the Old World resources, the *pacotille* that Jacques François had shipped off with him, and bought a sugar refinery. Enough said.

In 1721, when the Marquise de Balleroy was told that sugar could guarantee an annual income of 50,000 livres, she may have considered the statement a pipe dream. Well, still in the 1760s, every year Hubert's refinery was raking in between 60,000 and 90,000 in returns for his heirs.

Other advantages naturally came along with such vast wealth. Hubert soon acquired a title, Magoulet de Maisoncelle. And within decades, his descendants were forging the kinds of marriages that make the Daulmays' 1665 salt alliance with the Chevrots seem like small change.

Hubert and his wife Élisabeth Briochet had four children: a son, Hubert Michel, and three daughters: Marthe Élisabeth, Charlotte, and Jeanne. The first two daughters were married on the island: Marthe to Jean Joseph Bertrand, a financial administrator, and Charlotte to Gabriel Chicotteau, an infantry officer. For her marriage, Jeanne returned to the mainland. When her wedding contract was signed on October 8, 1754, she was residing with her uncle Jacques François in his handsome residence on the rue du Petit-Musc, in the shadow of the Marais' Saint-Paul Church. Jeanne's contract was drawn up by her uncle's notary, Augustin Loyson, the very man who early in his practice had arranged for his niece to marry Louis Chevrot.

Since both the bride's parents were by then deceased, her uncle Jacques François stood up for the twenty-two-year-old bride when she promised to marry Alexandre Jacques de Bongars. Bongars was then thirty-five and already had major titles appended to his name; he was most notably the *président à mortier*, or chief magistrate, of the Parlement of the northeastern French city of Metz. In exchange, the bride offered a splendid dowry: her share of her parents' property in the islands.

While Jeanne remained in France, her sisters, who had traveled for her wedding, resumed their lives on Saint-Domingue. Three years later, when Charlotte's husband died, she returned to France. Charlotte knew that her own end was in sight, and something was troubling her peace of mind. On March 27, 1757, she gave her brother-in-law Joseph Bertrand power of attorney to act for her in a matter for which she also asked the cooperation of both her sisters. The three sisters were joint owners of their family's extensive property in Saint-Domingue, and before her death, Charlotte wanted to end their rights to one part of that estate. Bertrand was still living in Cap Français; since the fulfillment of her wish would be legally complex, Charlotte asked him to retain an attorney who would make sure "that every necessary step will be correctly taken care of."

Charlotte's request was an amazing deathbed wish for a wealthy and privileged Frenchwoman in 1757. Decades before slavery would be officially and permanently abolished on Saint-Domingue, Charlotte wanted to be certain that "the negress named Renotte would be given her freedom."

In the years that followed Jeanne's wedding, her husband became an ever more powerful magistrate. On January 19, 1766, Alexandre Jacques de Bongars received the most influential posting of his career: he was appointed *intendant* of Saint-Domingue, the magistrate responsible for all matters relating to the judicial and financial administration, as well as all concerns relating to the infrastructure and public services, of the wealthiest French colonial possession.

On July 1, 1766, the Bongars family was formally welcomed upon their arrival at Cap Français. Jeanne, the daughter of a man shipped off to Saint-Domingue by an older brother desperate to be rid of him, had returned to the island of her birth among its notables.

Alexandre and Jeanne's daughters, Émilie and Adélaïde, came with them; a son, Alexandre-Louis, was born on Saint-Domingue. The family remained on the island until June 1771, when they returned to France. In February 1782, Bongars was again appointed *intendant*; he then served until April 9, 1785. In between his two terms, in January 1781, Alexandre and Jeanne presided over the marriage of their second child. It was the kind of alliance to which no previous Magoulet could ever have aspired.

As a sign of the families' significance, the notaries who drew up the marriage contract tied it up with a big deep blue ribbon. The ribbon would have been justified by the groom's status alone: Louis Claude René de Mordant, Marquis de Massiac, belonged to a venerable family; the bluest blood in France ran in his veins.

This "high and powerful lord" was not marrying Hubert Magoulet's granddaughter solely for her money, though her parents did settle 300,000 livres on Adélaïde. Louis Claude's uncle, Claude Louis d'Espinchal, minister and vice admiral of France's Navy, had named his nephew his sole heir; Louis Claude had thus come into a considerable estate of his own in 1778: total value over 100,000 livres, with an additional 24,000 in diamonds alone. At that time, he had also inherited the title of marquis as well as several sugarcane plantations on Saint-Domingue. Between those plantations and Hubert's refinery, the young couple functioned like a microcosm of Saint-Domingue's economy.

The marquis was already a lieutenant in the French navy, and this when France had finally achieved the kind of naval distinction Louis XIV and Colbert had coveted a century earlier. The decade from 1778, when the French fleet entered the American War of Independence, and 1789 was arguably the French navy's finest hour, the moment when it was fully the equal of its age-old English rival.

On the afternoon of January 8, 1781, the bride and groom and their notaries made the trip to Versailles in order to obtain for their marriage agreement the most impressive signatures in the land.

That day, a member of the Magoulet family that Antoine Chevrot had scorned as socially beneath him had a wedding agreement witnessed by the king and queen of France.

In a list that opens with a very prominent LOUIS, followed by Marie Antoinette (with the ink in *An* slightly smudged), and after scrolling through a list

*Signatures of the French royal family at the 1781 marriage of*
*Jacques I Magoulet's great-great-granddaughter.*

of names that includes those of Louis Stanilas Xavier, brother of Louis XVI
and future Louis XVIII, and his wife, Marie Joséphine, as well as the two oldest daughters of Louis XV and the head of the house of Bourbon-Condé, the
son of the prince who had funded two Magoulets' work at Chantilly, one finds
the name Magoulet de Maisoncelle Bongars.

Hubert Magoulet's daughter Jeanne—the great-granddaughter of a *gainier*
whose sense of self derived from the right to "follow the court," the

granddaughter of a man who collected the king's taxes and whose brother's self-importance was based on the privilege of embroidering for the queen of France—had taken the Magoulets to the top of the French social hierarchy. Her daughter Adélaïde de Bongars would not work for the court of France: she would be part of it. The Magoulets no longer had to wait for scraps from the table: by 1786, they were paying for the banquet.

The first years of her marriage to the Marquis de Massiac, at a time when French aristocrats were spending as if there were no tomorrow, must have been a giddy whirl for the young woman raised so far from the epicenter of French power. But of course Adélaïde got to the party as it was about to end, and, when it did, in August 1789, the regal Massiac family townhouse on one of Paris' grandest squares, the Place des Victoires, became the hub of a major rearguard movement.

In 1757, Adélaïde's aunt Charlotte had worked from France to free a slave still her property on Saint-Domingue. Three decades later, Adélaïde's husband helped found a political initiative designed to stop any attempt to change the economic status quo on the island. The new campaign began because Charlotte was far from the only *grand blanc*—"important white," as the sugar planters on Saint-Domingue were known—to believe that the island's dependence on slavery should be ended.

In 1789, 32,000 white settlers lived on Saint-Domingue and ran the plantations on which France's economy was so heavily reliant, but nearly 500,000 slaves labored on those plantations, as many as on all British sugar islands combined and close to the 700,000 slaves in the entire United States. Many of the wealthiest plantation owners lived in France and managed from afar the affairs on which their fortunes and their influence were dependent.

Early in 1789, those owners learned of a new association in Paris: an abolitionist group, the Société des Amis des Noirs (Society of the Friends of the Blacks). The colonial proprietors resolved to counter its influence, and only days after August 26, 1789, when the Declaration of the Rights of Man pronounced all men free and equal, the Marquis de Massiac and his fellow landowners established their headquarters in his townhouse on the Place des Victoires: the French antiabolitionist movement is still known as the Club Massiac, the Massiac Club. The founding member who gave the association its name was defending his wife's interests on Saint-Domingue: the Magoulet holdings encompassed two sugar refineries and a coffee plantation.

The club proved so effective in promoting its pro-slavery agenda that there was virtually no discussion of slavery in the French assemblies as long as it was active. Then, on August 10, 1792, the National Guard stormed the Tuileries

Palace and the royal family was obliged to take refuge with the Legislative Assembly: the monarchy's end was in sight. On August 16, Massiac's neighbors on the Place des Victoires reported to the police the sight of "flames pouring out of his residence's chimney." By the time officers arrived on the scene, most of the club's records had gone up in smoke.

In the final months of 1792, the Marquis and Marquise de Massiac fled to London. The marquis died in 1806, by which time slavery had been abolished on the island and Saint-Domingue had become the sovereign state of Haiti. The Haitian revolution of 1791 swept away the old world of Saint-Domingue, and with it the Magoulets' rights to the properties that had made them influential during the last gasp of the Bourbon monarchy.

Adélaïde lived until 1827, long enough to witness the two moments when the Bourbons were briefly restored to power, including the monarchy of one of those who had signed her marriage contract: Louis XVIII.

At 10 A.M. on November 21, 1827, Alexandre de Mordant, Marquis de Massiac, Adélaïde's son and sole surviving heir, authorized an inventory of his mother's possessions. Adélaïde had lived her final years in a fourth-floor walkup at 24 rue de l'Université. The colossal Magoulet-Bongars wealth had vanished: Adélaïde's total possessions were valued at 1,175 francs (more or less the equivalent of that sum in livres), plus 880 in cash. Also gone with the wind were the 24,000 livres' worth of diamonds her husband had offered as a wedding gift: Adélaïde's jewelry was estimated at a mere 40 francs.

Her inventory further records Adélaïde's long but ultimately fruitless struggle to win compensation for the extensive holdings on Saint-Domingue in the Magoulet-Bongars estate.

The rejection of her claim was the final trace of the Magoulet name in France's legal record.

In the end, sugar, like salt, came to naught.

# The Noise of Time
## The Chevrots: 1736–1790

I T WAS ONLY on May 12, 1736—a full six weeks after Louis Chevrot's death—that relatives and family friends gathered to appoint a guardian for his son, then three and a half. It had not been easy to find anyone willing to become legally involved in the boy's future.

In the end, the presiding magistrate managed to assemble seven people, but it was hardly an ideal group: not a single member of the child's immediate family had cared enough to assume responsibility for his welfare.

There were two glaring absences: Louis' brother Antoine Charles, the only close relation left on the Chevrot side, and the Loyson family in general. Not one near maternal relative showed up: not Marie Élizabeth's mother, the boy's only surviving grandparent; none of the male heads of the family, Marie Élizabeth's Loyson uncles, not even Augustin, the notary responsible for her marriage to Louis. Those who did participate were a lightly connected lot: five were described as cousins, but they were merely cousins-in-law, and distant ones at that. Claude Rimbault, for example, was the son of the man Antoine had attacked so viciously in print in 1700.

That May 12 meeting was a harbinger of what was ahead for Louis' son. The boy had a childhood that could have served to inspire novels written a full century later: *Oliver Twist* and *Jane Eyre*.

The assembly chose the boy's mother to serve as his guardian and a lawyer for the Parlement identified as "a friend" as substitute guardian. Marie Élizabeth had numerous family members living in Paris and living in ease: when Augustin Loyson died, those inventorying his estate found over 20,000 livres in cash in his apartment. But in her time of need his niece received no help from him or any family member.

Marie Élizabeth was soon so destitute that she parted with the only thing Louis had managed to hold on to during the years between Antoine's death and his own: his half of Antoine's position as annuities controller. At first his widow sold off bits of it. But on July 5, 1740, in desperation she handed over all that was left to another controller, Gallican François Dulaurens, in exchange for an annuity that paid her 200 in annual income. She received the first payment of 50 livres on the spot.

And just like that, the proof of status that had been so precious to Antoine Chevrot that he had held it over Louis' head for decades before finally depriving him of it in an attempt to keep his son and Louise Magoulet apart was gone. After that sale, Louis' son had little left to underwrite his future.

His next loss was far more devastating.

On May 19, 1741, Marie Élizabeth Loyson died. Her death was as sudden as her husband's had been five years before. The police were not called in, so there was no report. Marie Élizabeth's relatives later referred to her *dérange-ment*, derangement, a term then just beginning to be used to designate mental instability. Her death may have been thought a suicide: it would be easy to see why Marie Élizabeth had felt she could not go on.

By May 1741, Louis' widow had already spent her income for the entire year. She was far behind in her rent. She owed 21 livres to a widow named David who had sold her fruit on credit and over 350 more to other merchants who had helped her out in the same way. And she couldn't expect another penny before January 1742.

On May 19, the boy at least saw his mother buried in a churchyard: for Marie Élizabeth's last rites, her family handed over the princely sum of 40 livres (later deducted from Louis II's inheritance), the bare minimum required to avoid interment in a pauper's grave. No one was willing to contribute the extra 100 that would have ensured a respectable service.

On June 23, 1741, six weeks after Marie Élizabeth's death and exactly five years after the first assembly to select a guardian for Louis' son, a second such council was convened. One of the friends and three of the cousins-in-law who had been present for the meeting after Louis' death were back, among them Claude Rimbault, who by then had become an annuities controller, a develop-ment that would surely have driven Antoine wild. This time, both Augustin Loyson and another of Marie Élizabeth's Loyson uncles showed up, as well as her sister's husband, but their presence did not signify any wish to protect Marie Élizabeth's child. Anne Martin Loyson, Louis' grandmother, had agreed to become his guardian, and she wanted her male relatives' help in order to hold on to property. Antoine Charles had finally taken an interest, not in his nephew, mind you, but in the boy's small legacy. He was hoping to get sole ownership of the house on the rue du Perche, so the Loysons joined together to head off his move. This was the only assistance they ever gave the boy.

On July 4, an inventory of Marie Élizabeth Loyson's estate was drawn up. It was done at the request of Louis Chevrot, identified as "her only son, age 8," the exact age at which his father had lost his own mother. The inventory did not take long: when Louis Chevrot died, his possessions had a total value of 43 livres; Marie Élizabeth's came to only 39. In 1741, you couldn't buy a proper chair for that price.

Mother and son had shared a tiny room on the rue de la Mortellerie. They had shared a bed meagerly outfitted with old bedding worth 15 livres. They owned what the inventory listed as a "small" chest of drawers, three chairs, a "small" folding table, a "small broken" mirror, two glasses, one "small" candleholder, and a bit of "old" tapestry, the same tapestry that had been on the wall of the room in which Louis died. All their clothing combined was worth a paltry 3 livres. The wife of Marie Françoise Boulanger Chevrot's eldest son owned no gloves at all, and Marie Françoise's only grandchild didn't have a decent pair of shoes. The notary responsible for the inventory described every single garment as "in very bad shape," which meant that they had gone around virtually in rags.

Rather than the storybook early boyhood Louis Chevrot had lived, his son had known only deprivation. The social and financial ascension of a family that had been so carefully constructed for over a century had thus ended in a Chevrot heir's complete and utter indigence.

As he began life on his own, the only things the eight-year-old walked away with were a few souvenirs. There were six family portraits, unframed and therefore considered of no value: two were portraits of his father and mother. Since the household had never had a spare penny, these were surely the work of Louis Chevrot. And then there were the family papers placed in the boy's care. There were a few deeds to property and above all the voluminous records of Antoine's legal battle to have Louis' father's first marriage pronounced invalid. The eight-year-old might thus already have learned about the love of his father's life and what his grandfather had done to destroy it.

It may all have been too much for the boy to bear. The minute the inventory was completed, Louis fell so dangerously ill that it was touch-and-go all through the July and August after Marie Élizabeth's death. His health concerns during the summer of 1741 can be documented because the notary Augustin Loyson kept track of every cent spent for his care, later deducting the total cost from Louis' estate.

His relatives did not go overboard to keep the boy alive: two months of nursing, the fee for the surgeon who bled him, plus broth and medicine, all for 40 livres. And when "all his hair fell out," they bought him a wig, for which they paid 2 livres, also charged to his account. It's hard to imagine the kind of peruke available for such a paltry sum.

The next years were sheer precarity. On August 4, 1741, the boy's grand-mother asked the financier with whom his mother had taken out an annuity for an advance, but he refused: he was already holding eight promissory notes from Marie Élizabeth. No one in the Loyson clan was willing to contribute a farthing, not even Marie Élizabeth's sister Catherine, who lived a comfortable life thanks to her marriage to an artisan in a then booming sector of the luxury goods trade: porcelain.

And as for the boy's only close Chevrot relative, his uncle—well, Antoine Charles had serious difficulties of his own. He had sold off his share of Antoine's position and run through the proceeds. Antoine Charles had then borrowed money and offered the family farm in Courcelles as collateral on the loan.

On June 3, 1744, Louis' last remaining grandparent, Anne Martin Loyson, died. By June 25, when the third assembly to appoint a guardian for him was convened, Louis was still only eleven. This time, Claude Rimbault, the son of Antoine's old enemy, was selected. And as substitute guardian they chose some-one whose relation to the family was not made clear: Jacques Aubry. Aubry was given a precise mandate: to do the math on all of Louis II's inheritances, from his father, his mother, and his grandparents. The boy could never again expect a bequest, and his Loyson uncles wanted to know the bottom line. To give him the power to act in Louis II's name, Aubry was made guardian, the boy's fourth guardian in less than a decade.

The eleven-year-old was about to be cut loose.

Aubry would have been paid only a pittance for his services, but he was hardly short of funds. The eminent and eminently expensive positions that he occupied in the royal war administration had already brought him noble sta-tus and considerable wealth. Aubry had taken on this task out of loyalty to someone, but to whom? He performed his role admirably; on behalf of Louis' son, Aubry made the kind of decisions someone should have suggested to Louis and his brother when they had inherited from Antoine. In so doing, Aubry became a financial role model for his ward.

Aubry's first decision involved the boy's grandmother. Anne Martin had spent her final days in a single room rented for 50 livres a year, surrounded by

105 livres' worth of possessions. On November 10, 1744, in his ward's name, Aubry waived any further claim to her estate or to that of her late husband. This disengaged the boy from the months of complicated negotiations in which all other potential heirs were involved, and Aubry's instincts were proved correct. When all was said and done and everything was divided up, it became clear that Louis' mother had gotten more than her fair share with the money she had used as her dowry.

The next estate to be renounced was that of Antoine Charles. By February 1745, his financial affairs had gone from bad to disastrous. Losing the family farm in Courcelles seems to have been the last straw. On Sunday, September 24, 1747, it was all over for Antoine Charles Chevrot, age forty-three. After his death, the boy was the last Chevrot.

Did Antoine Charles take his own life? His uncle Henri Boulanger told the police that he had been with his nephew when he died and had "removed from the apartment a rifle that he recognized as having once been his." A rifle is not the first thing one imagines someone keeping in the small room, which rented for 60 livres a year, in which Antoine Charles had spent his life's final decade.

In contrast to his brother and sister-in-law, Antoine Charles had lived in a grand style. He had slept on a real bed carved of walnut and with a proper mattress and down pillows, protected from the cold by blue bed curtains trimmed with silk braid in a lemon-yellow hue. He had warmed himself by a fireplace equipped with the requisite tools. He owned three *chemises*, two collars, and three pairs of shoes. And a few touches of vestimentary elegance remained still in his wardrobe: a crimson satin vest and above all the traditional sign of the noble rank to which his father had falsely pretended: a sword. Antoine Charles' was adorned with a delicate design in silver filigree.

But many of the accoutrements of something like grandeur were merely borrowed. Henri Boulanger left that February day with the grand hat trimmed with gold braid that he had lent his nephew. The man who rented the room next door came for his dishes. A young woman "who refused to give her name" took away the sheets and the dressing gown that Antoine Charles had borrowed from her. Since no one else wanted it, she also took with her "a portrait of the deceased on canvas," probably another example of his brother Louis Chevrot's work.

On the financial side, Antoine Charles left only debt: thousands in promissory notes, rent due, court orders to repay creditors and to pay lawyers. In 1748, Aubry renounced in Louis II's name the inheritance of his father as well as that of his uncle, thereby severing the boy's last legal ties to the Chevrot estate. He also officially put an end in the boy's name to all outstanding litigation undertaken by Antoine Charles. And the lawsuits were numerous, for like his father, when in difficulty, Antoine Charles' first instinct had always been to turn to the courts.

Next, on December 20, 1748, his guardian reached a separate settlement with Claude Mongrolle, the vinegar merchant who had rented the Chevrot property on the rue du Perche since 1721. Antoine Charles had decided to ignore Louis' arrangement with the merchant and had taken legal action to force Mongrolle to resume rent payments. In his ward's name, Aubry ended all suits against Mongrolle and agreed to pay the legal fees that the merchant had incurred while defending himself against Antoine Charles. It would be many years before Louis saw income from the property, but the young man had retained control over the only remaining bit of the Chevrot estate, the last link to 150 years of his family's history in the city of his birth.

Finally, on June 27, 1750, Aubry drew up a blanket waiver: Louis wanted nothing to do with any lawsuits initiated by his mother or his great-uncle Henri Boulanger (who had gone after Antoine Charles' estate), a document intended to tie up any loose ends that the guardian might have missed. Louis, then seventeen, was at last free of the legal battles that had scarred the lives of two generations of Chevrots. On October 8, Antoine Charles' lawyer turned over to his nephew the records of litigation that Antoine Charles had accumulated, both his own lawsuits and his father's. The sight of that voluminous archive, testimony to the litigious obsession that had helped bring on his family's ruin, was another legal coming-of-age for the last of the Chevrots.

Was the 1700 pamphlet in which Antoine had attacked Hugues Rimbault part of that stash? If so, Louis might have been amazed to read his grandfather's self-characterization: "Lord Chevrot is not inclined to be litigious."

In his entire life, Louis II Chevrot did not initiate a single lawsuit or any type of legal proceeding. When his great-uncle Henri Boulanger died in 1759, leaving a tidy estate, Louis was the sole relative not to put in a claim.

Family documents always refer to Louis as "the orphan" and as a *boursier*, the recipient of funds earmarked by educational institutions for "indigent" students. Louis' education took place in a kind of establishment that first became common in Paris in the 1730s: a *pension* or boarding school run by a *maître de pension*, in his case, Pension Master Jean Antoine Desquinemare. His schooling cost Louis only 26 livres a year: the rest was covered by a scholarship.

The grandson of a man who had poured 71,000 livres into his post as annuities controller was thus dependent on the kindness of strangers to make his way in the world.

And he did make his way, a way with no precedent whatsoever in this story. Louis II Chevrot was a self-made man.

His independence from his past was fully evident in 1758, when he married. In eighteenth-century France, the institution of marriage remained defined, as it had been for centuries, as a union between two individuals that also created a bond between their two families. The list of signatures that concluded every marriage contract traditionally opened with those of the bride's and the groom's closest relatives, signatures that stood as evidence that their families had approved their union.

Louis' bride-to-be, Marguerite Toupet, was of age; her mother was deceased, but her father, Charles Toupet, was there to stand up for his daughter. On the groom's side, however, not a single Loyson or Boulanger was present. On January 8, 1758, when the document was drawn up, Louis had just turned twenty-five; he had clearly waited until he was of age and required no one's authorization to marry. The absence of any sign of family allegiance indicates that Louis had broken off all contact with the relatives who had shown an orphaned child no generosity. Did it also show that he was determined not to repeat his father's story?

To a man, Louis' Chevrot forebears had summoned on such occasions as many notable witnesses as possible from two worlds: the nobility and high finance. Louis showed no desire to follow in the footsteps of his ancestors: he had but a single person to stand up for him, identified as a "friend." Louis' lone witness came from neither of the spheres that had defined his family's aspirations: Marc Antoine Doublet was a man of the cloth and an educator. And those were the realms that would define Louis' life.

Doublet was a priest in a French religious order, the Oratorians, that had been founded in 1611 from a desire to amend the French Catholic Church in response to the Protestant Reformation. By 1758, Doublet had served his order for decades, during which time he had often fought for religious reform. He lived in the order's motherhouse in Paris on the rue Saint-Honoré. That church still stands directly opposite the Louvre; the French Oratory is now a Protestant church.

The Oratorians were a teaching order, and their schools were known for a resolutely modern type of curriculum. In the seventeenth and eighteenth centuries, Parisians educated in public establishments rather than by private tutors were most likely to be taught by Jesuits and to receive an education, in Latin, that was focused on the classics. The Oratorians taught in French and created a program of studies centered instead on contemporary literature, modern languages, and the sciences.

Louis' bride lived on a minuscule cul-de-sac just off the rue Saint-Honoré, around the corner from Doublet's church. Since Louis, too, resided nearby, their union was a neighborhood affair. It was also a positively brilliant match for a young man without a family to stand by him. Instead, just as in the case of Marie Magoulet's union, Louis married a woman who accepted his hand because she cared for him and believed in him.

Louis' net worth was hardly overwhelming: he received 200 livres a year from his annuity; the remaining farm in Cormeilles-in-Parisis brought in a bit of income; the house on the rue du Perche rented for 400 a year. While these were solid values, 700 a year was hardly enough to keep a household running.

However, Marguerite had a dowry, and quite a dowry it was: 10,000 livres, fully 6,000 in the best thing a bride could bring to the table—cash. Jacques Magoulet or Antoine Chevrot would have jumped at the chance to marry Marguerite Toupet. She also owned a full complement of furniture and house-hold linens, as well as clothing and personal items. Finally, she had an annuity of her own; the young couple handed over its income to her father "for his personal use during his lifetime." This was but the first example of the gener-osity that was a hallmark of their long marriage.

A second noted man of the cloth was another neighbor: Charles-Michel L'Épée, known to posterity as the Abbé de L'Épée. From 1739 on, L'Épée resided just behind another church on the rue Saint-Honoré, the Church of Saint-Roch, on the third floor of a building on the rue des Moulins. In 1758, Louis lived on the rue Saint-Roch; after their marriage, the young couple set up house on the rue des Orties, around the corner from L'Épée's residence. Like Doublet, the Abbé was an educator; like Doublet, he was known for his strictly principled stances, particularly with respect to a core belief on which Doublet and L'Épée found common ground: their defense of Jansenism.

For most of the seventeenth and eighteenth centuries, Jansenism was a force to be reckoned with in French society. This movement for theological reform within the Catholic Church was vehemently opposed by the Jesuits, who accused Jansenists of Calvinist leanings. The struggle between Jesuits and Jansenists was often intense: when the Catholic Church denounced Jansenism as a her-esy, that condemnation drove the faithful underground. The Jansenists had networks of sympathizers everywhere, and they helped their own.

Jansenist networks may well have aided Louis and Louise during their years on the run. When Louise moved to Auxerre, she chose one of the rare French cities whose church was governed by a bishop faithful to Jansenist principles, Bishop Charles de Caylus. In addition, she joined the congregation not of Auxerre's most prominent church, its cathedral, whose clergy were divided in their loyalty to their controversial bishop, but that of Saint-Eusèbe, whose clergy rallied roundly to Bishop Caylus' cause.

Had Louis shared Louise's beliefs?

His son surely did. Louis' choice of Doublet for his sole witness was an obvious signal of allegiance to this reform movement. And his next choice of mentor made that message loud and clear.

It's not known exactly when the Abbé de L'Épée founded a school in his home on the rue des Moulins, but the establishment was active before the time of Louis' marriage, and prior to his wedding, Louis was already collaborating with L'Épée, "helping the children with their homework and their practice." In the type of education in which L'Épée specialized, practice was key.

In the year or so that followed Louis' marriage, L'Épée made the decision to focus solely on children both deaf and mute. At that moment, he founded two *pensions*, one for girls and one for boys. The Abbé personally trained those whom he put in charge of boarding the children: several "respectable women" in the case of the girls, and in the case of the boys, one man alone: Louis Chevrot. Louis spent at least three decades of his life as the pension master responsible for a boarding school for deaf boys. During all that time, he and Marguerite Toupet housed, fed, and cared for these children. They helped them practice the sign language that L'Épée devised, and taught them according to his methods.

A young man who had known little care from age eight on thus devoted his life to creating an environment in which boys roughly as old as he had been at the time of his mother's death could thrive. Louis and Marguerite had no children of their own, but they had instead surrogate children by the dozen.

L'Épée was not the first educator to work with deaf children, but he is credited with two enormous firsts. To begin with, he was determined that the education he provided would not be reserved for the children of privileged families: his establishment was the first school for the deaf to be completely public and open to all, as well as free of charge for those unable to pay. In addition, L'Épée developed the first method of teaching via signs that influenced systems still in use today.

L'Épée called his methodology *signes méthodiques*, methodical or systematic signs, and he was a brilliant communicator who publicized his "systematic signs" in many ways. The Abbé was the author of six works published between 1772 and 1784 to explain how this "language of signs" functioned. Some recorded the demonstrations of the new language that took place at his school and were open to the public. In those public classes, held from three to five in the afternoon, L'Épée concentrated in particular on demonstrating that sign language was a language like any other, no more difficult to learn, and that all languages were alike for these children who had never heard any of them spoken. During those sessions, students signed their answers to questions posed in French and also to questions formulated in English, Spanish, Italian, German, and even Latin.

The Abbé admitted foreign pupils; he trained teachers, including foreign instructors, who later returned to their home countries and spread his method far and wide. Among those who received an education in the language of systematic signs by L'Épée's successor, Abbé Roch Ambroise Cucurrond Sicard, was Laurent Clerc, who joined with Thomas Gallaudet in 1817 to found in Hartford, Connecticut what is now the oldest existing establishment for the education of the deaf in North America. Clerc and Gallaudet based their instruction on L'Épée's methodical signs; the language used by Louis Chevrot and Marguerite Toupet to communicate with the boys in their care became the foundation of American Sign Language (ASL).

By 1773, Louis and his wife had moved to the rue d'Argenteuil, around the corner from the school: L'Épée had placed twenty-seven boys in their care. Twice a week, on Tuesday and Friday mornings from seven to twelve, the students had formal lessons with the Abbé. There were also the bi-weekly public lessons. Louis accompanied his pupils to and from these various sessions.

The expression "a good man" can seem vague or hackneyed, but in the case of Louis Chevrot, it feels truly justified. He devoted his life to improving the lot of young children who would otherwise have struggled to find a place in French society.

He also helped individuals for whom he was in no way officially responsible. On several occasions, elderly women who had never married and had no close relatives named him executor of their estates—one of them remarked in the document she had drawn up to formalize their arrangement, "as a proof of the friendship she bore him." These women left precise instructions for their executor: they wanted their money to be distributed in certain ways; sometimes, they did not want their heir apparent to get parts of their estate that they preferred to leave to someone who needed the money more. They realized that from a legal perspective their wishes might prove controversial. They trusted Louis to follow their instructions to the letter, and their confidence was rewarded. Their estates were divided just as they had wished; Louis fought off all attempts to invalidate their wills.

L'Épée named Louis *économe*, or bursar, in charge of his school's finances. Louis managed the budget, kept the account books, paid the bills. He clearly possessed the talent for sound financial management and decision making that might have saved his grandfather, father, or uncle and headed off the Chevrot family's disaster.

Soon, L'Épée rented a second property so that Louis' pupils could spend holidays at a remove from the traffic and pollution in the heart of Paris. The new home proved to everyone's liking: by about 1780, Louis and Marguerite and the boys boarding with them had moved there full time.

The property on the Right Bank in the shadow of the highest peak in Paris, the Butte Montmartre, where he and Marguerite Toupet lived during the last decade of their marriage, seems to have been a magical place, proof that Marie Françoise Boulanger's grandson had inherited her talent for designing spaces with children in mind.

When the couple moved to the rue des Martyrs, Montmartre was an independent territory not yet part of Paris. Its first mayor, Félix Desportes, was elected only in 1788; in the aftermath of the Revolution, in 1790, the territory became one of a number of small towns immediately surrounding the capital to be jointly administered. During this chaotic period and in this spot well removed from any of the homes the Chevrots had inhabited during the two centuries of the family's Parisian existence, Louis forged the kind of life no previous Chevrot could have imagined.

The home on the rue des Martyrs was a spacious affair: its private door gave access to a large garden; there was also an inner courtyard, and the living

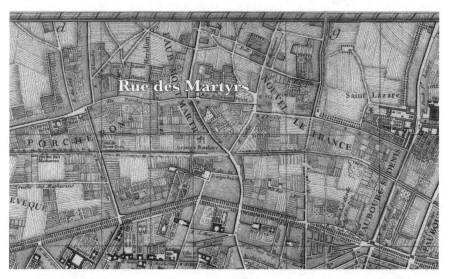

*The neighborhood where Louis II Chevrot's home for deaf boys was located.*

room's French doors opened onto it. Louis and Marguerite made these green spaces come alive with bright hues, offering their charges constant visual stimulation. Everywhere there were orange trees planted in large pots; colorful birds lived in ornamental cages: parrots and even a toucan. The house was well-stocked with toys, as well as barometers and telescopes and thermometers, tools to make science part of the boys' daily lives.

The boarders lived four by four in bedrooms that overlooked the garden. Each boy had a private space marked off with a partition. The house was equipped with dishes, cutlery, bowls, and glasses by the dozens, but the atmosphere was hardly institutional: the home was beautifully furnished and decorated. There were numerous large mirrors on the walls, fine furniture such as marble-topped chests of drawers, as well as a fancy chiming clock by François Gallois: Louis' home had that one thing in common with his grandfather's. The library was extensive—250 volumes—by far the largest of any Chevrot household. The couple slept in a bed with a graceful decorative canopy known as a *lit à la polonaise*, or Polish-style bed, a model then particularly fashionable; the canopy was crafted from cotton with a design depicting bouquets of red flowers against a blue background.

Both Louis and Marguerite dressed well. He owned two of everything: suits, shoes, hats. All her clothes were in fashionable painted cotton in bright colors and floral prints. Their life, while not luxurious, seems deeply inviting and comfortable, and by comparison with those of Louis' father, mother, uncle, and grandfather, their home was positively palatial. Louis' salary was modest, more than the 350 livres a year that tutors at the school were paid but not a fortune. He had no money for investments, in annuities or anything else, but unlike all Chevrots for two generations, he and his wife wanted for nothing, and they never had to fend off creditors.

The cost of a spot in L'Épée's school and Louis' home combined was not extravagant, 350 livres a year, and even that amount was paid only by families with sufficient means. The sum covered everything but wine, fruit, and dessert. If wealthier parents wanted "these additional little niceties" for their children, this added an extra 500 per year to their bill. All pupils had to supply two pairs of sheets, six towels, and a small trunk; each family had to furnish bedding or pay 50 livres to have it purchased. Poor families were responsible only for bedding, not a penny more. In exchange, their child received six years of free education and a well-rounded one at that: languages, mathematics, history, philosophy, religion.

The independent territory of Montmartre would have been a quiet place to sit out the events of the summer of 1789: its eleven hundred inhabitants probably hardly felt the turmoil of the Revolution's early months. But then on December 23, 1789, the Abbé de L'Épée died. Louis' snug little world was in for a revolution of its own.

L'Épée became a national hero, honored with the equivalent of a state funeral: political dignitaries and the regiment of municipal horse guards accompanied his remains to Saint-Roch's cemetery. In 1791, L'Épée was named "a benefactor of humanity." But officials wasted no time naming a successor: already on April 6, 1790, Abbé Sicard was appointed to be the new director of L'Épée's school. Louis continued in his functions under the new regime.

L'Épée's school was soon nationalized: it became the Institut National des Jeunes Sourds, the National Institute for Deaf Children, the first state-sponsored institution dedicated to the education of deaf children, an establishment that still exists in Paris. The modern era for the education of the deaf had begun, and Louis Chevrot played a key role at the start.

On Monday, August 30, 1790, Marguerite Toupet died. Only six days earlier, the National Assembly had received a delegation of teachers and students from Sicard's school begging for additional funds on the grounds that "they didn't have the means to meet the demand for this education." Soon after, plans were laid for a new building large enough to house "at least a hundred students," as opposed to the sixty-odd accommodated in L'Épée's day. Another institution was established in 1791: the National Institute for Blind Children. There was talk of appointing one person to manage the books of both new institutes.

By the time these plans were realized, in 1796, the Institute for Deaf Children had a new *maître de pension*. When the inventory of the boarding house's contents was drawn up after Marguerite's death, Louis, by then aged sixty-three, spoke of "the state of ill-health in which he found himself." It seems likely that Louis Chevrot did not long survive his wife.

There's no evidence that the paths of Marie Magoulet Beauvillain's son Claude Jacques and Louis Chevrot's heir crossed. But the only Magoulet and the only Chevrot to make the transition from an economy based on royal patronage to one founded on state sponsorship witnessed this transition at the same moment: Sainte-Geneviève became a French national monument in April 1791, while the school for the deaf was nationalized only three months later. In important and similar ways, these descendants of families whose destinies had for generations been shaped—and twisted—by the standards and the way of life that both Magoulets and Chevrots believed to be those of the aristocracy had turned away from those values.

On this score, Louis II Chevrot's trajectory was remarkable. When the first Antoine Chevrot arrived in Paris in 1604, he was already in the employ of the royal financial administration: from then on, every Chevrot male paid for the right to serve the French monarchy in some capacity—every Chevrot male until Louis II. Louis did not purchase any of his titles: instead he was hired to do a job. At no moment did this Louis Chevrot serve the crown.

The Magoulet name died out with the passing of Claude Magoulet. Louis and Marguerite had no children, so Louis was the last of the Chevrot line. And when Louis' wife died, the Chevrot estate was inventoried for the last time, this time, by notaries whose allegiance was to the French state rather than to a monarch.

In the end, not much was left. For the Chevrots, worldly things had indeed proved fleeting. There was one "perpetual annuity," set up in 1721 by Barthélemy Boulanger: in 1790, Boulanger's great-grandson still received 28 livres, 19 sous, and 3 deniers annually from that 1721 investment. There was the farm in Cormeilles, still rented to a vintner who every year paid 20 livres—and "a basket of grapes at harvest time."

And there was the jewel in the Chevrot family crown: the house on the rue du Perche. Number 3 rue du Perche, purchased by Nicolas Bajou in 1612, bequeathed to Antoine Chevrot in 1665, was in 1790 still the property of Antoine Chevrot's great-grandson. During all of Louis' life, the 400 livres a year in rent it brought in had been essential to his survival.

Geneviève Bajou, the aunt who left her home to her nephew Antoine Chevrot, also left a very detailed will. In it, she stressed repeatedly that if ever one of her Chevrot heirs was to die without heirs of his own, her property was to be given to Paris' Hôpital Général. The General Hospital where Louise Magoulet's dreams were destroyed had not changed appreciably in the decades between Louise's internment and 1790. Just as Paris was about to begin its transformation into the city that became known as "the Capital of the Nineteenth Century," an institution where countless Parisians had suffered as Louise did became the owner of the rue du Perche property. Profits from its sale helped the institution carry on its mission.

Upon his death, the last Chevrot left behind something no one would have wanted: copies of twenty-four documents related to his family's legal history: wills, legal separations, judgments of lawsuits, probate inventories, guardianships. There was also a document the notary described as "a letter from the king": the royal decree issued by Louis XV in December 1723 to declare Louis and Louise's marriage null and void. When the Chevrot dynasty ended, that stash of papers was lost. Many stories were consigned to a trash bin, above all, that of Louis Chevrot's long struggle to be allowed to live openly with Louise

Magoulet as man and wife, and of Antoine Chevrot's unrelenting opposition to their union.

Today an unexceptional house on Paris' rue du Perche is the only tangible reminder of all that generations of Magoulets and Chevrots fought so relentlessly to acquire.

# *A Father's Love*

I DON'T BELIEVE THAT the Magoulets and the Chevrots were typical French families: "Each unhappy family is unhappy in its own way," as Tolstoy so famously remarked.

The Magoulets to begin with were exceptionally mobile: professionally, socially, geographically. Very few Frenchmen of the day changed professions in a radical manner. To switch a mastership as a *gainier* for one as an embroiderer, as Jean I Magoulet did, was virtually unknown. And for someone who began his professional life as a financial administrator to make his name as an embroiderer, as Jean II did, was unheard of.

Some French families did travel widely and on occasion encouraged their children to emigrate to the outer reaches of the French empire. But few had family members crisscrossing the English Channel and various oceans with such regularity for two centuries. If there is a gene that encourages wanderlust, then it became evident in the Magoulet DNA with the generation born in the 1640s.

There are prominent examples of contemporary French families whose trajectories were marked by impressive social mobility, notably high-profile cases in which an individual parlayed his financial acumen into a noble title that was then passed on to future generations. But few families saw their fortunes rise and fall and rise again, in a sort of socioeconomic roller coaster.

In these areas and many more, their sheer unpredictability sets the Magoulets apart.

Above all, I in no way believe that the two Jean Magoulets and Antoine Chevrot were typical French fathers. Most of what we know about the behavior of actual eighteenth-century French fathers is information available only because of archival records such as those I studied. Those documents concern what was in all likelihood a small minority, fathers whose conduct provoked complaints that resulted in police investigations. The lives of good fathers, like those of happy families, went largely unrecorded.

Prior to the late seventeenth century, the subjects of fatherhood and parenting were only rarely invoked. Fathers seldom indicated their affection for their offspring, for example, by making a bequest in a will to a "beloved child." It was only in 1691, at the moment when the Queen's Embroiderer indentured his eldest son, that a French dictionary finally expanded the meaning of the word "love" to identify a kind of love never previously included: "paternal love." The lexicographer, Antoine Furetière, even described a father's love as "the most powerful kind of love."

From then on, French dictionaries mentioned paternal love as a matter of course. By the mid-eighteenth century, it was increasingly taken for granted that fathers were instinctively programmed to love and care for their children. In 1751, the greatest French dictionary ever, Diderot's *Encyclopedia*, decreed that "a father who has no love for his children is a monster."

Such evidence indicates that times had changed and along with them the expectations of how a father should behave. While I don't believe that either Jean Magoulet might have acted differently a few decades later, I do hope that at a later moment familial *omertà* might no longer have successfully dictated that those aware of their actions remain silent; more family members might have been willing to follow Noel Poisson's lead and oppose them. Louise Magoulet would not have been condemned as a prostitute and condemned to give birth in the Salpêtrière. Baby Jean Louis might have survived—and nothing else would have been the same.

Today, paternal love is taken for granted. And yet even as I was researching the lives of the Magoulets and the Chevrots, a state-sponsored French television station was running a public service announcement: "Help a child in danger. We all share this responsibility." New times have not altered the fact that fathers are still capable of horrendous violence against their children, nor the fact that many who learn of that violence choose to remain silently complicit with its perpetrators.

I thus felt that it was legitimate to describe as child abuse actions committed centuries before such terminology began to be used. These three fathers, both Queen's Embroiderers and Antoine Chevrot, were certainly not typical fathers in their day, but they did follow patterns typical of abusive fathers of any day.

As I was retelling their story, perhaps what troubled me most was the fact that the story of Jean and his daughter Louise seemed so current.

# *The Bourbons*

IN NOVEMBER 1700, the last Habsburg to rule over the Spanish empire, Carlo II, died childless. He willed his crown to Philippe de France, Duc d'Anjou, the second grandson of Louis XIV and Queen Marie-Thérèse. In February 1701, the seventeen-year-old duke reached Madrid and began his new life as Felipe V. He was destined to reign until 1746 and to become Spain's longest-ruling monarch. The current Spanish king, Felipe VI, is his direct heir.

Later in 1701, a Europe-wide coalition formed to prevent the possibility that the French and the Spanish thrones might be unified. The resulting War of the Spanish Succession (1701–1714) bankrupted France, paved the way for John Law's economic manipulations and the passion for quick riches that followed in their wake—and created thereby the climate in which Jean Magoulet was able to have his daughter Louise declared "fit for the islands."

Felipe V inherited his grandfather's and his father's instincts: he amassed fabulous paintings and beautiful objects of all kinds. The Spanish royal collections, the basis of Madrid's Prado museum, were much enriched by his acquisitions. From his grandmother, Queen Marie-Thérèse, he also inherited an appreciation for the work of master craftsmen. Among the masterpieces still part of the collection of the Spanish Royal Palace in Madrid are embroidered panels from 1733 in which the royal embroiderer Antonio Gómez de los Ríos depicted the life of Don Quixote. One panel is the earliest tour de force of embroidery done for a Bourbon monarch to have been signed.

After the death of Felipe V's father in 1711, Louis XIV sent to Madrid a large portion of his son's collection of precious objects, from crystal vases to Chinese

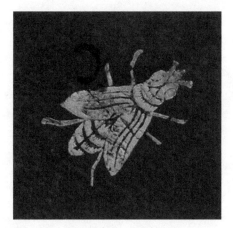

*Hubert Magoulet's mark: a golden bee.*

porcelain. Each object traveled in its specially designed and crafted leather case, each case a showpiece of the art of seventeenth-century French royal *gainiers*. Both the objects and their cases have survived intact: today they form what is known as the Dauphin's Treasure, housed in the Prado.

A number of those cases stand out because of the quality of their workmanship, noticeably finer than the rest.

Each such exceptional case features on the bottom the same mark: a golden bee. The identical bee also appears on several other leather containers that are part of the Prado's collections: these belonged to Queen Marie-Thérèse. All the cases "signed" with the golden bee were thus surely crafted in the workshop on the Quai de l'Horloge at the sign of the Golden Apple run by the queen's official casemaker, Hubert Magoulet.

In Madrid, the Bourbon legacy, the legacy of Versailles, and the Magoulet legacy all live on today.

ACKNOWLEDGMENTS

To begin at the beginning: it very quickly became apparent that the embroiderer on whom I was doing research was raising tricky questions. As soon as I saw huge problems looming, I contacted Daniel Roche. He questioned me for two hours, at the end of which he assured me that he could believe the story as I was reconstructing it. All along the way, Daniel Roche talked things through with the scholarly generosity and insightfulness that come naturally to him.

I would never have found my way through the archival maze created by the Magoulets and the Chevrots without the help of Robert Descimon, Philippe Florentin, and Jeffrey Merrick. Robert helped decipher particularly tricky documents; he ran down references in his personal databases; he was always willing to help interpret complex issues. Philippe gave me valuable tips about offbeat collections in the Archives Nationales and always cheered me up when things seemed hopelessly complicated. And he was there to give a second opinion when even I couldn't believe the latest scandal. Jeff generously discussed the interpretation of tough cases in areas ranging from spousal abuse to suicide; he was the perfect e-mail interlocutor all through the project.

Christian Baulez, another regular in the CARAN, provided key information on artists and artisans and the workings of their world. Alexandre Cojonnot had essential documents scanned in a flash. Robert Timon and his fellow genealogists in Auxerre and Vermenton went far, far beyond the call of duty to track down documents and even reconstruct a family tree. Aimery Caron shared his research on the French presence on Sainte Croix with enormous generosity. Lydia Mérigot found information on the rue du Perche in her files. Archivists at the Huguenot Society of London—Lucy Gwynn and Rachel

Stone in particular—were speedy, informative, and imaginative. Valérie Guitienne-Murger at the Bibliothèque de Port-Royal searched for possible Jansenist connections. Mathieu Da Vinha of the Centre de Recherche du Château de Versailles helped verify court functions.

Several scholars helped me understand the economic puzzles created by individuals key to this story. Daniel Dessert answered questions on all matters financial on numerous occasions, always with great patience and courtesy. Larry Neal, Chris Kobrak, and Joel Felix responded to inquiries about the workings of early modern finance, Michael Kwass to questions about the tax system. François Velde answered questions about John Law. Thierry Claeys kindly looked over transactions I found particularly opaque. Kate Desbarats discussed mint bills and card money and shared her discoveries.

Embroidery and textile experts were enormously generous with their time. Danièle Véron-Denise unhesitatingly shared her research on numerous Parisian embroiderers. Clare Brown discussed Jean I Magoulet's peculiarities. Linda Eaton gave a spirited introduction to Winterthur's collections and taught me a great deal about how embroiderers did business. Pilar Benito, Ana Cabrera, and Amalia Descalzo discussed Spanish embroidery. No one could have provided a more informed hands-on introduction to seventeenth-century Spanish embroidery than Maria Dolores Vila; I am very grateful to her and to colleagues from Madrid's Museum of Decorative Arts, especially Sofia Rodriguez, for their generosity during my visit. Lesley Miller discussed embroidery techniques and put me in touch with numerous Victoria and Albert colleagues, who never failed to share information promptly and carefully. Susan North gave me an unforgettable day in the V and A reserves: I'm grateful for her fine pedagogical skills and her patience in helping me understand difficult techniques.

Nick Humphrey discussed leather goods artisans and gave useful tips on their trade. Félix de la Fuente Andrés was a gold mine of information on the seventeenth-century French leather cases in the collections of the Museum of Decorative Arts and the Prado. I am especially grateful to Leticia Azcue Brea and colleagues from the Prado and the Museum of Decorative Arts, particularly Félix de la Fuente, for a magical morning in the Prado's reserves. That visit taught me to appreciate the *gainier*'s art.

Natalie Davis answered questions and put me in touch with scholars who offered their perspectives on problems of French marriage law. Sylvie Perrier helped me evaluate the specificity of guardianship documents. Philip Joseph Benedict, David Garrioch, and Keith Luria discussed cross-confessional godparenting. Alan Kors debated issues with me and uncovered documents on Jacques and Nicolas Magoulet. Jean-Marc Chatelain helped locate obscure factums on Jacques Magoulet and even did double duty as a photographer. Alexis Karakostas shared information on the Abbé de L'Épée. Drew Starling photographed a key signature and saved me a trip to still another archive.

Elsa Marguin of the Archives Nationales discussed the importance of signatures. Marc Smith looked at numerous photographs of signatures and offered expert advice, but he should not be blamed for my interpretations. Claire Lesage of the Bibliothèque de l'Arsenal greatly facilitated my work with the Archives de la Bastille. Phillippa Plock of Waddesdon Manor has discussed with me for many years now the image of Magoulet's shop held in its collections. I thank her for her always prompt responses, important information, and numerous insightful comments.

Myra Jehlen read and commented on early drafts at a time when I badly needed encouragement. Jerry Singerman patiently talked me through a rewrite of the first chapters. Robert Descimon generously reviewed several chapters and pointed me to new readings. Caroline Grubbs was a superb research assistant: thorough, imaginative, and consistently enthusiastic. She used online resources to track the Magoulets in ways that wouldn't have been possible a decade ago. Andrea Gottschalk provided creative designs for family trees.

Alice Martell was an encouraging first reader. And, last but certainly not least, my editor, Nancy Miller, was an exceptionally careful reader and talked me through major revisions.

I often quote precise sums: this is the only way to suggest the economic stakes of any business proposition. The following is an attempt to give a sense of price fluctuations in the Parisian marketplace, both low end and high.

## Food
1619: 1 livre bought two pounds of butter. This was the daily wage of a mason for a twelve-hour day in winter, fourteen in summer.

1690: 1 livre bought ten pounds of good bread.

July 1691: a *setier* (12 bushels) of wheat at Les Halles cost 10 livres.

September 1693: a *setier* of wheat cost 42 livres.

January 1708: a *setier* of wheat cost 10 livres.

May 1709: a *setier* of wheat cost 55 livres.

## Rent
Rents rose steadily during the first half of the seventeenth century. The same house in the Faubourg Saint-Honoré rented for 300 livres a year in 1608, for 410 in 1620, for 500 in 1632, and for 1,000 in 1659.

During the period from 1690 to 1725, 50 percent of the apartments in Paris rented for between 100 and 500 livres, while only 2 percent rented for more than 1,000.

## Clothing
1690: a duchess paid her shoemaker 22 livres for 4 pairs of shoes, her dressmaker 47 livres for several skirts.

1690: for an outfit embroidered in gold, a marquis paid his tailor 20 livres, and his embroiderer 580 livres.

1707: a master craftsman's entire wardrobe was worth 130 livres.

1720: a noble newly rich from financial speculation paid 900 livres for the embroidery in silver on a suit of clothes.

1721: another such noble paid 1,390 livres for the embroidery in gold on a single outfit.

1725: a noblewoman paid 1,725 for the embroidery in gold on a single outfit.

## Fine Art and Luxury Goods
1666: a painting by the contemporary French artist Jacques Stella was appraised at 60 livres, a small leather-covered coffer decorated with silver at 50 livres, a Turkish carpet at 15 livres, and a carpet embroidered in gold at 200 livres.

## Total Assets
During the period from 1600 to 1725, highly successful merchants and master craftsmen left estates worth between 3,000 and 10,000 livres.

From 1725 to 1789, the number who accumulated total assets worth over 10,000 livres more than quintupled.

NOTES

The following list of citations from works essential to my interpretation of the world of the Magoulets and the Chevrots includes references in the order in which they figure in each chapter.

## Chapter One: The Queen's Embroiderers
1. Decoration of Versailles' Grand Gallery: Havard, "broderie."
2. Embroiderers' presentation designs: Thunder (16–19, 26).

## Chapter Two: Star-Crossed
1. Royal decrees: 8 January 1719, 12 March 1719. Paris: Imprimerie Royale, 1719.
2. Louisiana in the late seventeenth century: White (chapter 1).
3. François Velde graciously converted Dangeau's stock quotes into the system used by most commentators.
4. Other prisoners, male and female, sent to Louisiana in 1719–1720: Giraud (3:216–264).

## Chapter Three: Upward Mobility 1: Salt and Taxes
1. The epithet "noble homme": Descimon (85).
2. Building boom in Paris: *Mercure françois* 1612 (475–476).
3. I am grateful to Robert Descimon for information on the Gillot family.
4. Female literacy in France: Dulong (405).
5. Child mortality: Lachiver (102).
6. "The fun part of town": Louis Liger (65).
7. For information on the rue du Perche in the early seventeenth century, I am grateful to Lydia Mérigot; see also her 1966 dissertation.
8. The cost of salt in 1680: Lachiver (91).
9. Antoine Chevot IV's position in the court of the Duchesse de Bourgogne: *État de la France*, 1702 edition (2:54–55).
10. Sale of offices: Doyle (chapter 2). *Conseiller du roi*: Doyle (45–46), *Encyclopédie* ("Conseiller du roi," 4:30–31).

## Chapter Four: Upward Mobility 2: Purveyor to the Crown

1. The number of master *gainiers*, embroiderers, and hatmakers in seventeenth-century Paris: AN Y9318. For the eighteenth century: Coquery (340).
2. "Prix du marc d'argent," Archives du CAEF, ms. 8 and ms. A-1.
3. Average cost of funerals: Croq 2012.
4. Number of merchants and artisans "suivant la cour": Delpeuch (53, 208); Thillay (394–396). Their privileges: Delpeuch (380, 409); Mousnier (2:119); Saint-Aubin (4–5).
5. Freedom enjoyed by artisans in privileged enclaves: Kaplan 1988.
6. Privileges enjoyed by artisans "suivant la cour": Saint-Aubin (4–5).
7. Importance of draftsmanship for embroiderers: Saint-Aubin (4).
8. Changing meaning of *bourgeois de Paris*: Croq (1997). Used to replace *marchand*: Bennini (334–335).

## Chapter Five: Salad Days

1. The most impressive dossier of complaints against Jacques Magoulet's administration is from Languedoc: AN H/748/214. Factums from other provinces are in the collections of the BNF.
2. Colbert's exchange with Foucault: Foucault (1:480).
3. Arrêts du Conseil d'État: Carondas Le Caron (2: 600–602; 924–931); Boutaric (346–367).
4. The 27 November 1683 decree of the Conseil d'État appeared in print, published by Sébastien Cramoisy.
5. Jacques' disgrace: Smedley-Weill (209–211).
6. Marie Freslin's guardian, Charles Olivier, served as *portier* in Queen Marie-Thérèse's household. *État de la France* 1683 edition (1:249).
7. Secrétaires du Roi: Marion.
8. Financiers' marriage contracts: Dessert (120–134).
8. When Jacques served as godfather to Jean's son François in November 1685, he identified himself as *premier commis de M. Legendre*; Legendre was described as *chef du domaine du roi* (Fichier Laborde: Magoulet).

## Chapter Six: Annual Income, Annual Expenditure

1. Evolution of the Maison du Roi: Boucher (368).
2. Evolution of financiers' investment preferences: Dessert (125–126, 146). After 1650–1670, many owned no real estate at all; they invested in only the most expensive *charges*.
3. The Lescots with whom Jean Magoulet had extensive financial dealings were not part of the family of celebrated Parisian *orfèvres*. I thank Michèle Bimbenet-Privat for confirming this. Debt collection proceedings against the Lescots: Jamet de La Guessière (3:719–740).
4. Sizes and prices of panes of glass for windows: DeJean 2009 (155–156). The panes of glass in the Galerie des Glaces: DeJean 2005 (chapter 9).
5. Stockpiling grain to create shortages: Calmette (40–41). Grain prices in the 1680s: Lachiver (128).
6. *Forbi v. Briet*: D'Auguesseau (3: 77–120); Jean Magoulet (98).

7. Infant and child mortality: Lachiver (195).

8. *Mercure historique et politique*, March 1687 (2:440–441, 477, 497). Advance war plans, details of operations, casualties (Quincy 2: 137–138). Size of Louis XIV's army: Lynn (53–54). Louis XIV's revenues: Dessert (155). Short-term loans: Dent (56).

9. The profession Dupré declared, *marchand grossier joaillier*, seems otherwise unknown.

10. For information on Sainte Croix under French rule, I am deeply indebted to Aimery Caron, both for his published work and for his unpublished research, which he graciously shared with me. A detailed census was regularly taken on Sainte Croix, but there is a break in the records during the War of the Grand Alliance (1688–1695), so Jean II's presence on the island cannot be accurately tracked. The notarial records for Dieppe stop in 1680, so no information on his exact departure date has survived.

## Chapter Seven: Secrets and Lies

1. Vauban's victories in Flanders: Cornette 1993 (chapters 1 and 6); Cornette 1997 (291ff.)

2. The climate, grain harvests, grain prices in the 1680s and 1690s: Lachiver (17–213).

3. Louis XIV's sudden departure from the battle front in 1693: Saint-Simon (1:235).

4. "Prix du marc d'argent," Archives du CAEF, ms. 8 and ms. A-1.

5. Casualties of the Nine Years' War: Lynn (250–253).

6. Death toll from famine in the 1690s: Lachiver (157–163). On 1693–1694: Lachiver (203–205).

7. Growth of war bureaucracy in the 1690s: Lynn (53–54). The role of a *commis*: Rowlands (138).

8. Standard procedure in naming guardians: Perrier (32–33).

9. The *garde du roi*: Mansel (13); Marion (352–353); Quincy (1: 377–378). Lists of the nobles serving were published every one to two years; I checked every list between 1686 and 1700: Magoulet never appears. Jean is listed in the 1687 *État de la France* as a *garçon de chambre du roi*; there is no mention of either Magoulet or Toulongeon in subsequent editions. The château and estate of Toulongeon belonged to an old noble family of noted military men from Burgundy. In the 1690s, Théodore Chevignard was Comte de Toulongeon.

10. François Gallois' participation in the Nine Years' War: Dessert (54, 588). The taxes owed by "femme Nicolas Magoulet": Buvat (1:206); Mouffle d'Angerville (181).

11. Marriage in France in the early 1700s: Lachiver (266).

12. Master craftsmen passed on or loaned out their names: Kaplan 2001 (335). Jean II was never listed in the *État de la France* in any capacity.

13. Rents of Parisian apartments between 1680 and 1726: Pardailhé-Galabrun (465).

## Chapter Eight: A Person of Consequence

1. The Du Lude marriage: Dessert (36).

2. The *Nouveau secrétaire de la cour* discusses ways of determining precise social rank and stresses that "those who do occupy such *charges* must never forget that they can never make them superior to those of higher birth" (429).

3. The financial administration of Paris' Hôtel de Ville: Marion (*contrôle, contrôleur, payeur, rentes*).

4. Clientele and market for *rentes* on the Hôtel de Ville: Béguin, Moulin.

5. Early eighteenth-century baby boom: Lachiver (266).

## Chapter Nine: The Great Winter

1. Climate and famine during the War of the Spanish Succession: Lachiver (264–383).

2. Princesse Palatine (2:12).

3. Death toll from the Great Winter: Lachiver (377–381).

4. The first children's rooms: DeJean 2009 (58–59, 174, 246).

5. Parenting and family life in the eighteenth century: Ariès (introduction).

6. Arrival of Peruvian silver in 1708: Cornette 1997 (493, 502).

7. Transport of children to the country: Delasselle (193–194).

8. The *dixième*: Cornette 1997 (515–516).

9. *Noblesse d'épée* hostile to new nobility: Cornette 1997 (521).

## Chapter Ten: The Deadly Years

1. *Billets de monnaie* in the early eighteenth century: Rowlands (108–111), Cornette 1997 (452–453, 479, 493, 508–509, 513). Law's 1707 treatise: Law, *Oeuvres complètes*, 1:198–207.

2. The climate and harvests from 1710 to 1714: Lachiver (390).

3. "The deadly years": Saint-Simon 1967 (46).

4. Paris opera ball: Legrave (501–506), Marais (1:274).

5. Separation of property, separation of body and domicile: Merrick 2011 (208–209).

6. The records for the Hôpital Général have not survived for these years, so it's impossible to verify the dates when the Magoulet girls were placed there. Information on the institution: Boucher, Carrez, Desgranges, El Ghoul, Williams 1979.

7. "Mint bills" and the French economy in 1716–1717: Faure (150–152, 645), Giraud (3:21–26), Law (3:323), Marais (1:88–90). A case when stolen bills from 1716 were replaced: AN Y 14930B, 29 March 1718.

8. The regent's letter from October 1716: White (24).

9. The distinction between the two types of prostitution: Benabou (24), Parent-Duchâtelet (2:288–292).

10. Family members who asked the state for help: Williams 1993 (47).

11. Climate and the death toll in 1718: Lachiver (410).

## Chapter Eleven: The Gold Rush

1. Death toll in 1718: 700,00; in 1715–1717: c. 600,000 a year (Lachiver 410).

2. Normally, seven to eight relatives were assembled (Perrier 32); Jean convoked only five "friends."

3. Early eighteenth-century opinions on annuities: Rowlands (73–75).

## Chapter Twelve: The Invention of Money

1. "Fièvre chaude": Balleroy (2:79); "people of our sort" (2:89). Saint-Simon (36:202).

2. "Suppression" of financial administrators in 1719: the *Nouveau Mercure galant*, September 1719 (121). The periodical also recorded the reorganization of the Tallow Farm (130–133).

3. Perspectives on John Law's project and its consequences for the French economy: see Faure; Garber (chapters 14–15); Harsin (in his edition of Law's *Oeuvres complètes*); Neal 1990 and 2002; Rowlands (chapter 6); and Velde.

4. "François Duval": *Nouveau Mercure galant*, March 1719 (184–188). On Duval: Giraud (3:140). Similar coverage of Louisiana is found in the September 1718 issue. On the *Mercure*'s coverage: Giraud (3:139).

5. Silver mines in Louisiana: *Nouveau Mercure galant*, April 1720 (96, 179). Contemporary travel accounts, such as Vallette de Laudun, encouraged this belief.

6. The Royal Bank in the contemporary press: *Nouveau Mercure galant*, January 1719 (157); *Gazette d'Amsterdam*, 15 December 1719. Law's million-livre purchase: Dangeau (18:163); Balleroy, 2:35. The ceiling Law commissioned for the Bank: Garas and Knox (150–156). The balustrade from the grand staircase that Law had installed was removed from its original location and moved to London in the 1870s. It is now part of the Wallace Collection. The bank's ceiling was destroyed in 1722.

7. Edict of April 22, 1719: *Nouveau Mercure galant*, May 1719 (68); gold's devaluation (73). The Balleroy correspondence repeats Law's reasoning on the superiority of paper money (2:129–130). Mob scene in the Royal Bank: *Gazette d'Amsterdam*, May 19 and May 23.

8. *Nouveau Mercure galant*, September 1718 (214); February 1719 (140). A handful of women arrived in New Orleans in June 1719 by mistake when their ship, bound for Martinique, was inexplicably rerouted.

9. First requests to send daughters to Louisiana: Giraud (3:216–264).

10. Law-Pancatalin interactions: Buvat (1:386–387). On Pancatalin: Desgranges (30–31, 37, 44–46). The "rebellion" on January 3, 1719: ms. 10,659 in the Arsenal Library; Giraud (3:261).

11. Bourlon was imprisoned in 1722 when many of those he had arrested denounced his corruption. Bibliothèque de l'Arsenal ms. 7557, fol. 101R. Thefts of banknotes in the bank building: ms. 10,700, fol. 37. Bourlon's cut: ms. 7557, fol. 35V, 45V, 48V.

12. Pollnitz (5:206).

13. Law in the *Gazette d'Amsterdam* (see issues from 14 February 1719, 30 December 1719, and 1 September 1719).

14. The Balleroy correspondence includes the greatest number of anecdotes about the newly wealthy (2:72, 84, 85, 113). The October issue of the *Nouveau Mercure galant* devotes a section to such tales.

15. "Millionaire": *Nouveau Mercure galant*, October 1719 (201).

16. "Seigneurs de la rue Quincampoix" and "dames du Mississippi": Balleroy (2:84, 113). Individuals "liés par l'agiotage": Balleroy (2:127).

17. Fate of babies born in the Salpêtrière: Delaselle (188, 195).

18. Heat wave and death toll in 1719: Lachiver (410–417).

19. Date of the prisoners' departure from Paris: ms. 10,632 (fol. 132V), Arsenal Library.

20. Saint-Simon (6:570). The *esclaves de la Louisiane*: (Giraud 3:270).

21. Influx of capital in September 1719: Faure (239–240). Stock fluctuations that fall: Velde (111). Law's manipulations of the stock market: Velde (106), Neal 1990 (74–75). Nobles used their cash to buy property: Balleroy, 2:107.

22. Law's visit to the rue Quincampoix: Buvat (1:409).

23. "Dividend" in French: *Nouveau Mercure galant*, December 1719 (216); Balleroy (2:87).
24. The king in *un habit chamarré de billets de banque*: (Buvat, 2:12–13).

## Chapter Thirteen: Personation: Clément Magoullet

1. Death Master File: *60 Minutes* (February 28, 2016); Saint-Simon (14:176–179, 233–239, 241–245). Importance of the turn of the eighteenth century in the history of identity: Denis (9–10), Hildesheimer (155–160), Ravel (165–168). Passports and identity papers: Denis (22), Durand.
2. The signature as the ultimate proof of a legal document's authenticity: Skupien (171–174).
3. Forgery convictions: Abad (171–172), Hildesheimer.
4. Reasons why individuals committed identity theft: Fontaine (116–120); Ravel.
5. *Billets de monnaie* in France in 1707: Isambert (20:519–521); Rowlands (30).
6. Guardians and the "emancipation" of children: Perrier (211).
7. How bigamy was punished and why often not prosecuted: Ravel (82–83).
8. *Supposition de personne*: Abad (171).

## Chapter Fourteen: "The Incredible Madness of the 20th Year of the Eighteenth Century"

1. Caumartin de Boissy: Balleroy (2:97).
2. Stair: Faure (348). Inflation in January 1720; Balleroy (2:121). Workers' wages: Barbier, 1:42.
3. *Le printemps écarlate*: Faure (387). Theft more frequent: Dangeau (18:267). Violence in the rue Quincampoix: Barbier (1:23–24); Balleroy (2:142, 151); Buvat (2:59–75).
4. The *bandouliers*: Buvat (2:77–78, 87); Balleroy (2:159–160). Revolts in Paris: Balleroy (2:159–160); Giraud (3:269–270). The decree ending deportation: AN/AD/259. The last chain gang: Arsenal ms. 12,708. The increase in slaves from Africa and the lingering fear of deportation: Giraud (3:270, 273–276).
5. Economic situation in the spring of 1720: Neal 1990 (71); Giraud (3:126); Levasseur (chapter 10). Fishmonger in Les Halles: Buvat (2:49). Rumors flying: Dangeau (18:290–291). Insider sales: Barbier (1:27). Ambassador Stair: Faure (465). The bank on May 22 and 25: Buvat (2:93).
6. Marais' diary (1:111–126, 1:253–255ff.). Barbier and Buvat confirm Marais' description.
7. De Mesmes and insider information: Dangeau (18:290).
8. Royal Bank in June: Barbier (1:27); Balleroy (2:173). June 11 decree: Marais (1:125). July 17 decree: *Nouveau Mercure galant*, August (106–107). Royal Bank's bankruptcy: Neal 1990 (71ff.). Louis XV refuses banknotes: Balleroy (2:181). Law and the end of his system: Law (3:230).
9. Paris in July and August: Balleroy (2:181–194); Faure (657–659); Levasseur (chapter 10); Marais (1:111–112).
10. The South Sea Bubble: Garber (109–121). The situation in London: *Amsterdam Gazette*, 10 and 13 September, 7 October 1720. Crisis in the English economy: Neal 1990 (72). Prices in London in September 1720: Balleroy (2:206–207).
11. The Sardinian Chapel: Evans (85–88); Harding (v, 13–18).
12. Moyses/Whitaker/Frankland/Franklin: Croft (198–199); Kelly (207); Sharratt (215).

No trace remains of the manuscript all of them cite, Moyses' "An Account of a Clerical and Missionary Life."

13. Prices of commodities fall in 1720: Barbier (1:139). Consequences of Law's system: Marais (1:131). Fall 1720 in London and Paris: *Gazette d'Amsterdam*, 20 September; Marais (1:240–241, 266). Caumartin de Boissy: Balleroy (2:206–207). Law's carriage stoned: Balleroy (2:195).

14. The aftermath of Law's system: Barbier (1:69); Marais (1:265, 269). Turning in shares: Marais (1:269); Barbier (1:58).

15. In late December 1720, notaries were drawing up huge annuities contracts: see, for example, MC ET CXIII 292. The Princesse de Conti put 48,000 livres into annuities; the Duchesse Du Lude 50,000; Antoine Crozat 200,000.

16. Colonists in New Orleans massacred: Buvat (2:29).

17. Voltaire (9–10). Law's modern defenders: Faure (466); Neal 1990 (chapter 4); Velde.

18. Louis XIV's war debt: *Nouveau Mercure galant*, September 1720 (139–148).

19. Circulation of Picart's print in Paris: Balleroy (2:256).

## Chapter Fifteen: Aftershocks

1. Paris in 1721: Marais (1:331–338, 391); *Lettres historiques* (May 1721, 554–555); Balleroy (2:297, 359).

2. Cartouche: Peveri 2010 (273, 278); Balleroy (2:336, 383–384). Judgment against Cartouche: AN X2/B946.

3. Requests to have daughters released from the Salpêtrière in 1719: AN O/1/368. Clément's letter is not part of this dossier, an indication that, if it was indeed sent, it never reached the proper authorities.

4. *Louis d'or de Noailles*: Faure (109).

5. *Rapt* and *rapt de séduction*: Cummings, Duguit, Fournel, Pacilly, Vautroys, as well as cases published in Chemin, ed., *Journal des principales audiences du Parlement* (5 May 1710, 27 June 1713). Louis XV's declaration: Sallé (583–592). Church retained authority over clandestine marriages: Hersent, *Optatus Gallus* (1640). Paternalistic bias in Parlement's rulings: Cummings (121, 125). Le Semelier/Noailles (371, 375).

6. Banknotes burned: Faure (605). The Bibliothèque du Roi: Balleroy (2:499). Néron's execution: Barbier (1:149). Paris as *coupe-gorge*: Balleroy (2:188). Annuities created: Balleroy (2:572). Louis XV's coronation: Barbier (1:156–157). The Regent diamond: Saint-Simon (31:353–356); Neal 2012 (46–50).

7. Masneuf: Félibien (4:365–366).

## Chapter Sixteen: Total Eclipse

1. "Sack dresses": Marais (1:199).

2. Père Maurice Bailly, la Petite Chapelle: Dangeau (3:202–203); Hébert (146); Maral (158); Saint-Simon, who suggests that Bailly had Jansenist leanings (4:400).

3. De Mesmes: *Mercure de France*, September 1719 (104), February 1720 (122); Saint-Simon (4:887–888, 380–381). His heavy debts: Barbier (1:21). Good wishes to Louis XV: AN O/1/370, fol. 24.

4. Maurepas' quarantine: AN O/1/370, fol. 105.

5. Punishments for *rapt de séduction*: Hanley (56).
6. The regent's death: Balleroy (2:549).
7. Total eclipse: Marais (2:773).
8. Prices of Compagnie des Indes stock in 1724: Balleroy (2:584–587).
9. Conditions in the Salpêtrière: Boucher (45–46); Williams (233). Prison's location: Carrez 2005 (10). Bailly: Desgranges (46–48, 70). A day in the Salpêtrière: *Réglement pour les supérieures* (fols. 54–70). Michel Cotel and his daughter: Bibliothèque de l'Arsenal, ms. 11,742 (fol. 270–286).
10. Requests to send children "to the islands" in 1724: AN O/1/371, fol. 662V and 663R.
11. Price of basic commodities in 1724: Barbier (1:202, 215).

## Chapter Seventeen: "A Diabolical Person"
1. Bread riots and d'Ombreval's resignation: Barbier (1:224); Williams 1979 (287).
2. No system for identifying dead bodies in eighteenth-century Paris: Denis (334).

## Chapter Eighteen: The Remains of the Day
1. Winter of 1728: Barbier (1:286).
2. I'm grateful to Thierry Claeys for calculating Antoine's yearly income from his position.
3. Average cost of funerals in the eighteenth century: Croq 2012 (180).
4. Académie de Saint-Luc: Guiffrey (3, 20, 25, 505).
5. Police investigations of suicide: Merrick 1989 and 2004; Denis (337). See article 12 in Louis XV's *Déclaration du roi concernant la forme de tenir les registres de . . . sépultures*, proclaimed at Versailles on April 9, 1736. I'm grateful to Jeff Merrick for this reference.
6. Cost of *convoi de la charité*: Croq 2012 (179).

## Chapter Nineteen: The Prince's Embroiderer, The Prince's Designer
1. The etching of Magoulet's shop is in the collections of Waddesdon Manor. Its size today is 255 by 214 mm; the print was trimmed from its original size.
2. Condé's investment in Law's stock: Harsin (21).
3. Condé's project at Chantilly: Fraisse/Garnier-Pelle (10–16), Le Duc 1996 (31–32), Miller 2001 (87–88).
4. Silk fabric produced at Chantilly: Petitcol (87, 94). Fraisse's work: Miller 2001.
5. Fraisse's influence on nineteenth-century textiles: Le Duc 1993 (15, 37).
6. Father Billet: Muller (153).
7. *L'Avant-coureur*: 17 July 1761 (472); 18 December 1761 (232). Claude Magoulet: Havard (4:232).

## Chapter Twenty: The King's Prosecutors
1. The La Vigne baptism and the Hervés: *Publications of the Huguenot Society of London* (26:67, 97, 99). French churches in London and the Savoy Church: Smiles (270–273).
2. Previous scholars, notably Benabou and Giraud, have speculated on how Prévost obtained access to information about *La Mutine*'s prisoners and their treatment. Benabou rehearsed the reasons why Prévost's model had to have been one of the women on the

ship's manifest (86–87). They were unable to recognize Louise Magoulet's exceptional status among those on Pancatalin's list because of the false claims made by her father.

3. The Billou/Billout family: Timon (81–84).

## Chapter Twenty-One: To the Islands

1. Sainte-Geneviève's history, Beauvillain's role there: Quatremère de Quincy (4, 9–10).
2. Both Soufflots and their work on Sainte-Geneviève/the Panthéon: Gallet (449–464).
3. Cost of Sainte-Geneviève: Quatremère de Quincy (15).
4. The Beauvillains on Réunion Island: Ricquebourg (105–107).

## Chapter Twenty-Two: A Royal Wedding

1. Making a fortune in Saint-Domingue: Balleroy (2:396).
2. Profits from Saint-Domingue's sugar industry: Blackburn (163), Debien (50), Popkin (221), Tarrade (2:740–753).
3. French navy in the 1780s: Monaque (chapter 6).
4. Slave populations on Saint-Domingue and elsewhere: Blackburn (163), Debien (50), Popkin (221).
5. Massiac and the Club Massiac: Debien (91–92). The club's effectiveness: Blackburn (167–172). The club's end: Debien (378).

## Chapter Twenty-Three: The Noise of Time

1. L'Épée and his method; Louis II's work for him: Berthier; Karakostas (37, 45, 50, 66); L'Épée (21).
2. Cost of boarding with Louis Chevrot: *Prospectus de la pension de l'institution* (1–3).

Unless otherwise specified, all documents are found in either the Archives Nationales or the Arsenal Library.

## *Related to the Magoulets:*

1. Jacques I
   24 October 1638 AN MC ET XVIII 253
   2 September 1659 AN MC ET XXXIV 155
   9 February 1661 AN MC ET XXXIV 159
   16 January 1662 AN MC ET XXXIV 162
   9 December 1663 AN MC ET XXXIV 169
   1 September 1663 AN MC ET XXXIV 172
   1 June 1669 AN MC ET XXXIV 187

2. Hubert
   24 July 1662 AN MC ET XXXIV 164
   23 February 1664 AN MC ET V 3 188
   10 October 1672 AN MC ET XCVII 33
   3 November 1673 AN MC ET XCVII 36, five documents
   27 February 1674 AN MC ET XXXIV 201
   14 January 1676 AN MC ET XCVII 41
   10 October 1676 AN MC ET XXIX 224
   1 October 1678 AN MC ET XXXIV 214
   18 July 1679 AN Y 9320
   15 September 1679 AN MC ET LXXXIV 196
   22 September 1703 AN MC ET LXXVI 128
   7 October 1703 AN MC ET LXVI 306
   16 December 1706 AN Y 10735

4 January 1707 AN MC ET LXVI 315
18 February 1707 AN MC ET LXVI 315
25 May 1707 AN MC ET LXVI 316
5 January 1709 AN MC ET LXVI 322

## 3. Claude I

22 July 1689 AN Y 9322

## 4. Jacques II

17 June 1681 BNF F-23639(5)
June 1681–27 November 1683 AN H 748 214
27 November 1683 BNF F-23639(342)
Late 1683 BNF Recueil Thoisy 147
21 February 1685 AN MC ET LXXIII 529
24 March 1687 Fichier Laborde: Jean Magoulet
29 December 1692 AN MC ET CXVIII 173
5 April 1698 AN Y 8949
13 April 1704 AN MC ET CXVII 194
26 November 1710 AN MC ET LIV 704
5 December 1710 AN Y 13739
15 December 1710 AN MC ET LIV 704
16 December 1710 AN Y 4208
18 December 1710 AN MC ET LIV 704
12 March 1714 AN MC ET LX 201
29 May 1714 AN Y 14049
26 June 1714 AN MC ET LIV 718
July 1716, 21 September 1716 AN MC ET LIV 728

## 5. Jean I

20 January 1667 AN MC ET XXXIV 180
16 April 1674 AN MC ET XXXIV 202
3 December 1675 AN MC ET LXXVII 338
1 August 1676 AN MC ET XXXIV 210
24 December 1677 AN O 1 3713 fol. 21V, 22R
21 December 1678 AN O 1 22 fol. 2
2 July 1679 AN MC ET XXXIV 217
3 August 1679 AN MC ET LXXVIII 357
13 August 1679 AN MC ET LXXVIII 357
23 September 1680 AN MC ET LXXVIII 364
28 March 1681 AN MC ET LXXVIII 367
22 May 1681 AN MC ET LXXVIII 368
11 August 1681 AN MC ET LXXVIII 369
4 October 1681 AN MC ET LXXVIII 370
20 November 1681 AN MC ET XXIV 482

28 December 1681 AN MC ET XXIV 482
18 February 1682 AN MC ET XXIV 483
16 March 1682 AN MC ET XXXIV 224
26 June 1682 AN MC ET XXIV 483
30 June 1682 AN MC ET XXIV 483
1 July 1682 AN MC ET XXIV 484
20 July 1682 AN MC ET XXIV 484
12 August 1682 AN MC ET XXIV 484
23 December 1682 AN MC ET LXXVIII 372
21 February 1685 AN MC ET LXXIII 529
24 March 1685 AN MC ET CXVIII 139
31 August 1686 AN MC ET LXXXII 24
6 October 1686 AN MC ET LXXXII 24
25 March 1687 Fichier Laborde: Jean Magoulet
28 May 1687 AN MC ET LXXVIII 398
June 1687 in Étude LXXXII missing; would have contained five documents concern-
     ing Jean
4 October 1687 AN MC ET LXXXII 25
6 March 1688 AN MC ET LXXXII 26
1 April 1688 AN MC ET LXXXII 26
29 May 1688 AN MC ET LXXXII 27
12 June 1688 AN MC ET LXXXII 27
21 July 1688 AN MC ET LXXXII 27
25 February 1689 AN MC ET LXXXII 28
3 March 1689 AN MC ET LXXXII 29
17 May 1689 AN MC ET LXXXII 29
23 May 1689 AN MC ET LXXXII 29
25 May 1689 AN MC ET LXXXII 29
4 June 1689 AN MC ET LXXXII 30
7 June 1689 AN MC ET LXXXII 30
15 June 1689 AN MC ET LXXXII 30, two documents
4 February 1690 AN MC ET LXXXII 31
15 February 1690 AN MC ET LXXXII 31
25 February 1690 AN MC ET CV 927
21 March 1690 AN MC ET LXXXII 31, two documents
5 May 1690 AN MC ET LXXXII 32
29 December 1690 AN MC ET LXXXII 33
1691 in Étude LXXXII missing; would have contained eight documents concerning Jean
6 March 1691 AN MC ET XLVI 151
9 July 1691 AN T 1123 13A
10 January 1692 AN MC ET LXXXII 34
12 July 1692 AN MC ET LXXXII 35
29 December 1692 AN MC ET CXVIII 173
26 February 1693 AN MC ET CXIX 56, three documents

18 March 1693 AN MC ET CXIX 56
4 May 1693 AN MC ET CXVIII 176
20 May 1693 AN MC ET CXVIII 176
2 January 1694 AN MC ET CXVIII 180
16 January 1694 AN MC ET XX 384
7 March 1694 AN MC ET XX 384
15 August 1694 AN MC ET CXVIII 183
17 November 1694 AN MC ET VII 150
18 January 1695 AN Y 15557
12 June 1695 AN MC ET CXVIII 188
4 October 1695 AN Y 4054 A
29 November 1695 AN MC ET CXVIII 190
14 February 1696 AN MC ET CXVIII 191
31 March 1696 AN MC ET CXVIII 192
4 May 1696 AN MC ET CXVIII 193
10 December 1697 AN MC ET XCVIII 202
14 December 1697 AN MC ET XCVIII 202
28 December 1697 AN MC ET XCVIII 202
17 January 1698 AN MC ET CXVIII 203
19 January 1698 AN MC ET CXVIII 203
28 March 1698 AN MC ET CXVIII 204
7 September 1699 Château de Sassenage, online archives
12 September 1699 Château de Sassenage (originals lost)
19 October 1699 AN MC ET CXVIII 213
6 June 1701 AN MC ET LXXXIII 231, two documents
20 May 1716 AN Y 4273 (tuon Marie Anne Magoulet)
11 April 1717 AN MC ET VI 642
27 May 1718 AN MC ET XXVII 120
8 February 1729 AN MC ET XXVII 172

## 6. Clément

11 June 1669 AN MC ET XXXIV 187
24 March 1687 Fichier Laborde: Jean Magoulet
16 December 1706 AN Y 10735
4 January 1707 AN MC ET LXVI 315
18 February 1707 AN MC ET LXVI 315
17 May 1708 AN MC ET XXXIV 340
5 January 1709 AN MC ET LXVI 322
15 December 1710 AN MC ET LIV 704
29 May 1714 AN Y 14049
2 June 1714 AN MC ET XCIV 146
July–November 1719 Arsenal ms. 10,654
20 May 1720 AN MC ET XXX 226
23 October 1720 AN MC ET LXXVIII 604

10 October 1721 AN MC ET XI 460

20 June 1723–October 1723 Arsenal ms. 10,700

30 September 1723 AN MC ET XXVII 152

18 November 1724 Arsenal ms. 10,155, fol. 18V

December 1724 Arsenal ms. 12,479 registres d'écrou

8 December 1724–18 January 1725 Arsenal ms. 10,843, fol. 40–73

14 July 1725 AN MC ET LXI 374

11 August 1725 AN Y 5291

16 November 1725 AN MC ET LXI 374

19 March 1730 AN MC ET XVII 661

14 May 1732 Archives de Paris microfilm 1102; see also AN MC ET L 428

1 December 1751 AN MC ET CXIII 366

## 7. Jean II

26 February 1682 Fichier Laborde: Jean Magoulet

12 June 1688 AN MC ET LXXXII 27

30 August 1695 AN AB 165 fol. 25V

4 October 1696 AN Y 4054 A

12 September 1699 Château de Sassenage, online archives (originals lost)

6 June 1701 AN MC ET LXXXIII 231, two documents

20 August 1703 AN MC ET CXV 317

1 February 1704 AN MC ET CVI 140

3 September 1704 AN MC ET CXVIII 240

28 September 1704 AN MC ET XCVIII 358

9 February 1705 AN MC ET XCVIII 359

26 May 1707 AN MC ET LXX 226

8 June 1708 AN Y 4178

30 July 1708 AN MC ET XXIV 541

9 June 1709 AN MC ET CI 129

15 June 1709 AN MC ET XCVIII 359

4 April 1714 AN MC ET XIII 179

27 October 1714 AN MC ET LIX 163

30 April 1715 AN Y 815

9–10 May 1715 AN Y 13472

24 May 1715 AN Y 8996

26 February 1717 AN Y 14928

18 April 1717 AN Y 14928

15 June 1717 AN Y 14928

5 November 1717 AN Y 14928

11 November 1718 AN Y 14930 B

18 November 1718 AN Y 4303

2 December 1718 AN MC ET LIX 175 B

27 May 1719 AN MC ET XXVII 120

3 June 1719 Fichier Laborde: Jean Magoulet

June–November 1719 Arsenal ms. 10,654
4 October 1720 AN Y 1899
20 December 1720 AN Y 4342
24 May–9 June 1721 Arsenal ms. 10,733
20 January 1722 AN MC ET LXXXV 397
24 March 1724 AN MC ET XXVII 152
June–August 1724 Arsenal ms. 10,843
1 January 1728 AN MC ET X 380
8 February 1729 AN MC ET XXVII 172
22 June 1729 AN MC ET XXVII 173
22 August 1729 AN MC ET XXVII 174
8 January 1731 AN Y 4463 A
18 March 1731 AN MC ET XXXIII 466
6 June 1731 AN Y 1899, two documents
11 May 1732 AN MC ET XXXVIII 263
9 December 1732 AN Y 14175
17 September 1732 AN MC ET XXVII 186
5 October 1732 AN MC ET XXXVIII 266
26 June 1733 AN MC ET XXVII 188
5 April 1734 AN MC ET CXVIII 381
12 April 1734 AN MC ET CXVIII 381
11 May 1735 AN MC ET XXVII 195
24 November 1735 AN Y 12577
16 December 1735 AN Y 9029
8 December 1737 AN MC ET XXXVIII 295
19 April 1738–39 September 1739 Arsenal ms. 11,437

## 8. Noel Poisson

1682 *État de la France*, "porte-manteau," court of the dauphine
18 April 1717 AN Y 14928
5 November 1717 AN Y 14928
25 May 1719 AN Y 14931

## 9. Louise Magoulet

5 August 1719 AN O 1 63 fol. 196 r and v
10 October 1719 AN O 1 63 fol. 284
10 November 1719 AN O 1 63 fol. 312
July–November 1719 Arsenal ms. 10,654
23 October 1720 MC ET LXXVIII 604
On Cartouche: AN X/72.
17 May 1721 AN X 4 B 288
3 December 1721 AN X 2 B 946
April–September 1723 Arsenal ms. 10,770 (Marie Louise Magoulet under name Chevrot)
26 April 1723 AN Y 15230

10 December 1723 AN X 1A 7082 fol. 234V-237V

June–September 1724 Arsenal ms. 10,843

December 1724–January 1725 Arsenal ms. 10,843 (in file on Clément Magoullet)

14 July 1725 AN MC ET LXI 374

11 August 1725 AN Y 5291

31 May 1729 Publications of the Huguenot Society: Quarto series, vol. 26, p. 67.

26 June 1733 AN MC ET XXVII 1889

November 1736 3 E 7/165, Archives Departementales de l'Yonne, Auxerre

21 November 1736 4 E 24/E 35. 5 Mi 100/2 (1730–1739), Archives Départementales de l'Yonne, Auxerre

## 10. Claude II

5 November 1717 AN Y 14928

16 September 1719 AN MC ET LXI 353

13 June 1720 AN MC ET LXI 357

Summer 1724 Arsenal ms. 10,843, fol. 90

30 July 1732 Archives départementales de l'Oise, État Civil, registre 1MI/ECA141R1

26 June 1733 AN MC ET XXVII 188

27 September 1737 Fichier Laborde: Claude Magoulet

October 1738–June 1739 Arsenal ms. 11,437

11 February 1743 AN MC ET XII 473

11 May 1745 Fichier Laborde: Claude Magoulet

## 11. Marie

July 1724 Arsenal ms. 10,843, fol. 86

26 June 1733 AN MC ET XXVII 188

11 May 1745 Fichier Laborde: Claude Magoulet

22 October 1787 AN MC ET LIV 1033

## *Related to the Chevrots:*

## 1. Antoine

22 February 1604 AN MC ET III 473 (Antoine I)

26 January 1665 AN MC ET LXVIII 195 (Antoine II)

21 May 1665 AN MC ET XXXIX 111 (Antoine II)

30 September 1679 AN Y 8892 (Antoine II)

25 October 1680 AN MC ET XXIII 345 (Boulanger-Perrin)

11 October 1692 AN MC ET XCIX 332 (Antoine II)

3 February 1698 AN O 1 3716

23 November 1698 AN MC ET XXVIII 42

23 December 1698 AN MC ET LXXV 436

1700 AN O 1 44, fol. 686

12 February 1700 AN MC ET LXVII 241

18 March 1700 AN MC ET LXVII 241

1700 BNF: *Réponse au mémoire de Rimbault, huissier-priseur, par Antoine Chevrot, valet de chambre ordinaire de Mme la duchesse de Bourgogne, contre Marie Périn femme separée de Rimbault et Barbe Pierre, leur servante.*

1702 *État de la France* 2:32

31 August 1702 AN MC ET LVII 216

13 August 1707 AN MC ET XV 409

5 March 1709 AN MC ET LXXV 436

20 April 1709 AN Y 4188

27 April 1709 AN MC ET XXVIII 99

3 November 1712 AN Y 15219

23 August 1713 AN MC ET XV 453

4 December 1715 AN Y 15222

8 January 1716 AN Y 15223

13 March 1719 AN MC ET XXXI 67, two documents

1 October 1719 AN MC ET LXX 260

1 September 1720 AN MC ET XXI 74

8 July 1720 in AN MC ET LXXXV 433, pièces annexes

17 October 1720 in AN MC ET LXXXV 433, pièces annexes

22 October 1720 AN MC ET XXVI 331

17 May 1721 AN X 4 B 288

18 July 1721 AN Y 15228

22 July 1721 AN MC ET XI 130

3 December 1721 AN X 2 B 946

1 December 1722 AN MC ET CXVI 236

19 May 1723 AN Y 4371

10 December 1723 AN MC ET LXXXV 429

1 July 1724 AN MC ET LXIX 573

24 November 1724 AN MC ET LXXXV 429

25 January 1726 AN Y 10747 (Du Lude)

14 April 1726 AN Y 10747 (Perrin)

6 December 1726 AN MC ET LXXXV 429

21 August 1729 AN Y 15323

21 August 1729 AN MC ET LXXXV 429

27 August 1729 AN MC ET LXXXV 429

## 2. Louis

8 July 1720 in AN MC ET LXXXV 433, pièces annexes

17 October 1720 in AN MC ET LXXXV 433, pièces annexes

23 October 1720 AN MC ET LXXVIII 604

17 May 1721 AN X 4 B 288

18 July 1721 AN Y 15228

3 December 1721 AN X 2 B 946

26 April 1723 AN Y 15230

19 May 1723 AN Y 4371

10 December 1723 AN MC ET LXXXV 429
29 August 1729 AN MC ET LXXXV 429
23 September 1729 AN MC ET LXXXV 429
8 November 1729 AN MC ET LXXXV 429
23 November 1729 AN Y 1005
3 January 1730 AN MC ET XXXIV 452
21 March 1730 AN Y 1010, two documents
30 August 1730 AN MC ET LXXXV 433
31 August 1730 AN MC ET LXXXV 433
26 September 1730 AN MC ET XCVI 380, two documents
6 October 1730 AN MC ET XCVI 380
8 November 1730 AN MC ET XCVI 380
10 January 1731 AN MC ET XCVI 380
22 October 1731 AN MC ET CXI 169
4 May 1734 AN MC ET XXXIV 452
19 August 1734 AN MC ET CXI 177
22–25 April 1735 AN MC ET CXI 179, several documents
19 March 1736 AN Y 15331, two documents
31 March 1736 AN Y 12030
4 June 1736 AN MC ET XXXIV 477

## 3. Louis II

12 May 1736 AN Y 4527 B
23 June 1741 AN Y 4588 B
4 July 1741 AN MC ET XXXIV 533
4 August 1741 AN MC ET XXXIV 533
27 July 1742 AN MC ET XXXIV 539
25 June 1744 AN Y 4624
13 July 1744 AN MC ET XXXIV 549
10 November 1744 AN MC ET XXXIV 551
1 February 1746 AN MC ET LXXXV 508
30 September 1746 AN MC ET LXXXV 510
3 October 1747 AN MC ET XXXIV 567
20 December 1748 AN MC ET LXXXV 519
27 June 1750 AN MC ET LXXXV 525
8 October 1750 AN MC ET LXXXV 526
8 January 1758 AN MC ET LXXIX 99
23 December 1767 AN MC ET XXXIV 663 (Boulanger)
22 April 1779 AN MC ET LXXIX 215
23 May 1780 AN MC ET LXXIX 224
10 October 1785 AN MC ET LXXIX 262
14 January 1790 AN MC ET LXXIX 300
30 August 1790 AN Z 2 2454

BIBLIOGRAPHY

Abad, Reynald. "Le Faux, un crime impardonnable? Le Procureur général du Parlement de Paris face aux demandes de grâce des faussaires au XVIIIe siècle." In *Juger le Faux (Moyen Âge—Temps Modernes)*. Ed. O. Poncet. Paris: École Nationale des Chartes, 2011: 163–178.

Acerra, Martine. "Les Avocats au Parlement de Paris: 1661–1715." *Histoire, Économie, Société*. 1982. 2:213–225.

Agnew, Reverend David C. A. *Protestant Exiles from France, Chiefly in the Reign of Louis XIV; or, The Huguenot Refugees and Their Descendants in Great Britain and Ireland*. 2 vols. London, 1886.

Aguesseau, Henri François d'. *Oeuvres complètes du Chancelier D'Aguesseau*. Paris: Fantin, 1819.

Ariès, Philippe. *Centuries of Childhood: A Social History of Family Life*. 1960. New York: Vintage, 1962.

Aubert, Gilbert. "'To Establish One Law and Definite Rules': Race, Religion, and the Transatlantic Origins of the Louisiana Code Noir." In Vidal: 21–43.

Audiger. *La Maison reglée et l'art de diriger la maison d'un grand seigneur*. Paris, 1692.

Balleroy, Marquise de. *Les Correspondants de la marquise de Balleroy*. Ed. É. de Barthélemy. 2 vols. Paris: Hachette, 1883.

Bancroft, Lundy, and Jay Silverman. *The Batterer as Parent: Addressing the Impact of Domestic Violence on Family Dynamics*. London: Sage, 2002.

———. *Why Does He Do That? Inside the Minds of Angry and Controlling Men*. New York: Putnam, 2002.

Barbier, E.J.F. *Journal historique et anecdotique du règne de Louis XV*. Ed. A. De La Villegille. 4 vols. Paris: Jules Renouard, 1847.

Béguin, Katia. "Estimer la valeur du marché des rentes d'État sous l'Ancien Régime." *Histoire et Mesure XXVI-2* (2011): 3–30.

Benabou, Erica-Marie. *La Prostitution et la police des moeurs au XVIIIe siècle*. Paris: Perrin, 1987.

Bennini, Martine. *Les Conseillers à la cour des aides (1604–1697)*. Paris: Champion, 2010.

Berthier, Ferdinand. *L'Abbé de l'Épée*. Paris: Michel Levy, 1852.

Bimbenet-Privat, Michèle. *Les Orfèvres et l'orfèvrerie de Paris au XVIIe siècle*. 2 vols. Paris: Association Paris-Musées, 2002.

Blackburn, Robin. *The Overthrow of Colonial Slavery, 1776–1848*. London: Verso, 1988.

Blondel, J. F. *Discours de la nécessité de l'étude de l'architecture*. Paris: Jombert, 1754.

Boucher, Jacqueline. "L'Évolution de la Maison du roi." *XVIIe siècle*. Vol. *34* (1982): 359–379.

Boucher, Louis. *La Salpêtrière, son histoire de 1656 à 1790*. Paris: Imprimerie de la Société de Typographie, 1883.

Boutaric, François de. *Traité des droits seigneuriaux et des matières féodales*. Paris: Pierre Prault, 1746.

Buvat, Jean. *Journal de la Régence (1715–1723)*. Ed. É. Campardon. *5* vols. Paris: Henri Plon, 1865.

Calmette, Jean-François. *La Rareté en droit public*. Paris: L'Harmattan, 2004.

Caron, Aimery. "Personnes et familles à Sainte-Croix au XVIIe siècle." *Bulletin de la Société d'histoire de la Guadeloupe*. Nos. 107–108 (1996): 1–290.

Carondas Le Caron, Louis. *Recueil des édits et ordonnances du roy, concernant les domaines et droits de la couronne*. 2 vols. Paris: Pierre Prault, 1735.

Carrez, Jean-Pierre. *Femmes opprimées à la Salpêtrière de Paris (1656–1791)*. Paris: Éditions Connaissances et Savoirs, 2005.

———. "Les Conditions à la Salpêtrière: XVIIe et XVIIIe siècles." *Revue de la Société française d'Histoire des Hôpitaux*. Number *118* (2/2005): 9–15.

Castelluccio, Stéphane. "Le Partage de la collection du Grand Dauphin." *L'Estampille/ L'Objet d'art*. No. *374* (May 2000): 56–72.

Colomer, J., and A. Descalzo, eds. *Spanish Fashion at the Courts of Early Modern Europe*. 2 vols. Madrid: CEEH, 2014.

Coquery, Natacha. *Tenir boutique à Paris au XVIIIe siècle*.Paris: Éditions du comité des travaux historiques et scientifiques, 2011.

Cornette, Joël. *Le Roi de guerre: Essai sur la souveraineté dans la France du Grand Siècle*. Paris: Payot, 1993.

———. *Chronique du règne de Louis XIV: De la fin de la Fronde à l'aube des Lumières*. Paris: SEDES, 1997.

Croft, Canon. *Historical Account of Lisbon College*. Barnet: St. Andrew's Press, 1902.

Croq, Laurence. "Le Prix de la mort." *Histoire et Mesure*. Vol. *XXVII*. No. 1 (2012): 161–214.

———. "Des Titulaires à l'évaluation sociale des qualités." *Dire et vivre l'ordre social*. Ed. F. Cosandey. Paris: Éditions de l'EHESS, 2005: 125–168.

———. *"Les Bourgeois de Paris" au XVIIIe Siècle: Identification d'une catégorie sociale polymorphe*. Thesis: Université de Paris I: 1997.

Cummings, Mark. "Elopement, Family and the Courts: The Crime of *Rapt* in Early Modern France." *Proceedings of the Annual Meeting of the Western Society for French History*. 1976: 118–125.

Dangeau, Philippe de Courcillon, Marquis de. *Journal*. Ed. M. Feuillet de Conches. *19* vols. Paris: Didot Frères, 1854–1860.

Davis, Natalie Zemon. *The Return of Martin Guerre*. Cambridge, MA: Harvard University Press, 1983.

Debien, Gabriel. *Les Colons de Saint-Domingue et la Révolution: Essai sur le Club Massiac (Août 1789–Août 1792)*. Paris: Colin, 1953.

Decrossas, Michaël and Marianne Grivel. "De l'Atelier de l'artisan au cabinet de l'amateur." *Ornements: Chefs-d'oeuvre de la collection Jacques Doucet*. Paris: INHA, 2014: 262–276.

DeJean, Joan. *The Age of Comfort: When Paris Discovered Casual—and the Modern Home Began*. New York: Bloomsbury, 2009.

———. *The Essence of Style: How the French Invented High Fashion, Fine Food, Style, Sophistication, and Glamour*. New York: Free Press, 2005.

Delasselle, Claude. "Les Enfants abandonnés à Paris au XVIIIe siècle." *Annales: Économies, Sociétés, Civilisations*. No. 1 (1975): 187–218.

Delpeuch, Emma. "Les Marchands et artisans suivant la cour." *Revue historique du droit français et étranger*. 1974: 379–413.

Denis, Vincent. *Une Histoire de l'identité: France, 1715–1815*. Paris: Champ Vallon, 2008.

Dent, Julian. *Crisis in Finance: Crown, Financiers, and Society in Seventeenth-Century France*. New York: Palgrave Macmillan, 1973.

Descimon, Robert. "Un Langage de la dignité: La Qualification de personnes dans la société parisienne à l'époque moderne." In *Dire et vivre l'ordre social*. Ed. F. Cosandey. Paris: Éditions de l'EHESS, 2005: 69–124.

Desgranges, Henry Légier. *Hospitaliers d'autrefois: Hôpital Général de Paris, 1656–1790*. Paris: Hachette, 1952.

Dessert, Daniel. *Argent, pouvoir, et société au Grand Siècle*. Paris: Fayard, 1984.

Doyle, William. *Venality: The Sale of Offices in Eighteenth-Century France*. Oxford: Oxford University Press, 1996.

Du Chemin, Michel, ed. *Journal des principales audiences du Parlement avec les arrêts qui y ont été rendus*. Paris: Durand, 1754.

Duguit, Léon. "Étude sur le rapt de séduction." *Nouvelle revue historique de droit français et étranger*. Vol. 10 (1886): 587–625.

Dulong, Claude. "De la conversation à la création." *Histoire des femmes en occident*. Ed. G. Duby and M. Perrot. Vol. 3: *XVIe-XVIIIe siècles*. Paris: Plon, 1991: 403–426.

Durand, Vincent. "Émigrations périodiques des ouvriers foréziens au XVIIe siècle.' *Bulletin de la Diana*. June–October 1890: 283–291.

El Ghoul, Fayçal. *Contribution à l'étude du régime des prisons en France sous le règne de Louis XIV*. Tunis: Publications de l'Université de Tunis, 1987.

Épée, Abbé Charles Michel de l'. *Institution des Sourds et Muets*. Paris: Butard, 1774.

*État de la France*. *3* vols. Paris: Étienne Loyson, 1702.

Evinson, Denis. *Catholic Churches of London*. Sheffield: Academic Press, 1998.

Faure, Edgar. *La Banqueroute de Law: 17 juillet 1720*. Paris: Gallimard, 1977.

Félibien, Father Michel. *Histoire de la ville de Paris, depuis son commencement jusqu'à présent*. 5 vols. Paris: Guillaume Despres, 1725.

Ferguson, Niall. *The Ascent of Money: A Financial History of the World*. New York: Penguin Press, 2008.

Ferrière, Claude de. *La Science parfaite des notaires*. 1682. Paris: H. J. Massé, 1699.

Fontaine, Laurence. "La Délinquance financière dans l'économie du privilège. Société de cour. Changements d'identité et 'affaires' à Paris au début du XVIIIe siècle." In *Cartouche, Mandrin, et autres brigands du XVIIIe siècle*. Ed. Lise Andries. Paris: Éditions Desjonquères, 2010: 115–132.

Foucault, Nicolas Joseph. *Mémoires de Nicolas Joseph Foucault*. Paris: Imprimerie Impériale, 1862.

Fournel, Jean-François. *Traité de la séduction considérée dans l'ordre judiciaire*. Paris: Demonville, 1781.

Fraisse, Jean Antoine. *Livre de desseins chinois*. Ed. Nicole Garnier-Pelle. Paris: Éditions Monelle Hayot, 2011.

Funck-Brentano, Frantz. *La Bastille des comédiens: Le For-l'Évêque*. Paris: Albert Fontemoing, 1903.

———. *Les Lettres de cachet à Paris, avec une liste des prisonniers à la Bastille*. Paris: Imprimerie Nationale, 1901.

Gallet, Michel. *Les Architectes parisiens du XVIIIe siècle*. Paris: Mengès, 1995.

Garas, Claire. "Le Plafond de la banque royale de G. A. Pellegrini." *Bulletin du Musée hongrois des beaux-arts*. Vol. *21* (1962): 75–93.

Garber, Peter. *Famous First Bubbles: The Fundamentals of Early Manias*. Cambridge, MA: MIT Press, 2000.

Giraud, Marcel. *Histoire de la Louisiane française*. *4* vols. Paris: Presses Universitaires de France, 1966.

Goetzmann, William, Catherine Labio, et al., eds. *The Great Mirror of Folly: Finance, Culture, and the Crash of 1720*. New Haven and London: Yale University Press, 2013.

Guiffrey, Jules. "Histoire de l'Académie de Saint-Luc." *Archives de l'art français*, Nouvelle période, t. *IX* (1915): 400–431.

Hanley, Sarah. "Engendrer l'état: Formation familiale et construction de l'État dans la France du début de l'époque moderne." *Politix, vol. 8*, 32 (1995): 45–65.

Harding, Johanna. *History of the Sardinian Chapel*. London: R. and T. Washbourne, 1905.

Harsin, Paul. "La Création de la Compagnie d'Occident (1717)." *Revue d'histoire économique et sociale*. Vol. *34*, no. 1 (1956): 2–42.

Hart, April, and Susan North. *Seventeenth- and Eighteenth-Century Fashion in Detail*. London: Victoria and Albert Publishing, 2010.

Havard, Henry. *Dictionnaire de l'ameublement et de la décoration: depuis le XIIe siècle jusqu'à nos jours*. *5* vols. Paris: Libraires Imprimeries Réunies, 1894.

Hayward, Maria. "William Green, Coffer-Maker to Henry VIII, Edward VI, and Mary I." *Furniture History*. Vol. *36* (2000): 1–13.

Hébert, François. *Mémoires du curé de Versailles, 1686–1704*. Paris: Éditions de France, 1927.

Herman, Judith. *Trauma and Recovery*. New York: Basic Books, 1992.

Hildesheimer, Françoise. "Le Faux devant le Parlement de Paris au XVIIIe siècle." In *Juger le Faux (Moyen Âge–Temps Modernes)*. Ed. O. Poncet. Paris: École Nationale des Chartes, 2011: 155–162.

Isambert et al. *Recueil des anciennes lois françaises depuis l'an 420 jusqu'à la Révolution de 1789*. Paris: Belin-Le Prieur, 1830.

Jaffe, Peter, Linda Baker, and Alison Cunningham. *Protecting Children from Domestic Violence: Strategies for Community Intervention*. New York: Guildford Press, 2004.

Jamet de La Guessière, François. *Journal des principales audiences du Parlement, avec les arrêts qui y ont été rendus, depuis l'année 1674 jusqu'en 1685*. *3* vols. Paris: Compagnie des Libraires Associés, 1757.

Kaplan, Steven. "Les Corporations, les 'faux-ouvriers,' et le faubourg Saint-Antoine au XVIIIe siècle." *Annales*. Vol. *43*, no. 2 (1988): 353–378.

———. *La Fin des corporations*. Paris: Fayard, 2001.

Karakostas, Alexis. *L'Institut national des sourds-muets de Paris de 1790–1800*. Thèse de doctorat en médecine, 1975.

Kelly, Bernard. *Historical Notes on English Catholic Missions*. London: Kegan Paul, 1907.

Knox, George. *Antonio Pellegrini, 1675–1741*. Oxford: Clarendon Press, 1995.

Lachiver, Marcel. *Les Années de misère: La Famine au temps du Grand Roi*. Paris: Fayard, 1991.

Lahalle, Agnès. *Les Écoles de dessin au XVIIIe siècle: Entre arts libéraux et arts mécaniques*. Rennes: Presses Universitaires de Rennes, 2006.

Lanchester, John. *I.O.U.: Why Everyone Owes Everyone and No One Can Pay*. New York: Simon and Schuster, 2010.

Laurent, Jean-Paul. "Le Grand Conseil." In Michel Antoine et al.*Guide des recherches dans le fonds judiciaire de l'ancien régime*. Paris: Imprimerie nationale, 1958: 27–64.

Law, John. *Oeuvres complètes*. Ed. P. Harsin. *3* vols. Paris: Librairie du Recueil Sirey, 1934.

Le Duc, Geneviève. *Porcelaine tendre de Chantilly au XVIIIe siècle*. Paris: Hazan, 1996.

———. *Chantilly: Un Certain regard vers l'extrème-Orient, 1730–1750*. London: French Porcelain Society, 1993.

Legrand, M. *Cartouche ou les voleurs, comédie*. Paris: Jean Musier, 1721.

Legrave, H. *Le Théâtre et le public à Paris de 1715 à 1750*. Paris: Klincksieck, 1972.

Leproux, Guy-Michel. "Les Recueils de mauresques et livres de broderie."*Ornements: XVe-XIXe siècles; Chefs d'oeuvre de la collection Jacques Doucet*. Paris: INHA, 2014: 96–106.

[Le Semelier, Père.]*Conférences ecclésiastiques de Paris sur le mariage, où l'on concilie la discipline de l'Église avec la jurisprudence du Royaume de France*. 1714. Paris: Veuve Étienne, 1748.

Lespinasse, René de. *Les Métiers et corporations de la ville de Paris*. *3* vols. Paris: Imprimerie Nationale, 1892–1997.

Levasseur, Émile. *Recherches historiques sur le système de Law*. Paris: Guillaumin, 1854.

Liger, Louis. *Le Voyageur fidèle, ou le Guide des étrangers dans la ville de Paris*. Paris: Pierre Ribou, 1715.

Lynn, John. *The Wars of Louis XIV, 1667–1714*. New York: Addison Wesley Longman, 1999.

Lyon-Caen, Nicolas. *Un Roman bourgeois sous Louis XIV? Récits de vies marchandes et mobilité sociale: les itinéraires des Homassel*. Limoges: Presses Universitaires de Limoges, 2008.

Mansel, Phillip. *Pillars of Monarchy: An Outline of the Political and Social History of Royal Guards (1400–1984)*. London: Quartet Books, 1984.

Marais, Mathieu. *Journal de la Régence*. Ed. H. Duranton and R. Granderoute. 2 vols. Saint-Étienne: Publications de l'Université de Saint-Étienne, 2004.

Maral, Alexandre. *La Chapelle royale de Louis XIV*. Paris: Arthéna, 2011.

———. *La Chapelle royale de Versailles sous Louis XIV: Cérémonial, lithurgie, et musique*. Paris: Mardagon, 2002.

Marion, Marcel. *Dictionnaire des institutions de la France aux XVIIe et XVIIIe siècles*. Paris: Picard, 1923.

Mérigot, Lydia. *La Place de France et le lotissement de la couture du Temple (1608–1630)*. Dissertation: École des Chartes, 1966.

Merrick, Jeffrey. "Gender in Pre-Revolutionary Political Culture." In Thomas Kaiser and

Dale Van Kley, eds. *From Deficit to Deluge: The Origins of the French Revolution.* Stanford: Stanford University Press, 2010: 198–219.

———."Marital Conflict in Political Context: Langeac vs. Chambonas, 1775." In S. Desan and J. Merrick, eds. *Family, Gender, and Law in Early Modern Europe.* University Park, PA: Pennsylvania State University Press, 2009: 137–181.

———."Patterns and Prosecution of Suicide in Eighteenth-Century France." *Historical Reflections: Réflexions historiques. 16.*1 (1989): 1–53.

Miller, Susan. "Images of Asia in French Luxury Goods: Jean Antoine Fraisse at Chantilly, c. 1729–36." *Apollo.* Vol. *154*, no. 477 (Nov. 2001): 3–12.

———."Jean Antoine Fraisse, 'Peintre en toile' at Chantilly." *Bulletin du CIETA.* 2001: 87–96.

Monaque, Rémi. *Une Histoire de la marine de guerre française.* Paris: Perrin, 2016.

Mouffle d'Angerville, Barthélemy François. *Vie privée de Louis XV, ou événements, particularités, et anecdotes de son règne.* London: J. P. Lyton, 1781.

Moulin, Mathilde. "Rentes sur l'Hôtel de Ville sous Louis XIV." *Histoire, économie, société.* Vol. *17, no. 4* (1998): 623–648.

Mousnier, Roland. *Les Institutions de la France sous la monarchie absolue, 1598–1789.* 2 vols. Paris: PUF, 1974.

Muller, Chanoine. "L'Historique de l'hospice Condé à Chantilly." *Comptes rendus et mémoires du Comité archéologique de Senlis 4* (1913): 107–247.

Nagle, Jean. *Un Orgueil français: La Vénalité des offices sous l'ancien régime.* Paris: Odile Jacob, 2008.

Neal, Larry. *"I Am Not Master of Events": The Speculations of John Law and Lord Londonderry in the Mississippi and South Sea Bubbles.* New Haven: Yale University Press, 2012.

———. *The Rise of Financial Capitalism: International Capital Markets in the Age of Reason.* Cambridge: Cambridge University Press, 1990.

*Nouveau secrétaire de la cour.* Paris: T. LeGras, 1761.

Pacilly, G. "Contribution à l'histoire de la théorie du rapt de séduction." *Revue d'histoire du droit.* Vol. *13* (1934): 306–319.

Palatine, Charlotte-Élisabeth, Duchesse d'Orléans, née Princesse. *Correspondance.* Ed. G. Brunet. 2 vols. Paris: Charpentier, 1857.

Pardailhé-Galabrun, Annick. *La Naissance de l'intime.* Paris: PUF, 1988.

Parent-Duchâtelet, A.-D.-B. *De la Prostitution dans la ville de Paris.* 1836. 2 vols.; Paris: Dallière, 1850.

Pellegrin, Nicole. "La Vertu de l'ouvrage: Recherches sur la féminisation des travaux d'aiguille (XVIe–XVIIIe siècles)." *Revue d'histoire moderne et contemporaine.* Vol. *46*: 4 (October–December 1999): 747–769.

Perrier, Sylvie. *Des Enfances protégées: La Tutelle des mineurs en France (XVIe au XVIIIe siècles).* Saint-Denis: Presses Universitaires de Vincennes, 1998.

Perrin-Khelissa, Anne. "La Question du relief au coeur des rapports entre l'estampe et l'objet décoratif au XVIIIe siècle."*Ornements: Chefs-d'oeuvre de la collection Jacques Doucet.* Paris: INHA, 2014: 250–259.

Petitcol, Xavier. "Une Chinoiserie imprimée sur satin au début du XVIIIe siècle." *Bulletin du CIETA.* 2002: 87–97.

Peveri, Patrice. "L'Exempt, l'archer, la mouche et le filou: Délinquance policière et contrôle des agents dans le Paris de la régence." In *Contrôler les agents de pouvoir*. Ed. Laurent Feller. Limoges: Presses Universitaires de Limoges, 2005: 245–271.

————. "La Criminalité cartouchienne: Vols, voleurs et culture criminelle dans le Paris de la Régence." In *Cartouche, Mandrin, et autres brigands du XVIIIe siècle*. Ed. Lise Andries. Paris: Desjonquières, 2010: 156–174.

————. "Littérature de colportage et contrôle de l'opinion: Une Relecture de 'L'Histoire de la vie et du procès de Louis Dominique Cartouche.'" In *Cartouche, Mandrin, et autres brigands du XVIIIe siècle*. Ed. Lise Andries. Paris: Éditions Desjonquières, 2010: 269–292.

Pollnitz, Baron de. *Lettres et mémoires*. 5 vols. Amsterdam: F. Changuion, 1737.

Popkin, Jeremy. "Saint-Domingue, Slavery, and the Origins of the French Revolution." In T. Kaiser and D. Van Kley, eds. *From Deficit to Deluge: The Origins of the French Revolution*. Stanford: Stanford University Press, 2010: 220–247.

*Pouvoir en actes: Fonder, dire, montrer, contrefaire l'autorité*. Paris: Somogy, 2013.

*Prospectus de la pension de l'institution nationale des sourds-muets*. Paris: Imprimerie des Sourds-Muets, 1792.

Quatremère de Quincy, Antoine Chrysostome. *Rapport sur l'édifice dit de Sainte-Geneviève*. Paris: Imprimerie Royale, 1791.

Quincy, Charles Sevin de. *Histoire militaire du règne de Louis-le-Grand*. 7 vols. Paris: 1726.

Ravel, Jeffrey. *The Would-be Commoner: A Tale of Deception, Murder, and Justice in Seventeenth-Century France*. New York: Houghton Mifflin, 2008.

*Registers of the Churches of the Chapel Royal, St. James, and Swallow Street. Publications of the Huguenot Society of London*. Vol. *28*. Ed. W. Minet and S. Minet. Machester: Sherratt and Hughes, 1924.

*Règlement pour les supérieures de la maison de Saint Louis de la Salpêtrière*. 8 August 1721. Bibliothèque de l'Arsenal. Ms. 2566.

Ricquebourg, L. J. Camille. *Dictionnaire généalogique des familles de l'Île Bourbon (la Réunion): 1665–1810*. Ricquebourg (self-published), 1983.

Rosenfeld, Sophia. "The Political Uses of Sign Language: The Case of the French Revolution." *Sign Language Studies*. Vol. *6*, no. 1 (Fall 2005): 17–37.

Rowlands, Guy. *The Financial Decline of a Great Power: War, Influence, and Money in Louis XIV's France*. Oxford: Oxford University Press, 2012.

Saint-Aubin, Charles Germain, de. *L'Art du brodeur*. Paris: 1770.

Saint-Simon, Louis de Rouvroy, Duc de. *Mémoires*. Ed. A. de Boislisle. *43* vols. Paris: Hachette, 1879–1930.

————. *Parallèle des trois premiers rois Bourbon*. 1746. Paris: De Bonnet, 1967.

Sallé, M. *L'Esprit des ordonnances et des principaux édits et déclarations de Louis XV, en matière civile, criminelle et bénéficiale*. Paris: Saugrain, 1759.

Schneider, Daniel, Kristen Harknett, and Sara McLanahan. "Intimate Partner Violence in the Great Recession." Article available online at works.bepress.com/kristenharknett/16, doi: 10.1007/s13524=016=0462=1.

Scott, Rebecca, and Jean Hébrard. *Freedom Papers: An Atlantic Odyssey in the Age of Emancipation*. Cambridge, MA: Harvard University Press, 2012.

Sévigné, Marie de Rabutin Chantal, Marquise de. *Correspondance*. Ed. R. Duchêne. *3* vols. Paris: Gallimard, 1978.

Sharrett, Michael, ed. *Lisbon College Register: 1628–1813*. London: Catholic Record Society, 1991.

Skupien, Raphaële. "La Signature." In *Le Pouvoir en actes: Fonder, dire, montrer, contrefaire l'autorité*. Ed. Elsa Marguin-Hamon. Paris: Archives Nationales, 2013: 171–183.

Smedley-Weill, Anette. *Les Intendants de Louis XIV*. Paris: Fayard, 1995.

Smiles, Samuel. *The Huguenots: Their Settlements, Churches, and Industries in England and Ireland*. New York: Harper and Brothers, 1867.

Tarrade, Jean. *Le Commerce colonial de la France à la fin de l'Ancien Régime*. 2 vols. Paris: PUF, 1972.

Thillay, Alain. *Le Faubourg Saint-Antoine et ses faux-ouvriers: La Liberté du travail aux XVIIe et XVIIIe siècles*. Paris: Champ Vallon, 2002.

Thunder, Moira. *Embroidery Designs for Fashion and Furnishings*. London: Victoria and Albert Museum, 2014.

Timon, Robert. *Revue de la Société généalogique de l'Yonne*. No. 143 (2014): 81–84.

[Vallette de Laudun]. *Journal d'un voyage à la Louisiane fait en 1720*. La Haye [Paris]: Musier, 1768.

Vautroys, Abbé Alexandre. *Étude historique et juridique sur le consentement des parents au mariage de leurs enfants*. Paris: Arthur Rousseau, 1889.

Velde, François. "Was John Law's System a Bubble? The Mississippi Bubble Revisited." In J. Atack and L. Neal. *The Origins and Development of Financial Markets and Institutions: From the Seventeenth Century to the Present*. Cambridge: Cambridge University Press, 2009: 99–120.

Vidal, Cécile, ed. *Louisiana: Crossroads of the Atlantic World*. Philadelphia: University of Pennsylvania Press, 2014.

Voltaire, François Marie Arouet, known as. *Oeuvres complètes de Voltaire: Politique et législation*. Vol. *1*. Paris: Baudouin Frères, 1827.

Wardle, Patricia. "The King's Embroiderer: Edmund Harrison (1590–1667)." *Textile History 26*, 2 (1995): 139–184.

White, Sophie. *Wild Frenchmen and Frenchified Indians: Material Culture and Race in Colonial Louisiana*. Philadelphia: University of Pennsylvania Press, 2012.

Williams, Alan. *The Police of Paris: 1718–1789*. Baton Rouge: Louisiana State University Press, 1979.

———. "Patterns of Conflict." *Journal of Family History*. Vol. *18* (1993): 39–52.

ILLUSTRATION CREDITS

Front-matter map: Abbé Delagrive. Map of Paris. 1728. Author's collection.

2   Trade image for Jean Magoulet's shop. Etching and engraving. 1680s. Waddesdon Manor, the Rothschild Collection (The National Trust). Photograph: University of Central England.

5   Jean Berain (drawing). Jean Le Pautre (engraving). *Le Mercure galant.* January 1678, *extraordinaire.* Photo: Patrick Lorette for Joan DeJean.

11   Nicolas de Fer. 1718. "La Louisiane." Private collection.

13   "Bonnes pour les isles." 1719. Archives de la Bastille. Bibliothèque de l'Arsenal.

25   Abbé Delagrive. Map of Paris. 1728. Detail. Author's collection.

28   Abbé Delagrive. Map of Paris. 1728. Detail. Author's collection.

28   Antoine Chevrot's marriage contract. 1698. Archives Nationales: MC ET XXVIII 42.

37   Seventeenth-century leather case crafted by a Parisian *gainier.* Museo Nacional del Prado, Madrid.

37   Octagonal coffer with cameos. Paris. Mid-seventeenth century. Museo Nacional del Prado, Madrid.

41   "La Galerie du Palais." Anonymous engraving. C. 1640. Musée Carnavalet. Photo: Gérard Leyris.

44  Attributed to Charles Beaubrun. Queen Marie-Thérèse and her son, the Dauphin of France. c. 1665. Museo Nacional del Prado, Madrid.

49  Jean I Magoulet. Signature. 1679. Archives Nationales: MC ET LXXVIII 357.

64  Abbé Delagrive. Map of Paris. 1728. Detail. Author's collection.

65  Advertisement for Jean Magoulet's shop. Etching and engraving. 1680s. Waddesdon Manor, the Rothschild Collection (The National Trust). Photograph: University of Central England.

66  Claude Perrault. "Élévation de la pricipale façade au côté de Saint-Germain-l'Auxerrois." Jacques-François Blondel. *Architecture française*. University of Pennsylvania Libraries.

67  *Le Mercure galant*. August 1682. Author's collection.

71  Abbé Delagrive. Map of Paris. 1728. Detail. Author's collection.

80  Alexandre Le Roux. "Distribution du pain." Engraving. 1693. Private collection.

94  Jean II Magoulet. Signature. 1701. Archives Nationales: MC ET LXXXIII 231.

126  Abbé Delagrive. Map of Paris. 1728. Detail. Author's collection.

128  Diderot and d'Alembert. *Encyclopédie*. University of Pennsylvania. Van Pelt Libraries. Rare Books and Special Collections.

130  "Billet de l'état." 1716. Musée Carnavalet.

131  Gérard Jollain. 1717. "Trade between the Indians of Mexico and the French in the Port of the Mississippi." Private collection.

133  Louise Poisson. Signature. 1701. Archives Nationales: MC ET LXXXIII 231.

147  Ballustrade of the staircase built for the Royal Bank. Paris. 1719. The Wallace Collection, London.

148  Billet. Banque royale. 1719. Musée Carnavalet.

152  Antoine Humblot. "La Rue Quincampoix." 1720. Private collection.

164  Compagnie des Indes. Dividende d'une action. 1721. Musée Carnavalet. Photo: Gérard Leyris.

280   Louise Magoulet and Guillaume Billout. Signatures. 1736.

289   Jacques Germain Soufflot. Sainte-Geneviève Church. University of Pennsylvania Libraries.

298   Signatures of the French royal family. 1781. Archives Nationales: MC RS 1548.

311   Abbé Delagrive. Map of Paris. 1728. Detail. Author's collection.

319   Leather case. Mid-seventeenth century. Museo Nacional del Prado, Madrid.

## COLOR PLATES

Attributed to Charles Beaubrun. Queen Marie-Thérèse and her son, the Dauphin of France. c. 1665. Museo Nacional del Prado, Madrid.

Embroidered panel. French. Early 1680s. Metropolitan Museum of Art.

Embroidered firescreen. French. c. 1720. Metropolitan Museum of Art.

Waistcoat. French. 1730s. Detail. Victoria and Albert Museum, London.

Waistcoat. French? 1730s. Victoria and Albert Museum, London.

Mantua. London. C. 1740. detail. Madame Leconte, embroideress. Victoria and Albert Museum, London.

Mantua. London. C. 1740. Madame Leconte, embroideress. Magdalene Giles, mantua maker. Victoria and Albert Museum, London.

Leather case. French. 1660s? Museo Nacional del Prado, Madrid.

Octagonal coffer with cameos. Paris. Mid-seventeenth century. Museo Nacional del Prado, Madrid.

Giovanni Pellegrini. Design for ceiling, Banque Royale. 1719. Petit Palais, Paris.

Wallet. French. 1719. Archives de la Bastille. Bibliothèque de l'Arsenal.

Textile. French. 1730s? Victoria and Albert Museum, London.

Porcelain jar. Chantilly. 1730s. Metropolitan Museum of Art.

INDEX

Note: Page numbers in *italics* refer to illustrations.

A NOTE ON THE AUTHOR

Joan DeJean has been Trustee Professor at the University of Pennsylvania since 1988. She previously taught at Yale and at Princeton. She is the author of eleven books on French literature, history, and material culture of the seventeenth and eighteenth centuries, including most recently *How Paris Became Paris: The Invention of the Modern City* (2014); *The Age of Comfort: When Paris Discovered Casual and the Modern Home Began* (2009); *The Essence of Style: How the French Invented High Fashion, Fine Food, Chic Cafés, Style, Sophistication, and Glamour* (2005).

She lives in Philadelphia and, when in Paris, around the corner from the house where, in 1612, this story began.